PRIMARYPLOTS® 2

PRIMARYPLOTS™ 2

*A Book Talk Guide
for Use with Readers Ages 4–8*

By Rebecca L. Thomas

R. R. BOWKER®
A Reed Reference Publishing Company
New Providence, New Jersey

Published by R. R. Bowker
A Reed Reference Publishing Company
Copyright © 1993 by Reed Publishing (USA) Inc.
All rights reserved
Printed and bound in the United States of America
Primaryplots is a trademark of Reed Properties Inc., used under license.
Except as permitted under the Copyright Act of 1976,
no part of this publication may be reproduced or transmitted
in any form or by any means, or stored in any information storage
and retrieval system, without prior written permission of
R. R. Bowker, 121 Chanlon Road, New Providence, New Jersey 07974.

Primaryplots 2 is part of Bowker's Booktalking Series of "plot" books.

The covers of these books are designed to correspond to the complexity of the plots
contained in each volume. The "roads" on the *Primaryplots* cover therefore are very
simple; those on companion volumes *Middleplots, Juniorplots,* and *Seniorplots* are
increasingly intricate. Circles, squares, and other geometric shapes that highlight capital
letters also move from the simple to the elaborate, reflecting the ascending age levels of
the readers.

Library of Congress Cataloging-in-Publication Data
Thomas, Rebecca L.
    Primaryplots 2 : a book talk guide for use with readers ages 4-8 /
  by Rebecca L. Thomas.
      p.   cm.
  Includes bibliographical references and index.
  ISBN 0-8352-3411-8 : $41.00
    1. Children's literature—Book reviews. 2. Children—Books and
reading. 3. Children's literature—Stories, plots, etc. 4. Book
talks. I. Title. II. Title: Primary plots 2. III. Title: Primaryplots two
Z1037.A1T46 1993
028.5'344—dc20   93-21138
                                   CIP

ISBN 0-8352-3411-8

9 780835 234115

Contents

v

Preface

There have been many changes in the world of children's books since *Primaryplots* was published in 1989. The whole-language philosophy has been embraced by many educators. One key aspect of that philosophy is providing a literature-based curriculum. Typically, teachers who are interested in whole-language activities are moving away from packaged reading programs and are looking for quality fiction and nonfiction materials. They are focusing on literature not only in the reading/language arts program but also in other areas of the curriculum. Many school districts are focusing on trade books in the sciences and social studies. Books with math tie-ins are also featured, as well as other curricular areas such as art and music.

The use of literature and the incorporation of a whole-language philosophy in classrooms has increased the use of many school and public libraries. As teachers look for books to use in their classrooms, librarians assist them by providing information about new titles and selection sources. Reference books that feature thematic units linking titles by topics and suggesting related activities have received increased use by teachers and librarians.

Primaryplots 2 features 150 recent picture books that will interest children from preschool through age 8. All the highlighted titles in *Primaryplots 2* have been selected from books published between 1988 and 1992. Attention has been given to linking books with curriculum areas, as well as suggesting activities and projects to extend the featured books. More books with multicultural themes or experiences have been selected, reflecting the growth in publishing in this area. The purpose of *Primaryplots 2* is to serve as a guide for book talks, story programs, classroom activities, and reading guidance.

The 150 titles in *Primaryplots 2* are divided into 8 chapters. They are (1) Enjoying Family and Friends, (2) Developing a Positive Self-Image, (3) Celebrating Everyday Experiences, (4) Finding the Humor in Picture Books, (5) Exploring the Past, (6) Learning about the World around You, (7) Analyzing Illustrations, and (8) Focusing on Folktales.

In order to focus on high quality materials, the "best books" and "notable" lists from standard reviewing and evaluation sources were consulted, including *School Library Journal*'s "Best Books," the Association of Library Services to Children's "Notable Books," *Booklist*'s "Editor's Choice," and the International Reading Association's "Children's Choices." Subject area lists were also consulted, such as the annual "Notable Children's Trade Books in the Field of Social Studies" list from the National Council for the Social Studies–Children's Book Council and the "Outstanding Science Trade Books for Children" list produced by the National Science Teachers Association. The 16th edition and supplements of *Children's Catalog* (Wilson, 1991–92) were also consulted.

In selecting books from these lists to be featured in *Primaryplots 2*, consideration was given to providing titles that could be used at different levels from preschool to the middle grades in elementary school. Books were chosen that offered natural extension activities or that connected with specific curriculum areas. An effort was also made to feature a variety of types of books, including counting and alphabet books, poetry, nonfiction, and books using different styles of illustration. Still, the final selection of a featured title was a personal decision.

Each featured title includes:

1. *Bibliographic Information.* Each main-entry book gives the author(s), title, illustrator(s), publisher, date of publication, paperback information, and suggested use level. If the main-entry book is available in an enlarged "Big Book" format, this is noted.

2. *Plot Summary.* Even though many picture books can be read very quickly, this brief retelling of the plot allows librarians and teachers to make decisions about using a book without having the book at hand.

3. *Thematic Material.* The eight chapter headings represent overall themes for many of the books; however, this section provides more specific information to help librarians and teachers as they select books.

4. *Book Talk Material and Activities.* This section presents suggestions for book talks, discussions, programs, and other activities. There are also ideas for writing, dramatizing, comparing, analyzing, and other extension activities. Some books have been correlated with curriculum areas, such as science, social studies, or art. Other books offer opportunities for studying characters, making murals, charting sequential events, or using puppets. Suggestions include having children use books as models for their own writing and illustrating efforts. The suggestions for book talks, story pro-

grams, and activities are based on the experiences of the author, a school librarian in the Shaker Heights (Ohio) City Schools since 1976. The activities have been designed to provide opportunities for children to interact with books in a variety of ways and to develop their critical skills as readers. Ideas are included that could be adapted to the school or public library or to the classroom.

5. *Audiovisual Adaptation.* The OCLC cataloging database was searched for information about the availability of a title in audiovisual format. Recent catalogs of audiovisual materials were also examined.

6. *Related Titles.* The materials in this section are annotated to describe themes or activities that relate to the highlighted book. *A to Zoo,* 3rd edition (Bowker, 1989), and *Children's Catalog,* 16th edition and supplements (Wilson, 1991–92), as well as the "best books" lists were consulted for suggested titles. At least five related titles are included for each highlighted book. If a related title is featured in *Primaryplots* (Bowker, 1989), that is noted.

7. *About the Author and Illustrator.* Information about the author and the illustrator is included here, if available. Biographical resources that are easily available to school and public librarians were consulted, including *Something about the Author* (Gale, 1971–1988) and *The Sixth Book of Junior Authors* (Wilson, 1989) and its five companion titles.

Children need many opportunities to interact with books as they learn to read and make decisions about books. The *Primaryplots* volumes are intended to help teachers and librarians provide a variety of books and activities that will encourage children to develop a love for books and reading.

Many people have helped with the preparation of this manuscript. Special thanks should be given to Gary Raymont, Connie Brown and Hylah Schwartz, who read and reacted to many of the chapters. Pat Baird provided computer access that proved invaluable. Madeleine Obrock assisted with the OCLC searches, often on very short notice. The teachers and children at Fernway and Boulevard Elementary Schools in Shaker Heights, Ohio, read many of the books and participated in the activities, providing their personal reactions to themes and projects. The librarians at the Shaker Heights Public Library were especially helpful in providing reference services. Ellen Stepanian, Director of Library Media of the Shaker Heights City Schools, has been a source of support and encouragement. Her leadership and commitment to library services serve as a model for me. And my family's pride in this accomplishment has been an ongoing source of support which I appreciate.

Catherine Barr, Senior Editor at Bowker, has provided invaluable assistance in the preparation of the manuscript. Assistant Editor Judith M. Balsamo oversaw corrections and editing. Finally, I must thank Marion Sader, Publisher of Professional and Reference Books at Bowker. She selected me for the first *Primaryplots* and has encouraged me to continue with this project.

1

Enjoying Family and Friends

How did you feel when you started school? Perhaps you worried about having friends, like *Chrysanthemum*. Or you wondered *What Will Mommy Do When I'm at School?* Has your class ever taken a special trip (as in *Arthur Meets the President*) or is your school like Timmy Roybal's in *Pueblo Boy?* The books in this chapter feature experiences that will be familiar to many children. Family celebrations, like Christmas and birthdays; special journeys, like a trip to Florida or an imaginary flight over New York City; and everyday experiences in many locations, including an urban neighborhood, a pueblo in New Mexico, and a houseboat in Hong Kong. Sharing these books with children will promote discussions and activities about families and friends.

Aliki.   *Christmas Tree Memories*
   Illus. by the author. Harper, 1991, LB (0-06-020008-1)
   Suggested Use Level: Gr. 1–3

Plot Summary
   As a family gathers around the Christmas tree on Christmas Eve, they remember past celebrations. Specific ornaments provide the spark that leads to a sharing of family memories. A pine-cone angel made on a visit to Granny's, origami decorations made after a visit to the museum, and a decorated starfish from a summer vacation are among the remembered moments. The family remembers loved ones and traditions before going to sleep until Christmas Day.

Thematic Material
   Holidays are special times for families. The Christmas holiday provides this family with an opportunity to reflect on the past, to remember both

people and traditions. *Christmas Tree Memories* celebrates the feeling of family togetherness.

Book Talk Material and Activities

Librarians and teachers who work with young children organize many programs around holidays. Finding new books to read and booktalk adds interest to these annual activities. *Christmas Tree Memories* could be the focus of a program for children and their families. After reading the book, family members could share some of their memories of Christmas. A display of ornaments accompanied by brief descriptions of their importance would also extend this book. Of course, there should be many other Christmas books available for circulation. Librarians and teachers may want to focus on some more recent titles in which family memories and traditions are celebrated, like *Chita's Christmas Tree*, by Elizabeth Fitzgerald Howard; *Tree of Cranes*, by Allen Say; and *Night Tree*, by Eve Bunting. Valerie Worth's collection of poems, *At Christmastime*, provides more images of this holiday. Legends and folktales, like *The Legend of Old Befana* and *Babushka*, would also extend the mood of a program celebrating Christmas memories.

Related Titles

At Christmastime, poems by Valerie Worth. Illustrated by Antonio Frasconi. Harper, 1992. Free verse poems focus on Christmas images, including wreaths, tinsel, ornaments, angels, and stockings.

Babushka: An Old Russian Folktale, retold and illustrated by Charles Mikolaycak. Holiday, 1984. A young woman named Babushka is cleaning her cottage when a procession marches past, searching for a star and a King. At first, Babushka refuses to join them, but she changes her mind. Although she does not find the procession, Babushka brings gifts to children hoping to find the King. (Condensed in *Primaryplots*, Bowker, 1989, pp. 316–318.)

Chita's Christmas Tree, by Elizabeth Fitzgerald Howard. Illustrated by Floyd Cooper. Bradbury, 1989. In Baltimore, Chita and Papa take the buggy and go out into the country to select a Christmas tree. Papa carves Chita's name on it and promises that Santa will bring the tree on Christmas Eve. The traditions of this African-American family could be compared to those of the family in *Christmas Tree Memories*.

The Legend of Old Befana: An Italian Christmas Story, retold and illustrated by Tomie dePaola. Harcourt, 1980. Old Befana is a bad-tempered woman who spends her time cleaning and cooking. When a bright star appears, Old Befana does not leave her work to search for the Child King.

Night Tree, by Eve Bunting. Illustrated by Ted Rand. Harcourt, 1991. Like Chita and Papa in *Chita's Christmas Tree,* this contemporary family drives to the forest and chooses a Christmas tree, which they trim with food for the woodland animals.

Tree of Cranes, written and illustrated by Allen Say. Houghton, 1991. In Japan, a young boy's mother describes the Christmas she remembers from California.

About the Author and Illustrator

ALIKI (BRANDENBERG)

Illustrators of Children's Books: 1957–1966, Vol. III, comp. by Lee Kingman, Grace Allen Hogarth, and Harriet Quimby. Horn Book, 1978, pp. 72, 206; *1967–1976, Volume IV,* 1978, pp. 94–95, 177–178.

Something about the Author, ed. by Anne Commire. Gale, 1971, Vol. 2, pp. 36–38; 1984, Vol. 35, pp. 49–55.

Third Book of Junior Authors, ed. by Doris de Montreville and Donna Hill. Wilson, 1972, pp. 8–9.

Brown, Marc.   *Arthur Meets the President*
Illus. by the author. Little, Brown, 1991 (0-316-11265-8); pap. (0-316-11291-7)
Suggested Use Level: Gr. K–3

Plot Summary

Arthur's class is studying the presidents of the United States. Their teacher, Mr. Ratburn (a rat), tells them about an essay contest with the theme "How I Can Help Make America Great." The prize is a trip to Washington, D.C., and the White House for the winner and for the class. Arthur and his classmates, who are all depicted as animals, enter the contest, and Arthur wins. Of course, Arthur is nervous about meeting the president (a bear) and reciting his speech, but he and his family and friends prepare for the trip. In Washington, the class visits the Washington Monument, the Capitol Building, the Museum of Natural History, and the White House. In the Rose Garden, Arthur's notes for his speech are blown away when the president's helicopter lands, but his sister, D.W., saves the day when she climbs a tree, hangs upside down, and holds up a poster with Arthur's speech printed on it.

Thematic Material

Arthur Meets the President is a recent book in the popular series of books about Arthur and his family and friends. Arthur's trip to Washington could spark an interest in this city, the presidency, and the government.

Book Talk Material and Activities

Arthur is a popular character in children's literature. He and his sisters, D.W. and Kate, have many experiences that children can relate to. For example, in *Arthur's Baby*, Arthur learns he can be a helpful big brother to a baby. In *Arthur's Pet Business*, Arthur shows he can be responsible enough to have his own pet. *Arthur Meets the President* takes Arthur and his family and friends to Washington, D.C., where they meet a fictional president. Young children could be introduced to informational books about the presidency and the government of the United States, such as *The Buck Stops Here*.

In *Arthur Meets the President*, Arthur and his friends visit several tourist attractions in Washington, D.C. Books about other points of interest could be booktalked and displayed. Jill Krementz's photoessay, *A Visit to Washington, D.C.*, is a particularly good selection, since it focuses on the experiences of one child and his family. Roxie Munro's drawings for *The Inside-Outside Book of Washington, D.C.* would provide another look at the attractions.

Audiovisual Adaptation

Arthur Meets the President. American School Publishers, cassette/book, 1992; filmstrip/cassette, 1992; videorecording, 1992.

Related Titles

Arthur's Baby, written and illustrated by Marc Brown. Little, Brown, 1987. Arthur is nervous about having a new baby in the family. His confidence is restored when he stops Kate's crying. (Condensed in *Primaryplots*, Bowker, 1989, pp. 3–5.)

Arthur's Pet Business, written and illustrated by Marc Brown. Little, Brown, 1990. Arthur wants a dog, so he finds a way to earn money and to prove he is responsible. This is one of the more recent books about Arthur.

The Buck Stops Here, written and illustrated by Alice Provensen. Harper,

1990. Rhymes describe each president, and the illustrations include information about their lives and accomplishments.

The Inside-Outside Book of Washington, D.C., written and illustrated by Roxie Munro. Dutton, 1987. The only text for this book is the locations and items being depicted, such as "The Library of Congress" and "The White House, East Room." The detailed color drawings provide opportunities for discussion and encourage additional research. Information about the locations and experiences is given after the illustrations.

The President's Cabinet and How it Grew, written and illustrated by Nancy Winslow Parker with an introduction by Dean Rusk. Harper, 1991. Each cabinet post is featured and the responsibilities are described.

A Visit to Washington, D.C., written and photographed by Jill Krementz. Scholastic, 1987. Color photographs describe a trip to Washington, D.C., by six-year-old Matt Wilson and his family. Sites include the Vietnam Memorial, the Washington Monument, the Air and Space Museum, and the White House.

Washington, D.C., by Dennis Brindell Fradin. Illustrated with photographs and maps. Childrens Pr., 1992. The history, geography, and people of Washington, D.C., are presented in this book, which is part of the From Sea to Shining Sea series. Interesting places to visit and famous people from the city are highlighted.

We the People: The Constitution of the United States of America, illustrated by Peter Spier. Doubleday, 1987. The preamble of the Constitution is the text for Peter Spier's detailed drawings. There are usually more than 25 drawings on each page, and they depict many aspects of the phrases of the Constitution. Many scenes of Washington, D.C., are included; for example, the Pentagon is shown on the page accompanying the phrase "provide for the common defense."

The White House, written by Leonard Everett Fisher. Illustrated with photographs and drawings. Holiday, 1989. This book focuses on the history of this building and the people who have lived there.

About the Author and Illustrator

BROWN, MARC

Fifth Book of Junior Authors and Illustrators, ed. by Sally Holmes Holtze. Wilson, 1983, pp. 54–55.

Something about the Author, ed. by Anne Commire. Gale, 1976, Vol. 10, pp. 17–18; 1988, Vol. 53, pp. 9–18.

Greenfield, Eloise.   *Grandpa's Face*

Illus. by Floyd Cooper. Philomel, 1988 (0-399-21525-5); pap., Philomel/
Sandcastle (0-399-22106-9)
Suggested Use Level: Gr. 1–3

Plot Summary

Tamika and her grandpa share some special times together, especially
when they go for walks and Grandpa tells her stories. Grandpa participates in local theater productions, and one day Tamika is frightened by
the face her grandpa makes while he practices for a performance.
Tamika worries that he will make that mean face at her. Grandpa takes
her for a "talk-walk," and they discuss her fear. Grandpa reassures her
that his love for her will always be there, shining in his face when he
looks at her.

Thematic Material

In *Grandpa's Face*, Grandpa is an active older adult who has a caring
relationship with his granddaughter, Tamika. Grandpa understands her
fears and helps her overcome them. This book presents an extended
African-American family.

Book Talk Material and Activities

There are many children's books that provide positive images of older
adults. In these books, the characters are interesting and active. In
Grandpa's Face, Grandpa is involved in a theater group. He also has a very
special relationship with Tamika, his granddaughter, and she turns to him
for support and reassurance. *Song and Dance Man* by Karen Ackerman
focuses on another grandfather whose past success as a vaudeville per-
former delights his grandchildren. Once again, Grandpa has a special
relationship with his grandchildren.

Older adults often volunteer to participate in school and library activities with children. A weekly "Book Buddies" program involves several
retired adults who read to children. Often these adults have children and
grandchildren in another town, and they enjoy working with children,
sometimes developing a mentoring relationship with a few children. A
book talk program featuring books with active older adults provides chil-

dren with opportunities to read and discuss intergenerational relationships.

Related Titles

I Know a Lady, by Charlotte Zolotow. Illustrated by James Stevenson. Greenwillow, 1984. A little girl shares her impressions of her elderly neighbor, who lives independently.

Knots on a Counting Rope, by Bill Martin, Jr., and John Archambault. Illustrated by Ted Rand. Henry Holt, 1987. A young Native American boy and his grandfather share stories by a campfire. (Condensed in *Primaryplots*, Bowker, 1989, pp. 61–63.)

Old Henry, by Joan Blos. Illustrated by Stephen Gammell. Morrow, 1987. Old Henry is an eccentric stranger who lives alone. His independent spirit at first alienates him from his neighbors, who do come to appreciate his individuality. (Condensed in *Primaryplots*, Bowker, 1989, pp. 43–45.)

Song and Dance Man, by Karen Ackerman. Illustrated by Stephen Gammell. Knopf, 1988. Grandpa puts on a show in the attic for his grandchildren. They enjoy remembering the good old vaudeville days with him.

We Can't Sleep, written and illustrated by James Stevenson. Greenwillow, 1982. Louie and Mary Ann can't sleep. Of course, Grandpa remembers a night when he couldn't sleep. Grandpa's exaggerated experiences make Louie and Mary Ann realize there is no reason to worry.

Where the River Begins, written and illustrated by Thomas Locker. Dial, 1984. Two boys hike along the river with their grandfather, sharing his knowledge of life and nature.

About the Author

GREENFIELD, ELOISE

Fifth Book of Junior Authors and Illustrators, ed. by Sally Holmes Holtze. Wilson, 1983, pp. 137–139.

Something about the Author, ed. by Anne Commire. Gale, 1980, Vol. 19, pp. 141–143; Gale, 1990, Vol. 61, pp. 89–102.

Greenfield, Eloise.   *Night on Neighborhood Street*
Illus. by Jan Spivey Gilchrist. Dial, 1991, LB (0-8037-0778-9)
Suggested Use Level: Gr. 2–4

Plot Summary

Seventeen poems describe life on Neighborhood Street during the evening and night. In the early evening, the street is a busy place, with families and friends playing, talking, and laughing together. In the homes, some children are getting ready for bed, as described in "Little Boy Blues," "Goodnight, Juma," and two poems about new babies. There are problems on Neighborhood Street, such as "The Seller" with his "packages of death." Sometimes there are discussions; sometimes there are arguments, as described in "The Meeting." One poem tells of the empty, boarded-up houses. But there are many good times, such as "Fambly Times," describing a family playing games and enjoying their time together. Some poems feature children, as in "Nerissa" and "Karen." One is about a boy, "Darnell," who is afraid of the dark. Another poem describes a slumber party. Another tells of a boy who dreams of dancing.

Thematic Material

The images in *Night on Neighborhood Street* are of an African-American community. They show experiences in an urban neighborhood, focusing on the feelings of friends and families.

Book Talk Material and Activities

Some children will be familiar with the kind of urban neighborhood described in these poems. Others may not know this neighborhood, but they will understand the feelings in these poems—such as Buddy's dreams of dancing and Juma's efforts to put off going to bed. The poems in this collection show a variety of experiences, including negative images of drug dealing and arguments. They also describe loving families, fun with friends, and celebrating in church. In one poem, neighborhood rhymes are mentioned, such as "Li'l Liza Jane" and "Rise, Sally, Rise." Children could learn some of these songs in *Shake It to the One That You Love the Best*, a collection of songs from African-American traditions.

Many of the poems in this collection focus on individual children, such as "Darnell," who is afraid of the dark; "Karen," who listens to her older sister; and "Nerissa," who tries to make her parents happy. Gwendolyn Brooks's *Bronzeville Boys and Girls* also includes poems about different children, including "Tommy," who wants his seed to grow; and "Narcissa," who uses her imagination to be a queen or a bird. In *Nathaniel Talking*, Eloise Greenfield features a nine-year-old boy who raps about his life. Lee Bennett Hopkins has a collection of poems about friendship, *Best Friends*. Children will enjoy looking for other poems that describe the everyday experiences of children and their friends.

Night on Neighborhood Street could also be correlated with picture books about friends and growing up. *Matthew and Tilly* and *Cherries and Cherry Pits* provide images of urban neighborhoods.

Related Titles

Best Friends, selected by Lee Bennett Hopkins. Illustrated by James Watts. Harper, 1986. The eighteen poems in this collection show many moods and moments of friendship. Everyday activities like laughing, talking, fighting, and making up are featured. (Condensed in *Primaryplots*, Bowker, 1989, pp. 16–17.)

Bronzeville Boys and Girls, by Gwendolyn Brooks. Illustrated by Ronni Solbert. Harper, 1956. Brooks's poems deal with the individual experiences of children. "The Admiration of Willie" describes how one child feels about grownups.

Cherries and Cherry Pits, written and illustrated by Vera B. Williams. Greenwillow, 1986. Bidemmi loves to draw and to tell stories about her pictures. Each story in this book tells about people who share cherries. In the last story, Bidemmi imagines how everyone in the neighborhood will enjoy "eating cherries and spitting out the pits." (Condensed in *Primaryplots*, Bowker, 1989, pp. 282–284.)

Matthew and Tilly, by Rebecca C. Jones. Illustrated by Beth Peck. Dutton, 1991. These two friends enjoy the time they spend together in their urban neighborhood, even though they sometimes disagree. The illustrations show that Matthew is white and Tilly is African-American.

Nathaniel Talking, by Eloise Greenfield. Illustrated by Jan Spivey Gilchrist. Black Butterfly Children's Books, 1988. Nathaniel is nine, and he raps and rhymes about his life, including "Missing Mama," "Making Friends," and "Watching the World Go By." He tells about some people who are important to him.

Shake It to the One That You Love the Best: Play Songs and Lullabies from Black Musical Traditions, collected and adapted by Cheryl Warren Mattox. Illustrations from the works of Varnette P. Honeywood and Brenda Joysmith. Warren-Mattox Productions, 1989. A cultural notation accompanies each song; for example, "Loop De Loo" is an African-American ring game, and "Ya, Ya, Ya" is a lullaby from the Congo. The pages are bordered with photographs of fabrics woven in colors and designs associated with African traditions.

The Way I Feel . . . Sometimes, by Beatrice Schenk de Regniers. Illustrated by Susan Meddaugh. Clarion, 1988. "Feeling Mean, Mostly," "Feeling Better," "Feeling Wishful," and "Feeling OK, After All" are the chapters in this collection of poems.

About the Author

GREENFIELD, ELOISE

Fifth Book of Junior Authors and Illustrators, ed. by Sally Holmes Holtze. Wilson, 1983, pp. 137–139.

Something about the Author, ed. by Anne Commire. Gale, 1980, Vol. 19, pp. 141–143; Gale, 1990, Vol. 61, pp. 89–102.

Henkes, Kevin.   *Chrysanthemum*

Illus. by the author. Greenwillow, 1991, LB (0-688-09700-6)
Suggested Use Level: Gr. K–2

Plot Summary

When this little mouse was born, her parents knew she would be special, so they gave her a special name, Chrysanthemum. As she grows, Chrysanthemum knows she is special, and she loves her special name. But when she goes to school, Chrysanthemum's name causes problems. It is too long for the name tag, and her classmates tease her for being named after a flower. At home, her parents reassure her that she is special and so is her name. At school, however, the teasing continues, until Chrysanthemum dreads going to school. When Mrs. Twinkle, the ebullient music teacher, learns of the teasing, she tells the children her name, Delphinium. Chrysanthemum is delighted, and the classmates who have teased her all give themselves flower names. When Mrs. Twinkle's daughter is born, she is given a special name, Chrysanthemum.

Thematic Material

In this story, Chrysanthemum is able to accept herself even when others tease and criticize her. The theme of feeling secure about who you are is expressed in this book.

Book Talk Material and Activities

Most children have experienced being teased or mocked. Like Chrysanthemum, they have had to deal with the experience and maintain a positive self-image. When children have unpleasant experiences, they often feel isolated and alone. Hearing stories like *Chrysanthemum* lets children know they are not alone. After reading several stories in which the main characters face everyday problems, a group of children could develop a problem-solving chart (see Chart 1 below).

Other books could be read and discussed and then added to the chart (see Related Titles for more suggestions). This chart could provide ideas for dealing with problems in other situations. Children could discuss possible solutions for their own problems. Many schools help children learn to mediate their own arguments, and offering a program that fea-

Chart 1

Book Title	Problem	How Was It Solved?
Chrysanthemum	She is teased about her name.	Her music teacher helps Chrysanthemum feel special by sharing her own unusual name.
Ira Sleeps Over	Ira wants to take his teddy bear on an overnight visit to Reggie's.	Ira goes home and gets his bear. He discovers that his friend sleeps with a teddy bear too.
King of the Playground	Sammy won't let Kevin play at the playground.	Kevin stands up to Sammy and they play together.
Bus Stop Bop	The bus breaks down and the people get tired of waiting.	The people on the bus entertain each other—singing, dancing, tumbling, and more.

tures book characters coping with problems could provide samples for mediation activities.

Related Titles

Bus Stop Bop, by Robin Kingsland. Illustrated by Alex Ayliffe. Viking, 1991. When the bus breaks down, the people on the bus become annoyed, until they take turns entertaining each other. When the bus is repaired, they sing "The Wheels on the Bus."

Cornelius, written and illustrated by Leo Lionni. Pantheon, 1983. Cornelius feels left out because the other crocodiles don't appreciate his special skills.

Ira Sleeps Over, written and illustrated by Bernard Waber. Houghton Mifflin, 1972. Ira worries that his friend Reggie will make fun of him for bringing his toy bear along on an overnight visit.

King of the Playground, by Phyllis Reynolds Naylor. Illustrated by Nola Langner Malone. Atheneum, 1991. When Sammy threatens Kevin, Kevin leaves the playground and goes home. Kevin's father helps him talk about his problem and think of some solutions. Kevin decides to stand up to Sammy, and together they build a sand fort.

Louis the Fish, written by Arthur Yorinks. Illustrated by Richard Egielski. Farrar, 1980. Louis is unhappy as a man. He dreams of being a fish. If only his dream could come true.

Oliver Button Is a Sissy, written and illustrated by Tomie dePaola. Harcourt, 1979. When Oliver takes dancing classes, his friends make fun of him, until they find out how helpful the classes are.

Shy Charles, written and illustrated by Rosemary Wells. Dial, 1988. Although Charles is very shy, when his help is needed, Charles knows what to do.

Timothy Goes to School, written and illustrated by Rosemary Wells. Dial, 1981. Timothy feels so inadequate that he is ready to quit school. He isolates himself from his classmates until he realizes that Violet feels left out too. Together, they find they can enjoy school and each other.

About the Author and Illustrator

HENKES, KEVIN

Sixth Book of Junior Authors and Illustrators, ed. by Sally Holmes Holtze. Wilson, 1989, pp. 123–124.

Something about the Author, ed. by Anne Commire. Gale, 1986, Vol. 43, pp. 110–112.

Henkes, Kevin. *Julius, the Baby of the World*
Illus. by the author. Greenwillow, 1990, LB (0-688-08944-5)
Suggested Use Level: Gr. K–2

Plot Summary

Lilly, a mouse, plans to be a wonderful big sister to the new baby. When the baby is born, Lilly changes her mind. Julius gets so much attention from their parents. Lilly has to share her room with him and play quietly while he sleeps. Lilly's parents love Julius, but Lilly thinks he is just in the way. Her parents try to be understanding, but sometimes Lilly misbehaves so much that she is sent to the "uncooperative chair." No matter what Lilly does, her parents still love Julius. When the relatives come to the party to celebrate Julius's birth, Cousin Garland is not impressed with Julius. Lilly defends her brother and demands that Cousin Garland call him "The Baby of the World." Lilly now claims her role as Julius's older sister and protector.

Thematic Material

Although the characters in this book are mice, this is a story of sibling rivalry.

Book Talk Material and Activities

Anyone with younger brothers and sisters can identify, and perhaps sympathize, with Lilly's resentment of Julius. They will be amused by her antics, which often lead to her being sent to the "uncooperative chair." Lilly's behavior in *Julius, the Baby of the World* is similar to the independence she displayed in *Chester's Way*. Lilly is a very opinionated character. In *Chester's Way,* her wild, unpredictable behavior alienates Chester and his friend, Wilson. However, when Chester and Wilson need help and Lilly assists them, they find they can learn from each other.

Kevin Henkes has written and illustrated books that present the everyday concerns of children. In many of his books, the humor is conveyed through the illustrations, particularly in the comments written in the pictures. In *Julius,* Lilly takes back her toys, saying "These are *mine!*" When her parents count and sing the alphabet to Julius, Lilly says the numbers and letters to him in random order. In *Chester's Way,* Lilly introduces herself saying "I'm Lilly! I am the Queen! I like EVERYTHING!" Other characters in books by Kevin Henkes demonstrate their independent spirits. *Jessica* (see chapter 2) insists she has an imaginary friend; *Sheila Rae, the Brave* is an intrepid adventurer; and *Chrysanthemum* (elsewhere in this chapter) learns to accept her individuality. Children reading Kevin Henkes's books smile as they recognize some of their own behaviors and experiences.

Related Titles

Arthur's Baby, written and illustrated by Marc Brown. Little, Brown, 1987. Arthur is nervous that he will not be a good big brother, but he is the one who is able to get Kate to stop crying. (Condensed in *Primaryplots*, Bowker, 1989, pp. 3–5.)

A Baby Sister for Frances, by Russell Hoban. Illustrated by Lillian Hoban. Harper, 1964. A classic story of the anxieties felt by Frances the badger when a new baby badger is coming.

Chester's Way, written and illustrated by Kevin Henkes. Greenwillow, 1988. Chester and Wilson are best friends. They are very conservative and do everything alike. When Lilly, who wears disguises and can talk backwards, moves into their neighborhood, the boys are dismayed, until they need her help.

I'll Fix Anthony, by Judith Viorst. Illustrated by Arnold Lobel. Harper, 1969. Here's a story of how a little brother feels about his big brother. Compare this boy's plans for Anthony with Lilly's plans for Julius. What might Julius think about doing to Lilly?

Jamaica Tag-Along, by Juanita Havill. Illustrated by Anne Sibley O'Brien. Houghton, 1989. When Ossie goes to the park to play basketball, Jamaica follows him. Later, when Jamaica is playing, she is bothered by a toddler named Berto.

Sheila Rae, the Brave, written and illustrated by Kevin Henkes. Greenwillow, 1987. Sheila Rae decides she will prove her bravery by walking home from school a new and unknown way. When she gets lost, her timid sister, Louise, comes to her rescue.

The Very Worst Monster, written and illustrated by Pat Hutchins. Greenwillow, 1985. When a baby boy monster is born to the monster family, everyone expects him to grow up to be the Worst Monster in the World. Hazel, the baby's older sister, feels left out and thinks of many ways to get attention. (Condensed in *Primaryplots*, Bowker, 1989, pp. 129–131.)

Where's the Baby, written and illustrated by Pat Hutchins. Greenwillow, 1988. Baby Monster creates a huge mess wherever he goes. Hazel is surprised by Grandma's accepting reaction.

About the Author and Illustrator

HENKES, KEVIN

Sixth Book of Junior Authors and Illustrators, ed. by Sally Holmes Holtze. Wilson, 1989, pp. 123–124.

Something about the Author, ed. by Anne Commire. Gale, 1986, Vol. 43, pp. 110–112.

Howard, Elizabeth Fitzgerald. *Aunt Flossie's Hats (and Crab Cakes Later)*

Illus. by James Ransome. Clarion, 1991 (0-395-54682-6)
Suggested Use Level: Gr. 1–4

Plot Summary

In Baltimore, Sarah and Susan go to visit their Great-Great-Aunt Flossie for tea and stories. Aunt Flossie's house is filled with mementos of her life, including hats. Each hat reminds Aunt Flossie of a special story, which she shares with the girls. One time, when Aunt Flossie was a young girl, there was a fire in Baltimore, and Aunt Flossie and her mother went out into the night. Aunt Flossie still smells the smoke in her hat. Another hat reminds Aunt Flossie of a parade. Seeing Aunt Flossie's favorite hat reminds the girls of the time the hat blew into the water and was rescued by a boy and his dog. After sharing stories, Sarah, Susan, their parents, and Aunt Flossie go out for crab cakes, and Aunt Flossie is wearing her favorite hat.

Thematic Material

The themes of family togetherness and respect for the past are important in this story. This book presents an African-American family and emphasizes how much they care for each other.

Book Talk Material and Activities

When Elizabeth Fitzgerald Howard visited the Shaker Heights (Ohio) schools in the fall of 1992, we prepared by reading her books, *Aunt Flossie's Hate (and Crab Cakes Later)*, *The Train to Lulu's*, and *Chita's Christmas Tree*. Many children worked on extension activities for the books, such as a diorama of Chita and her tree, a mural of the train, and, of course, hats. First-grade students took paper bowls, turned them upside down, and decorated them with paint, feathers, sequins, and ribbons. They read other hat books, such as *A Three Hat Day*, *Hats, Hats, Hats*, and *Whose Hat?*

Fourth-grade children brought in a special hat from home and wrote about it. Each story about a hat was paired with a picture of the child wearing the hat. The day of Ms. Howard's visit was "Aunt Flossie's Hat Day" with everyone wearing a special hat.

During her presentation to classes, Elizabeth Fitzgerald Howard focused on her books as reminiscences, adding additional details from her memories that were not in the books. Other family stories, such as *When I Was Young in the Mountains* and *In Coal Country*, were displayed in the library.

Related Titles

Chita's Christmas Tree, by Elizabeth Fitzgerald Howard. Illustrated by Floyd Cooper. Bradbury, 1989. In Baltimore, Chita and Papa take the buggy and go out into the country to select a Christmas tree. Papa carves Chita's name on it and promises Santa will bring the tree on Christmas Eve.

Hats, Hats, Hats, by Ann Morris. Photographs by Ken Heyman. Lothrop, 1989. This book depicts many cultures, focusing on different varieties of hats. An index of the locations is included.

In Coal Country, by Judith Hendershot. Illustrated by Thomas B. Allen. Knopf, 1987. In this memoir, a girl recalls her father and his work in the coal mines of Ohio. (Condensed in *Primaryplots*, Bowker, 1989, pp. 172–174.)

A Three Hat Day, by Laura Geringer. Illustrated by Arnold Lobel. Harper, 1985. R.R. Pottle the Third is so fond of hats that he sometimes wears more than one. (Condensed in *Primaryplots*, Bowker, 1989, pp. 51–53.)

The Train to Lulu's, by Elizabeth Fitzgerald Howard. Illustrated by Robert Casilla. Bradbury, 1988. Beppy and Babs are taking the train to visit their Great-Aunt Lulu. This book is based on an experience from the author's childhood.

When I Was Young in the Mountains, by Cynthia Rylant. Illustrated by Diane Goode. Dutton, 1982. The repetition of the title phrase evokes a sense of nostalgia as the author describes childhood moments. This book was a Caldecott Honor book in 1983.

Whose Hat?, written and illustrated by Margaret Miller. Greenwillow, 1988. Photographs of different hats are accompanied by the question "Whose Hat?" This book could correlate with a discussion of jobs people do, such as baker, police officer, and construction worker.

Johnson, Angela. *The Leaving Morning*
Illus. by David Soman. Orchard Books, 1992, LB (0-531-08592-9)
Suggested Use Level: Gr. 1–3

Plot Summary

Two children, a brother and sister, are moving from their apartment. They have said goodbye to their friends, neighbors, and family. Now the morning to leave has arrived. The truck is loaded, and the children and their parents sit together for one last time in their apartment. Then they go to their car and wave goodbye.

Thematic Material

The two children in *The Leaving Morning* are apprehensive about moving. They are sad to be leaving so many people they know and love. Many children will identify with these feelings. This story focuses on the experiences of an African-American family.

Book Talk Material and Activities

Moving is a common experience in the lives of most children. They may have experienced moving to a new home or school; they may have said goodbye to a friend or neighbor who moved away. In *The Leaving Morning*, the reasons for the family's move are not presented; in the illustrations, however, the mother appears to be pregnant, so perhaps the family needs a larger home. After hearing this story, children could talk about where they live now and what they like about their home. What would they miss the most? Is there anything they would change? Have they ever lived anywhere else? A book talk program could include other stories in which characters move, including *Goodbye House* and *Ira Says Goodbye*.

Older children will enjoy hearing this story and then finding out about some of the moves their family has made. Where did their parents grow up? Their grandparents? Other stories about families could extend this discussion, including *Watch the Stars Come Out* and *Molly's Pilgrim*.

Taking time to talk about personal experiences helps children get to know one another and feel more comfortable together. Children could discuss what other changes they have experienced, including the start of a new school year or the birth of a new brother or sister. When children talk about their feelings, they learn to express themselves. They hear about the experiences of others, and they build relationships by sharing what they have done. Book discussions can encourage children to think about and react to different situations.

Related Titles

Goodbye House, written and illustrated by Frank Asch. Prentice Hall, 1986. It is moving day for Baby Bear and his family. All the rooms are now empty, and Baby Bear and his father move from room to room remembering and saying goodbye. (Condensed in *Primaryplots*, Bowker, 1989, pp. 77–79.)

Ira Says Goodbye, written and illustrated by Bernard Waber. Houghton, 1988. Reggie, Ira's best friend, is moving away. As Ira remembers all the good times they have shared, he feels sad. But when Reggie seems to be looking forward to the move, Ira feels angry. The two boys realize they are both upset about the move.

Molly's Pilgrim, by Barbara Cohen. Illustrated by Michael J. Deraney. Lothrop, 1983. Molly and her family have come to America from Russia, and Molly feels like an outsider. When her class studies Thanksgiving and the Pilgrims, Molly begins to see her place in her new homeland.

Watch the Stars Come Out, by Riki Levinson. Illustrated by Diane Goode. Dutton, 1985. A little girl listens while her grandma tells her a special story. When the grandma was a little girl, she and her brother left their home and traveled by boat to America. (Condensed in *Primaryplots*, Bowker, 1989, pp. 179–180.)

We Are Best Friends, written and illustrated by Aliki. Greenwillow, 1982. When Peter moves away, Robert learns how to remain his friend and how to make new friends.

About the Author

JOHNSON, ANGELA
Something about the Author, ed. by Donna Olendorf. Gale, 1992, Vol. 69, p. 118.

Johnson, Dolores. *What Will Mommy Do When I'm at School?*
Illus. by the author. Macmillan, 1990 (0-02-747845-9)
Suggested Use Level: PreS–Gr. 1

Plot Summary

As a little girl prepares to begin school, she wonders how her mother will spend the day without her. Will Mommy be scared? Will she miss making muffins together? Mommy won't dance and sing, or watch cartoons. The two of them won't comb each other's hair, shop for groceries, or have a pretend tea party. Daddy tries unsuccessfully to reassure her. Finally, the little girl and her mother agree they are both worried about the changes they are facing. The little girl is apprehensive about school and the mother about a new job. They will have lots to share at the end of the day. Both agree they will help each other face the new situations.

Thematic Material

The focus of this story is the caring relationship between a little girl and her mother. This is also a story about facing new experiences, in this case, starting school. This book depicts a loving African-American family.

Book Talk Material and Activities

This is a reassuring story of a caring family experience. The narrator of the book tells of her concern for her mother without directly acknowledging her own fears about starting school. She is comforted by both her parents. The security of the family relationship is very satisfying, making this especially right for preschool children.

A preschool story program could focus on books in which characters share special times with their families or are reassured by them. In *Say It!* and *What Alvin Wanted,* two children make demands only their mothers can fulfill. *Jonathan and His Mommy* enjoy their own way of walking together, and Bea's father pays a special visit to her school in *Bea and Mr. Jones.* After sharing several family stories, children may want to write a note or draw a picture about their day and to take it home with them.

Related Titles

Bea and Mr. Jones, written and illustrated by Amy Schwartz. Bradbury, 1982. Bea and her father decide to trade places for the day. Ask children to think about who they might want to trade places with and what they think might happen.

Jonathan and His Mommy, by Irene Smalls-Hector. Illustrated by Michael Hays. Little, Brown, 1992. Walking around their urban neighborhood, an African-American boy and his mother use many creative ways of moving, including giant steps, zigzag steps, even bunny steps.

Mama, Do You Love Me? by Barbara Joosse. Illustrated by Barbara Lavallee. Chronicle Books, 1991. An Inuit mother reassures her daughter that she is loved. Cultural information about the Inuit follows the text.

Say It! by Charlotte Zolotow. Illustrated by James Stevenson. Greenwillow, 1980. As a mother and daughter go for a walk, the mother talks about the beauty of the time they spend together. The little girl wants to hear her mother say "I love you."

Side by Side: Poems to Read Together, collected by Lee Bennett Hopkins. Illustrated by Hilary Knight. Simon & Schuster, 1988. Sharing poems about familiar experiences, like playing or going to bed, could be included in a program for families.

What Alvin Wanted, written and illustrated by Holly Keller. Greenwillow, 1990. Alvin is unhappy and no one can find out why. When Mama comes home, she knows what he needs.

About the Author and Illustrator

JOHNSON, DOLORES
Something about the Author, ed. by Donna Olendorf. Gale, 1992, Vol. 69, pp. 118–119.

Keegan, Marcia. *Pueblo Boy: Growing Up in Two Worlds*
Photographs by the author. Dutton, 1991 (0-525-65060-1)
Suggested Use Level: Gr. 2–4

Plot Summary

This photoessay features Timmy Roybal, a Pueblo Indian boy who is ten years old. Timmy, whose Indian name is Agoyo-Paa, which means "Star Fire," lives in New Mexico. Timmy is in the fifth grade and, like many children, he rides his bike to school. The photographs show Timmy working on his math and on a computer. After school, Timmy's activities include playing with his cousins and playing baseball. Timmy also enjoys pocket pool and fishing. From his family, Timmy learns about the art and ceremonies of the Pueblo Indians. The traditions of the Pueblo Indians are passed down orally, and Timmy's father teaches him a Tewa prayer (Tewa is the language of the people of the San Ildefonso Pueblo, where Timmy and his family live). Information about the clans of the Pueblo Indians is included, as are details about the importance of corn. Timmy visits a historical site near his home, Bandelier National Monument, which contains artifacts from people who lived there many centuries ago. He also participates in many ceremonial activities that reflect the culture of the Pueblo Indians, including the Corn Dance, and photographs show some of the activities of the San Ildefonso feast day.

Thematic Material

This book describes the everyday activities of a ten-year-old boy, Timmy Roybal. Many familiar home and school activities are included, along with information about the ceremonies and traditions of the Pueblo Indians. This book could be incorporated into a study of families around the world.

Book Talk Material and Activities

The recent emphasis on multicultural materials has resulted in many fine books depicting the daily activities of children from many parts of the world. These books introduce children to the variety of cultures and traditions. *Pueblo Boy* describes the experiences of one child in New Mexico. An excellent companion book is *Pueblo Storyteller* by Diane Hoyt-Goldsmith. This book focuses on April Trujillo, who lives in the Cochiti Pueblo in New Mexico. Her Indian name is KU-tsi-ya-t'si, which means "Lady Antelope" in Keres, the language of the Cochiti people. The daily activities of her life are described, some of which will be familiar to many children, such as playing with her cousin or playing golf with her grandfather. Baking bread is an important tradition, and April describes how she and her grandmother prepare the dough and bake it in an outdoor oven. Other chapters are entitled "Making the Pottery," "Making the Cochiti Drum," "The Buffalo Dance," and "Pueblo Storyteller." A Pueblo legend, "How the People Came to Earth," is also included, along with a glossary. Looking at the Pueblo life of Timmy Roybal and comparing it to April Trujillo's activities help children realize that even within one cultural group, there are similarities and differences.

Legends of the Pueblo Indians, such as *Arrow to the Sun* and *Quail Song*, could be shared along with *Pueblo Boy*. Children might also be interested in some other cultural groups; booktalking *Totem Pole* and *Hoang Anh: A Vietnamese-American Boy* would extend that interest.

Related Titles

Arrow to the Sun: A Pueblo Indian Tale, adapted and illustrated by Gerald McDermott. Viking, 1974. A boy must survive four tests to prove his identity and find his father. This book received the Caldecott Medal in 1975.

Hoang Anh: A Vietnamese-American Boy, by Diane Hoyt-Goldsmith. Photographed by Lawrence Migdale. Holiday, 1992. Describes the daily activities of Hoang Anh and his family. Hoang Anh enjoys everyday activities similar to those of many children, such as playing football, but he also learns and appreciates the customs from his Vietnamese heritage.

Pueblo Storyteller, by Diane Hoyt-Goldsmith. Photographed by Lawrence Migdale. Holiday, 1991. Describes the daily life and experiences of April Trujillo, focusing on her family's respect for the traditions of the Pueblo Indians.

Quail Song: A Pueblo Indian Tale, adapted by Valerie Scho Carey. Illustrated by Ivan Barrett. Putnam, 1990. Quail uses her wits to trick Coyote.

Totem Pole, by Diane Hoyt-Goldsmith. Photographed by Lawrence Migdale. Holiday, 1990. David is a member of the Eagle Clan, a family group of the Tsimshian tribe on the northwest coast of North America. David describes the traditions of this group, particularly their skill carving wood. "The Legend of the Eagle and the Young Chief: A Tsimshian Tale" is included, along with chapters entitled "Carving the Pole" and "Raising the Pole." A glossary is included.

About the Author and Illustrator

KEEGAN, MARCIA
Something about the Author, ed. by Anne Commire. Gale, 1976, Vol. 9, pp. 121–122.

Keller, Holly. *The Best Present*
Illus. by the author. Greenwillow, 1989, LB (0-688-07320-4)
Suggested Use Level: K–Gr. 2

Plot Summary

Rosie's grandmother is in the hospital and Rosie wants to visit her. Rosie is eight years old, and the hospital has a rule that children must be at least ten years old to visit. With the help of her friend, Kate, Rosie tries to make herself look older. She goes to the hospital, planning to visit her grandmother and give her some flowers, but she finds that she cannot break the rule. Rosie hands the flowers to someone on the elevator and, dejected, returns home. When her grandmother is released from the hospital, Rosie goes to visit her. Her grandmother shows Rosie some of the gifts she received, including Rosie's flowers. Grandma tells Rosie the flowers were "the best present of all."

Thematic Material

Rosie's grandmother understands how much Rosie cares about her. Even though Rosie does not get into the hospital, her grandmother helps Rosie feel proud of her accomplishment. There is a feeling of family togetherness in this story. *The Best Present* is also a story about being considered too little or too young to do things.

Book Talk Material and Activities

The Best Present is a very satisfying story to share with young children. They relate to Rosie's disappointment at being excluded from visiting her grandmother. They appreciate the love and understanding her grandmother shows Rosie. Young children often feel "left out." In *The Best Present*, Rosie's grandmother understands that feeling. Grandma appreciates what Rosie tried to do, and she helps Rosie feel special just for trying.

There are many books that feature characters who are insecure and who feel what they do is not good enough. In *Shy Charles*, other characters seem to expect Charles to be more outgoing. When someone needs his help, Charles is able to speak and act, although he is still very shy. Jay is another very shy boy whose teacher helps him overcome his shyness and talk about his cricket in *A Pocketful of Cricket*. Sophie the mouse feels left out because Wendell is bossy in *A Weekend with Wendell*.

There are many books about children and their grandparents. Booktalking some recent books would extend the reading of *The Best Present.* In some of these books, children learn about problems that can occur for older adults. *Grandpa's Song* describes a grandfather who is having trouble remembering. The characters in *Wilfrid Gordon McDonald Partridge* also have failing memories. Other books show grandparents helping their grandchildren, like the grandfather in *Grandpa's Face* (elsewhere in this chapter) and the grandmother in *Oma and Bobo.* These books introduce children to a variety of images of older adults.

Related Titles

Grandpa's Song, by Tony Johnston. Illustrated by Brad Sneed. Dial, 1991. Grandpa has always been very outgoing, but now he has become forgetful. His grandchildren help him remember his favorite song.

Happy Birthday, Grampie, by Susan Pearson. Illustrated by Ronald Himler. Dial, 1987. Martha and her parents go to visit Grampie at the nursing home, and Martha's special card helps him remember the love they have shared.

Oma and Bobo, written and illustrated by Amy Schwartz. Bradbury, 1987. On her birthday, Alice is delighted to learn that she will be allowed to have a dog. Her grandmother, Oma, is not pleased, but she ends up helping Alice train Bobo. (Condensed in *Primaryplots,* Bowker, 1989, pp. 111–113.)

A Pocketful of Cricket, by Rebecca Caudill. Illustrated by Evaline Ness. Holt, 1964. Jay catches a cricket, and it becomes his friend. At school, he overcomes his shyness to talk about his cricket.

Shy Charles, written and illustrated by Rosemary Wells. Dial, 1988. Although Charles is very shy, when his help is needed, Charles knows what to do.

A Weekend with Wendell, written and illustrated by Kevin Henkes. Greenwillow, 1986. When Wendell comes to visit, Sophie cannot wait for him to leave. He is bossy, and he plays tricks on her. After Sophie stands up to him, they enjoy being together.

Wilfrid Gordon McDonald Partridge, by Mem Fox. Illustrated by Julie Vivas. Kane-Miller, 1984. Wilfrid lives next door to an old people's home. By collecting special objects, he helps his friend, Miss Nancy, remember some past experiences. (Condensed in *Primaryplots,* Bowker, 1989, pp. 49–51.)

About the Author and Illustrator

KELLER, HOLLY

Something about the Author, ed. by Anne Commire. Gale, 1986, Vol. 42, p. 123.

Khalsa, Dayal Kaur. *My Family Vacation*
Illus. by the author. Clarkson N. Potter, 1988 (0-517-56697-4)
Suggested Use Level: Gr. 1-2

Plot Summary

May, Richie, and their parents are taking a vacation to Miami, Florida. This is the first vacation May has been on, and she is eager and apprehensive. They pack the car and head south, leaving just as snow is beginning to fall. May loves staying in the motels along the way. She loves collecting souvenirs, making sure to get a little bar of soap from each motel bathroom. She does not love being tormented by her older brother, Richie, but she is used to it. The family stops for sightseeing along the way, visiting an aquarium and the Parrot Jungle. Continuing south, May and Richie squabble in the back seat. In Miami Beach, Richie reminds May that he has dared her to jump off the high diving board. Gathering her courage, May jumps, and, for once, Richie is impressed. Then, while their parents sit by the pool, Richie and May go to the penny arcade and the bowling alley and play miniature golf. The family goes out to celebrate the last night of their stay in Miami. They head back home, with the weather becoming colder and colder, arriving to see their house covered with snow. May has souvenirs and memories of her first family vacation.

Thematic Material

May is very excited about going on her first vacation, but she is also a bit nervous. There is a feeling of family togetherness in this story, although, like ordinary siblings, May and Richie do not always get along.

Book Talk Material and Activities

Where might May and her family live? How far might they travel to reach Miami Beach? What is the longest trip you have ever taken? How did you travel? Every child has visited somewhere, often on a car trip similar to the one in *My Family Vacation*. They have played games to pass the time and collected souvenirs and mementos. A group of children could talk about their experiences and compare them to those in this book. Sharing information about similar experiences lets children learn about each other. Related activities could include charting the length (in miles or in days) of the longest trip; discussing the styles of transportation; selecting a destination and planning a vacation; and preparing a book of games to play while traveling.

Other books in which characters travel could be presented, including *Just Us Women* and *Stringbean's Trip to the Shining Sea*. *The Relatives Came* looks at a family trip from the perspective of a character who is being visited by relatives. *Dinosaurs Travel* describes the preparations for a trip, some common experiences, and different types of traveling. Children will enjoy reading other books about May: *How Pizza Came to Queens* and *I Want a Dog*.

Related Titles

Dinosaurs Travel: A Guide for Families on the Go, by Laurene Krasny Brown and Marc Brown. Little, Brown, 1988. This book is filled with useful information about traveling, including getting ready and coming home.

Emma's Vacation, written and illustrated by David McPhail. Dutton, 1987. The bears take a trip and have several adventures, but Emma's favorite time is when she and her parents spend some quiet time together.

How Pizza Came to Queens, written and illustrated by Dayal Kaur Khalsa. Clarkson N. Potter, 1989. When Mrs. Pelligrino comes from Italy to visit, May and her friends are fascinated. And when Mrs. Pelligrino makes pizza, May and her friends are delighted.

I Want a Dog, written and illustrated by Dayal Kaur Khalsa. Clarkson N. Potter, 1987. May wants a dog, and she works hard to convince her parents she would be responsible. She practices by putting a skate on a leash and caring for it like a dog.

Just Us Women, by Jeannette Caines. Illustrated by Pat Cummings. Harper, 1982. A girl and her aunt plan a trip together. The girl describes their preparations and some of the things they hope to do.

Ralph's Secret Weapon, written and illustrated by Steven Kellogg. Dial, 1983. Aunt Georgiana has some special plans for Ralph while he visits her for his summer vacation. Ralph is willing to try to please his aunt, but he does let her know when he needs to do things for himself. (Condensed in *Primaryplots*, Bowker, 1989, pp. 22–23.)

The Relatives Came, by Cynthia Rylant. Illustrated by Stephen Gammell.

Bradbury, 1985. One summer the relatives from Virginia come to visit. They crowd into the house, and there is a celebration of family togetherness. (Condensed in *Primaryplots*, Bowker, 1989, pp. 31–33.)

Stringbean's Trip to the Shining Sea, by Vera B. Williams. Illustrated by Vera B. Williams and Jennifer Williams. Greenwillow, 1988. Stringbean and his brother, Fred, are taking a trip to the Pacific Ocean. Most of the pages in this book are designed to look like postcards, which Stringbean and Fred send home to their family in Kansas.

The Train to Lulu's, by Elizabeth Fitzgerald Howard. Illustrated by Robert Casilla. Bradbury, 1988. Beppy and Babs are taking the train to visit their Great-Aunt Lulu. This book is based on an experience from the author's childhood.

About the Author and Illustrator

KHALSA, DAYAL KAUR

Something about the Author, ed. by Anne Commire. Gale, 1990, Vol. 62, pp. 98–100.

Levinson, Riki.   *Our Home Is the Sea*

Illus. by Dennis Luzak. Dutton, 1988 (0-525-44406-8); pap., Puffin (0-14-054552-2)

Suggested Use Level: Gr. K–2

Plot Summary

On his last day of school, a boy hurries home. He rushes through the city streets of Hong Kong to catch the tram. On the tram, he sees the market area; he passes children meeting their amahs; he sees tall apartment buildings. Running through the park, he sees a man selling birds, and he sees a peacock. At the harbor, the boy sees his houseboat. He waves to his family and waits for his mother to come for him in the sampan. At home on the houseboat, he sits with his two younger brothers, and they have bowls of congee and some tea. The next morning his father is there. Together, they travel out to the grandfather's boat for a day of fishing. Three generations work together on the sea.

Thematic Material

This book focuses on the everyday experiences of a boy in another part of the world. Specific words and activities are included that tell about life in Hong Kong. This could be included in a social studies unit on families and homes around the world.

Book Talk Material and Activities

How do children learn about others in the world? Sharing a book like *Our Home Is the Sea* introduces children to another part of the world and a different way of life. The boy in this story has some things in common with American children. He is on his way home from school with his report card. He is eager to get home and to see his family, especially his father. He is looking forward to spending some time fishing with his father and grandfather. This boy is also very different from American children. He travels through busy streets where it is common to see open markets selling fish and poultry. The signs that he sees are written in another language. His home is a houseboat, which he reaches on a sampan, a smaller boat. There are many details in the text and illustrations that children could list as similarities and differences. Specific terms like tram, amah, sampan, and congee could be defined in context using information from the text and the illustrations.

Hong Kong is depicted in the photographs in *Houses and Homes* and *On the Go,* and both of these would expand children's understanding of *Our Home Is the Sea. The House I Live In* features different houses in America. An activity for children could be to draw or bring a photograph of their home. Or the class could take a survey to find out what kinds of homes they come from, such as single family, apartments, and so on. The homes in *Houses and Homes* could provide some possible categories for the survey. Sharing these books could help children understand the variety of peoples and ways of life in the world.

Related Titles

The House I Live In: At Home in America, written and illustrated by Isadore Seltzer. Macmillan, 1992. Twelve houses are featured, including a houseboat in Northern California. The influences of geography and history are reflected in many of the houses.

Houses and Homes, by Ann Morris. Photographed by Ken Heyman. Lothrop, 1992. Color photographs show a variety of homes around the world, including tents, mud huts, and cabins. Places featured include France, India, Hong Kong, and Kenya.

My Place in Space, by Robin Hirst and Sally Hirst. Illustrated by Roland Harvey and Joe Levine. Orchard, 1990. When the bus driver asks Henry where he lives, Henry describes the street, town, country, hemisphere, planet, solar system, solar neighborhood, galaxy, supercluster, and universe.

On the Go, by Ann Morris. Photographed by Ken Heyman. Lothrop, 1990. Different methods of travel are described in the simple text and pictured in the color photographs. Vehicles powered by animals and engines are depicted. The places shown include Peru, Hong Kong, Bali, Somalia, Germany, the United States, and the moon.

A Road Might Lead to Anywhere, by Rachel Field. Illustrated by Giles Laroche. Little, Brown, 1990. In this poem, a young girl dreams of the places she might visit someday. Some of the locations are everyday; some are exotic.

This Is the Way We Go to School: A Book about Children around the World, by Edith Baer. Illustrated by Steven Björkman. Scholastic, 1990. A rhyming text describes the ways many children go to school. After the story there is a list of where each child lives and a map showing the locations.

About the Author

LEVINSON, RIKI

Sixth Book of Junior Authors and Illustrators, ed. by Sally Holmes Holtze. Wilson, 1989, pp. 170–172.

Something about the Author, ed. by Anne Commire. Gale, 1987, Vol. 49, pp. 156–157; 1988, Vol. 52, pp. 113–116.

Mora, Pat.   *A Birthday Basket for Tia*
Illus. by Cecily Lang. Macmillan, 1992 (0-02-767400-2)
Suggested Use Level: Gr. K–2

Plot Summary

Cecilia is excited about Great-Aunt Tia's ninetieth birthday, but she is worried about finding a gift. She decides to fill a basket with mementos of special times she has shared with her great-aunt—a favorite book, a teacup, a red ball, and some fresh flowers. At the surprise birthday party, Tia is delighted with Cecilia's gifts. The family celebrates with a piñata, music, and a dance performed by Tia and Cecilia.

Thematic Material

This book focuses on a birthday celebration in a Mexican-American family. Special emphasis is given to the relationship between Cecilia and her great-aunt.

Book Talk Material and Activities

Birthday celebrations have different traditions around the world. In *A Birthday Basket for Tia*, Cecilia and her mother prepare a piñata for the party, and they make *bizcochos,* sugar cookies. Children hearing this story relate to the universal experience of the birthday, but they also experience some of the cultural details of the lives of Cecilia and her family. Gail Gibbons's *Happy Birthday!* is a nonfiction book that describes some of the traditions and beliefs associated with birthdays.

After hearing *A Birthday Basket for Tia*, children could discuss the relationship between Cecilia and her Great-Aunt Tia. What does Tia do to make Cecilia feel special? Children could tell about a time when someone made them feel special. This kind of discussion helps children relate Cecilia's story to their own lives. *A Birthday Basket for Tia* is reminiscent of other stories. Creating a basket filled with special items occurs in *Mr. Rabbit and the Lovely Present. Ask Mr. Bear* is a story about finding a present. Choosing special items to spark memories happens in *Wilfrid Gordon McDonald Partridge.* These books could be booktalked for children to sign out after hearing *A Birthday Basket for Tia.*

Related Titles

Ask Mr. Bear, written and illustrated by Marjorie Flack. Macmillan, 1932. A little boy wants to find a special gift for his mother. He gets some advice from Mr. Bear.

Happy Birthday!, written and illustrated by Gail Gibbons. Holiday, 1986. Why are there candles on a birthday cake? Why is there a cake? Gail Gibbons provides background information on some common birthday experiences.

Mr. Rabbit and the Lovely Present, by Charlotte Zolotow. Illustrated by Maurice Sendak. Harper, 1962. Mr. Rabbit helps the little girl choose just the right present for her mother.

Oma and Bobo, written and illustrated by Amy Schwartz. Bradbury, 1987. Although this story does not include a birthday, Alice and her grandmother, Oma, work together to train Bobo, Alice's dog. Alice and her grandmother have a strong relationship. (Condensed in *Primaryplots,* Bowker, 1989, pp. 111–113.)

Some Birthday!, written and illustrated by Patricia Polacco. Simon & Schuster, 1991. This family has a very unusual way to celebrate a birthday—they look for the Monster in the Clay Pit Bottoms.

Wilfrid Gordon McDonald Partridge, by Mem Fox. Illustrated by Julie Vivas. Kane-Miller, 1984. Wilfrid lives next door to an old people's home. By collecting special objects, he helps his friend, Miss Nancy, remember some past experiences. (Condensed in *Primaryplots,* Bowker, 1989, pp. 49–51.)

Pinkney, Gloria Jean.   *Back Home*

Illus. by Jerry Pinkney. Dial, 1992, LB (0-8037-1169-7)
Suggested Use Level: Gr. 2–4

Plot Summary

Ernestine, who is eight, has traveled by train to visit her relatives in North Carolina. Her uncle June meets her at the train and takes her to see her aunt Beula and her cousin Jack. They have not seen Ernestine since she was a baby. Ernestine sleeps in the bedroom that was her mama's when she was growing up. She even gets to wear her mama's old overalls. Although she wants to be friends with Jack, Ernestine cannot seem to make him like her. He teases her about her fancy clothes and city ways. When the family visits the abandoned house where Ernestine was born, Ernestine plans to come back someday and fix the house. As she prepares to leave, Ernestine realizes she and Jack have become friends, and she looks forward to her next visit to her family home.

Thematic Material

The feeling of togetherness in this African-American family is a central theme in *Back Home.* Although it is not stated, this story is set in the past, perhaps in the 1930s or 1940s. There is a sense that this is a personal reminiscence, which is supported by the note about the author and by the dedication to the memory of the author's mother, Ernestine.

Book Talk Material and Activities

Many authors write about their own memories and experiences. These nostalgic reminiscences are often filled with loving memories of special times with friends and family. Books with the theme of family togetherness could be shared before holidays and could be the focus of classroom writing projects. Many children in the middle grades of elementary school are developing an understanding for the past. They can look back on some of their own experiences and begin to talk or write about them. After reading *Back Home,* children could write or talk about where they were born or about a special family gathering. They could talk with other relatives about their memories of family experiences. *Grandaddy's Place* could be compared and contrasted with *Back Home,* as both books feature children who are visiting relatives in the country for the first time. Books such as *When I Was Nine, The Train to Lulu's,* and *When I Was Young in the Mountains* would also extend the theme of family reminiscences.

Jerry Pinkney, the author's husband, has included many details of the family's life in his illustrations. He conveys the rural setting by showing Uncle June and Cousin Jack at work on the farm. There are illustrations of farm animals and fields. The illustrations also convey the time period of the book, showing Cousin Jack in knickers and vehicles that are very dated. When the family goes to visit the grave of Ernestine's grandmother, the dates are 1887–1928. This would be another book to include when studying the art of Jerry Pinkney (see *Turtle in July* in chapter 7).

Related Titles

Grandaddy's Place, by Helen V. Griffith. Illustrated by James Stevenson. Greenwillow, 1987. Janetta and Momma are going to visit Grandaddy, whom Janetta has never met. This is also Janetta's first trip to the country. (Condensed in *Primaryplots,* Bowker, 1989, pp. 11–13.)

I Go with My Family to Grandma's, by Riki Levinson. Illustrated by Diane Goode. Dutton, 1986. For this family gathering, each of the five cousins comes by a different mode of transportation from a different part of New York City.

The Train to Lulu's, by Elizabeth Fitzgerald Howard. Illustrated by Robert Casilla. Bradbury, 1988. Beppy and Babs are taking the train to visit their Great-Aunt Lulu. This book is based on an experience from the author's childhood.

When I Was Nine, written and illustrated by James Stevenson. Greenwillow, 1986. A man reminisces about his childhood, including his dog, his family, his neighborhood, and some of his everyday activities. (Condensed in *Primaryplots,* Bowker, 1989, pp. 190–192.)

When I Was Young in the Mountains, by Cynthia Rylant. Illustrated by Diane Goode. Dutton, 1982. The repetition of the title phrase evokes a sense of nostalgia and yearning as the author describes childhood memories.

About the Illustrator

PINKNEY, JERRY

Illustrators of Children's Books: 1957–1966, Volume III, comp. by Lee Kingman, Grace Allen
Hogarth, and Harriet Quimby. Horn Book, 1978, pp. 158, 235; *Volume IV, 1967–76,*
1978, pp. 151, 205.
Sixth Book of Junior Authors and Illustrators, ed. by Sally Holmes Holtze. Wilson, 1989, pp.
225–227.
Something about the Author, ed. by Anne Commire. Gale, 1983, Vol. 41, pp. 164–174.
Talking with Artists, comp. and ed. by Pat Cummings. Bradbury, 1992, pp. 60–65.

Reid, Margarette S.   *The Button Box*
Illus. by Sarah Chamberlain. Dutton, 1990 (0-525-44590-0)
Suggested Use Level: Gr. K–2

Plot Summary

A young boy opens his grandmother's button box and sorts through the
buttons, selecting his favorites. He selects painted buttons, jeweled buttons,
fabric-covered buttons, metal buttons, leather buttons, even buttons from
shoes. There are shiny buttons from uniforms and brightly colored buttons. He looks at details on the buttons, including what they are made of,
how many holes they have, and unusual shapes and sizes. His grandmother shows him a button game and talks about what some of the
buttons are made of. Then the buttons go back into the button box to be
played with on another day. After the story, a brief history of buttons is
included.

Thematic Material

This book looks at a special collection of items, in this case buttons. It
also presents a shared experience between a boy and his grandmother.

Book Talk Material and Activities

In 1978, the first Sunday after Labor Day was designated National
Grandparents' Day. *The Button Box* could be included in a story or book
talk program for this day. Grandparents or other older adults could be
invited to special school or library activities in their honor. They could
read favorite stories from when they were children or just tell what it was
like when they were growing up. Some may even want to share a special

collection with the group. Children need to see the contributions older adults can make, and this would be a special time for sharing. *Aunt Flossie's Hats (and Crab Cakes Later)* (elsewhere in this chapter), *The Hundred Penny Box*, and *Wilfrid Gordon McDonald Partridge* are other stories about memories and collections.

In *The Button Box*, the little boy enjoys sorting and classifying the buttons. This activity could extend into some classroom projects involving "hands-on" math experiences. Certainly, this book should be enjoyed as a lovely family story and not be force-fed as a math "project book"; however, some playful activities could be related to the book. Children could also see the similarities between *The Button Box* and "A Lost Button" in *Frog and Toad Are Friends*. They may enjoy looking at many buttons and seeing similarities and differences, and a "button box" could be in an activity area for children to explore.

Related Titles

Blackberries in the Dark, by Mavis Jukes. Illustrated by Thomas B. Allen. Knopf, 1985. This book takes place during the first summer after Austin's grandpa died. Austin's memories of the time he and his grandfather had together show how much he loved his grandfather.

The Hundred Penny Box, by Sharon Bell Mathis. Illustrated by Leo Dillon and Diane Dillon. Viking, 1975. Michael's Great-Great-Aunt Dew keeps a box with a penny for every year of her life—one hundred pennies. She counts them with Michael and tells a story about each one.

"A Lost Button" in *Frog and Toad Are Friends*, written and illustrated by Arnold Lobel. Harper, 1970. Toad loses his button, and Frog helps him search for it. They find many buttons, but they do not find Toad's button. Annoyed, Toad returns home—and finds his button. Now, he must find a way to thank Frog for all the looking he did.

A Three Hat Day, by Laura Geringer. Illustrated by Arnold Lobel. Greenwillow, 1985. R.R. Pottle the Third is so fond of hats that he sometimes wears more than one. He wishes he could find someone who would appreciate him and his hats. (Condensed in *Primaryplots*, Bowker, 1989, pp. 51–53.)

Wilfrid Gordon McDonald Partridge, by Mem Fox. Illustrated by Julie Vivas. Kane-Miller, 1984. Wilfrid collects items to help his elderly friend, Miss Nancy, remember. He gives his collection to her, and as she holds each object, it brings a special memory to her. (Condensed in *Primaryplots*, Bowker, 1989, pp. 49–51.)

Ringgold, Faith. *Tar Beach*
Illus. by the author. Crown, 1991, LB (0-517-58030-6)
Suggested Use Level: Gr. 1–3

Plot Summary

Eight-year-old Cassie Louise Lightfoot thinks about the hot summer nights when her family and friends go up to the roof of their apartment building in Harlem. This is their "Tar Beach." From the roof, Cassie sees the lights and buildings, the stars, and, most especially, the George Washington Bridge, which opened in 1931, the year Cassie was born. Cassie's father was on the construction crew that built the bridge, making it even more important to her. Cassie feels the bridge is hers. She feels she can fly over the city, looking at her bridge, soaring over the Union Building (which excludes her own father because of his race), and gliding past the ice cream factory. As her family prepares for a dinner up on Tar Beach, Cassie plans her next flight, taking her young brother Be Be along. Together they will fly among the stars, free to go anywhere.

Thematic Material

Cassie is part of a loving African-American family. In this reminiscence, she reflects on some special times with family and friends. *Tar Beach* was a Caldecott Honor Book in 1992.

Book Talk Material and Activities

Abuela is another imaginative fantasy involving flight. In this book, Rosalba is riding on the bus to the park with her grandmother, her "Abuela." Seeing the many birds at the park, Rosalba imagines she and her Abuela can fly. Together they glide above the city, the harbor, the Statue of Liberty, and the airport. They visit relatives and fly through the clouds, returning to the park for a boat ride. Spanish words are used throughout the story, and a glossary is included.

Looking at *Tar Beach* and *Abuela* could promote a discussion of fantasy trips. What do Cassie and Rosalba see on their trips? What would you see if you could fly? Who would you take with you on your trip? Other flying fantasies include *I'm Flying!* and *Aunt Harriet's Underground Railroad in the Sky*, which is another flying adventure for Cassie and Be Be.

The illustrations for *Tar Beach* feature details from one of Faith Ringgold's story quilts. The story is illustrated with paintings. A border of quilted fabric pieces runs along the bottom of each page. A photograph of the original "Tar Beach" story quilt is included at the end of the book, accompanied by information about Faith Ringgold and her art.

Related Titles

Abuela, by Arthur Dorros. Illustrated by Elisa Kleven. Dutton, 1991. The collage illustrations are filled with details and effectively use changing perspectives to convey the joy of this imaginative fantasy.

Aunt Harriet's Underground Railroad in the Sky, written and illustrated by Faith Ringgold. Crown, 1992. While flying, Cassie and Be Be meet Harriet Tubman. Be Be rides on the train in the sky, and Cassie follows the route to freedom on the ground.

I'm Flying!, by Alan Wade. Illustrated by Petra Mathers. Knopf, 1990. A little boy uses helium and balloons to get rid of things he doesn't like, such as his math book and his mom's purple dress. Finally, he decides to fly away.

Jim Flying High, by Mari Evans. Illustrated by Ashley Bryan. Doubleday, 1979. Jim is a flying fish that gets stuck in a tree. He will not admit he has a problem, but his family and friends still help him.

Tonight Is Carnaval, by Arthur Dorros. Illustrated with *arpilleras* sewn by the Club de Madres Virgen del Carmen of Lima, Peru. Dutton, 1991. In the Andes Mountains of South America, a family prepares for Carnaval. The illustrations for this book are photographs of fabric wall hangings, *arpilleras.* After the story is a description of how the *arpilleras* were made and a glossary of some of the terms in the book.

About the Author and Illustrator

RINGGOLD, FAITH

Something about the Author, ed. by Diane Telgen. Gale, 1993, Vol. 71, pp. 159–164.

Rylant, Cynthia.   *Henry and Mudge and the Long Weekend: The Eleventh Book of Their Adventures*
  Illus. by Suçie Stevenson. Bradbury, 1992 (0-02-778013-9)
  Suggested Use Level: Gr. 1–2

Plot Summary

It is a cold, boring Saturday. Henry and his dog, Mudge, have nothing to do. Even Henry's parents are bored, until Henry's mother comes up with a plan. Working together in the basement, Henry, his parents, and Mudge take some large boxes, paint, and other supplies and create a castle. The boring weekend becomes two days of family fun.

Thematic Material

The books about Henry and Mudge are a very popular series for beginning readers. They emphasize the friendship between Henry and his dog and often focus on family activities and togetherness.

Book Talk Material and Activities

The five chapters in this book are accessible to children who are developing independence as readers. *Henry and Mudge and the Long Weekend* is the eleventh book about these two characters. Many children ask for series books, like the Henry and Mudge books, because they feel comfortable with the familiar characters. The format of this book (short chapters, large print, wide spacing between words and lines of text) makes it very appropriate for beginning readers. Sharing some of the Henry and Mudge books could introduce children to the concept of a series in which the same characters have different adventures in different books. Several of the books follow Henry and Mudge through the seasons: spring *(Henry and Mudge in Puddle Trouble)*, summer *(Henry and Mudge and the Forever Sea* and *Henry and Mudge in the Green Time)*, fall *(Henry and Mudge under the Yellow Moon)*, and winter *(Henry and Mudge in the Sparkle Days)*. These could be correlated with other seasonal stories. *Henry and Mudge and the Wild Wind* is the newest book about these two friends.

A book talk program could focus on other series books in the first reader format, including the Penrod stories, the books about Old Turtle and his friends, and the books about Oliver Pig and his family. Sharing these books with a group of children is especially enjoyable because there are enough books available for each child to choose one following the program.

Related Titles

The Henry and Mudge books, written by Cynthia Rylant and illustrated by Suçie Stevenson, include:

Henry and Mudge: The First Book of Their Adventures. Bradbury, 1987. When Henry finally is allowed to have a dog, Mudge is just a puppy. He grows to be a very large dog and becomes Henry's best friend.

Henry and Mudge and the Bedtime Thumps: The Ninth Book of Their Adventures. Bradbury, 1991. Henry worries about taking Mudge to visit Grandmother. Will she like Mudge? Will Mudge stay out of trouble?

Henry and Mudge and the Forever Sea: The Sixth Book of Their Adventures. Bradbury, 1989. On a hot summer day, Henry, Mudge, and Henry's father go to the beach. This is Mudge's first trip to the ocean.

Henry and Mudge and the Happy Cat: The Eighth Book of Their Adventures. Bradbury, 1990. When a shabby cat comes to the door, Henry, Mudge, and Henry's father let it in. The whole family comes to love the cat. The owner, a police officer, claims the cat, and Henry and Mudge miss their friend.

Henry and Mudge and the Wild Wind: The Twelfth Book of Their Adventures. Bradbury, 1992. During a thunderstorm, Henry and Mudge stay inside and try to find things to do.

Henry and Mudge Get the Cold Shivers: The Seventh Book of Their Adventures. Bradbury, 1989. First, Henry gets a cold and then Mudge gets a cold. Both of them need to take their medicine to get well again.

Henry and Mudge in Puddle Trouble: The Second Book of Their Adventures. Bradbury, 1987. There are three spring stories in this book. In the first, Mudge eats a flower. Then, Henry and Mudge play in a huge puddle—and Henry's father joins them. In the third story, Mudge protects some kittens from another dog.

Henry and Mudge in the Green Time: The Third Book of Their Adventures. Bradbury, 1987. In the three stories in this book, Henry and Mudge go on a picnic, Henry gives Mudge a bath, and Henry plays "King of the Green Hill," with Mudge as the dragon.

Henry and Mudge in the Sparkle Days: The Fifth Book of Their Adventures. Bradbury, 1988. In the winter, the two friends play in the snow, share Christmas Eve dinner, and take long, cold walks.

Henry and Mudge Take the Big Test: The Tenth Book of Their Adventures.

Bradbury, 1991. Henry takes Mudge to Papp's Dog School. Then Henry worries, because Mudge is not a very good student.

Henry and Mudge under the Yellow Moon: The Fourth Book of Their Adventures. Bradbury, 1987. In the fall, the two friends enjoy the leaves and celebrate Halloween and Thanksgiving.

Some other series books for beginning readers:

Old Turtle's Soccer Team, written and illustrated by Leonard Kessler. Greenwillow, 1988. Old Turtle, Cat, Rabbit, Frog, Duck, and the rest of their friends play soccer. Chapters in this book also focus on the rules of soccer and on preparing to play.

Penrod's Pants, by Mary Blount Christian. Illustrated by Jane Dyer. Macmillan, 1986. The five stories in this book focus on the adventures of Penrod the porcupine and Griswold the bear, including going on a shopping trip and pulling a loose tooth.

Tales of Oliver Pig, by Jean Van Leeuwen. Illustrated by Arnold Lobel. Dial, 1979. This is the first book in this series. Oliver's sister, Amanda, is a baby. In other books, Amanda and Oliver grow and change. The most recent book in the series is *Amanda Pig on Her Own,* illustrated by Ann Schweninger. Dial, 1991.

About the Author

RYLANT, CYNTHIA

Sixth Book of Junior Authors and Illustrators, ed. by Sally Holmes Holtze. Wilson, 1989, pp. 255–256.

Something about the Author, ed. by Anne Commire. Gale, 1986, Vol. 44, pp. 167–168; 1988, Vol. 50, pp. 182–188.

Say, Allen. *The Lost Lake*

Illus. by the author. Houghton, 1989 (0-395-50933-5); pap. (0-395-63036-3)

Suggested Use Level: Gr. 2–4

Plot Summary

A young boy, Luke, has traveled to spend the summer with his father. His father, who works at home, is very busy, and Luke becomes bored.

When his father notices some pictures Luke has cut from magazines, he takes Luke on a surprise trip to the mountains. They are going to Lost Lake, a special place where Luke's father had hiked with his father. They hike together, although Luke is not used to hiking, so he lags behind. His father keeps encouraging him, and they reach a lake. The lake is crowded with people, so Luke and his father continue hiking, even after it begins to rain. They finally stop and set up their tent. As they eat dinner, Luke's father apologizes for taking Luke to the crowded lake. He wanted Luke to see the lake as he remembered it, isolated and beautiful. They decide to continue hiking, to look for a lake that can become their Lost Lake. The next day, they leave the other hikers behind and go through a forest. As they leave the forest, it is dark, so they settle down for the night, sleeping outside. In the morning, the sun rises over the mountains and shines down on a beautiful lake.

Thematic Material

In this story, Luke does not have a close relationship with his father. Their hiking and camping trip helps them develop a friendship. The theme of appreciating the beauty of nature is also evident in *The Lost Lake*.

Book Talk Material and Activities

This is a lovely story of a caring relationship that develops between a father and son. When Luke first comes to stay with his father, he does not know his father well. The time they spend in the mountains gives them the opportunity to be together and to learn about each other. They make a commitment to continuing the family tradition of finding a Lost Lake. In *Dawn* by Uri Shulevitz, a grandfather and his grandson sleep outside and wake to a beautiful sunrise. *Where the River Begins* is also a story about sharing a special time in the outdoors, as is *Owl Moon*.

The illustrations for *The Lost Lake* show that Luke and his father have an Asian heritage. This information is not contained in the text. Literature with multicultural images has received a lot of attention. Many educators are looking for literature that is inclusive, presenting the images and experiences of many children. They want all children to be able to see themselves in the stories and pictures of the books they read. Children also need to learn about the experiences of others. *The Lost Lake* presents a father and son who learn how much they care for each other. It tells a story many children will relate to, while providing some children with a visual image of themselves. Allen Say's illustrations for *How My Parents Learned to Eat* and *The Bicycle Man* provide some past and present images of Japan.

Related Titles

The Bicycle Man, written and illustrated by Allen Say. Houghton, 1982. Two American soldiers visit the Japanese school on Sportsday and add to the fun of that special day in this memoir of the author's experience as a first-grader.

Dawn, written and illustrated by Uri Shulevitz. Farrar, 1974. A boy and his grandfather spend the night outside, waking just before dawn and watching the sun rise. The illustrations begin with a small blue-and-black oval and grow in size to fill the pages with bright green, blue, and yellow.

How My Parents Learned to Eat, by Ina R. Friedman. Illustrated by Allen Say. Houghton, 1984. A young girl whose mother is Japanese and whose father is American tells about her family. (Condensed in *Primaryplots,* Bowker, 1989, pp. 215–217.)

Owl Moon, by Jane Yolen. Illustrated by John Schoenherr. Philomel, 1987. A young girl goes owling with her father on a moonlit winter night. The girl becomes cold and tired, but she knows she must be patient. She and her father do see a beautiful owl. (Condensed in *Primaryplots,* Bowker, 1989, pp. 240–243.)

Three Days on a River in a Red Canoe, written and illustrated by Vera B. Williams. Greenwillow, 1984. After they buy a red canoe, a girl and her mother, aunt, and cousin plan a trip. This book is written like a journal as the girl describes the preparations for the trip and some of the activities that occurred on the trip.

Where the River Begins, written and illustrated by Thomas Locker. Dial, 1984. Two boys hike along the river with their grandfather, sharing his knowledge of life and nature.

About the Author and Illustrator

SAY, ALLEN

Sixth Book of Junior Authors and Illustrators, ed. by Sally Holmes Holtze. Wilson, 1989, pp. 266–268.

Something about the Author, ed. by Anne Commire. Gale, 1982, Vol. 28, p. 179; ed. by Donna Olendorf, Gale, 1992, Vol. 69, pp. 181–183.

Tsutsui, Yoriko.   *Anna in Charge*
Illus. by Akiko Hayashi. Viking, 1988 (0-670-81672-8); pap., Puffin
(0-14-050733-7)
Suggested Use Level: K–Gr. 2

Plot Summary

When she has to run an errand, Anna's mother leaves Anna at home
with her younger sister, Katy. Katy is taking a nap, but as soon as Mother
is gone, she wakes up. Anna and Katy play outside together. Anna draws
a train track out of chalk so she and Katy can play "choo-choo," but when
she looks up from her work, she realizes Katy has wandered away. Anna
searches the neighborhood for Katy, finding her playing in the sand in the
park. Anna is relieved to have found her little sister, and she gives her a
big hug.

Thematic Material

As Anna discovers, being an older sibling can bring responsibilities and
concerns. This story was originally published in Japan in 1979. The
Japanese setting provides an opportunity to relate the theme of caring
about your family to other cultures.

Book Talk Material and Activities

Have you ever had to watch a younger child? What was it like? How
did the child behave? Being an older brother or sister can be fun and
frustrating. Reading *Anna in Charge* encourages children to talk about their
own experiences. They can relate to Anna's concern when her sister is
missing and to her relief when she finds Katy. They talk about how much
more they know or can do than a baby or toddler. They feel proud of what
they have accomplished. A book talk program could feature other stories
of older children taking responsibility for someone younger, like *Two and
Too Much* and *Max's Dragon Shirt* (elsewhere in this chapter).

The illustrations for *Anna in Charge* provide many details about Japan
that children could be encouraged to observe and discuss. Questions could
include: Looking at the setting, what is different from our homes? What
is similar? How does the clothing compare with what we wear? Other
books about Japan, both fiction and nonfiction, could be featured, like
How My Parents Learned to Eat and *A Family in Japan*. Two other books about

Anna—*Anna's Secret Friend* and *Anna's Special Present*—could also be featured.

Related Titles

Anna's Secret Friend, by Yoriko Tsutsui. Illustrated by Akiko Hayashi. Viking, 1987. Anna and her family move, and Anna misses her old friends. At her new house, someone puts flowers in the mailbox, then there is a letter, then a paper doll. Anna finally meets the little girl who has given her these gifts, and they play together.

Anna's Special Present, by Yoriko Tsutsui. Illustrated by Akiko Hayashi. Viking, 1988. When Katy is in the hospital, Anna is very worried. She wants to do something that will help Katy feel better and show Katy how much she loves her, so Anna gives Katy her special doll.

Cooking the Japanese Way, by Reiko Weston. Photographed by Robert L. Wolfe and Diane Wolfe. Lerner, 1983. After a brief introductory overview of Japan, recipes are presented for some typical Japanese foods. Descriptions of a Japanese table and eating with chopsticks are included.

A Family in Japan, by Peter Otto Jacobsen and Preben Sejer Kristensen. Illustrated with photographs. Bookwright, 1984. The everyday experiences of one family in Japan are the focus for this book. Information is given about their home, work, school, food, and recreation.

How My Parents Learned to Eat, by Ina R. Friedman. Illustrated by Allen Say. Houghton, 1984. A young girl whose mother is Japanese and whose father is American tells about her family. (Condensed in *Primaryplots*, Bowker, 1989, pp. 215–217.)

Journey to Japan, by Joan Knight. Illustrated by Kinuko Craft. Viking, 1986. Children are fascinated by pop-up books, and this one gives some basic information about Japanese life and customs. The paper engineering of this book demonstrates the movement on an assembly line, a drum being played at a festival, and workers exercising.

A Place for Ben, written and illustrated by Jeanne Titherington. Greenwillow, 1987. Ben feels he needs a place that belongs to him, but his little brother, Ezra, just won't leave him alone. (Condensed in *Primaryplots*, Bowker, 1989, pp. 68–69.)

That Bothered Kate, written and illustrated by Sally Noll. Greenwillow, 1991. Tory does everything her sister Kate does, and that bothers Kate. But when Tory wants to be alone, Kate is bothered by that, too.

Two and Too Much, by Mildred Pitts Walter. Illustrated by Pat Cummings. Bradbury, 1990. Brandon watches his two-year-old sister, Gina, while their mother gets ready for some guests. Brandon finds a two-year-old can be a handful.

Vincent, Gabrielle.   *Feel Better, Ernest!*
Illus. by the author. Greenwillow, 1988, LB (0-688-07726-9)
Suggested Use Level: PreS-Gr. 1

Plot Summary

Celestine, a young mouse, awakens one morning and finds that her friend Ernest, a bear, is ill. She hurries to get the doctor, who tells Ernest he must stay in bed. Little Celestine says she will take care of him. She brings him hot tea and, when he becomes bored, she entertains him. When Ernest is better, Celestine prepares a special supper to celebrate. The two friends enjoy their meal and make plans to go to the market—to replace the dishes Celestine has broken.

Thematic Material

There are many books about the friendship between Ernest, a large, older bear who cares for Celestine, a young mouse. In *Feel Better, Ernest!*, the roles are reversed as Celestine takes the responsibility for caring for Ernest when he is sick. The themes of caring for a friend and having the smaller, younger character take charge are evident in this book.

Book Talk Material and Activities

Young children feel very satisfied when Celestine takes charge in *Feel Better, Ernest!* They enjoy it when she becomes a bit bossy, giving Ernest tea when he wants coffee and ordering him to stay in bed. When Celestine tries to keep Ernest from feeling bored, there is a double-page spread of illustrations. Celestine sings, draws pictures, makes faces, plays dress-up, and reads a book while Ernest stays in his bed and laughs at her antics. At the end of these games, Celestine becomes very efficient, ordering Ernest to rest. When Ernest is better, children enjoy the illustrations showing the kitchen—and the mess Celestine has made. They know, however, that Ernest will clean up the mess and that, instead of being annoyed with Celestine, he will appreciate all she has tried to do for him.

After hearing this book, many children want to look at other Ernest and Celestine books, like *Ernest and Celestine's Picnic*, *Where Are You Going, Ernest and Celestine?*, and the first book, *Ernest and Celestine*. They like to talk about the relationship between these two characters. For example, Ernest tries to do whatever Celestine wants, even having a picnic in the rain. They notice how the story is told through conversation. They also notice how the illustrations capture Celestine's personality—she droops when she is sad; she leaps into the air or stands on her toes when she is happy. Children enjoy seeing the different experiences shared by these two friends. These experiences could be added to the "What do friends do?" chart described for *Mr. Nick's Knitting* (elsewhere in this chapter).

Other books about being sick could be shared or booktalked along with *Feel Better, Ernest!* Try *Henry and Mudge Get the Cold Shivers* and *What the Mailman Brought*.

Related Titles

Ernest and Celestine, written and illustrated by Gabrielle Vincent. Morrow, 1986. On a walk in the snow, Celestine loses her toy duck, Gideon. Although it is difficult, Ernest is able to replace him. Ernest also has a surprise Christmas party to welcome the new Gideon.

Ernest and Celestine's Picnic, written and illustrated by Gabrielle Vincent. Greenwillow, 1982. Even though it is raining, Ernest takes Celestine out for a picnic. They meet a wealthy bear, who invites them to visit his home, where Celestine plays with the young mice that he cares for.

Henry and Mudge Get the Cold Shivers: The Seventh Book of Their Adventures, by Cynthia Rylant. Illustrated by Suçie Stevenson. Bradbury, 1989. First, Henry gets a cold, and then Mudge gets a cold. Both of them need to take their medicine to get well again.

What the Mailman Brought, by Carolyn Craven. Illustrated by Tomie de Paola. Putnam, 1987. William is sick, and he is bored with the inactivity. When he receives some unusual mail, he begins to feel better.

Where Are You Going, Ernest and Celestine?, written and illustrated by Gabrielle Vincent. Greenwillow, 1986. When he applies for a job at the museum, Ernest is told he cannot bring Celestine with him. Even though he loves art, Ernest does not take the job. As they leave the museum, Celestine becomes lost. When they are reunited, Ernest reassures her that he loves her more than anything.

About the Author and Illustrator

VINCENT, GABRIELLE

Sixth Book of Junior Authors and Illustrators, ed. by Sally Holmes Holtze. Wilson, 1989, pp. 305–307.

Something about the Author, ed. by Anne Commire. Gale, 1990, Vol. 61, p. 196.

Wells, Rosemary. *Max's Dragon Shirt*

Illus. by the author. Dial, 1991, LB (0-8037-0945-5)

Suggested Use Level: PreS–Gr. K

Plot Summary

Max, a young bunny, is going shopping with his older sister, Ruby. Ruby has decided Max needs new pants, even though Max wants a dragon shirt. In the store, Ruby is distracted by some dresses. While she tries them on, Max wanders off. He finds a dragon shirt in the boys' department and tries it on. When he wants to show it to Ruby, Max realizes he is lost. Meanwhile, Ruby realizes Max is missing. She finds Max eating ice cream with two policemen. Because Max has spilled ice cream on the dragon shirt, Ruby must use all her money to pay for the shirt.

Thematic Material

Like many older sisters, Ruby tries to boss Max around, but he is able to get his way. Young children may be worried when Max is lost, but they will be relieved when he is rescued and feel a sense of satisfaction when Max gets the shirt he wants.

Book Talk Material and Activities

Many toddlers will be familiar with the cardboard books about Max, including *Max's New Suit* and *Max's Birthday.* These books are small (about 4 inches square) and have sturdy pages that are great for very young children, because they are easier for them to manipulate. Some of the more recent stories about Max, like *Max's Dragon Shirt* and *Max's Christmas,* are presented as picture books, which are more suitable for sharing with groups. A preschool story program could feature the Max books. The picture books could be read aloud to young children, with the board books available for them to look at on their own.

After reading *Max's Dragon Shirt,* other books about young children and clothes could be featured. Jessie in *Shoes from Grandpa* has grown so much that she gets new clothes from her family. Like Max, the main character in *You'll Soon Grow Into Them, Titch* has a problem with his older siblings, who give him their hand-me-down clothes. Children could talk about how Titch and Max deal with their concerns. *How Do I Put It On?* and *Jesse Bear, What Will You Wear?* both feature bears wearing, and playing with, clothes.

Related Titles:

Aaron's Shirt, by Deborah Gould. Illustrated by Cheryl Harness. Bradbury, 1989. Aaron loves his shirt with red and white stripes. Even when it is too small, Aaron wants to wear his favorite shirt. He solves his problem by putting the shirt on his teddy bear.

How Do I Put It On? Getting Dressed, by Shigeo Watanabe. Illustrated by Yasuo Ohtomo. Philomel, 1979. This book shows a young bear getting dressed.

Jesse Bear, What Will You Wear? by Nancy White Carlstrom. Illustrated by Bruce Degen. Macmillan, 1986. The rhyming text in this book describes Jesse Bear getting dressed and then pretending to wear a flower, the sun, his chair, and other items he encounters throughout the day. (Condensed in *Primaryplots*, Bowker, 1989, pp. 47–49.)

Mary Wore Her Red Dress and Henry Wore His Green Sneakers, adapted and illustrated by Merle Peek. Clarion, 1985. This song is about clothes and colors, including green shoes, purple pants, and violet ribbons. The musical arrangement is included.

Max's Birthday, written and illustrated by Rosemary Wells. Dial, 1985. Max is chased by a wind-up dinosaur. The cardboard pages of this book make it more durable for young children.

Max's Christmas, written and illustrated by Rosemary Wells. Dial, 1986. It is Christmas Eve, and Max, a bunny, is waiting for Santa. His sister, Ruby, has tried to tell him the truth about Santa, but Max does not believe her. (Condensed in *Primaryplots*, Bowker, 1989, pp. 37–39.)

Max's New Suit, written and illustrated by Rosemary Wells. Dial, 1979. Max the bunny wants to dress himself. The results are not quite right, but very funny. Preschoolers will enjoy this series of Very First Books about Max.

Peter's Pockets, by Eve Rice. Illustrated by Nancy Winslow Parker. Greenwillow, 1989. When Peter gets a new pair of pants, he realizes they do not have any pockets. His mother helps him by sewing special pockets on his pants.

Shoes from Grandpa, by Mem Fox. Illustrated by Patricia Mullins. Orchard, 1989. Because she has grown so much, Jessie gets new clothes from her family. Grandpa buys her shoes, and then he buys her some jeans so she can ride on her skateboard.

You'll Soon Grow Into Them, Titch, written and illustrated by Pat Hutchins. Greenwillow, 1983. Titch gets everyone's hand-me-downs until Dad buys Titch some new clothes of his own. The arrival of a new baby gives Titch the satisfaction of having someone who will get his hand-me-down clothes.

About the Author and Illustrator

WELLS, ROSEMARY

Fourth Book of Junior Authors and Illustrators, ed. by Doris de Montreville and Elizabeth D. Crawford. Wilson, 1978, pp. 343–345.

Illustrators of Children's Books: 1967–1976, Volume IV, comp. by Lee Kingman, Grace Allen Hogarth, and Harriet Quimby. Horn Book, 1978, pp. 13, 168, 213.

Something about the Author, ed. by Anne Commire. Gale, 1980, Vol. 18, pp. 296–298; ed. by Donna Olendorf, Gale, 1992, Vol. 69, pp. 214–217.

Wild, Margaret.   *Mr. Nick's Knitting*
Illus. by Dee Huxley. Harcourt, 1989 (0-15-200518-8)
Suggested Use Level: Gr. K–2

Plot Summary

Mr. Nick and Mrs. Jolley knit while they ride on the train to the city. Mrs. Jolley makes toy animals; Mr. Nick makes sweaters of all sizes. They often help each other with their knitting problems. The other passengers on the train enjoy the sounds of their knitting. One Monday, Mrs. Jolley is not on the train. She is not there on Tuesday or Wednesday. Mr. Nick and the other passengers miss her. On Thursday, Mr. Nick is told that Mrs. Jolley is in the hospital. He goes to visit her, bringing special gifts, and he finds that Mrs. Jolley is very ill and will be in the hospital for quite some time. She tells him how she misses their trips on the train and their knitting. Away from the hospital, Mr. Nick begins to knit something for Mrs. Jolley. He knits for a week, including when he is in the bathtub. When he is finished, he takes his gift to the hospital. Mrs. Jolley is sad and lonely in the hospital. She opens Mr. Nick's gift and finds a quilt filled with squares depicting happy faces, houses, a sailboat, trees, and many other everyday scenes. Mrs. Jolley can look at all the activity in the quilt. It will help her be too busy to be sad. The next morning, Mr. Nick knits on his trip to the city while Mrs. Jolley knits in her hospital bed.

Thematic Material

Being a friend means you care about another person and will help that person even if it means extra work. When Mrs. Jolley is sick, Mr. Nick finds a way to help her feel better.

Book Talk Material and Activities

Mr. Nick's Knitting could be the featured book at a library program where children bring a friend with them. Before reading this book, have children talk about how they help their friends. They could tell about a special time when their friend needed them or they could discuss some of the everyday experiences they share. This discussion could also feature books in which the characters help each other, such as those listed on this chart:

According to *Chase's Annual Events, 1993* (Contemporary, 1992), August 1 is Friendship Day. A program for friends featuring friendship books would be very appropriate. Children could add to the "What do friends do?" chart as they find more books about friends.

Related Titles

Best Friends, written and illustrated by Steven Kellogg. Dial, 1986. Kathy and Louise share everything. When Louise goes on vacation, Kathy expects her to be miserable. She is upset when she finds Louise is having fun. The two friends find a way to stay friends. (Condensed in *Primaryplots,* Bowker, 1989, pp. 20–22.)

Chester's Way, written and illustrated by Kevin Henkes. Greenwillow,

Chart 2

What do friends do?
Mr. Nick knits a special quilt for Mrs. Jolley in *Mr. Nick's Knitting*.
Toad rakes leaves for Frog and Frog rakes leaves for Toad in *Frog and Toad All Year*.
Harold shows Lizzie how to play cat's cradle in *Lizzie and Harold*.
Lilly rescues Chester and Wilson from the rude older boys in *Chester's Way*.

1988. Chester and Wilson, two conservative mice, are very good friends. When Lilly moves into their neighborhood, they are surprised by her wild ways. The boys try to exclude her until she rescues them from some troublemakers.

Frog and Toad All Year, written and illustrated by Arnold Lobel. Harper, 1976. Follow these friends through a year of activities. How do they help each other? There are three other books about Frog and Toad.

George and Martha, written and illustrated by James Marshall. Houghton, 1972. This is the first book in the series about two hippo friends. In one of the stories, George eats Martha's split pea soup, even though he does not like split pea soup.

Jamaica Tag-Along, by Juanita Havill. Illustrated by Anne Sibley O'Brien. Houghton, 1989. Jamaica's brother will not let her play with him and his friends. Later, when a toddler named Berto wants to play with Jamaica, she tries to ignore him until she realizes she is treating Berto the way her brother has treated her. She and Berto play together, and they let Jamaica's brother join them.

Lizzie and Harold, by Elizabeth Winthrop. Illustrated by Martha Weston. Lothrop, 1986. Lizzie wants a best friend. Even though her neighbor, Harold, wants to be her friend, Lizzie chooses a girl named Christina, who ignores her. It takes a while, but Lizzie realizes Harold is the friend she has been looking for. (Condensed in *Primaryplots,* Bowker, 1989, pp. 39–41.)

2

Developing a Positive Self-Image

CHILDREN often need to be reassured about the changes in their lives. Even as they develop a sense of independence, they still need to feel accepted. Taking risks and trying new experiences are featured in many of the books in this chapter. Grace dreams of starring in *Peter Pan* while Matthew dreams of being an artist. *Koala Lou* worries that she is not special while Harry worries about his lost library card. Many children will identify with the fears, mistakes, hopes, and triumphs of the characters in the books in this chapter.

Bunting, Eve.   *The Wednesday Surprise*
   Illus. by Donald Carrick. Clarion, 1989. (0-89919-721-3); pap. (0-395-54776-8)
   Suggested Use Level: Gr. 1–3

Plot Summary
   Anna and her grandma are planning a surprise for Anna's father's birthday. On Wednesdays, Grandma watches Anna, while everyone else is busy with work and basketball practice. Grandma makes hot dogs for dinner and then she and Anna begin to read the books Grandma has brought with her. When Anna's brother comes home, the three of them play cards until it is time for Grandma to leave. There is no mention of the books. Anna's father, a truck driver, comes home on the weekend, bringing something special for Anna, Sam, and their mother. While Dad sleeps, the rest of the family prepares for his birthday celebration. Grandma comes over, and the family has dinner followed by the birthday cake. Everyone gives Dad his presents. Then Anna and Grandma share their surprise. Grandma begins to read a book, and the family discovers

Anna has helped Grandma learn to read. Grandma reads them every book in her book bag. Anna and Grandma are proud of their accomplishment.

Thematic Material

Respect for older adults is one theme in this book, which portrays a positive relationship between generations. This story focuses on the feeling of satisfaction Grandma and Anna have about their accomplishment.

Book Talk Material and Activities

Children like to see themselves helping others and accomplishing things that are important. When Anna helps her grandmother learn to read, she does it as a surprise for her family. But she also does it because it is important to her grandmother. Anna knows she has done something very special. *The Wednesday Surprise* features an older adult who takes on new challenges and who is willing to learn new things. *Sea Swan* (elsewhere in this chapter) and *I Know a Lady* also feature older characters who stay active and involved. *Song and Dance Man* shows a grandfather whose abilities are appreciated by his grandchildren.

The Wednesday Surprise could be featured in a program about taking risks and trying new things. Children who hear this book are often surprised that the grandmother cannot read. In one class, the second graders talked about things they thought they would never be able to do. One girl said she was sure she would never learn to ride a two-wheeler, but now she can. Another girl told how she used to worry about doing math. These children liked the idea that Anna was the teacher and they admired Anna's grandmother for being willing to learn something new. Miriam Cohen's books about childhood concerns fit very well with this discussion (such as *When Will I Read?*). The reading focus of this book makes it a good sharing book for Children's Book Week (in November), especially since Grandma uses some well-known children's books to help her learn.

Audiovisual Adaptations

The Wednesday Surprise. Houghton, cassette/book, 1991; Learning Corporation of America, videorecording, 1991.

Related Titles

I Know a Lady, by Charlotte Zolotow. Illustrated by James Stevenson. Greenwillow, 1984. Sally's elderly neighbor is a very caring person. She takes an interest in the activities of Sally and her friends and is involved in many activities in the neighborhood.

The Midnight Eaters, by Amy Hest. Illustrated by Karen Gundersheimer. Four Winds, 1989. Samantha and Nana make a fire in the fireplace and share a midnight snack—ice cream sundaes.

Miss Maggie, by Cynthia Rylant. Illustrated by Thomas DiGrazia. Dutton, 1983. Miss Maggie lives alone in a deteriorating house. Nat is afraid of her until one day, when she needs his help, he discovers she is lonely and afraid too. Nat overcomes his fears to help Miss Maggie.

Song and Dance Man, by Karen Ackerman. Illustrated by Stephen Gammell. Knopf, 1988. When his grandchildren come to visit, Grandpa takes them to the attic and puts on a show just for them. They love to see their grandpa perform.

A Special Trade, by Sally Wittman. Illustrated by Karen Gundersheimer. Harper, 1978. This very positive story describes the changing relationship between a little girl and her neighbor. Each finds ways to help the other and to show how much they care for each other.

When I Am Old with You, by Angela Johnson. Illustrated by David Soman. Orchard, 1990. A young boy tells about the times he will share with his grandfather, imagining they are both old. They will go fishing, play cards, look at old pictures, spend time with friends, go to the ocean, take long walks, and sit and rest in their rocking chairs. They will enjoy being old together, as they enjoy the times they share now.

When Will I Read?, by Miriam Cohen. Illustrated by Lillian Hoban. Greenwillow, 1977. Jim wonders if he will ever learn to read. His understanding teacher gives him encouragement and time.

Wilfrid Gordon McDonald Partridge, by Mem Fox. Illustrated by Julie Vivas. Kane-Miller, 1984. Wilfrid lives next door to an old people's home. One of the residents, Miss Nancy, cannot remember things, and Wilfrid thinks of a way to bring her some special memories. (Condensed in *Primaryplots,* Bowker, 1989, pp. 49–51.)

About the Author

BUNTING, EVE

Fifth Book of Junior Authors and Illustrators, ed. by Sally Holmes Holtze. Wilson, 1983, pp. 60–61.

Something about the Author, ed. by Anne Commire. Gale, 1980, Vol. 18, pp. 38–39; 1991, Vol. 64, pp. 60–69.

About the Illustrator

CARRICK, DONALD

Fourth Book of Junior Authors and Illustrators, ed. by Doris de Montreville and Elizabeth D. Crawford. Wilson, 1978, pp. 71–72.

Illustrators of Children's Books: 1967–1976, Vol. IV, comp. by Lee Kingman, Grace Allen Hogarth, and Harriet Quimby. Horn Book, 1978, pp. xiii, 106, 183.

Something about the Author, ed. by Anne Commire. Gale, 1975, Vol. 7, p. 40; 1991, Vol. 63, pp. 19–22.

Cooney, Barbara. *Island Boy*
Illus. by the author. Viking, 1988 (0-670-81749-X); pap., Puffin, 1991 (0-14-050756-6)
Suggested Use Level: Gr. 2–4

Plot Summary
Pa built the house and brought the family to the island that would now be named after them—Tibbetts Island. The twelve children in the Tibbetts family, six boys and six girls, enjoyed their life on the island. There was work to do with Pa, clearing the land and planting. In the house, Ma taught the children to read and write. Matthias, the youngest, often watched the activities of the older children, and as he grew, he joined them. He went fishing with Pa and, once, he caught a wild bird, a seagull, and tamed it, keeping it as a pet until the day came for the bird to return to the wild. When he was older, Matthias left the island, serving as cabin boy on a ship, and later, becoming the captain. Although he traveled to many wonderful places, he remembered his home on Tibbetts Island. He married a schoolmistress, Hannah, and returned to the island to raise a family. When their three daughters grew up and left the island, Matthias and Hannah remained. The islands and coves around them had become popular vacation homes, but they loved their solitude and seclusion. When Hannah died, Matthias stayed on the island, sometimes joined by his grandson, little Matthias. Later, little Matthias and his mother, Annie, came to live with Matthias on the island. They worked together, growing food and selling it to the vacationers. During a storm, Matthias's boat was swamped and washed ashore. Matthias was found nearby and buried on Tibbetts Island. Young Matthias thinks of his grandfather and the good life he has lived.

Thematic Material

Island Boy focuses on the life of one person, Matthias Tibbetts. The importance of home and family are emphasized.

Book Talk Material and Activities

Many books describe situations and people that are familiar to children. There are stories about friends, school, siblings, and everyday experiences. *Island Boy* introduces children to a character who has a very different life. Matthias Tibbetts lives in New England on an isolated island. He values his home, his family, and his independence. Barbara Cooney's *Miss Rumphius* is also a spirited, independent character who lives in a New England coastal town. When sharing these books with children, encourage them to focus on the characters. These two books describe the lives of people from their childhood through adulthood. Included is information about their families, travels, and work. *Island Boy* and *Miss Rumphius* show characters who make choices that reflect their values.

Several books could be featured in a program on independent characters. *Kite Flier* and *The Man Who Lived Alone* describe characters who choose to lead isolated lives. *The Old, Old Man and the Very Little Boy* follows the life of one person in an African village. Besides being independent, do the characters share any other attitudes or values? What is important to each character? How is each character depicted in the illustrations? Asking children to analyze characters encourages them to look more closely at personalities and the details the author and illustrator include to develop their characters.

Related Titles

Kite Flier, by Dennis Haseley. Illustrated by David Wiesner. Four Winds, 1986. The man who makes kites is admired and respected. When his son is born and his wife dies, the man stops making kites. As his son grows, Kite Flier begins to make kites again. (Condensed in *Primaryplots*, Bowker, 1989, pp. 55–57.)

The Man Who Lived Alone, by Donald Hall. Illustrated by Mary Azarian. Godine, 1984. A man's unhappy childhood leads him to a life of solitude as an adult. He is self-sufficient and satisfied with the life he has chosen.

Miss Rumphius, written and illustrated by Barbara Cooney. Viking, 1982. Miss Rumphius is satisfied with her life. She shares her happiness by planting lupines and making the world more beautiful.

The Old, Old Man and the Very Little Boy, by Kristine L. Franklin. Illustrated by Terea D. Shaffer. Atheneum, 1992. In an African village, a little boy enjoys an old man's stories. When the boy is older and the old man has died, the boy is so busy he barely remembers the times they spent together. But when the little boy has grown to be an old man, he remembers, and he shares his stories with the young boys of the village.

When I Am Old with You, by Angela Johnson. Illustrated by David Soman. Orchard, 1990. A young boy tells about the times he will share with his grandfather, imagining they are both old. They will enjoy being old together, as they enjoy the times they share now.

About the Author and Illustrator

COONEY, BARBARA

More Junior Authors, ed. by Muriel Fuller. Wilson, 1963, pp. 53–54.

Something about the Author, ed. by Anne Commire. Gale, 1974, Vol. 6, pp. 49–51; 1990, Vol. 59, pp. 46–55.

Fleischman, Sid. *The Scarebird*

Illus. by Peter Sis. Greenwillow, 1988, LB (0-688-07318-2)
Suggested Use Level: Gr. 1–3

Plot Summary

A farmer called Lonesome John makes a scarecrow out of some old clothes and straw. Even though the scarecrow does not have a head, it keeps the birds away from the field. But after a while, Lonesome John makes the scarebird a head, with eyes and a mouth, and he begins to speak to the scarebird. In the morning, he greets it; in the evening, he plays the harmonica for it. When the wind starts to blow, John gives the scarebird shoes and gloves, and he replaces the straw that has blown away. When the sun comes out, John gives the scarebird his own hat. When the rains come, John gives the scarebird a yellow slicker. Finally, John takes his checkerboard out to the field and begins to play a game of checkers with the scarebird, although John makes all the moves himself. When a young man named Sam comes to the farm looking for work, Lonesome John is suspicious, but he lets him stay. Slowly, John develops a friendship with Sam, and when Sam needs work gloves, John takes them from the scarebird. He also gives Sam the scarebird's hat, shoes, and yellow slicker. When it looks as though there is no more work, Sam prepares to leave. The evening before he goes, Sam sits on the porch with John and plays his harmonica. Lonesome John joins him and then asks him to help with the harvest. Sam stays to help John on the farm and to be his friend. As the sun goes down, John and Sam begin a game of checkers.

Thematic Material

Lonesome John leads an isolated life. He wants a friend, so he creates one in the scarebird. When Sam comes, John is able to find a real friend. This book features an independent character who reaches out to find friendship.

Book Talk Material and Activities

Many children are concerned about getting along with others. They often feel isolated and alone. *The Scarebird* could be the focus for a discussion about needing others and making friends. Because his farm is so far from town and his family is gone, Lonesome John is lonely. He is so lonely he befriends a scarecrow, which he calls the scarebird. When Sam comes to the farm, John is reluctant to give up his friendship with the scarebird. Eventually, he and Sam become friends, and they enjoy the companionship they share. While few children have the isolated situation of Lonesome John, many children relate to his feelings. They understand his friendship with the scarebird, since many of them have toys they consider friends. They are satisfied when John makes friends with Sam, even though it changes his relationship with the scarebird.

Children need opportunities to share their concerns, or at least to hear about experiences that focus on more serious emotions. After hearing *The Scarebird*, several second graders talked about times they felt alone or left out. The teacher shared some other books in which characters are alone, different, or left out, and the group discussed how the characters handled these situations. *The Man Who Kept His Heart in a Bucket* was a very popular book with this class. They enjoyed hearing how the man really did keep his heart in a bucket, to protect his heart from being hurt again. The students also enjoyed the elements of humor in *The Scarebird*, particularly when Lonesome John gave the scarebird some clothes and when he began to play checkers with it. Other books such as *Kite Flier* and *Cornelius* also deal with being hurt, alone, and feeling left out.

Related Titles

Cornelius, written and illustrated by Leo Lionni. Pantheon, 1983. Cornelius, a crocodile, is able to walk on his hind legs. He feels left out because the other crocodiles do not appreciate his special ability. Cornelius comes to realize the other crocodiles put him down because he is special.

Kite Flier, by Dennis Haseley. Illustrated by David Wiesner. Four Winds, 1986. The man who makes magnificent kites is admired and respected by the people in the village. When his son is born, his wife dies. It is a long time before Kite Flier will make any kites. (Condensed in *Primaryplots,* Bowker, 1989, pp. 55–57.)

The Man Who Kept His Heart in a Bucket, by Sonia Levitin. Illustrated by Jerry Pinkney. Dial, 1991. Jack's heart was broken one time. Now he keeps it in a bucket, until he meets a maiden who helps him find love.

The Man Who Lived Alone, by Donald Hall. Illustrated by Mary Azarian. Godine, 1984. A man's unhappy childhood leads him to a life of solitude as an adult. He is self-sufficient and satisfied with the life he has chosen.

Old Henry, by Joan W. Blos. Illustrated by Stephen Gammell. Morrow, 1987. Old Henry is an eccentric stranger who moves into a deserted house. At first, his neighbors are happy to see the house occupied. When they realize Henry is not going to fix the house, they become annoyed. After Henry moves away, the people miss him. And Henry finds he misses his neighbors too. (Condensed in *Primaryplots,* Bowker, 1989, pp. 43–45.)

Witch Hazel, by Alice Schertle. Illustrated by Margot Tomes. Harper, 1991. Johnny makes a scarecrow from the branches of a witch hazel bush. One windy night, Johnny and his scarecrow have an unusual adventure.

About the Author

FLEISCHMAN, SID

Third Book of Junior Authors, ed. by Doris de Montreville and Donna Hill. Wilson, 1972, pp. 86–87.

Something about the Author, ed. by Anne Commire. Gale, 1976, Vol. 8, pp. 61–63; 1990, Vol. 59, pp. 89–95.

About the Illustrator

SIS, PETER

Sixth Book of Junior Authors and Illustrators, ed. by Sally Holmes Holtze. Wilson, 1989, pp. 279–281.

Something about the Author, ed. by Donna Olendorf. Gale, 1992, Vol. 67, pp. 178–185.

Fox, Mem. *Koala Lou*
Illus. by Pamela Lofts. Harcourt, 1989 (0-15-200502-1)
Suggested Use Level: PreS–Gr. 1

Plot Summary

Everyone loves Koala Lou, especially her mother, who says "Koala Lou, I DO love you!" But as time passes and more koalas come into the family, Koala Lou begins to feel left out. She longs for her mother's attention and wants to hear how much her mother loves her. Koala Lou decides that if she wins the gum-tree climbing event in the Bush Olympics, her mother will notice her and remember how much she loves Koala Lou. Koala Lou trains for her event, and she is ready when the big day arrives. Tough Koala Klaws climbs first, and her time is incredible. Koala Lou knows she must do better than Koala Klaws, but when the race is over, Koala Klaws wins and Koala Lou is second. Dejected, Koala Lou leaves the Olympics and cries. When Koala Lou goes home, her mother is waiting. She hugs Koala Lou and says, "Koala Lou, I DO love you!"

Thematic Material

The love the mother koala feels for Koala Lou is there even though she does not always say it. Animals of Australia are mentioned throughout this reassuring story of family love.

Book Talk Material and Activities

This story of the love between a mother and her child is very satisfying for young children. Koala Lou worries that her mother is too busy to love her. She feels she must be special in order to get her mother's attention. Children who hear this story are reassured that Koala Lou's mother loves her just as she is. This book would be appropriate to share before Mother's Day (the second Sunday in May). In Koala Lou, the characters are animals from Australia. Other books have a similar theme and use a variety of characters. For example, in *Say It!* and *Amifika*, the characters are people, and in *What Alvin Wanted* the characters are mice.

Children enjoy the Australian setting of *Koala Lou*. Mem Fox's *Possum Magic* and David Cox's *Bossyboots* are two other picture books with an Australian connection.

Related Titles

Amifika, by Lucille Clifton. Illustrated by Thomas DiGrazia. Dutton, 1977. Amifika's father has been away, and now he is coming home. Amifika, an African-American boy, is not sure his father will remember him.

Bossyboots, written and illustrated by David Cox. Crown, 1985. Abigail, who lives in Australia, is very bossy. When the stagecoach in which she is riding is stopped by an outlaw, Abigail's bossiness becomes a virtue.

Possum Magic, by Mem Fox. Illustrated by Julie Vivas. Harcourt, 1983. Grandma Poss turns Hush, her possum granddaughter, invisible. But she cannot make her visible again. Grandma Poss and Hush travel around Australia eating special Australian foods, hoping to find the right magic to make Hush visible again.

Say It!, by Charlotte Zolotow. Illustrated by James Stevenson. Greenwillow, 1980. As a mother and daughter go for a walk, the mother talks about the beauty of the time they spend together. The little girl wants to hear her mother say "I love you."

What Alvin Wanted, written and illustrated by Holly Keller. Greenwillow, 1990. When the mama mouse is away, Alvin begins to cry and will not stop. No one can find out why he is crying. When Mama comes home, she remembers to give him a good-bye kiss.

About the Author

Fox, Mem

Sixth Book of Junior Authors and Illustrators, ed. by Sally Holmes Holtze. Wilson, 1989, pp. 88–89.

Something about the Author, ed. by Anne Commire. Gale, 1988,. Vol. 51, pp. 65–70.

Gauch, Patricia Lee. *Dance, Tanya*
Illus. by Satomi Ichikawa. Philomel, 1989 (0-399-21521-2)
Suggested Use Level: Gr. K–2

Plot Summary

Tanya is a toddler who likes to imitate her older sister, Elise, as she practices her ballet. Sometimes Tanya dances on her own or with her stuffed bear. Tanya loves to be the swan when her mother plays the music from *Swan Lake.* But Tanya is too little to take ballet lessons, and she is sad when Elise goes to her class. When Elise's dance recital approaches, Tanya is caught up in the excitement of the preparations. Relatives come for the performance, and Tanya is delighted to watch Elise, although she ends up falling asleep on her mother's lap. At home, after the recital, Tanya wakes up and puts on her own recital for her family. For her Christmas present, Tanya receives a leotard and slippers and begins to take dance lessons with Elise.

Thematic Material

Dance, Tanya describes a very young child who has a great enthusiasm for performing. Her parents encourage and support her dancing. Tanya's story continues in *Bravo, Tanya.*

Book Talk Material and Activities

Many children participate in activities that involve performing. Ballet, gymnastics, theater, soccer, and hockey are among these events. The children take lessons and go to clinics; they work out and perform. Reading a story like *Dance, Tanya* could promote a discussion of the talents and experiences of children in the group. A related library program for parents could feature some of the recreational classes and services that are available for children in the community.

In *Dance, Tanya,* Tanya loves to dance. *Bravo, Tanya* continues the story of Tanya and her dance lessons. When she begins to take classes, it is difficult for her to adjust to the formal requirements of training. *Going to My Ballet Class* could be shared with the stories about Tanya, since it focuses on a real class and describes some of the preparations involved in learning to dance. *Amazing Grace* (elsewhere in this chapter) also features a character who dreams of performing.

A book talk program could feature other books that highlight children as performers. It would be especially effective to include a variety of opportunities, including ballet *(Opening Night)*, gymnastics *(Going to My Gymnastics Class)*, theater *(A Very Young Actress)*, and sports *(Baseball Kids* and *A Very Young Skier).*

Related Titles

Baseball Kids, written and photographed by George Sullivan. Dutton, 1991. Players from two Little League teams are featured in this photoessay. Some of the players discuss their skills on the field, others describe batting techniques.

Bravo, Tanya, by Patricia Lee Gauch. Illustrated by Satomi Ichikawa.

Philomel, 1992. Now that Tanya is in dance class, she must adjust to the routine of practice and repetition, and she loses some of her enjoyment. The woman who plays the piano for the dance class helps Tanya remember that she loves to dance.

Going to My Ballet Class, written and illustrated by Susan Kuklin. Bradbury, 1989. Jami loves her ballet class. She learns about counting the beat of the music and warming up. Color photographs show Jami and her class as they demonstrate basic ballet positions.

Going to My Gymnastics Class, written and illustrated by Susan Kuklin. Bradbury, 1991. Color photographs depict Gaspar and his classmates at their gymnastics activities. Doing stretches before class and learning the correct movements are highlighted.

Opening Night, written and illustrated by Rachel Isadora. Greenwillow, 1984. Heather and her friend, Libby, are appearing in a ballet production. Heather has practiced and prepared to be ready for her performance. (Condensed in *Primaryplots*, Bowker, 1989, pp. 57–58.)

A Very Young Actress, written and photographed by Jill Krementz. Knopf, 1991. The text and color photographs describe the experiences of Lauren Gaffney, who is ten, as she prepares for the role of "Annie."

A Very Young Skier, written and photographed by Jill Krementz. Knopf, 1990. Stephanie Cimino enjoys skiing. The photographs show Stephanie demonstrating some of the basics of skiing. Stephanie enjoys skiing with her family and friends.

About the Author

GAUCH, PATRICIA LEE

Fifth Book of Junior Authors and Illustrators, ed. by Sally Holmes Holtze. Wilson, 1983, pp. 130–132.

Something about the Author, ed. by Anne Commire. Gale, 1982, Vol. 26, pp. 81–83.

About the Illustrator

ICHIKAWA, SATOMI

Illustrators of Children's Books, 1967–1976, Vol. IV, ed. by Lee Kingman, Grace Allen Hogarth, and Harriet Quimby. Horn Book, 1978, p. 24.

Something about the Author, ed. by Anne Commire. Gale, 1984, Vol. 36, p. 121; 1987, Vol. 47, pp. 132–136.

Gibbons, Gail. *Marge's Diner*
Illus. by the author. Crowell, 1989, LB (0-690-04606-5)
Suggested Use Level: Gr. 1–3

Plot Summary

At Marge's Diner, people come for food and conversation. It is open twenty-four hours a day. In the morning, people stop for breakfast. Some are in a hurry, while some are happy to stop and sit. Bill cooks at the grill; Marge and the waitresses take orders, serve food, and clean up. Later, Marge goes to the kitchen to work on the food for lunch and dinner. When things get busy, everyone helps out. They wash dishes and work the cash register. At lunchtime, Marge lists the specials. After lunch, Marge places orders for food for the diner. During the quiet time in the afternoon, the workers prepare for dinner. Right after school, the diner is filled with teens playing music and talking. Marge's daughter, Molly, comes by for a snack and to start her homework. Later, Marge's husband joins Molly and Marge at the diner for dinner. More people fill the diner for their evening meal. Marge has a surprise for one of her regular customers. It is Mr. Reynolds's birthday, and Marge has a cake for him. As things slow down, Marge gets ready to go home, checking the supplies and menu for tomorrow. Marge says good-bye to the night crew, drops off money at the bank, and goes home.

Thematic Material

Going out to eat is a familiar experience for most children. In *Marge's Diner*, children receive a "behind-the-scenes" look at a restaurant. *Marge's Diner* also features a woman as the owner of this business.

Book Talk Material and Activities

Gail Gibbons has written many books that focus on community resources and services. *Marge's Diner* looks at the work involved in a food service business. Marge employs many people; she orders food and materials from suppliers; she serves the community. Children are surprised by the many people who are involved in *Marge's Diner*. *We Keep a Store, The Milk Makers,* and *Where Food Comes From* look at the experiences of others who supply food.

Learning about community services introduces children to the many people who help others. *Check It Out!* provides information about libraries, *Fill It Up!* describes service stations, and *The Post Office Book* tells how the mail is delivered. *Department Store* describes the items and services in a store. Teachers or librarians could share some of these books with children as part of a program on the community. Guest speakers from different occupations could visit classes or the library. Other books that describe jobs and services, such as *How a Book Is Made* and *Up Goes the Skyscraper!*, could be displayed.

Audiovisual Adaptation

Marge's Diner. Library Learning Resources, kit (book, activity cards, guide), 1990.

Related Titles

Check It Out! The Book about Libraries, written and illustrated by Gail Gibbons. Harcourt, 1985. Libraries are a part of the lives of most children, and this book describes several kinds of libraries, focusing on the services at a public library.

A Chef, written and illustrated by Douglas Florian. Greenwillow, 1992. Describes the daily work of a chef, including planning the menu, assigning the work, and cooking. One double-page spread focuses on a pastry chef making blueberry pies. The final page depicts some basic utensils that a chef would use.

Department Store, written and illustrated by Gail Gibbons. Crowell, 1984. The text and illustrations feature different people and activities in a department store. Customers, salespeople, stockroom workers, and display artists are some of the people included.

Fill It Up! All about Service Stations, written and illustrated by Gail Gibbons. Crowell, 1985. Details about what goes on at a service station are presented. Clear, well-labeled illustrations highlight information such as how a hydraulic lift works and where gasoline is stored.

How a Book Is Made, written and illustrated by Aliki. Crowell, 1986. A clear and well-illustrated description of the process of publishing a book. Specific careers are described.

The Milk Makers, written and illustrated by Gail Gibbons. Macmillan, 1985. Follows the production of milk from the cow to the store. The last page in the book uses illustrations and captions to show milk and other dairy products. (Condensed in *Primaryplots*, Bowker, 1989, pp. 89–91.)

The Post Office Book, written and illustrated by Gail Gibbons. Crowell, 1982. Some of the activities of postal employees, including sorting the mail, loading it onto trucks and planes, and delivering it, are described.

Up Goes the Skyscraper!, written and illustrated by Gail Gibbons. Four Winds, 1986. Jobs in the construction industry are described as a skyscraper is designed, contracted, and built.

We Keep a Store, by Anne Shelby. Illustrated by John Ward. Orchard, 1990. A family runs a small store in a rural community. This fiction book focuses on the camaraderie of family and friends at the store. Children play in the store, and adults gather there and share stories. Some details about operating the store are incorporated in the story.

Where Food Comes From, by Dorothy Hinshaw Patent. Photographs by William Muñoz. Holiday, 1991. Color photographs depict the source of different foods, including grains, fruits, and dairy products.

About the Author and Illustrator

GIBBONS, GAIL

Sixth Book of Junior Authors and Illustrators, ed. by Sally Holmes Holtze. Gale, 1989, pp. 96–97.
Something about the Author, ed. by Anne Commire. Gale, 1981, Vol. 23, pp. 77–78.

Grifalconi, Ann. *Osa's Pride*
Illus. by the author. Little, Brown, 1990 (0-316-32865-0)
Suggested Use Level: Gr. 1–3

Plot Summary

Osa's father went to fight in a war and did not come back. In her African village, Osa hides her feelings of sadness and loss behind boastful stories of her father's accomplishments. She brags so much to her friends that her friends will not play with her. Her family watches her, and finally, Gran'ma intervenes. Using a special story cloth, she tells Osa of a proud girl who is carrying eggs in a basket on her head. The girl tilts her head to be admired, and the eggs begin to fall out. The story cloth is not finished, so Gran'ma asks Osa to complete the story. Osa realizes that she has been as proud as the girl in the story. Her grandmother hugs her, and later, Osa tells her Gran'pa and Uncle Domo what she has learned about being too proud.

Thematic Material

Osa makes up stories about her father because she misses him. With the help of her grandmother, Osa comes to understand her own feelings and learns to accept her situation.

Book Talk Material and Activities

Within *Osa's Pride* is a story about a girl carrying eggs on her head. A similar story is available in a picture book, *The Woman with the Eggs*, and it is in several collections of fables, including *Borrowed Feathers*. Children are surprised to see versions of a story from different locations. They become aware that telling stories is an activity that occurs in many places and that stories travel around the world. The grandmother's use of a story cloth shows that telling stories is a respected tradition in this African community. *Knots on a Counting Rope* shows the importance of stories to a Native American family. Children also enjoy the other story about Osa, *Darkness and the Butterfly*.

Many children relate to the difficulties Osa has in getting along with her friends. There are many books that provide children with situations in which characters learn to solve their problems. By reading these books, children learn different ways to deal with difficult situations. *Osa's Pride*, *Bartholomew the Bossy*, and *Chester's Way* all present characters that learn to get along.

Related Titles

Bartholomew the Bossy, by Marjorie Weinman Sharmat. Illustrated by Normand Chartier. Macmillan, 1984. Bartholomew the skunk has been elected president of the neighborhood club. He tries to boss his friends into changing the way they behave. Bartholomew must learn to accept his friends as they are. (Condensed in *Primaryplots*, Bowker, 1989, pp. 33–35.)

Borrowed Feathers and Other Fables, edited by Bryna Stevens. Illustrated by Freire Wright and Michael Foreman. Random, 1977. Here are seven fables from Aesop. The story of the greedy milkmaid could be compared to the story Gran'ma tells in *Osa's Pride*.

Chester's Way, written and illustrated by Kevin Henkes. Greenwillow, 1988. Chester and Wilson have to learn to get along with Lilly, a very flamboyant character.

Darkness and the Butterfly, written and illustrated by Ann Grifalconi. Little, Brown, 1987. This story, set in Africa, describes how the Wise Woman helps Osa learn to overcome her fear of the dark. (Condensed in *Primaryplots*, Bowker, 1989, pp. 258–260.)

Knots on a Counting Rope, by Bill Martin, Jr., and John Archambault. Illustrated by Ted Rand. Holt, 1987. A young Native American boy and his grandfather sit by the campfire and tell the story of the boy's courage. When the story ends, the grandfather adds a knot to the counting rope that marks the times this story has been told. (Condensed in *Primaryplots,* Bowker, 1989, pp. 61–63.)

Once a Mouse: A Fable Cut in Wood, written and illustrated by Marcia Brown. Scribner, 1961. A hermit transforms a mouse into ever larger animals, until the mouse, who is now a tiger, is overcome by his own pride. This book received the Caldecott Medal in 1962.

The Woman with the Eggs, by Hans Christian Andersen. Adapted by Jan Wahl. Illustrated by Ray Cruz. Crown, 1974. A proud, haughty woman envisions the fine life she will have with the money she makes from selling eggs. Unfortunately, she forgets the eggs are on her head when she raises her head to look down at everyone.

About the Author and Illustrator

GRIFALCONI, ANN

Illustrators of Children's Books; 1957–1966, Vol. III, comp. by Lee Kingman, Grace Allen Hogarth, and Harriet Quimby. Horn Book, 1968, pp. 3, 17, 222; *1967–1976, Vol. IV,* 1978, pp. 68, 124, 191.

Something about the Author, ed. by Anne Commire. Gale, 1971, Vol. 2, pp. 125–126; ed. by Donna Olendorf, Gale, 1991, Vol. 66, pp. 97–107.

Third Book of Junior Authors and Illustrators, ed. by Doris de Montreville and Donna Hill. Wilson, 1972, pp. 111–113.

Henkes, Kevin. *Jessica*
Illus. by the author. Greenwillow, 1989, LB (0-688-07830-3); pap., Puffin, 1990 (0-14-054194-2)
Suggested Use Level: Gr. K–2

Plot Summary

Ruthie has a best friend that only Ruthie can see. Jessica and Ruthie play together and read together; sometimes they even get in trouble together. Even though Ruthie's parents do not believe in Jessica, Ruthie does. When Ruthie goes to kindergarten, she brings Jessica with her, only to meet a real girl named Jessica, who becomes Ruthie's real best friend.

Thematic Material

The need for friends is one theme in this book, but there is also the celebration of an independent spirit. Ruthie's insistence that there is a Jessica overcomes the objections of her parents. Ruthie is able to leave her imaginary friend when she has the opportunity to make a real friend.

Book Talk Material and Activities

This book could be the focus of a discussion on friends. In a group, children could list some of the important qualities of a friend. Later, they could write advertisements for a friend, focusing on the qualities most important to them. They could make "Wanted" posters for a friend. Other books could extend the activity, such as *Daniel's Dog*, in which the imaginary friend is a dog; *The Dragon in the Clock Box*, where the imaginary friend is a dragon; and the poem "Changing" by Mary Ann Hoberman (in Lee Bennett Hopkins's *Best Friends*), which encourages children to think about another's point of view. Some children may want to do journal writing about why they are a good friend. Books about making new friends, such as Miriam Cohen's *Will I Have a Friend?*, Aliki's *We Are Best Friends*, and Amy Ehrlich's *Leo, Zack and Emmie* could be part of a friendship book talk program.

Related Titles

Best Friends, written and illustrated by Steven Kellogg. Dial, 1986. Kathy and Louise share everything, until Louise goes on vacation and Kathy feels left out. (Condensed in *Primaryplots,* Bowker, 1989, pp. 20–22.)

"Changing," by Mary Ann Hoberman, in *Best Friends,* edited by Lee Bennett Hopkins. Illustrated by James Watts. Harper, 1986. This poem looks at the idea of changing places and thinking about another's point of view. (Condensed in *Primaryplots,* Bowker, 1989, pp. 16–17.)

Daniel's Dog, by Jo Ellen Bogart. Illustrated by Janet Wilson. Scholastic, 1990. Daniel has an imaginary dog named Lucy. Even when his mother is busy with the new baby, Lucy has time for Daniel.

The Dragon in the Clock Box, by M. Jean Craig. Illustrated by Kelly Oechsli. Norton, 1962. Joshua's family is very busy, so Joshua creates a fantasy about a dragon's egg that he keeps in a clock box. Joshua's family becomes very interested in his dragon.

Leo, Zack and Emmie, by Amy Ehrlich. Illustrated by Steven Kellogg.

Dial, 1981. When Emmie moves into a new neighborhood, it takes some time before the boys, Leo and Zack, will be her friends.

We Are Best Friends, written and illustrated by Aliki. Greenwillow, 1982. When Peter moves away, Robert learns how to remain his friend and how to make new friends.

Will I Have a Friend?, by Miriam Cohen. Illustrated by Lillian Hoban. Macmillan, 1967. One in a series of books about Jim and his friends. Some other titles are *Best Friends* (Macmillan, 1971); *See You in Second Grade* (Greenwillow, 1989); and *It's George!* (Greenwillow, 1988).

About the Author and Illustrator

HENKES, KEVIN

Sixth Book of Junior Authors and Illustrators, ed. by Sally Holmes Holtze. Wilson, 1989, pp. 123–124.

Something about the Author, ed. by Anne Commire. Gale, 1986, Vol. 43, pp. 110–112.

Hoffman, Mary.   *Amazing Grace*
Illus. by Caroline Binch. Dial, 1991 (0-8037-1040-2)
Suggested Use Level: Gr. 1–3

Plot Summary

Grace has listened to and read stories, and she loves them. She especially loves to act them out. In her play-acting, Grace is Joan of Arc or Anansi the Spider; she is an explorer or a pirate. Grace takes the most exciting part. Sometimes, when she is alone, she acts out all the parts. At school, Grace wants to star in *Peter Pan,* but her classmates chide her because she is a girl and because she is black. At home, Grace tells her Ma and her grandmother, Nana, about the comments of her classmates, and they are dismayed. Nana takes Grace to see a ballet in which the lead is being danced by the granddaughter of a friend of Nana's from Trinidad. Grace sees a beautiful black ballerina dance as Juliet in *Romeo and Juliet.* At home, Grace dances and dreams of future accomplishments. When the auditions for the play are held, Grace is the unanimous choice for Peter Pan. Grace is proud and confident; she is amazing.

Thematic Material

This book affirms individuality. Grace finds she does not have to conform to the expectations of others. Grace's independent spirit is restored with the help of her mother and grandmother.

Book Talk Material and Activities

Although Grace enjoys challenges, her confidence is shaken by the remarks of her classmates. Her mother and grandmother encourage her and provide her with the support she needs. With this support, Grace has a positive self-image; she believes any achievement is possible for her. *Amazing Grace* celebrates one child's independent spirit and creativity. *Matthew's Dream* (elsewhere in this chapter) and *Musical Max* also feature characters with creative abilities, while *Cowboy Dreams* (elsewhere in this chapter) celebrates the imaginative spirit of children.

One activity that could correlate with this book is making paper cutouts. Each child lies down on a large sheet of paper (for example, from a roll of white butcher paper), and other children help trace the child's outline. Children illustrate their outlines to look like themselves, then cut them out and display them. A follow-up activity might have the children suggest positive words or sentences about each other and themselves and then write them on the cutout. The children could think about what is "amazing" about themselves. Related books could focus on other independent characters, like Louise in *Louise Builds a House*, William in *Which Horse Is William?*, and Henry in *Old Henry*.

Related Titles

Louise Builds a House, written and illustrated by Louise Pfanner. Orchard, 1987. When Louise builds her house, she adds details that meet her needs. She creates a house that is as individual as she is. Louise's imagination appears again in *Louise Builds a Boat* (Orchard, 1989).

Musical Max, by Robert Kraus. Illustrated by Jose Aruego and Ariane Dewey. Simon & Schuster, 1990. Max loves to practice playing music on many instruments. His family and neighbors do not always appreciate his talent. When Max stops playing, though, everyone misses his music.

Nicolas, Where Have You Been?, written and illustrated by Leo Lionni. Knopf, 1987. Nicolas, a mouse, goes looking for a new berry patch and is befriended by some birds. When he returns home, he helps his friends overcome their prejudices toward birds. The mice and the birds learn to be more tolerant of each other.

Old Henry, by Joan Blos. Illustrated by Stephen Gammell. Morrow, 1987. Old Henry is an eccentric stranger who moves into a deserted house. His neighbors hope he will fix the dilapidated structure, but Henry is content with the house as it is. (Condensed in *Primaryplots,* Bowker, 1989, pp. 43–45.)

Something Special for Me, written and illustrated by Vera B. Williams. Greenwillow, 1983. Rosa needs to find the present that is just right for her. At first, she thinks she will get something all her friends have, but she decides to demonstrate her independence. (Condensed in *Primaryplots,* Bowker, 1989, pp. 70–72.)

Tessa Snaps Snakes, written and illustrated by Alison Lester. Houghton, 1991. Ernie, Celeste, Rosie, Nicky, Tessa, Frank, and Clive are friends, but each has his or her own way of doing things. They all laugh, but at different things. They earn money doing different jobs. They keep different secrets, dislike different things, and eat different midnight snacks. Their differences make them unique and interesting.

Which Horse Is William?, written and illustrated by Karly Kuskin. Greenwillow, 1992. William's mother knows him even when he is a horse, a skunk, a lamb, a duck, a mouse, a songbird, a rabbit, a dog, or a pig. William's unique personality always shines through. New artwork updates this book, originally published in 1959.

About the Author

HOFFMAN, MARY

Something about the Author, ed. by Anne Commire. Gale, 1990, Vol. 59, pp. 101–103.

Johnson, Angela. *Do Like Kyla*
Illus. by James Ransome. Orchard, 1990, LB (0-531-08452-3)
Suggested Use Level: PreS–Gr. 1

Plot Summary

All day long, a little girl follows her older sister, Kyla, and imitates her behavior. They tap on the window to attract the birds, stretch and get dressed, braid their hair, eat breakfast, and kiss the dog. Later, they go to the store, wearing similar coats and boots. They crunch in the snow and follow their own footsteps home. At the end of the day, they read a book together. As they get ready for bed, the sisters look out the window at the birds and the little sister taps on the window. Following her lead this time, Kyla taps too.

Thematic Material

Little brothers and sisters often follow their older siblings. Many children will relate to the situations in *Do Like Kyla*, enjoying the everyday experiences of these two African-American children.

Book Talk Material and Activities

What do you like about being with your brother or sister? What do you like about being alone? Is there anything you don't like? Children often want to discuss their everyday experiences, and they often need to talk about what they like and what they don't like. By sharing information about their homes and families, children learn about each other. They build relationships and see similarities and differences. In a classroom or library, children could make a chart listing things they like to do with a sibling or friend.

Do Like Kyla could be included in a book talk program on relationships between brothers and sisters. *That Bothered Kate* has a similar plot, only Kate is not so accepting of her young sister as Kyla is. In *Jamaica Tag-Along*, Jamaica realizes she has treated a little boy named Berto the same way her brother Ossie treated her. Jamaica lets Berto help her build a sand castle and, later, lets Ossie help them both. In *A Place for Ben*, the focus is on two brothers, Ben and Ezra. Pat Hutchins's books about Titch (such as *You'll Soon Grow Into Them, Titch*) and about the Monster family *(The Very Worst Monster)* also focus on the relationships between siblings. In classrooms or libraries, the experiences of these book characters could be added to the chart about siblings.

Related Titles

Hard to Be Six, by Arnold Adoff. Illustrated by Cheryl Hanna. Lothrop, 1991. A little boy is frustrated that he cannot do everything his older sister can do. When he visits his grandfather's grave with his grandmother, he is reassured by the loving feelings that are shared. This multiracial family enjoys many activities together.

Jamaica Tag-Along, by Juanita Havill. Illustrated by Anne Sibley O'Brien. Houghton, 1989. When Ossie goes to the park to play basketball, Jamaica follows him. Later, when Jamaica is playing, she is bothered by a toddler named Berto.

A Place for Ben, by Jeanne Titherington. Greenwillow, 1987. Ben feels he needs a place that belongs to him, but his little brother, Ezra, just won't leave him alone. (Condensed in *Primaryplots,* Bowker, 1989, pp. 68–69.)

That Bothered Kate, written and illustrated by Sally Noll. Greenwillow, 1991. Tory does everything her sister Kate does, and that bothers Kate. But when Tory wants to be alone, Kate is bothered by that, too.

The Very Worst Monster, written and illustrated by Pat Hutchins. Greenwillow, 1985. In the Monster family, everyone pays attention to the new baby and ignores Hazel. Hazel finds a way to get her family's attention. (Condensed in *Primaryplots,* Bowker, 1989, pp. 129–131.)

You'll Soon Grow Into Them, Titch, written and illustrated by Pat Hutchins. Greenwillow, 1983. As in *Titch* (Macmillan, 1971), this story describes the dilemma of being the youngest.

About the Author

JOHNSON, ANGELA
Something about the Author, ed. by Donna Olendorf. Gale, 1992, Vol. 69, p. 118.

Khalsa, Dayal Kaur. *Cowboy Dreams*
Illus. by the author. Clarkson N. Potter, 1990, LB (0-517-57491-8)
Suggested Use Level: Gr. 2–4

Plot Summary

A woman reminisces about her childhood dream of being a cowboy. She pretended she was a cowboy and her bike was a horse. The illustrations show her riding a rocking horse, riding on the back of a man, and riding on a merry-go-round. At the museum, the girl looked at pictures of the West. At the movies, she saw Westerns. She thought about having a horse of her own, even planning to turn the garage into a stable. She entered a contest for a horse but did not win, so she rode the coin-operated horse in front of the store. When she saw an almost life-sized horse at the toy store, she begged to have it, although she knew it was too expensive. So she pretended that the banister was a horse. She would ride it and sing cowboy songs. Her story concludes with some of the words to "Home on the Range," "Poor Lonesome Cowboy," "The Streets of Laredo," and "Red River Valley." As an adult, she still remembers wanting to be a cowboy, and she still hums the cowboy songs.

Thematic Material

This is a book about the dreams of childhood. Told as a reminiscence, it is a reflection on a time when everything seemed possible.

Book Talk Material and Activities

Like *Amazing Grace* (elsewhere in this chapter), *Cowboy Dreams* is a story about being hopeful and having dreams. The mood of each book is very different, however. Grace believes she can achieve her dreams; she looks ahead to her future. The narrator in *Cowboy Dreams* is looking back on her childhood. While there is a sense of nostalgia and yearning, there is also a feeling of happiness. Most children realize it is unlikely that the little girl in *Cowboy Dreams* would ever become a cowboy, and they enjoy her imaginative spirit and the way she acted out her dream. *Bea and Mr. Jones* is another story in which the characters try out different roles.

Several books that look back and reflect on childhood experiences could serve as models for similar memory books. This would be very appropriate for children in the middle elementary grades (grades 3 and 4) who are beginning to have a sense of their own past. Working on an illustrated memory book could be a project for children and their families. *Cowboy Dreams, When I Was Nine,* and *My Album* would all relate to these activities.

Related Titles

Bea and Mr. Jones, written and illustrated by Amy Schwartz. Bradbury, 1982. Bea and her father decide to trade places for the day. Their switch is so successful that they stay in their new roles.

Howdy!, by LaVada Weir. Illustrated by William Hoey. Steck-Vaughn, 1972. Luke, an African-American child, wears his cowboy hat and says "Howdy" to everyone. Pretty soon, everyone is saying "Howdy."

My Album, written and illustrated by Eleanor Schick. Greenwillow, 1984. A girl looks at photographs of herself and her family and describes each scene. The "photographs" are actually drawings, and children could prepare a similar project using either real photographs or their own drawings.

One Good Horse: A Cowpuncher's Counting Book, by Ann Herbert Scott.

Illustrated by Lynn Sweat. Greenwillow, 1990. Items that would be familiar to a Western setting are counted, like sagebrush and mountain quail. Numbers from one to ten are included, then fifty and one hundred.

When I Was Nine, written and illustrated by James Stevenson. Greenwillow, 1986. Walking alone, a man reminisces about his childhood, remembering his family, his dog, his neighborhood, and some of his everyday activities. (Condensed in *Primaryplots,* Bowker, 1989, pp. 190–192.)

White Dynamite and Curly Kidd, by Bill Martin, Jr., and John Archambault. Illustrated by Ted Rand. Holt, 1986. At the rodeo, a cowboy tells a child about riding White Dynamite, a white bull. On the last page, the child's cowboy hat is removed, showing a girl, who dreams of following her father.

About the Author and Illustrator

KHALSA, DAYAL KAUR
Something about the Author, ed. by Anne Commire. Gale, 1990, Vol. 62, pp. 98–100.

Lasky, Kathryn.   *Sea Swan*
Illus. by Catherine Stock. Macmillan, 1988 (0-02-751700-4)
Suggested Use Level: Gr. 1–3

Plot Summary
Elzibah Swan is a widow living in Boston in the house built by her great-grandfather. With her cat for company and the household help of Mr. and Mrs. Fortly, Elzibah enjoys her life, which is filled with regular activities such as the symphony and the Great Books club. When her grandchildren come to visit, Elzibah abandons her schedule to spend time with them. After they leave, she returns to her solitude and her schedule. On her seventy-fifth birthday, Elzibah decides to find a challenge for herself; she decides to learn to swim. She takes lessons, learning to kick, breathe, and stroke. Finally, she is able to swim. Now her schedule is filled with this new activity. She spends hours at a rocky cove, enjoying the salt water and the blue sky. In the fall, Elzibah works on the plans for a new house—a house by the sea. As the weather becomes colder, Elzibah buys a wet suit and swims in the cove while a light snow falls. On the coldest

days of winter, Elzibah swims at an indoor pool, and she learns how to cook—making pancakes, eggs, and chowder. When the warm weather returns, she supervises the construction of her new home, and she learns to dive and breathe through a snorkel tube. Elzibah's house is finally done, and she moves into it with her cat and Mr. and Mrs. Fortly. Elzibah is content to face new challenges in her home by the sea.

Thematic Material

Sea Swan presents an image of an older adult who is vibrant and active. Elzibah's life is safe and secure, yet she chooses to look for challenges.

Book Talk Material and Activities

Children need many opportunities to interact with older adults. A story or book talk program could focus on books that present a variety of images of older adults. Included could be books in which the older adult takes an active role in the world, as in *Miss Rumphius* and *I Know a Lady*. Other books could stress a loving relationship between a child and an older relative or adult, as in *Grandpa's Face* (see chapter 1) and *Grandaddy's Place*. After hearing *Sea Swan* and looking at some related titles like *Miss Rumphius* and *Grandaddy's Place*, children could share a special feeling or experience they have had with an older relative or friend.

An additional activity could involve a community services department that works with older adults. A trip could be arranged to a retirement center. Children could read favorite books to some of the residents, and a "pen pal" activity could be initiated. In many communities, grandparents and neighbors are encouraged to participate in school activities. They are invited to special programs; sometimes they volunteer to work with children. Books about older adults can help children understand and appreciate the involvement of older adults.

Related Titles

Aunt Flossie's Hats (and Crab Cakes Later), by Elizabeth Fitzgerald Howard. Illustrated by James Ransome. Clarion, 1991. Susan and Sarah love to visit their great-great-aunt Flossie. She always lets them play with her hats, and she tells them a story about each hat (see chapter 1).

Georgia Music, by Helen V. Griffith. Illustrated by James Stevenson.

Greenwillow, 1986. In this companion book to *Grandaddy's Place*, Grandaddy now lives with Janetta and Momma. Janetta helps him learn to accept this new situation.

Grandaddy's Place, by Helen V. Griffith. Illustrated by James Stevenson. Greenwillow, 1987. Janetta is nervous about meeting her grandaddy for the first time. At his house in the country, Janetta is afraid of all the animals and the noises. Grandaddy reassures her, and they become friends. (Condensed in *Primaryplots*, Bowker, 1989, pp. 11–13.)

Grandpa and Bo, written and illustrated by Kevin Henkes. Greenwillow, 1986. Bo visits his grandpa in the country. They enjoy walking and talking with each other, and even though it is summer, they celebrate Christmas, because they will not see each other in December.

I Know a Lady, by Charlotte Zolotow. Illustrated by James Stevenson. Greenwillow, 1984. A young girl describes the special relationship she has with an elderly neighbor.

Miss Maggie, by Cynthia Rylant. Illustrated by Thomas DiGrazia. Dutton, 1983. Miss Maggie lives alone in a deteriorating house. A young neighbor, Nat, is afraid of her. When Miss Maggie needs his help, Matt finds out that she is lonely and afraid, too.

Miss Rumphius, written and illustrated by Barbara Cooney. Viking, 1992. Miss Rumphius has promised she will do something to make the world more beautiful.

My Island Grandma, by Kathryn Lasky. Illustrated by Emily McCully. Morrow, 1993. A little girl shares her feelings of love for her grandmother when she describes the summers they spend together.

About the Author

LASKY, KATHRYN

Sixth Book of Junior Authors and Illustrators, ed. by Sally Holmes Holtze. Wilson, 1989, pp. 160–161.

Something about the Author, ed. by Anne Commire. Gale, 1978, Vol. 13, pp. 124–125; ed. by Donna Olendorf, Gale, 1992, Vol. 69, pp. 129–132.

About the Illustrator

STOCK, CATHERINE

Something about the Author, ed. by Donna Olendorf. Gale, 1991, Vol. 65, pp. 197–199.

Lionni, Leo. *Matthew's Dream*
Illus. by the author. Knopf, 1991, LB (0-679-91075-1)
Suggested Use Level: Gr. 1–3

Plot Summary
Matthew, a mouse, wonders about his future. His parents have their expectations, but Matthew is not sure what he will become. On a class visit to a museum, Matthew sees incredible treasures. He sees paintings in a variety of artistic styles and using many different materials. He meets another mouse, Nicoletta, who shares his admiration of the art. Later, Matthew dreams that he and Nicoletta enter a beautiful painting. Waking in his shabby home, Matthew is disappointed. Then he looks more closely at his surroundings. He sees shapes and colors and textures. He is inspired to become a painter. He marries Nicoletta, and his life is filled with satisfaction and joy.

Thematic Material
Matthew's Dream is a book about creativity and independence. It celebrates the artist.

Book Talk Material and Activities
Matthew makes some choices that take him in an unusual direction. His parents hope he might become a doctor, yet Matthew is interested in art. By pursuing his own dream, Matthew finds success and fulfillment. Many children feel it is important to conform, to be "one of the gang." Stories like *Matthew's Dream* and *Cherries and Cherry Pits* focus on characters who do not do what is expected. They provide characters who are independent.

Art is a focus of *Matthew's Dream,* and other art-related books could be featured. Tomie dePaola's *The Art Lesson* describes the frustration a child feels when conformity is valued over creativity. *Bear Hunt* by Anthony Browne features a character who uses his artistic talent to solve problems. *Matthew's Dream* could be read before a trip to an art museum, as could *Visiting the Art Museum* and *Picture This*.

Related Titles
The Art Lesson, written and illustrated by Tomie dePaola. Putnam, 1989. Tommy creates beautiful paintings at home, but at school his creativity is not encouraged.

Bear Hunt, written and illustrated by Anthony Browne. Doubleday, 1979. With his pencil, Bear draws his way out of the problems he encounters from hunters.

Cherries and Cherry Pits, written and illustrated by Vera B. Williams. Greenwillow, 1986. Bidemmi loves to draw. As she draws with her markers, she tells stories about her pictures. (Condensed in *Primaryplots,* Bowker, 1989, pp. 282–284.)

Frederick, written and illustrated by Leo Lionni. Pantheon, 1967. While the other mice prepare for winter, Frederick does not seem to be helping. Yet when the cold, dreary winter days arrive, Frederick shares his colors, feelings, and words.

The Incredible Painting of Felix Clousseau, written and illustrated by Jon Agee. Farrar, 1988. Many artists enter their work in the art contest, but the winner is Felix Clousseau, whose paintings have unusual powers.

Musical Max, by Robert Kraus. Illustrated by Jose Aruego and Ariane Dewey. Simon & Schuster, 1990. Max loves to practice music on many instruments. His family and neighbors do not always appreciate his talent. When Max stops playing, though, everyone misses his music.

Picture This: A First Introduction to Paintings, by Felicity Woolf. Illustrated with reproductions. Doubleday, 1989. From illuminated manuscripts to surrealistic and abstract paintings, this book provides information about different types of art and ways to look at and learn about it.

Visiting the Art Museum, written and illustrated by Laurene Krasny Brown and Marc Brown. Dutton, 1986. A family's visit to the museum is told through conversation balloons. The pictures and objects they see are described more completely in the "More about the Art" section at the end of the book.

About the Author and Illustrator

LIONNI, LEO

Illustrators of Children's Books: 1957–1966, Vol. III, comp. by Lee Kingman, Grace Allen Hogarth, and Harriet Quimby. Horn Book, 1968, pp. 3, 16, 140, 229; *1967–1976, Vol. IV,* 1978, pp. 7, 11, 139–140, 198.

Something about the Author, ed. by Anne Commire. Gale, 1976, Vol. 8, pp. 114–115.

Third Book of Junior Authors, ed. by Muriel Fuller. Wilson, 1963, pp. 179–180.

Polacco, Patricia.   *Thunder Cake*
Illus. by the author. Philomel, 1990 (0-399-22231-6)
Suggested Use Level: Gr. K–2

Plot Summary

A little girl is visiting her grandmother. There is a thunderstorm coming, and the girl is frightened. Grandma, however, seems pleased there will
be a storm because she can make a Thunder Cake. After calling her
granddaughter out from under the bed, Grandma checks the recipe and
counts the seconds between seeing the lightning and hearing the thunder.
The storm is ten counts away when the two begin to gather the ingredients. They get eggs and milk from the animals in the barn, then chocolate
and sugar from the dry shed. Finally, they get some overripe tomatoes and
some strawberries. They mix the ingredients and put the cake in the oven;
the storm is three counts away. While the cake bakes, Grandma tells her
granddaughter how proud she is of her bravery. She reminds her of all
they accomplished during the storm. As the thunderstorm passes over-
head, the cake is finished, and grandmother and granddaughter enjoy
eating their Thunder Cake. A recipe for the cake follows the story.

Thematic Material

In *Thunder Cake*, a grandmother helps her granddaughter overcome her
fear of the thunderstorm. This story presents a positive relationship between a child and an older adult.

Book Talk Material and Activities

When *Thunder Cake* was shared with a class of second graders, it led to
a discussion of bravery. The librarian asked the children to describe what
it meant to be brave and to think about times they had been brave. For
many children, being brave meant facing danger or doing something
dangerous. Several said police officers and firefighters were brave. One
child said, "If you save someone from in front of a car, you are brave."
Another said, "Brave means to risk your life." About being brave themselves, one child said, "I am brave when I go up to the attic by myself."
Others talked about going into the basement or going outside in the dark.
One girl said, "I am brave when I tell the truth and I know I will be
punished." Several children felt the girl in *Thunder Cake* was not that brave

because she did not face her fears on her own. The class had heard *Brave Irene,* and many children felt Irene was "more brave" because she took the risk on her own.

Children often enjoy grouping books into categories, like "Brave Books" or "Facing Fears." Doing this helps them focus on the themes of the stories. After reading *Thunder Cake* and *Brave Irene,* these second graders looked for other books that had characters who faced danger or overcame their fears. They suggested *Doctor DeSoto* because the mouse dentist was kind when he agreed to help the fox, and he was brave when he faced the fox after realizing the fox planned to eat him. They remembered the book *Once When I Was Scared* and talked about how Daniel, the main character, went out into the night to bring back hot coals to restart the fire in the cabin. They added Wiley and his mother in *Wiley and the Hairy Man* to their list of brave characters because they faced the Hairy Man together.

Audiovisual Adaptation

Thunder Cake. Spoken Arts, cassette/book, 1990.

Related Titles

Brave Irene, written and illustrated by William Steig. Farrar, 1986. Irene's mother makes a dress for the duchess, but she becomes ill and cannot deliver it. Irene bravely walks through a storm to get the dress to the duchess in time for the ball. (Condensed in *Primaryplots,* Bowker, 1989, pp. 65–68.)

Do Not Open, written and illustrated by Brinton Turkle. Dutton, 1981. When Miss Moody opens the bottle (even though it is marked "Do Not Open"), a monster appears. Miss Moody must stay calm to outwit the monster.

Doctor DeSoto, written and illustrated by William Steig. Farrar, 1982. Doctor DeSoto, a dentist who is a mouse, will not treat dangerous animals. One day, a fox needs his help, and Doctor DeSoto must decide what to do.

Once When I Was Scared, by Helena Clare Pittman. Illustrated by Ted Rand. Dutton, 1988. On a stormy night, Daniel goes to the neighbor's house to bring back hot coals for the fire. He imagines he is transformed into several animals, including an eagle that frightens a bear. This story is told by Daniel, now a grandfather, to his grandson.

Storm in the Night, by Mary Stolz. Illustrated by Pat Cummings. Harper,

1988. During a storm that has cut off the electricity, a grandfather and grandson sit together in the dark and enjoy the sounds, smells, and feelings of the rain. The grandfather describes a stormy night from his childhood and how he had to overcome his fear of the dark.

Wiley and the Hairy Man, adapted from an American folktale and illustrated by Molly Bang. Macmillan, 1976. The Hairy Man wants Wiley. Three times he tries to get Wiley, and three times he fails. Now he cannot harm Wiley again.

Porte, Barbara Ann.   *Harry in Trouble*
Illus. by Yossi Abolafia. Greenwillow, 1989, LB (0-688-07722-6); pap., Dell, 1990 (0-440-40370-7)
Suggested Use Level: Gr. K–2

Plot Summary

Harry has a problem. He has lost his library card . . . for the third time! The first time, his dog ate it. His next card went through the wash. He put his third card in a very safe place, but now he can't remember where it is. His friend Dorcas tries to help Harry by telling him all the things she has lost. Harry even talks to his father and his Aunt Rose about losing things. Harry's father tells him that his mom, who died when Harry was one, was very organized. Aunt Rose tells Harry that Harry's dad used to lose thing when he was younger. When Harry goes to the library to tell Ms. Katz about losing another card, she is exasperated. She decides she will make him one more card but keep it at her desk for him. Harry is happy that she is so helpful, and that he can still sign out books. He hurries to tell Aunt Rose, who reminds him that he left his card in her piano bench. Now Harry has two cards.

Thematic Material

An important theme here is learning to deal with everyday problems. Harry wants to do his best. He accepts the responsibility for losing his library card, and he receives support and understanding from his friends, family, and his librarian.

Book Talk Material and Activities

When some kindergartners heard *Harry in Trouble*, it led to a discussion of things that worried them. One child talked about a lost library book, another about being lost, another about being afraid of dogs, and another about being afraid of some older children. They felt Harry was right to be worried about losing things, and they were reassured that the librarian and his Aunt Rose helped him with his problem.

Many books present situations that allow children to deal with their own concerns. In *Lost in the Museum*, Paul and Jim and some classmates are on a class trip. They become separated from their teacher, and Jim goes to look for her. He leads her back to the rest of the group. *Sheila Rae, the Brave* becomes lost when she takes a different route home. *Annabelle Swift, Kindergartner* worries that she will not behave correctly at school. Using these books in a program could help children understand that many of their problems are shared by others.

Related Titles

Annabelle Swift, Kindergartner, written and illustrated by Amy Schwartz. Orchard, 1988. Before Annabelle starts school, her older sister, Lucy, coaches her in some everyday activities. When Annabelle gets to school, Lucy's suggestions are not that helpful.

Ghost's Hour, Spook's Hour, by Eve Bunting. Illustrated by Donald Carrick. Clarion, 1987. On the night of the big storm, there is a power failure. Jake is apprehensive about being in the dark, and with his dog, Biff, he begins to look for his parents. (Condensed in *Primaryplots*, Bowker, 1989, pp. 79–81.)

Jamaica's Find, by Juanita Havill. Illustrated by Anne Sibley O'Brien. Houghton, 1986. When Jamaica finds a stuffed toy at the park, she wants to keep it. When she turns it into the park lost and found, she makes a new friend.

Lost in the Museum, by Miriam Cohen. Illustrated by Lillian Hoban. Greenwillow, 1979. Even though they have been told to stay with the group, Paul and Jim and some of their classmates become separated from their teacher.

Sheila Rae, the Brave, written and illustrated by Kevin Henkes. Greenwillow, 1987. Sheila Rae decides to prove how brave she is by taking a different route home from school. She is lucky her little sister, Louise, has followed her and knows the way home.

Tales of Amanda Pig, by Jean Van Leeuwen. Illustrated by Ann Schweninger. Dial, 1983. In one of the five stories in this book, Amanda's father helps Amanda overcome her fear of the dark and of the hall clock that looks like a monster. (Condensed in *Primaryplots*, Bowker, 1989, pp. 35–37.)

About the Author

PORTE, BARBARA ANN

Sixth Book of Junior Authors and Illustrators, ed. by Sally Holmes Holtze. Wilson, 1989, pp. 231–232.
Something about the Author, ed. by Anne Commire. Gale, 1986, Vol. 45, p. 168; 1989, Vol. 57, pp. 148–149.

About the Illustrator

ABOLAFIA, YOSSI

Sixth Book of Junior Authors and Illustrators, ed. by Sally Holmes Holtze. Wilson, 1989, pp. 4–5.
Something about the Author, ed. by Anne Commire. Gale, 1987, Vol. 46, p. 21; 1990, Vol. 60, pp. 1–3.

Rockwell, Anne.   *What We Like*

Illus. by the author. Macmillan, 1992 (0-02-777274-8)
Suggested Use Level: PreS–Gr. 1

Plot Summary

Ten categories describe "What We Like." Included are "What We Like . . . " to Make, to Look At, to Wear, to Do Outside, to Do Inside, to Feel, to Eat, to Smell, to Say, and to Hear. The illustrations show young animals and their families and friends depicting the specific concepts. For example, there are ten pictures of "What We Like to Wear," including warm pajamas, snowsuits, and Halloween costumes. The characters include cats, bears, dogs, pigs, foxes, and rabbits. On the last page, a kitten encourages readers to talks about what they like.

Thematic Material

As children learn more about each other, they realize people have similarities and differences. They also learn to accept each other and develop friendships. *What We Like* encourages children to talk about themselves.

Book Talk Material and Activities

Sharing *What We Like* with young children leads naturally to activities about likes and dislikes. One group of preschoolers made a mural depicting some of their preferences. "We like . . . " and "We don't like . . . " were the headings on the mural. The children drew pictures of their likes and dislikes and then dictated words or sentences to accompany them. Some of their likes were "hearing stories," "ice cream," and "riding my bike." Their dislikes included "my brother," "going to bed," and "eating cooked carrots."

In a first grade class, children made a spiral-bound book called "What We Like About School." Each child drew a picture and wrote a brief caption. Some children noticed that Anne Rockwell used cartoon-style panels to illustrate *What We Like*, so they tried that, too. Many of the books by Anne and Harlow Rockwell focus on daily activities, and these books were included in a library program featuring everyday experiences and activities, such as being at home *(In Our House)* or going to the beach *(At the Beach)*. These books provided students with ideas for their own likes and dislikes lists. Stories where the characters had strong likes and dislikes were also presented, including *I Like Me*, *I'll Fix Anthony*, and *Chester's Way*. A follow-up activity in the library resulted in a book called "What We Like to Read."

Related Titles

At the Beach, written and illustrated by Anne Rockwell and Harlow Rockwell. Macmillan, 1987. Many children enjoyed talking about their trip to the beach after hearing this book. They remembered other water activities they had enjoyed.

Chester's Way, written and illustrated by Kevin Henkes. Greenwillow, 1988. Chester and his friend Wilson have very definite opinions about everything. At first, they do not like Lilly, who seems too unconventional. When she comes to their aid, Chester and Wilson accept her as their friend.

Feelings, written and illustrated by Aliki. Greenwillow, 1984. A variety of emotions, including sadness, anger, and joy, are described in this book.

I Like Me, written and illustrated by Nancy Carlson. Viking, 1988. The young pig in this book is self-confident. She knows she can have fun even if she is alone.

I'll Fix Anthony, written by Judith Viorst. Illustrated by Arnold Lobel. Harper, 1969. The little brother in this book describes the things he does not like about his brother, Anthony. Then he describes how he will "fix Anthony."

In Our House, written and illustrated by Anne Rockwell. Crowell, 1985. A young bear takes the reader on a tour of his house, describing things that happen in each room.

On Our Vacation, written and illustrated by Anne Rockwell. Dutton, 1989. What happens when you go on vacation? This family of bears describes some of their fun activities.

School Days, by B. G. Hennessy. Illustrated by Tracey Campbell Pearson. Viking, 1990. An activity-filled day at school is described in this book.

About the Author and Illustrator

ROCKWELL, ANNE

Fifth Book of Junior Authors and Illustrators, ed. by Sally Holmes Holtze. Wilson, 1983, pp. 264–266.

Illustrators of Children's Books: 1967–1976, Vol. IV, comp. by Lee Kingman, Grace Allen Hogarth, and Harriet Quimby. Horn Book, 1978, pp. 6, 154–155, 207.

Something about the Author, ed. by Anne Commire. Gale, 1983, Vol. 33, pp. 170–174; ed. by Diane Telgen, Gale, 1993, Vol. 71, pp. 165–168.

Wood, Audrey. *Elbert's Bad Word*

Illus. by Audrey Wood and Don Wood. Harcourt, 1988 (0-15-225320-3)

Suggested Use Level: Gr. 1–3

Plot Summary

At a party, Elbert overhears a new word. It is not a pleasant word. Putting the word in his pocket, Elbert mingles with the guests. The word jumps into Elbert's mouth, so that when his toe is mashed by Sir Hilary's mallet, Elbert says the word. The guests are aghast. Elbert's mother makes him wash his mouth with soap, although the word is no longer in his mouth. Elbert wants to be rid of the word, so he visits the gardener, who is also a wizard. The wizard makes a little cake, with a special ingredient of sparkling words. Elbert eats the cake and returns to the party. When his toe is again mashed with Sir Hilary's mallet, the guests wait for Elbert's reaction. He uses the words the wizard has given him, such as "MY STARS" and "ZOUNDS AND GADZOOKS." The bad word disappears down a hole in the ground.

Thematic Material

The humor in this book is present in the story and the illustrations. The bad word begins as a dirty cloud and grows to be a shocking beast. Learning to deal with anger and with angry words are related themes in this book.

Book Talk Material and Activities

When their teacher read *Elbert's Bad Word,* a class of second graders talked about how the "bad word" was never said. Most of them realized the author and illustrator presented the word as an angry creature so children would relate this to their own situations. Knowing the actual word was not as important as learning other words and behaviors for dealing with anger and painful situations. They talked about some of the things they did when they had problems, like yelling, throwing tantrums, crying, and getting into fights. Several children said that doing these things often just made their problems worse. They liked the way Elbert got rid of the bad word, although there was a feeling that it is not always that easy. The class read *I'll Fix Anthony* and continued their discussion of dealing with difficult feelings. When they compared the two books, most of the children felt they were more like the brother in *I'll Fix Anthony* than like Elbert. They thought the brother probably felt better for planning to get even with Anthony, although he did not really ever do what he planned. They enjoyed the wizard and the magic word cake in *Elbert's Bad Word* and felt that this humorous and magical solution let them think about the problem of using unacceptable language. Making a menu of words they could use to deal with problems was a follow-up activity.

Aliki's *Feelings* presents information about many different emotions and can lead to discussions about different kinds of feelings. Often, children cannot explain exactly what they are feeling. Hearing stories and poems about characters who cope with different moods and emotions lets children relate to these situations and learn more about themselves.

Audiovisual Adaptation

Elbert's Bad Word. MCA/Universal Home Video, videorecording, 1992.

Related Titles

Dinah's Mad, Bad Wishes, by Barbara Joosse. Illustrated by Emily Arnold McCully. Harper, 1989. Dinah and Mama are both very angry. At first, they think mean things about each other, but finally they make up.

Feelings, written and illustrated by Aliki. Greenwillow, 1984. Cartoon drawings show children experiencing many feelings, including anger, sadness, and joy.

I'll Fix Anthony, by Judith Viorst. Illustrated by Arnold Lobel. Harper, 1969. Here's a story of how a little brother feels about his big brother. Anthony had better watch out!

"I'm in a Rotten Mood!" in *The New Kid on the Block,* by Jack Prelutsky. Illustrated by James Stevenson. Greenwillow, 1984. This poem would be great to say after reading *Elbert's Bad Word.* Other poems in this collection describe different feelings. *Something Big Has Been Here* (Greenwillow, 1990) is a companion volume of verses.

Mean Soup, written and illustrated by Betsy Everitt. Harcourt, 1992. Horace's mother helps him deal with his angry feelings—they make mean soup, using his emotions as ingredients.

The Way I Feel . . . Sometimes, by Beatrice Schenk de Regniers. Illustrated by Susan Meddaugh. Clarion, 1988. "Feeling Mean, Mostly," "Feeling Better," "Feeling Wishful," and "Feeling OK, After All" are the chapters in this collection of poems.

About the Author and Illustrator

Wood, Audrey

Sixth Book of Junior Authors and Illustrators, ed. by Sally Holmes Holtze. Wilson, 1989, pp. 320–321.

Something about the Author, ed. by Anne Commire. Gale, 1986, Vol. 44, p. 214; 1988, Vol. 50, pp. 218–224.

Wood, Don

Sixth Book of Junior Authors and Illustrators, ed. by Sally Holmes Holtze. Wilson, 1989, pp. 322–323.

Something about the Author, ed. by Anne Commire. Gale, 1986, Vol. 44, p. 214; 1988, Vol. 50, pp. 224–231.

3

Celebrating Everyday Experiences

OPPOSITES, shadows, fractions, shapes, numbers, colors, and the alphabet are some of the concepts featured in the books in this chapter. Everyday experiences like playing with toys, learning about trains, telling time, sending letters, and going to the doctor are also featured. As children read about familiar activities, they see how their lives are similar to those of other children. The books in this chapter not only introduce children to simple concepts, such as colors, as in *I Went Walking,* but also describe more complex relationships, such as mixing colors in *Color Dance.* Numbers and counting are introduced in *Count!,* while money, banking, and investments are presented in *If You Made a Million.* Many of the books in this chapter could be models for projects, such as a museum trip book like *Dinosaurs, Dragonflies & Diamonds* or a theme alphabet book, such as *Eating the Alphabet.* Using familiar experiences, children could write, illustrate, and publish their own books.

Aliki.   *My Feet*
   Illus. by the author. Crowell, 1990, LB (0-690-04815-7); pap., Trophy (0-06-445106-2)
   Suggested Use Level: PreS–Gr. 1

Plot Summary
   This informational book describes the parts of the foot: the toes, the toenails, the sole, and the heel. Facts about caring for feet are presented. Using feet for walking, running, jumping and other activities is discussed.

The strong heel bone supports weight, while the ball of the foot is used for jumping. Wearing shoes and boots is discussed, as is enjoying bare feet.

Thematic Material

My Feet could be included in a program for young children on the human body. In schools, it could be in a science or health unit.

Book Talk Material and Activities

A book talk or story program for young children could focus on some beginning informational books about the body and health habits. Aliki's *My Feet, My Hands,* and *My Five Senses* could all lead to discussions of ways the children in the group use their feet, hands, and senses. A mural or collage of feet, shoes, and activities could be an extension activity for *My Feet.* Animals and their feet could be added to the mural. *What Neat Feet!* shows the feet of different animals and describes how they assist that animal. Included are the webbed foot of a swan, the flipper of a seal, the fuzzy foot of a rabbit, the hoof of a goat, the padded foot of a cat, the two-toed foot of a camel, and the flat, round foot of an elephant. *Whose Shoe?* matches shoes with the people and animals that wear them, such as a horseshoe with a horse.

Learning healthy habits correlates with the health curriculum in many schools. Sharing books like *Dinosaurs Alive and Well!, How Many Teeth,* and *Splash! All About Baths* could lead to a discussion of daily routines that help children stay healthy. *When I See My Doctor . . .* (elsewhere in this chapter) could be included in this unit.

Related Titles:

Dinosaurs Alive and Well! A Guide to Good Health, written and illustrated by Laurene Krasny Brown and Marc Brown. Little, Brown, 1990. A community of dinosaurs presents information about health and nutrition.

Here Are My Hands, by Bill Martin, Jr., and John Archambault. Illustrated by Ted Rand. Holt, 1985. In this rhyming text, children celebrate their hands, feet, head, nose, and other body parts.

How Many Teeth, revised edition, by Paul Showers. Illustrated by True Kelley. Harper, 1991. Caring for teeth is one part of this nonfiction book, which also includes information about why children lose their baby teeth.

I'm Growing, written and illustrated by Aliki. Harper, 1992. This Let's-Read-and-Find-Out science book provides a simple description of human growth and development.

My Five Senses, revised edition, written and illustrated by Aliki. Harper, 1989. A young child describes some everyday experiences, focusing on how his senses give information in each setting.

My Hands, revised edition, written and illustrated by Aliki. Crowell, 1990. Fingers, palms, fingernails, and thumbs are all parts of hands. Hands help with many everyday tasks, including carrying, waving, and buttoning.

Splash! All about Baths, by Susan Kovacs Buxbaum and Rita Golden Gelman. Illustrated by Maryann Cocca-Leffler. Little, Brown, 1987. A penguin, an elephant, a cat, and other cartoon animals answer some questions about bathtime.

What Neat Feet! written and photographed by Hana Machotka. Morrow, 1991. In this informational book, a close-up color photograph of an animal's foot is shown, followed by a photograph of and information about that animal. Included are a swan, a seal, a rabbit, a goat, a cat, a camel, and an elephant.

Whose Shoe?, written and photographed by Margaret Miller. Greenwillow, 1991. In a question-and-answer format, shoes are matched with people and animals, including a clown, a ballet dancer, a horse, a runner, and a baby.

Your Insides, by Joanna Cole. Illustrated by Paul Meisel. Putnam & Grosset, 1992. This book provides an overview of the body and its systems. One special feature is the see-through pages of the skin, muscles and bones, heart and lungs, and stomach and intestines.

Your Skin and Mine, revised edition, by Paul Showers. Illustrated by Kathleen Kuchera. Harper, 1991. This book describes the layers of skin, how skin heals after a cut, and how the amount of melanin in the skin influences skin color. Some safety and health tips are included.

About the Author and Illustrator

ALIKI (BRANDENBERG)

Illustrators of Children's Books: 1957–1966, Vol. III, comp. by Lee Kingman, Grace Allen Hogarth, and Harriet Quimby. Horn Book, 1978, pp. 72, 206; *1967–1976, Vol. IV,* 1978, pp. 94–95, 177–178.

Something about the Author, ed. by Anne Commire. Gale, 1971, Vol. 2, pp. 36–38; 1984, Vol. 35, pp. 49–55.

Third Book of Junior Authors, ed. by Doris de Montreville and Donna Hill. Wilson, 1972, pp. 8–9.

Aylesworth, Jim. *Country Crossing*
Illus. by Ted Rand. Atheneum, 1991 (0-689-31580-5)
Suggested Use Level: Gr. K–2

Plot Summary
On a summer night in the country, there are the sounds of crickets and an owl. The engine of a car can be heard in the distance, gradually becoming louder as it approaches the railroad tracks. Suddenly, the night is filled with noise. There is the clanging of the bell at the railroad crossing. The car stops as the gates come down. There is the sound of the train whistle and the rumbling of the train engine and wheels, closer and closer, louder and louder. The flashing red lights of the crossing sign are joined by the bright yellow headlight of the train. The train engine goes by, followed by the freight cars, rolling rhythmically past the car. Finally, the caboose passes by, and the train is gone. The car crosses the tracks and moves down the road. The sound of its engine soon fades. At the railroad crossing, there are crickets chirping and the sound of an owl.

Thematic Material
The descriptive sound words ("Puttaputt," "Churrrrrr," and "Chooachoo") capture the feeling of the sudden appearance of the train at the quiet railroad crossing. *Country Crossing* could be read along with other books about the night as well as with books about trains.

Book Talk Material and Activities
In *Country Crossing*, the quiet night is interrupted by the arrival of the freight train. The author's use of descriptive language adds to the drama of the moment as the warning bell rings "CLANG" and the train rushes past "CHOOACHOO CHOO CHOO" and "WHOOAWOO WHOOAWOOOOOO." These words are set in larger type as the train roars through the crossing, and there are sound words incorporated into the illustrations. This is a great book to read aloud with lots of opportunities for participation. A contrasting experience is described in *Night in the Country* by Cynthia Rylant. In this book, it is so quiet you can even hear an apple fall from the tree. *City Night* would provide another look at the night.
Many public libraries offer evening story hours, and *Country Crossing*

would be a good book to share with children and their parents. After the story, the group could even meet outside and listen to the evening noises around them. What animals do you hear? Can you hear any cars? Any trucks? Any trains? Each adult-child pair could try to write the sounds they heard, developing some descriptive sound words. Then the group could get back together and share some of the sounds they heard. *Trains* by Anne Rockwell (elsewhere in this chapter) could be booktalked along with *Country Crossing*.

Related Titles

City Night, by Eve Rice. Illustrated by Peter Sis. Greenwillow, 1987. The text describes the noises and activities in the city. The illustrations show a dark blue sky with yellow light coming from windows and street lamps. How do the sounds of the city compare to those at the railroad crossing?

The Goodnight Circle, by Carolyn Lesser. Illustrated by Lorinda Bryan Cauley. Harcourt, 1984. Deer, foxes, turtles, and frogs all prepare to go to sleep, but owls, beavers, opossums, and raccoons are busy throughout the night.

Night in the Country, by Cynthia Rylant. Illustrated by Mary Szilagyi. Bradbury, 1986. In the country, the darkness is filled with animals and sounds—swooping owls, singing frogs—as people and animals move slowly through the night. (Condensed in *Primaryplots*, Bowker, 1989, pp. 232–234.)

Night Noises, by Mem Fox. Illustrated by Terry Denton. Harcourt, 1989. The night noises in this story are those made by Lily Laceby's family as they sneak into her house to give her a surprise party.

Night Owls, by Sharon Phillips Denslow. Illustrated by Jill Kastner. Bradbury, 1990. In the summer, William goes to the country to visit his Aunt Charlene. They enjoy some special nighttime activities, such as counting lightning bugs and climbing a tree.

THUMP, THUMP, Rat-a-Tat-Tat, by Gene Baer. Illustrated by Lois Ehlert. Harper, 1989. The sounds and excitement of a marching band are captured in the rhythm of the words and the bright colors and design of the illustrations. The words become larger as the band comes nearer.

About the Author

AYLESWORTH, JIM
Something about the Author, ed. by Anne Commire. Gale, 1985, Vol. 38, p. 35.

About the Illustrator

RAND, TED

Sixth Book of Junior Authors and Illustrators, ed. by Sally Holmes Holtze. Wilson, 1989, pp. 238–239.

Berger, Melvin. *Switch On, Switch Off*
Illus. by Carolyn Croll. Crowell, 1989, LB (0-690-04786-X); pap., Trophy (0-06-445097-X)
Suggested Use Level: Gr. 1–3

Plot Summary

When you enter a dark room, you flip a switch up and a light comes on. When you want the room dark, you flip the switch down, and the light goes off. Electrical energy works the lights, the radio, the electric stove, the air conditioner, and other household appliances. Directions are given for making a simple coil generator. Explanations are given for how electricity flows through wires, how it is generated, how it is distributed to houses and other buildings, and how it is distributed throughout a house. Circuits are described, along with the inner workings of a light bulb and a lamp. The book ends with a boy turning off his light and going to bed.

Thematic Material

This nonfiction book provides introductory information about electricity.

Book Talk Material and Activities

After reading *Switch On, Switch Off,* it would be fun to have children do some simple activities. *The Science Book of Electricity* provides many suggestions for "hands-on" science experiences. The experiments with static electricity are simple and can be done by children. Most involve using balloons to show how electrical charges attract and repel objects. Activities demonstrating current electricity include making a simple circuit and then operating it with a switch.

Ghost's Hour, Spook's Hour and *Storm in the Night* tell about the experiences of children when there is a power failure. A story program could feature these stories as well as other stories about characters who are afraid of the dark, like Osa in *Darkness and the Butterfly* and Eugene in *Eugene the Brave*.

Related Titles

Darkness and the Butterfly, written and illustrated by Ann Grifalconi. Little, Brown 1987. Osa, a young girl, lives in Africa. During the day, she is happy and carefree, but at night, she is filled with fear. During a dream, she learns to face the night without fear. (Condensed in *Primaryplots*, Bowker, 1989, pp. 258–260.)

Eugene the Brave, by Ellen Conford. Illustrated by John M. Larrecq. Little, Brown, 1978. With the help of his sister Geraldine, Eugene the possum learns to overcome his fear of the dark.

Experiments with Electricity, by Helen J. Challand. Illustrated with photographs and drawings. Childrens Pr., 1986. The information in this book is slightly more complex than that in *Switch On, Switch Off.* Static electricity is described, along with some simple activities. Lightning, switches, fuses, and batteries are explained.

Ghost's Hour, Spook's Hour, by Eve Bunting. Illustrated by Donald Carrick. Clarion, 1987. On the night of the big storm there is a power failure. Jake wakes up and is afraid of the dark. He moves through the house and is reassured when he finds his parents in the living room. (Condensed in *Primaryplots*, Bowker, 1989, pp. 79–81.)

The Science Book of Electricity, by Neil Ardley. Photographs by Dave King. Harcourt, 1991. The simple activities presented in this book demonstrate concepts like static electricity, positive and negative charges, electrical fields, and current electricity. Adults could use these activities as demonstrations for younger children. Older children could do many of the activities themselves.

Storm in the Night, by Mary Stolz. Illustrated by Pat Cummings. Harper, 1988. During a storm that has cut off the electricity, a grandfather and grandson sit together in the dark and enjoy the sounds, smells, and feelings of the rain. The grandfather describes a stormy night from his childhood and how he had to overcome his fear of the dark.

About the Author

Berger, Melvin

Fifth Book of Junior Authors and Illustrators, ed. by Sally Holmes Holtze. Wilson, 1983, pp. 30–31.

Something about the Author, ed. by Anne Commire. Gale, 1973, Vol. 5, pp. 21–22.

About the Illustrator

CROLL, CAROLYN

Something about the Author, ed. by Anne Commire. Gale, 1988, Vol. 52, p. 31; 1989, Vol. 56, p. 38.

Burton, Marilee Robin. *Tail Toes Eyes Ears Nose*

Illus. by the author. Harper, 1988, LB (0-06-020874-0); pap., (0-06-443260-2)

Suggested Use Level: PreS–Gr. 1

Plot Summary

The tail, toes, eyes, ears, and nose of nine animals are depicted and then followed by an illustration of the animal. Included are a horse, a pig, a mouse, a cat, a dog, a rabbit, an elephant, a bird, and a boy.

Thematic Material

Young children need simple informational books. The concepts in this book could be shared in a unit on animals, as well as in a health unit discussion of the body.

Book Talk Material and Activities

Tail Toes Eyes Ears Nose introduces some basic body parts of animals. Other books build on these concepts, such as *But Not Like Mine* by Margery Facklam and *Spots, Feathers, and Curly Tails* by Nancy Tafuri. Each book focuses on physical characteristics and allows children to become familiar with similarities and differences between species. As children learn more about themselves, they could make a word bank of descriptive terms. *Tail Toes Eyes Ears Nose* could also be featured before a trip to a farm or the zoo, and a class book of the animals observed on the trip could be created. Eric Carle's *The Mixed-Up Chameleon,* which tells of a chameleon who wishes he could have certain characteristics of the zoo animals he sees, would further extend the concepts.

Related Titles

But Not Like Mine, by Margery Facklam. Illustrated by Jeni Bassett. Harcourt, 1988. Children learn about some of the physical characteristics of animals and fold out the page to find they are "not like mine." The creative format and patterned text encourage children to join in the reading.

A Children's Zoo, written and illustrated by Tana Hoban. Greenwillow, 1985. Each color photograph of a zoo animal is accompanied by three descriptive words about the animal's behavior and appearance.

The Mixed-Up Chameleon, written and illustrated by Eric Carle. Crowell, 1984. A chameleon wishes he could be like some of the animals in the zoo.

So Can I, by Margery Facklam. Illustrated by Jeni Bassett. Harcourt, 1988. Animals act out action words, and the reader folds out the page to reveal a child in the same activity.

Spots, Feathers, and Curly Tails, by Nancy Tafuri. Greenwillow, 1988. Farm animals are the focus of this look at physical characteristics.

About the Author and Illustrator

BURTON, MARILEE

Something about the Author, ed. by Anne Commire. Gale, 1987, Vol. 46, pp. 33–34.

Conrad, Pam. *The Tub People*
Illus. by Richard Egielski. Harper, 1989, LB (0-06-021341-8)
Suggested Use Level: Gr. 1–3

Plot Summary

The tub people are little wooden toys that are used in the bathtub. There are seven tub toys: father, mother, grandmother, doctor, policeman, child, and dog. In the tub, the people play at being on a raft of floating soap. The father is the captain, and he rescues the child when he falls in the water. One evening, the tub child is separated from the family. As the water swirls down the drain, the tub child goes too. All the tub toys are very sad. Without the child, they will not play games. When a man comes to work on the tub drain, the tub toys hope the child will come back. The child is found, but he and all the tub toys are taken away from the tub. They are moved into the bedroom, where they play mountain climbers on the rumpled bedsheets. The child pretends to fall off the mountain, and the father saves him. At night, all the toys are lined up on the windowsill together.

Thematic Material

Stories about toys and their adventures are very common in picture books for children.

Book Talk Material and Activities

When children play with their toys, they use their imaginations to create new worlds and to try out different experiences. In *The Tub People*, the child playing with the toys is never seen but is present as the one controlling the action. The feelings and emotions in the story are very childlike; the perspective of many of the pictures is through the eyes of the child who plays with and loves these toys. The reader is brought into the drama of the tub people, taking on the role of this unseen child. Many schools and libraries have special days when children bring a favorite toy with them. A display case of books and toys would build on this interest. Small toys could be grouped with *The Tub People;* stuffed animals would go with *Corduroy* and *This Is the Bear;* cars, trucks, and other vehicles could be displayed near Anne Rockwell's *Big Wheels* and *Cars* or with *My First Look at Things That Go.*

The Tub People could be shared with a group of older children to discuss perspective. Related books such as *George Shrinks, I'm Coming to Get You,* and *Ben's Dream* could be used to look at the changing point of view of the main character. Writing a story from the point of view of a toy would correlate with these books.

Audiovisual Adaptations

The Tub People. Scholastic, cassette/book, 1990; Library Learning Resources, kit (book, activity cards), 1990.

Related Titles

Ben's Dream, written and illustrated by Chris Van Allsburg. Houghton, 1982. While studying for his social studies test, Ben falls asleep and dreams he is visiting all the places he has been studying. The shifts in perspective provide a challenge to children as they try to identify where Ben is.

Big Wheels, written and illustrated by Anne Rockwell. Dutton, 1986. Large vehicles, including cranes, cement mixers, and snowplows, are the focus of this book. The illustrations show a community of pigs doing construction and farm work.

Cars, written and illustrated by Anne Rockwell. Dutton, 1984. This is a very simple book about the importance of cars. These illustrations show animals driving cars and other vehicles.

Corduroy, written and illustrated by Don Freeman. Viking, 1968. During the day, Corduroy waits in the department store for someone to buy him. At night, Corduroy leaves the toy department to look for a button. What do you think your toys do while you are asleep?

George Shrinks, written and illustrated by William Joyce. Harper, 1985. After dreaming that he has shrunk, George wakes up to find his dream has come true. How would you feel if you were suddenly small? (Condensed in *Primaryplots,* Bowker, 1989, pp. 134–135.)

I'm Coming to Get You, written and illustrated by Tony Ross. Dial, 1984. The end of this book is a surprise, as the giant monster is really no bigger than a mouse. Children can discuss how the illustrations make the reader think the monster is big.

My First Look at Things That Go, edited by Andrea Pinnington and Charlotte Davies. Photographs by Steve Gorton. Random, 1991. Color photographs of toy vehicles for construction, farm, water, and the road are included here.

This Is the Bear, by Sarah Hayes. Illustrated by Helen Craig. Lippincott, 1986. In this rhyming story, a stuffed bear named Fred is involved in a series of mishaps. (Condensed in *Primaryplots,* Bowker, 1989, pp. 95–97.)

About the Author

CONRAD, PAM

Sixth Book of Junior Authors and Illustrators, ed. by Sally Holmes Holtze. Wilson, 1989, pp. 64–66.

Something about the Author, ed. by Anne Commire. Gale, 1987, Vol. 49, p. 75; 1988, Vol. 52, pp. 29–31.

About the Illustrator

EGIELSKI, RICHARD

Illustrators of Children's Books: 1967–1976, Vol. IV, comp. by Lee Kingman, Grace Allen Hogarth, and Harriet Quimby. Horn Book, 1978, pp. 116, 187.

Sixth Book of Junior Authors and Illustrators, ed. by Sally Holmes Holtze. Wilson, 1989, pp. 85–86.

Something about the Author, ed. by Anne Commire. Gale, 1977, Vol. 11, pp. 89–90; 1987, Vol. 49, pp. 90–96.

Ehlert, Lois.   *Eating the Alphabet: Fruits and Vegetables from A to Z*
Illus. by the author. Harcourt, 1989 (0-15-224435-2)
Suggested Use Level: PreS–Gr. 1

Plot Summary
Collage illustrations on a white background depict a variety of vegetables and fruits. Organized alphabetically, common and uncommon foods include avocado, apple, beet, fig, grapes, kohlrabi, mango, okra, pumpkin, radicchio, watermelon, and zucchini. At the back of the book is a glossary of the foods and some additional information about each one, including the origin.

Thematic Material
The alphabet is used to present a variety of fruits and vegetables. This book could tie in to studies of plants, food, and nutrition.

Book Talk Material and Activities
Librarians and teachers know the importance of relating books to everyday experiences. Many young children have limited contact with books outside the school, day care, or library setting. They need opportunities to use literature and language and to connect it to familiar experiences. Activities that focus on food build on what children already know. Many of the fruits and vegetables in *Eating the Alphabet* are very familiar to children: banana, lettuce, orange, potato; many are not that common: kumquat, parsnip, pomegranate. Sharing this book could lead to a discussion of food likes and dislikes. A survey could be conducted of favorite fruits and vegetables, and children could chart the results. Teachers and librarians could even arrange a tasting of some of the less-familiar fruits and vegetables.

Other books about foods, both fiction and nonfiction, should be available not only to expand the discussion but also to introduce more literature in this experience. Bruce McMillan's *Growing Colors,* Douglas Florian's *Vegetable Garden,* and Lois Ehlert's *Eating the Alphabet* enable children to experience similar books with different styles of illustrations: photography in *Growing Colors,* pen and ink and watercolor in *Vegetable Garden,* and collage in *Eating the Alphabet.* Nonfiction books such as *A Book of Vegetables* and *In My Garden* could introduce informational books.

Using the framework of the alphabet in *Eating the Alphabet,* children could make their own alphabet of foods. They could even make a mural of their foods using the collage technique of Lois Ehlert. By building on a familiar experience, all children could participate. *Alligator Arrived with Apples* is another food and alphabet book that could extend the activity.

Related Titles

Alligator Arrived with Apples: A Potluck Alphabet Feast, written by Crescent Dragonwagon. Illustrated by Jose Aruego and Ariane Dewey. Macmillan, 1987. In alphabetical order, animals bring appropriate items to a banquet, so there are animals and foods from A to Z. Along with alligator's apples, there are mouse's mousse and zebra's zucchini.

A Book of Vegetables, by Harriet L. Sobol. Photographed by Patricia A. Agre. Dodd, 1984. Cabbage, eggplant, lettuce, peppers, zucchini, and other vegetables are described and depicted.

Growing Colors, written and photographed by Bruce McMillan. Lothrop, 1988. Photographs of fruits and vegetables are used to depict colors, including orange carrots, brown peppers, and purple plums.

Growing Vegetable Soup, written and illustrated by Lois Ehlert. Harcourt, 1987. Colorful pictures show the process of growing vegetables, from planting to watering and weeding to picking and, finally, to eating. Information is contained in the labels for the illustrations, which indicate which plants are growing and what tools are used.

In My Garden: A Child's Gardening Book, by Helen Oechsli and Kelly Oechsli. Macmillan, 1985. This nonfiction book describes organizing and caring for a garden. Specific information for beans, carrots, lettuce, radishes, tomatoes, and zucchini is given. Suggestions are provided for outdoor and indoor gardening activities.

Vegetable Garden, written and illustrated by Douglas Florian. Harcourt, 1991. A rhyming text describes the activities of a family working in their garden.

About the Author and Illustrator

EHLERT, LOIS

Illustrators of Children's Books: 1957–1966, comp. by Lee Kingman, Grace Allen Hogarth, and Harriet Quimby. Horn Book, 1968, pp. 103, 203, 216; *1967–1976, Vol. IV,* 1978, pp. 116, 187.

Something about the Author, ed. by Anne Commire. Gale, 1984, Vol. 35, pp. 97–98; ed. by Donna Olendorf, Gale, 1992, Vol. 69, pp. 50–53.

Talking with Artists, comp. and ed. by Pat Cummings. Bradbury, 1992, pp. 36–41.

Ernst, Lisa Campbell.   *Ginger Jumps*
Illus. by the author. Bradbury, 1990 (0-02-733565-8)
Suggested Use Level: Gr. 1–2

Plot Summary

Ginger is a small dog who has spent her life with the circus. It is a very busy place, so busy that no one has time for Ginger. Even the other dogs are too busy practicing with Sir Deedrick for his daredevil dog act. Eventually, Ginger learns some tricks and joins the daredevil dogs. When she is performing, Ginger begins to watch the audience. Maybe someday she will find a family with a little girl who will play with her. Prunella, the star daredevil dog, sneers at Ginger, but Ginger is convinced she will find her little girl. Time passes as she searches the circus crowds, and Ginger is chosen to learn a new trick and work with some new clowns. Ginger is to climb to the top of a very tall staircase, jump onto a trampoline, and land in the arms of one of the new clowns. Ginger practices jumping from the lower steps and does very well, but when it is time to jump from the top steps, Ginger will not jump. Prunella takes over and does the trick; she will work with the new clowns. On the night that Prunella is to work with the clowns and perform the trick in public for the first time, there is a problem. Prunella trips, and the little girl clown laughs. Ginger knows that is the laugh of her little girl, so she runs past Prunella, hurries up the stairs, and jumps into the little girl's arms. She has found success in the circus, and more importantly, she has found her little girl.

Thematic Material

This story has a circus setting and focuses on a character who is a part of the circus but who dreams of a more ordinary life.

Book Talk Material and Activities

In one kindergarten, the teachers organized a circus. The children acted as clowns and other circus performers. Some children even dressed up as circus animals and performed tricks, including a lion jumping through a hula hoop and a seal doing addition problems on a horn. These children read and discussed many circus books before their performance. They talked about the acts in a circus, including animals that perform.

Several books with similar themes could be compared and contrasted with *Ginger Jumps*. Lisa Campbell Ernst has also written and illustrated

When Bluebell Sang, about a cow who sings and leaves the farm to perform. How does Bluebell feel about her success? What advice might she give Ginger? Bill Peet has many books with a circus or performance theme, including *Pamela Camel, Ella,* and *The Whingdingdilly.* Compare the feelings of the characters in these books to the way Ginger feels. Children enjoy discussing books and making connections among stories.

Related Titles

Daisy, written and illustrated by Brian Wildsmith. Pantheon, 1984. Farmer Brown and his cow, Daisy, both enjoy watching television. When Daisy accidentally becomes famous, she leaves the farm. Her new life is exciting and glamorous, but eventually Daisy returns to the farm. (Condensed in *Primaryplots,* Bowker, 1989, pp. 280–282.)

Dial-a-Croc, by Mike Dumbleton. Illustrated by Ann James. Orchard, 1991. Vanessa catches a crocodile, and they go into business together, until the crocodile insists he be allowed to go home.

Ella, written and illustrated by Bill Peet. Houghton, 1964. Ella the elephant is the star of the circus. When something at the circus annoys Ella, she hides and is left behind when the circus leaves town. Ella finds her new life is not what she expected.

Pamela Camel, written and illustrated by Bill Peet. Houghton, 1984. Pamela Camel works for the circus. She is too clumsy to be in a circus act, so she is part of a menagerie of wild animals that people stare at and poke. She runs away from the circus, stops a train from crossing some broken railroad tracks, and returns to the circus as a star. (Condensed in *Primaryplots,* Bowker, 1989, pp. 146–148.)

When Bluebell Sang, written and illustrated by Lisa Campbell Ernst. Bradbury, 1989. Bluebell the cow can really sing. She becomes a concert star, but she misses her life on the farm.

The Whingdingdilly, written and illustrated by Bill Peet. Houghton, 1970. Scamp is not happy being a dog. When a witch changes him into a "whingdingdilly," Scamp becomes a featured attraction at an animal museum. Scamp wishes he had been satisfied just being himself.

About the Author and Illustrator

ERNST, LISA CAMPBELL

Something about the Author, ed. by Anne Commire. Gale, 1986, Vol. 44, p. 80; 1989, Vol. 55, pp. 25–26.

Talking with Artists, ed. by Pat Cummings. Bradbury, 1992, pp. 42–47.

Field, Rachel. *General Store*
Illus. by Nancy Winslow Parker. Greenwillow, 1988, LB (0-688-07354-9)
Suggested Use Level: PreS–Gr. 1

Plot Summary

Rachel Field's poem is presented as a picture book. The poem lists the items that would be found in a general store, including fabric, candy, kitchen utensils, seeds, and food. The poem closes with an image of a child "playing" store.

Thematic Material

This book presents some images of an old-fashioned store. In many libraries and classrooms, a store is a play area.

Book Talk Material and Activities

Many children enjoy "playing" store. Like the child in the poem *General Store,* they organize the items they will sell, and they keep money in a toy cash register. Reading this poem would extend the fun of this play area. Giles Laroche also has illustrated a picture book of this poem. His cut-paper pictures are very different from Nancy Winslow Parker's drawings. They are much more detailed and seem to be set in a more modern time. Comparing these two versions gives children ideas for their own art activities.

Visiting a local store or market would be a natural extension for this book. Gail Gibbons's *Department Store* would give some background information about the many people who work at a store. *We Keep a Store* describes the activities at a small country store. Stories like *The Purse* look at characters who visit a store.

Related Titles

Department Store, written and illustrated by Gail Gibbons. Crowell, 1984. The text and illustrations feature different people and activities in a department store. Customers, salespeople, stockroom workers, and display artists are some of the people included.

Everything from a Nail to a Coffin, written and illustrated by Iris Van Rynbach. Orchard, 1991. In 1874, two brothers began to build the Goodrich General Store. This book describes how the store has served the small Connecticut town throughout the years.

General Store, by Rachel Field. Illustrated by Giles Laroche. Little, Brown, 1988. The detailed cut-paper illustrations for this book show a very cluttered store.

My First Look at Shopping, photographed by Steve Gorton. Random, 1991. Different kinds of stores and what they sell are highlighted in this book, including the bakery and the toy store.

The Purse, written and illustrated by Kathy Caple. Houghton, 1986. Katie buys a new purse, but then she has no money to put in it.

We Keep a Store, by Anne Shelby. Illustrated by John Ward. Orchard, 1990. A young African-American girl describes the activities in her family's rural store. Besides buying food and supplies at the store, neighbors spend time there talking and telling stories.

About the Author

FIELD, RACHEL

Something about the Author, ed. by Anne Commire. Gale, 1979, Vol. 15, pp. 106–113.

About the Illustrator

PARKER, NANCY WINSLOW

Fifth Book of Junior Authors and Illustrators, ed. by Sally Holmes Holtze. Wilson, 1983, pp. 233–235.

Illustrators of Children's Books: 1967–1976, Volume IV, comp. by Lee Kingman, Grace Allen Hogarth, and Harriet Quimby. Horn Book, 1978, pp. 149, 203–204.

Something about the Author, ed. by Anne Commire. Gale, 1976, Vol. 10, pp. 113–114; ed. by Donna Olendorf, Gale, 1992, Vol. 69, pp. 152–154.

Fleming, Denise. *Count!*
Illus. by the author. Holt, 1992 (0-8050-1595-7)
Suggested Use Level: PreS–Gr. 1

Plot Summary
Animals are the focus of this colorful counting book. Numbers from one to ten feature a gnu, zebras, crocodiles, kangaroos, giraffes, cranes, worms, toucans, fish, and lizards. Counting continues by tens from ten to fifty, featuring lizards, butterflies, snails, frogs, and bees. For each number, the numeral is printed, the word is spelled out, the illustrations depict the number of items being featured, and there are also that number of colored blocks. Action words often accompany the animals, like "Stretch, giraffes!" and "Line up, lizards."

Thematic Material
This book encourages active participation in counting; children could demonstrate some of the numbers, such as "Bounce, kangaroos!"

Book Talk Material and Activities
Just when you think there couldn't be another counting book, a book like *Count!* appears. This book could be shared in a primary classroom as part of a unit on counting and numbers. Children loved acting out some of the numbers. They jumped, wiggled, and fluttered. They got into groups based on the numbers and then moved like the animals. For example, ten children lined up like lizards. After the children heard *Count!* and responded to it, they shared several other counting and number books, including *Willy Can Count* and *Fish Eyes*, both of which encourage participation. In *Willy Can Count*, there are opportunities to predict what Willy will count. In *Fish Eyes*, children enjoyed the die-cut holes.

The Related Titles section below lists a selection of recent counting and number books. These books could be booktalked for preschool and primary grade teachers to help them update their lessons and activities. These books feature different approaches to counting and numbers, including having the counting activities as part of a story, as in *Mouse Count*, and having the counting activity focus on a theme, like the dinosaurs in *Count-a-saurus*. *Each Orange Has 8 Slices* has a question-and-answer approach that could require counting as well as some simple arithmetic activities. Teachers always appreciate seeing new books, especially when they correlate with their classroom activities.

Related Titles

Count-a-saurus, by Nancy Blumenthal. Illustrated by Robert Jay Kaufman. Four Winds, 1989. This book introduces numbers from one to ten by featuring different dinosaurs. The rhyming text adds to the humor of the presentation, as does the "Append-a-Saurus," which gives brief facts about the dinosaurs.

Each Orange Has 8 Slices: A Counting Book, by Paul Giganti, Jr. Illustrated by Donald Crews. Greenwillow, 1992. This book encourages counting as well as other math skills, such as addition and multiplication. Younger children could count the items in the illustrations to answer questions about how many seeds the eight oranges have, while older children could multiply eight oranges times two seeds each to find the answer.

Fish Eyes: A Book You Can Count On, written and illustrated by Lois Ehlert. Harcourt, 1990. A rhyming text introduces the sequence of numbers from one to ten in this book. Die-cut holes show the eyes of the fish. There is some simple addition in this book, as a small fish appears on each page and is added on to the number on that page.

From One to One Hundred, written and illustrated by Teri Sloat. Dutton, 1991. This interesting counting book encourages children to apply their understanding of numbers. There are items on each page that correlate to the number. For example, on the page for "1," children are to find one castle, one marshmallow, one dragon, and so on. The numbers go in order from one to ten and then are presented by tens from ten to one hundred. Children will need a lot of time to find and count the one hundred children.

Mouse Count, written and illustrated by Ellen Stoll Walsh. Harcourt, 1991. A snake catches ten mice and puts them into a jar. The mice must use their wits to escape. This is a story that incorporates counting into the plot.

My First Look at Numbers. Random, 1990. Color photographs on a white background make this a fine introductory counting book. The words and photographs are large enough to share with a group.

Nine Ducks Nine, written and illustrated by Sarah Hayes. Lothrop, 1990. In this story, the ducks seem to be ignoring the danger from the fox, but in the end they outwit him. The reader counts backwards from nine to one. There is a lot of humor in the remarks the ducks make.

Numbers at Play: A Counting Book, by Charles Sullivan. Illustrated. Rizzoli, 1992. This book introduces counting and art; the counting rhymes refer to well-known paintings and other works of art. For example, Jasper Johns's "Numbers in Color" is featured for the number seven. There are two rhymes and illustrations for each number from one to ten. Brief background information about the illustration and the artist is also included.

One Bear with Bees in his Hair, written and illustrated by Jakki Wood. Dutton, 1991. Count the bears as they add on one by one to this rhyming story.

One Good Horse: A Cowpuncher's Counting Book, by Ann Herbert Scott. Illustrated by Lynn Sweat. Greenwillow, 1990. Items that would be familiar in a Western setting are counted, such as sagebrush and mountain quail. Numbers from one to ten are included, then fifty and one hundred. This could be a springboard for making theme counting books.

One Magic Box, by Roger Chouinard and Mariko Chouinard. Illustrated by Roger Chouinard. Doubleday, 1989. When a mysterious box appears, numbered items from one to fourteen try to open it. The wizard finds the box, with fifteen stars on it. He opens it, and all the other items are drawn into the box.

What Comes in 2's, 3's, and 4's? by Suzanne Aker. Illustrated by Bernie Karlin. Simon & Schuster, 1990. Simple, familiar items are used to illustrate number groups, such as two wings on a bird, three meals a day, and four seasons.

Willy Can Count, written and illustrated by Anne Rockwell. Arcade, 1989. Willy goes for a walk with his mother, who encourages him to count. Willy does not count the obvious items, but there are clues about what Willy will count.

Gibbons, Gail. *Dinosaurs, Dragonflies & Diamonds: All About Natural History Museums*
Illus. by the author. Four Winds, 1988 (0-02-737240-5)
Suggested Use Level: Gr. 1–3

Plot Summary

Natural history museums collect and exhibit many items about people and the natural world. Specific exhibits are presented, such as a habitat exhibit of animals and a display of gems. A permanent exhibit is described; in this case, it is the dinosaur skeletons. A special exhibit on gold is featured as an example of a temporary exhibit. Some of the behind-the-scenes activities are described, like preparing the exhibit and maintaining the collection. Museum jobs—for example tour guide and lecturer—are also discussed. A detailed explanation of how a new rattlesnake exhibit is made is included.

Thematic Material

Visiting a museum is a common school and family experience. *Dinosaurs, Dragonflies & Diamonds* could be included in social studies units on community resources.

Book Talk Material and Activities

Before taking a trip to the Cleveland Museum of Natural History, a class of second graders prepared by reading about museums. The classroom teacher asked the children to work in small groups and to suggest some questions about their trip. Their questions included "How long will it take to get there?" "What will we see?" and "Who works at the museum?" *Dinosaurs, Dragonflies & Diamonds* was a focus book for this class. It provided them with background information and suggested some specific details they could watch for on their trip. One group decided to take notes about how many different exhibits they saw. Another group wanted to find the dinosaur exhibit. Several children were interested in information about rocks and minerals, particularly gemstones. As the children planned for this trip, they talked about other museums they had visited. Most had been on school trips to the Cleveland Museum of Art, whereas others had visited the museums of the Smithsonian on family vacations.

After the trip, the children prepared oral reports, which were shared with another class before its trip to the museum. Again, the children worked in small groups, which provided many opportunities for cooperative learning. In the classroom, other books about museums and collecting were available, including *Bones, Bones, Dinosaur Bones* (see chapter 5), *Visiting the Art Museum*, and *My Visit to the Dinosaurs*. Several children brought in their collections from home, including some hats and a doll collection. They talked about their collections, telling how long they had been collecting and how they got started.

Opportunities to work together and to develop oral skills are an important aspect of the whole-language philosophy. In their small groups, these children talked about their trip and made decisions about the topic for their oral reports. They argued about what was "the most interesting thing" and about who should go first. They wrote down what they wanted to say; they practiced their presentation; they used the library for additional information. While the finished oral reports were very brief, many language and cooperation skills were involved in preparing them.

Related Titles

Lost in the Museum, by Miriam Cohen. Illustrated by Lillian Hoban. Greenwillow, 1979. On a class trip to the museum, Jim and some of his friends become separated from their group. Jim helps bring everyone back together.

My Visit to the Dinosaurs, revised edition, written and illustrated by Aliki. Harper, 1985. Going to the natural history museum provides information about archaeology and paleontology as well as facts about several dinosaurs.

Picture This: A First Introduction to Paintings, by Felicity Woolf. Illustrated with reproductions. Doubleday, 1989. From illuminated manuscripts to surrealistic and abstract paintings, this book provides information about different types of art and ways to look at and learn about it.

Prehistoric Pinkerton, written and illustrated by Steven Kellogg. Dial, 1987. The little girl who owns Pinkerton is studying dinosaurs in school. She takes the big dog on a class trip to the museum. (Condensed in *Primaryplots,* Bowker, 1989, pp. 137–140.)

A Visit to the Natural History Museum, by Sandra Ziegler. Illustrated with photographs. Childrens Pr., 1989. In this nonfiction book, a class trip to the Field Museum of Natural History in Chicago is presented. It would be interesting to compare this book to *Dinosaurs, Dragonflies & Diamonds*.

Visiting the Art Museum, written and illustrated by Laurene Krasny Brown and Marc Brown. Dutton, 1986. A family's visit to the museum is told through conversation balloons. The pictures and objects they see are described more completely in the "More About the Art" section at the end of the book.

About the Author and Illustrator

GIBBONS, GAIL

Sixth Book of Junior Authors and Illustrators, ed. by Sally Holmes Holtze. Gale, 1989, pp. 96–97.
Something about the Author, ed. by Anne Commire. Gale, 1981, Vol. 23, pp. 77–78.

Hale, Sarah Josepha. *Mary Had a Little Lamb*
Photographs by Bruce McMillan. Scholastic, 1990 (0-590-43773-9)
Suggested Use Level: PreS–Gr. 1

Plot Summary
This version of "Mary Had a Little Lamb" is illustrated with color photographs. In the photographs, Mary is a contemporary African-American child attending a small school in Maine. Her teacher is a white man and her classmates are from a variety of ethnic backgrounds. Four verses of the rhyme are featured in the book; the complete rhyme is included along with the Afterword. An excerpt from a lesson on this nursery rhyme from the 1857 *McGuffey's Old Second Reader* is also included, along with a description of the preparation of this book.

Thematic Material
Children learn nursery rhymes and songs at home, at preschool, and with friends. The multicultural images in this book expand the audience that can identify with this well-known rhyme.

Book Talk Material and Activities
Music and nursery rhymes are included in many programs for young children. Including rhymes from different cultures allows broader participation. In Bruce McMillan's photographs for *Mary Had a Little Lamb,* a traditional poem has been given a contemporary setting. Including images of children from different cultural backgrounds allows more children to see themselves in books. When they identify with characters and experiences,

children develop an affinity for books; they see a personal purpose for reading. The illustrations in *Read-Aloud Rhymes for the Very Young* depict children from different backgrounds, as do the illustrations in *Sing a Song of Popcorn* and *Talking Like the Rain*. The poems of Eloise Greenfield *(Honey, I Love* and *Under the Sunday Tree)* and Lucille Clifton *(Some of the Days of Everett Anderson)* provide images of African-American children; many of Byrd Baylor's books *(Hawk, I Am Your Brother* and *I'm in Charge of Celebrations)* focus on Native American experiences.

This version of "Mary Had a Little Lamb" could be compared with the version by Tomie dePaola. DePaola's illustrations use an old-fashioned setting to interpret this nineteenth-century rhyme. A display of other picture books of simple rhymes, such as *Little Bo Peep* and *Three Little Kittens,* could be prepared.

Related Titles

Hawk, I Am Your Brother, by Byrd Baylor. Illustrated by Peter Parnall. Scribner, 1976. Rudy Soto, a young Native American boy, dreams of flying. By helping an injured hawk and then setting it free, Rudy is able to feel the joy of flight as the hawk soars through the sky. Parnall's illustrations received a Caldecott Honor award in 1977.

Honey, I Love and Other Love Poems by Eloise Greenfield. Illustrated by Leo Dillon and Diane Dillon. Crowell, 1972. Jumping rope, dressing up, and other familiar experiences celebrate the life of a young girl.

I'm in Charge of Celebrations, by Byrd Baylor. Illustrated by Peter Parnall. Scribner, 1986. The girl in this book creates her own special celebrations honoring the beauty of her desert world. Included are "Rainbow Celebrations Day" and "Coyote Day."

Little Bo Peep, illustrated by Paul Galdone. Clarion, 1986. This version of the nursery rhyme includes the familiar verse and some that are not as well known.

Mary Had a Little Lamb, by Sarah Josepha Hale. Illustrated by Tomie dePaola. Holiday, 1984. Besides the well-known opening verse, there are additional verses about how the teacher sends the lamb away, how and why the lamb is devoted to Mary, and how all children should be kind to animals. (Condensed in *Primaryplots,* Bowker, 1989, pp. 93–95.)

Read-Aloud Rhymes for the Very Young, selected by Jack Prelutsky. Illustrated by Marc Brown. Knopf, 1986. The poems in this collection are arranged in subject groupings, including animals, feelings, and everyday experiences.

Sing a Song of Popcorn: Every Child's Book of Poems, selected by Beatrice Schenk de Regniers, Eva Moore, Mary Michaels White, and Jan Carr. Illustrated by nine Caldecott Medal artists. Scholastic, 1988. Eighteen poems are included in the "Mostly People" section, including poems by Nikki Giovanni and Eve Merriam. Compare the everyday experiences of these people to Mary and her classmates.

Some of the Days of Everett Anderson, by Lucille Clifton. Illustrated by Evaline Ness. Holt, 1970. Poems follow Everett Anderson through a very busy week of walking in the rain, visiting the candy shop, talking with his mother, missing his father, and watching the stars.

Talking Like the Rain: A Read-to-Me Book of Poems, selected by X. J. Kennedy and Dorothy M. Kennedy. Illustrated by Jane Dyer. Little, Brown, 1992. "Play," "Families," "Just For Fun," and poems about other everyday experiences are included in this book.

Three Little Kittens, illustrated by Paul Galdone. Clarion, 1986. Children who hear this rhyme enjoy joining in on the meows and purrs.

Under the Sunday Tree: Poems, by Eloise Greenfield. Illustrated by Amos Ferguson. Harper, 1988. Life in the Bahamas is captured in these poems and paintings.

About the Author and Illustrator

McMillan, Bruce

Sixth Book of Junior Authors and Illustrators, ed. by Sally Holmes Holtze. Wilson, 1989, pp. 194–196.

Something about the Author, ed. by Anne Commire. Gale, 1981, Vol. 22, pp. 183–184; ed. by Donna Olendorf and Diane Telgen, Gale, 1993, Vol. 70, pp. 156–160.

Hoban, Tana. *Exactly the Opposite*
Photographs by the author. Greenwillow, 1990, LB (0-688-08862-7)
Suggested Use Level: PreS–Gr. 1

Plot Summary

Twenty-eight color photographs illustrate a variety of opposites. There is a picture of two hands, one open with the palm up and one closed into a fist. Another pair of pictures shows two views of a sunflower, front and back. There is a picture of a fire paired with a picture of a glass containing ice. The wordless presentation allows different possibilities to be suggested.

Thematic Material

Exactly the Opposite is a wordless collection of color photographs that depict the concept of opposites.

Book Talk Material and Activities

Wordless books allow children to present their own interpretations of what they see. They can express their own possibilities. In small groups, children can look at many wordless books and discuss what they see. Working with their peers, children learn new words and see another's point of view. *Exactly the Opposite* is an open-ended presentation that promotes discussion. For many of the pictures, children could suggest different opposites. For example, in one pair of pictures, there is a picture of a large bear and then a picture of three small bears. Of course, this could illustrate large and small or big and little, but it could also illustrate near and far, as the large bear is photographed in a close-up. This picture could also illustrate one and many. Discussing possibilities encourages children to be creative with language. Tana Hoban's *Is It Larger? Is It Smaller?* and *Push, Pull, Empty, Full* also present images of opposites. After using these books, many children enjoy looking for photographs to create collages of opposites.

Bruce McMillan also has several photographic concept books, including *Becca Backward, Becca Frontward* and *Dry or Wet?* These could also be book-talked for children to select and sign out.

Related Titles

Becca Backward, Becca Frontward: A Book of Concept Pairs, written and photographed by Bruce McMillan. Lothrop, 1986. Color photographs depict a girl in everyday situations that illustrate word pairs such as *above/below, full/empty,* and *far/near.*

Delivery Van: Words for Town and Country, written and illustrated by Betsy Maestro and Giulio Maestro. Clarion, 1990. Following a delivery van on its route, readers are introduced to many terms about the town and the country. Children could decide which terms are opposites and suggest some other words that apply to the town and to the country.

Dry or Wet?, written and photographed by Bruce McMillan. Lothrop, 1988. Color photographs show situations that depict the concepts of dry and wet, including a girl on a diving board (dry) and the splash made when she jumps into the pool (wet).

Fast-Slow, High-Low: A Book of Opposites, written and illustrated by Peter Spier. Doubleday, 1972. Detailed pictures encourage discussions about the opposites being presented, including over/under and young/old.

Is It Larger? Is It Smaller?, written and photographed by Tana Hoban. Greenwillow, 1985. Items in color photographs illustrate the concepts of large and small in this wordless book. For example, one picture shows a sow and some piglets, another a toy car and a real car.

Push, Pull, Empty, Full: A Book of Opposites, written and photographed by Tana Hoban. Macmillan 1972. Black-and-white photographs illustrate fifteen pairs of opposites. For examples, elephants are shown for the word *thick,* and flamingos are depicted for *thin.* The illustrated word is printed on the photograph.

Traffic: A Book of Opposites, written and illustrated by Betsy Maestro and Giulio Maestro. Crown, 1981. Following a car on a journey, children are introduced to some opposite pairs, such as slow/fast and far/near.

About the Author and Illustrator

HOBAN, TANA

Fourth Book of Junior Authors and Illustrators, ed. by Doris de Montreville and Elizabeth D. Crawford. Wilson, 1978, pp. 178–179.

Illustrators of Children's Books: 1967–1976, Volume IV, comp. by Lee Kingman, Grace Allen Hogarth, and Harriet Quimby. Horn Book, 1978, p. 176.

Something about the Author, ed. by Anne Commire. Gale, 1981, Vol. 22, pp. 158–159; ed. by Donna Olendorf and Diane Telgen, Gale, 1993, Vol. 70, pp. 87–91.

Hoban, Tana.   *Shadows and Reflections*
Photographs by the author. Greenwillow, 1990, LB (0-688-07090-6)
Suggested Use Level: PreS–Gr. 1

Plot Summary

In this wordless book, clear color photographs, most set in urban areas, illustrate the concepts of shadows and reflections. Windows, water, and the hoods of cars reflect, whereas shadows are formed on sidewalks and sand.

Thematic Material

This book correlates with science studies of shadows and reflections. It also provides opportunities for language experiences and observation.

Book Talk Material and Activities

Tana Hoban's photoessays encourage children to study the world around them. Her photographs illustrate basic concepts and relate them to everyday experiences. Books such as *Shadows and Reflections, All about Where,* and *Dots, Spots, Speckles, and Stripes* provide children with opportunities to talk about the photographs and then to look around them for more examples of the concepts. Her books could be the focus of a cooperative experience between older and younger elementary children. Pairs of children could meet, each with a Tana Hoban book, and talk about what they see. The older child might even write down some of the observations. Later, the pair could take a walk around the school or neighborhood looking for more examples of the concepts and, again, writing some down. When they return to the group, each pair could talk about what they observed.

In elementary science programs, *Shadows and Reflections* could correlate with studies of the earth's rotation, day and night, and the sun. Nonfiction books could be presented to provide additional information, including *Me and My Shadow* and *Sun Up, Sun Down.*

Related Titles

All about Where, written and photographed by Tana Hoban. Greenwillow, 1991. Twenty-six color photographs illustrate words that show locations, including above, behind, over, and around (see chapter 6).

Bear Shadow, written and illustrated by Frank Asch. Prentice Hall, 1985. Bear is trying to fish, but his shadow keeps getting in the way, so Bear tries to lose his shadow.

Dots, Spots, Speckles, and Stripes, written and photographed by Tana Hoban. Greenwillow, 1987. In this wordless book, color photographs of a peacock, a child with freckles, a zebra, confetti, and other familiar objects illustrate the concepts in the title.

Me and My Shadow, written and illustrated by Arthur Dorros. Scholastic, 1990. This nonfiction book provides clear information about how light produces shadows.

My Shadow, by Sheila Gore. Photographs by Fiona Pragoff. Doubleday,

1990. The activities suggested in this nonfiction book could provide children with direct experiences in making and studying shadows.

Shadows Are About, by Ann Whitford Paul. Illustrated by Mark Graham. Scholastic, 1992. In a rhyming text, the author describes the day, following the shadows that are formed.

Sun Up, Sun Down, written and illustrated by Gail Gibbons. Harcourt, 1983. In this introductory nonfiction book about the sun, there is information about light, seasons, weather, and shadows.

About the Author and Illustrator

HOBAN, TANA

Fourth Book of Junior Authors and Illustrators, ed. by Doris de Montreville and Elizabeth D. Crawford. Wilson, 1978, pp. 178–179.

Illustrators of Children's Books: 1967–1976, Volume IV, comp. by Lee Kingman, Grace Allen Hogarth, and Harriet Quimby. Horn Book, 1978, p. 176.

Something about the Author, ed. by Anne Commire. Gale, 1981, Vol. 22, pp. 158–159; ed. by Donna Olendorf and Diane Telgen, Gale, 1993, Vol. 70, pp. 87–91.

Jonas, Ann. *Color Dance*

Illus. by the author. Greenwillow, 1989, LB (0-688-05991-0)

Suggested Use Level: PreS–Gr. 1

Plot Summary

Three young girls wearing leotards are holding colorful scarves that match their leotards—red, yellow, and blue. As the girls dance, their scarves overlap, creating colors. Red and yellow make orange. Yellow and blue make green. Red and blue make purple. Shades of colors are created by adding layers of the basic colors. Chartreuse, green, and aquamarine are made by yellow and blue. Magenta, purple, and violet are made by red and blue. Marigold, orange, and vermillion are made by red and yellow. Mixing many colors, the girls dance and make browns and grays. A young boy dances in, bringing scarves that are white, gray, and black. As the dance ends, the scarves are placed on the floor to form a color wheel. The color wheel is described on the page after the text.

Thematic Material

This book introduces colors as well as the concept of mixing colors.

Book Talk Material and Activities

As young children learn the names of colors, they could also learn some simple scientific concepts associated with colors. *Color Dance* shows how colors can be layered and mixed to create other colors. Layers of one color can also create shades of that color. This introductory information could be extended by some demonstrations, such as those found in *The Science Book of Color*. One simple activity involves weaving colored plastic sheets (from the covers of plastic folders). Where the colors overlap, different colors are created. For another project, circles of different colors are drawn on blotting paper with felt markers. When water soaks into the paper, the colors separate. There are other simple activities in this book that demonstrate other properties of color.

Sharing stories about color also extends children's understanding of this concept. *Little Blue and Little Yellow* is a classic story in which two small circles hug each other and create a new green circle. The different items depicted for the colors in *If You Take a Paintbrush* emphasize the shades of a color; for example, there is a yellow sun shining on the sandy desert with a golden camel. Tana Hoban's photographic concept books encourage children to look for colors, first in the photographs in the books and then in their own world. Children could make a collage of colors, grouping shades of colors together.

Related Titles

Freight Train, written and illustrated by Donald Crews. Greenwillow, 1978. In this Caldecott Honor book, the cars of the train are different colors: red, orange, yellow, green, blue, purple, and black. As the train begins to move, the colors flow and appear to merge.

If You Take a Paintbrush: A Book of Colors, written and illustrated by Fulvio Testa. Dial, 1983. Each page features one color. The text is simple, highlighting one item, but the illustrations show other items in that color.

Is It Red? Is It Yellow? Is It Blue? An Adventure in Color, written and photographed by Tana Hoban. Greenwillow, 1978. Circles of color at the bottom of each photograph highlight the color featured in the photograph. Children can look and find other colors, too.

Little Blue and Little Yellow: A Story for Pippo and Ann and Other Children, written and illustrated by Leo Lionni. Astor, 1959. A little blue circle has many friends, but his best friend is a little yellow circle. When they hug, they make a green circle.

Of Colors and Things, written and photographed by Tana Hoban. Greenwillow, 1989. Color photographs of everyday objects encourage children to look for specific colors in the pictures and in the world around them. On each page, there are four photographs for the color being featured. That color dominates three of the pictures, but it is not that prominent in the fourth picture, so children must look more closely at that picture.

The Science Book of Color, by Neil Ardley. Photographed by Pete Gardner. Harcourt, 1991. Making invisible ink, creating colorful patterns, and using vegetables for dyes are some of the activities in this book that would extend children's understanding of color.

About the Author and Illustrator

JONAS, ANN

Something about the Author, ed. by Anne Commire. Gale, 1986, Vol. 42, p. 122; 1988, Vol. 50, pp. 106–109.

Kuklin, Susan.   *When I See My Doctor . . .*
Photographs by the author. Bradbury, 1988 (0-02-751232-0)
Suggested Use Level: PreS–Gr. 1

Plot Summary
Thomas, who is four years old, is visiting Dr. Mitchell, his pediatrician, for a routine checkup. His visit is clearly documented through color photographs and a simple text. Dr. Mitchell describes the procedures to Thomas and lets him see the instruments that will be used. Photographs of the instruments are included, including a stethoscope, otoscope, tongue depressors, reflex hammer, lancet and hemoglobinometer, and sphygmomanometer. Pronunciation guides are given, as needed. Dr. Mitchell checks Thomas's heart and allows him to listen too. He listens to Thomas breathe and checks his ears, eyes, and throat. He checks over Thomas's bones and joints. A nurse runs a blood test, takes Thomas's blood pressure, and gives him a polio vaccination. Thomas is happy and healthy as he leaves his doctor's office.

Thematic Material
Many young children are apprehensive about visiting their doctors. *When I See My Doctor . . .* is a factual account of one child's checkup. It

provides information and offers children a chance to talk about their own experiences.

Book Talk Material and Activities

In writing this book, the author/photographer visited a nursery school in New York City. One of the children from that school, Thomas Gilliland, is the child depicted in the book. The author also interviewed the pediatrician, Dr. Michael Mitchell. As a result, this book provides a very straightforward account of a checkup. Many young children will recognize the situations described in this book. They will be interested in the descriptions and photographs of the instruments the doctor uses. Teachers and librarians will want to read *When I See My Doctor . . .* and the companion book *When I See My Dentist . . .* to young children. Children can discuss their own experiences and, perhaps, add details to those in the books. Fred Rogers's *Going to the Hospital* and *Going to the Dentist* could also be shared as part of a program focusing on good health habits.

The two *When I See My . . .* books could serve as springboards for writing projects for children. Children could suggest other subjects for study, such as the teacher or their parents, and look at the workplace and materials that are used. They could describe the materials used at home—for example, in cooking or cleaning, or even for homework.

Related Titles

Body Sense, Body Nonsense, by Seymour Simon. Illustrated by Dennis Kendrick. Lippincott, 1981. Does "an apple a day keep the doctor away"? Can "drafts cause colds"? In this book some common sayings about the body, both true and false, are examined.

Dinosaurs Alive and Well!, written and illustrated by Laurene Krasny Brown and Marc Brown. Little, Brown, 1990. A community of dinosaurs presents information about health and nutrition.

A Doctor's Tools, by Kenny DeSantis. Photographs by Patricia A. Agre. Dodd, 1985. Before visiting the doctor, many children will want to see and discuss some of the instruments and procedures that may occur.

Germs Make Me Sick!, by Melvin Berger. Illustrated by Marilyn Hafner. Crowell, 1985. Simple information about illness is provided, along with suggestions for maintaining good health.

Going to the Dentist, by Fred Rogers. Photographs by Jim Judkis. Putnam, 1989. Some of the typical events that occur during a regular visit to the dentist are described.

Going to the Hospital, by Fred Rogers. Photographs by Jim Judkis. Putnam, 1988. Mr. Rogers presents some reassuring information about what happens during a stay in the hospital.

My Doctor, written and illustrated by Harlow Rockwell. Macmillan, 1973. With colorful illustrations and a brief text, this book describes a visit to the doctor for a checkup.

Taking My Cat to the Vet, written and illustrated by Susan Kuklin. Bradbury, 1988. This is part of a group of books for preschoolers that use color photographs and a simple text to present information for young children. Also in the series is Kuklin's *Taking My Dog to the Vet* (Bradbury, 1988.) Both books focus on the experiences of preschool children and their pets.

When I See My Dentist . . . , written and photographed by Susan Kuklin. Bradbury, 1988. In this companion book to *When I See My Doctor . . . ,* color photographs and a simple text document one young girl's trip to the dentist. Each step of the cleaning and examination is explained, and photographs depict the instruments.

Why I Cough, Sneeze, Shiver, Hiccup, & Yawn, by Melvin Berger. Illustrated by Holly Keller. Harper, 1983. This Let's-Read-and-Find-Out Science book explains some of the reflex actions of the body.

About the Author and Illustrator

KUKLIN, SUSAN

Something about the Author, ed. by Anne Commire. Gale, 1991, Vol. 63, pp. 80–85.

Leedy, Loreen. *Messages in the Mailbox: How to Write a Letter*
Illus. by the author. Holiday, 1991 (0-8234-0889-2)
Suggested Use Level: Gr. 2–4

Plot Summary

Some children and animals ask their teacher, Mrs. Gator, about receiving mail, and she teaches them about writing letters. "Friendly Letters," "Invitations," "Thank-You Notes," "Get-Well Letters," "Love Letters," "Sympathy Letters," "Congratulations," "Form Letters," "Fan Letters," "Business Letters," "Requests," "Complaints," "Protests," and "Letters to the Editor" are featured. Addressing the envelope and mailing the letter are also discussed. Suggestions for creative content and format are given. The information is presented in the text and also in the speech balloons of the characters. The illustrations are arranged in cartoon-style panels. A list of the state and territorial abbreviations follows the text.

Thematic Material

Writing letters and receiving mail is one way children can apply their writing and reading skills. *Messages in the Mailbox* could also be featured in a study of the post office and other community services.

Book Talk Material and Activities

The whole-language philosophy encourages teachers and children to find ways to use language. Making lists, writing directions, taking surveys and charting the results, interviewing family and friends, presenting information orally, and keeping a journal are some possible activities. So is writing letters. *Messages in the Mailbox* is a good book to keep in the writing center. In addition to describing different types of letters, there are suggestions about who to write or what to write about. Specific features of letters are described, such as the heading, salutation, body, closing, signature, and postscript of a friendly letter.

A book talk and display of stories in which characters write letters could spark additional interest in this activity. In "The Letter," Frog writes a letter to his friend Toad. One group of students wrote Toad some letters too. They told him they liked the stories about him and felt they were his friends. Their librarian read their letters and answered each one as if she were Toad. Many children enjoy writing letters and cards to nursery rhyme and fairy tale characters after reading *The Jolly Postman* and *The Jolly Christmas Postman*. Children made a list of books in which characters wrote letters, such as *Old Henry*, *A Letter to Amy*, and *Dear Mr. Blueberry*, and they watched for other books to add to their list. They displayed the list in the writing center, encouraging their classmates to write letters.

After writing, sending, and receiving letters, a trip to the post office would be a natural follow-up. Gail Gibbons's *The Post Office Book* would provide some background information about this community service.

Related Titles

Dear Mr. Blueberry, written and illustrated by Simon James. Macmillan, 1991. Emily writes to Mr. Blueberry about the whale in her pond, and Mr.

Blueberry answers her, although he doubts the information she has given him. Emily and Mr. Blueberry continue their correspondence until Emily's whale returns to the ocean.

Frog and Toad Are Friends, written and illustrated by Arnold Lobel. Harper, 1970. Here are five stories about two good friends. In one, Toad feels sad because he does not get any mail, so his friend, Frog, writes him a letter.

The Jolly Christmas Postman, written and illustrated by Janet Ahlberg and Allan Ahlberg. Little, Brown, 1991. Characters from folktales and nursery rhymes send Christmas greetings and gifts, including a board game for Red Riding Hood and a jigsaw puzzle for Humpty Dumpty. There is also a pleated "peep" book for the postman.

The Jolly Postman: Or Other People's Letters, written and illustrated by Janet Ahlberg and Allan Ahlberg. Little, Brown, 1986. The postman delivers the mail from and to well-known nursery-rhyme and folktale characters, like Goldilocks and Cinderella. The format of this book is very creative, with some pages designed as envelopes that contain different letters and notes. (Condensed in *Primaryplots,* Bowker, 1989, pp. 244–246.)

A Letter to Amy, written and illustrated by Ezra Jack Keats. Harper, 1968. Peter writes an invitation for Amy to come to his birthday party. His mother has to remind him of what needs to be included. Children could use *Messages in the Mailbox* to learn how to write an invitation.

Old Henry, by Joan W. Blos. Illustrated by Stephen Gammell. Morrow, 1987. At the end of this book, Henry writes a letter to the mayor, asking if he can come back to his home. Children can discuss the way the mayor might respond to this letter. (Condensed in *Primaryplots,* Bowker, 1989, pp. 43–44

The Post Office Book, written and illustrated by Gail Gibbons. Crowell, 1982. The activities performed by postal employees that are described include sorting the mail, loading it onto trucks and planes, and delivering it.

Stringbean's Trip to the Shining Sea, by Vera B. Williams. Illustrated by Vera B. Williams and Jennifer Williams. Greenwillow, 1988. Most pages in this book are designed to look like postcards, which Stringbean and his brother, Fred, send home to their family in Kansas.

About the Author and Illustrator

Leedy, Loreen

Something about the Author, ed. by Anne Commire. Gale, 1988, Vol. 50, pp. 123–124; 1989, Vol. 54, p. 38.

McMillan, Bruce. *Eating Fractions.*
Photographs by the author. Scholastic, 1991 (0-590-43770-4)
Suggested Use Level: PreS–Gr. 3

Plot Summary

Color photographs show children sharing food. Beginning with one whole banana, two children share it when it is cut into halves. A sweet roll is broken into three pieces, a pizza is cut into four pieces, an ear of corn is divided into two pieces, some pear salad is split for three servings, and a small strawberry pie is cut into four pieces. Each fraction—whole, halves, thirds, and fourths—is depicted in the color photograph of the item and also in a small drawing next to the printed word for the fraction. Four recipes are included.

Thematic Material

The mathematical concept of some simple fractions—whole, halves, thirds, and fourths—is explained in this photoessay.

Book Talk Material and Activities

Many teachers are using children's literature to investigate math concepts. *Eating Fractions* is a great way to introduce the concept of fractions to children. The use of food in the photographs leads to some natural extension activities in the library or classroom. The two children in the photographs clearly enjoy their experiences with food and fractions. After looking at *Eating Fractions,* children could work in groups to divide and share some food. Graham crackers work especially well for breaking into halves and quarters. Pat Hutchins's *The Doorbell Rang* is a story that focuses on dividing cookies among an ever-increasing group of children.

Once children understand the concept of fractions, they would enjoy the activities in *Ed Emberley's Picture Pie.* In this book, the circle is the basic shape, and it is divided into fractions, including halves and fourths. These pieces are then used to create a picture. For example, a whole red circle is decorated with a line down the middle, two black dots, and some antenna to be a ladybug. Or half of a circle becomes the head and two whole circles become the cheeks of a walrus, with a fourth of a circle for the nose. In one class of third graders, the children "showed their work" as they made these projects. They cut two sets of the fractions they needed.

One set became the picture; one set was labeled to show the fractions that made the picture. This activity allowed students to play with the concept of fractions.

Related Titles

Angles Are as Easy as Pie, by Robert Froman. Illustrated by Byron Barton. Crowell, 1976. Cutting pies into pieces for hungry alligators is the premise for this simple explanation of geometry. The connection between food and math is similar to that in *Eating Fractions.*

The Doorbell Rang, written and illustrated by Pat Hutchins. Greenwillow, 1986. Ma makes a dozen cookies for Sam and Victoria to share, but then guests begin to come. The dilemma of more guests and fewer cookies continues until Grandma arrives with more cookies.

Ed Emberley's Picture Pie: A Circle Drawing Book, written and illustrated by Ed Emberley. Little, Brown, 1984. Beginning with a circle and then dividing it into fractions, children can make many pictures and designs, including birds, fish, and insects.

Gator Pie, written and illustrated by Louise Mathews. Dodd, 1979. The alligators have to keep cutting their pie so they can have enough pieces to go around.

What Comes in 2's, 3's, and 4's?, by Suzanne Aker. Illustrated by Bernie Karlin. Simon & Schuster, 1990. Simple familiar items are used to illustrate number groups, such as two wings on a bird, three meals a day, and four seasons.

About the Author and Illustrator

McMILLAN, BRUCE

Sixth Book of Junior Authors and Illustrators, ed. by Sally Holmes Holtze. Wilson, 1989, pp. 194–196.

Something about the Author, ed. by Anne Commire. Gale, 1981, Vol. 22, pp. 183–184; ed. by Donna Olendorf and Diane Telgen, Gale, 1993, Vol. 70, pp. 156–160.

McMillan, Bruce. *Fire Engine Shapes*
Photographs by the author. Lothrop, 1988, LB (0-688-07843-5)
Suggested Use Level: PreS–Gr. 1

Plot Summary
Seven shapes—a square, a rectangle, a diamond, a triangle, a hexagon, an oval, and a circle—are introduced on the front endpapers. Full-color close-up photographs of a fire engine follow, and readers may look for shapes within each picture.

Thematic Material
This wordless book introduces simple shapes, but it could also be used before a trip to a fire station or as part of a study of community helpers.

Book Talk Material and Activities
Like Tana Hoban, Bruce McMillan provides books with excellent photographs designed to introduce concepts and encourage observation. His books could be used to provide language experience activities for young children. Using *Fire Engine Shapes,* a librarian or teacher could encourage children to talk about the shapes they see on a trip, in the classroom, or at home. Given a list of simple shapes, children could work in small groups to find items that represent each shape. Tana Hoban's *Shapes, Shapes, Shapes* could be included in this activity, as could stories in which shapes are introduced, such as *The Shapes Game.* Children would enjoy using other photographic concept books from Bruce McMillan, such as *Growing Colors, Becca Backward, Becca Frontward,* and *Dry or Wet?*

Related Titles
Becca Backward, Becca Frontward: A Book of Concept Pairs, written and photographed by Bruce McMillan. Lothrop, 1986. Color photographs depict a girl in everyday situations that illustrate word pairs like *above/below, full/empty,* and *far/near.*

Circles, Triangles, and Squares, written and photographed by Tana Hoban. Macmillan, 1974. The black-and-white photographs in this book depict everyday scenes in the city. A circle, a triangle, and a square appear on the endpapers.

Dry or Wet?, written and photographed by Bruce McMillan. Lothrop, 1988. Color photographs show situations that depict the concepts of dry and wet, including a girl on a diving board (dry) and the splash made when she jumps into the pool (wet).

Fire Engines, written and illustrated by Anne Rockwell. Dutton, 1986. Dalmatians work at this fire department, which has a variety of vehicles to serve different needs—including a fire engine boat.

Fire! Fire!, written and illustrated by Gail Gibbons. Crowell, 1984. Fire-fighting equipment is described, as are the different responsibilities of firefighters, including searching for people in a burning building and operating an aerial ladder.

Growing Colors, written and photographed by Bruce McMillan. Lothrop, 1988. Color photographs of fruits and vegetables introduce children to colors in the world around them.

If You Look around You, written and illustrated by Fulvio Testa. Dial, 1983. Beginning with a point, this book describes increasingly complex shapes, including a triangle, a cylinder, and a sphere—which, from far out in space, looks like a point.

Listen to a Shape, written and photographed by Marcia Brown. Watts, 1979. Poetic verses and color photographs encourage children to look for shapes in the world around them.

My First Look at Shapes, photography by Stephen Oliver. Random, 1990. Color photographs of simple shapes are clearly labeled for young children to "point and say" the item and the shape.

The Shapes Game, by Paul Rogers. Illustrated by Sian Tucker. Holt, 1989. Circles, triangles, squares, stars, ovals, crescents, rectangles, spirals, and diamonds are described in the rhyming text. Bright, colorful pictures depict the items and the shapes.

Shapes, Shapes, Shapes, written and photographed by Tana Hoban. Greenwillow, 1986. Hoban introduces eleven shapes and then provides color photographs of everyday scenes in which the shapes can be observed. (Condensed in *Primaryplots*, Bowker, 1989, pp. 97–99.)

About the Author and Illustrator

McMILLAN, BRUCE

Sixth Book of Junior Authors and Illustrators, ed. by Sally Holmes Holtze. Wilson, 1989, pp. 194–196.

Something about the Author, ed. by Anne Commire. Gale, 1981, Vol. 22, pp. 183–184; ed. by Donna Olendorf and Diane Telgen, Gale, 1993, Vol. 70, pp. 156–160.

McMillan, Bruce. *Time to . . .*
Photographs by the author. Lothrop, 1989, LB (0-688-08856-2)
Suggested Use Level: Gr. K–2

Plot Summary

Color photographs follow a young boy through a typical day. On every verso page is a photograph of a standard analog clock at a particular hour; the same time is printed on a digital clock; and the time is also written in words. For example, on one page, the analog clock has the long hand on twelve and the short hand on seven; the digital clock reads "7:00 AM"; and the text reads "SEVEN O'CLOCK IN THE MORNING." The recto page reads "TIME TO . . . " followed by an activity, such as "WAKE UP." Activities such as eating, being at school, and playing are depicted. The boy's day is presented from 7:00 A.M. until 9:00 P.M., when he goes to bed. Some additional information about clocks and telling time follows the text, as does information about the photographs.

Thematic Material

Learning to tell time is emphasized throughout the primary grades. *Time to . . .* provides very clear information about one child's day.

Book Talk Material and Activities

Children's literature is being used throughout the school curriculum, including mathematics. *Time to . . .* shows everyday activities that would be familiar to many children. Those activities are correlated with the hour-by-hour passage of time on a standard analog clock and a digital clock. In *The Grouchy Ladybug,* an hour-by-hour account of the ladybug's day is given. *Around the Clock with Harriet* follows a similar pattern. Charting the different times and activities would reinforce the concept of time with young children. After filling in the chart, children could circle the areas where activities are very similar. Having children draw pictures of themselves doing activities throughout a day would further reinforce the concept. *My First Book of Time* has a foldout clock that can be adjusted to show different times.

Gail Gibbons provides facts about clocks in *Clocks and How They Go,* while Pat Hutchins gives a humorous look at the passing of time in *Clocks and More Clocks.* Both books would be good choices to read or booktalk

Chart 3

At 8:00 A.M.	
Time to . . .	Shows a boy eating breakfast.
The Grouchy Ladybug . . .	"Came across a praying mantis."
Around the Clock with Harriet	"When Harriet woke up the next day, her watch said 8 o'clock."
and I	Get ready for school.
At 4:00 P.M.	
Time to . . .	Shows a boy riding his bike.
The Grouchy Ladybug . . .	"Encountered an elephant."
Around the Clock with Harriet	"When her watch said 4 o'clock, Harriet was shopping."
and I	Have my after-school snack.

along with *Time to . . .*, as would Jesse Bear's playful look at his daily activities in *It's About Time, Jesse Bear*.

Related Titles

Around the Clock with Harriet: A Book about Telling Time, written and illustrated by Betsy Maestro and Giulio Maestro. Crown, 1984. Harriet the elephant has a very busy day. Her activities are described in this hour-by-hour account.

Bear Child's Book of Hours, written and illustrated by Anne Rockwell. Harper, 1987. Children can follow Bear Child through a day of activities.

Clocks and How They Go, written and illustrated by Gail Gibbons. Crowell, 1979. Details about the history of clocks is provided, along with information on different kinds of clocks.

Clocks and More Clocks, written and illustrated by Pat Hutchins. Macmillan, 1970. Mr. Higgins has many clocks, and he finds it difficult to set them to tell the same time.

The Grouchy Ladybug, written and illustrated by Eric Carle. Crowell, 1977. Throughout the day, the bad-tempered ladybug creates problems. A clock face shows the changing time.

It's About Time, Jesse Bear and Other Rhymes, by Nancy White Carlstrom. Illustrated by Bruce Degen. Macmillan, 1990. Jesse Bear gets up, gets dressed, eats breakfast, and enjoys his day in these lighthearted verses.

My First Book of Time, by Claire Llewellyn. Illustrated by Julie Carpenter.

Photographed by Paul Bricknell. Dorling Kindersley, 1992. Many aspects of time are presented, including days, weeks, and seasons. This oversized book has a foldout clock with hands that can be moved to show different times. There are activities in the book that encourage children to use this clock.

About the Author and Illustrator

McMILLAN, BRUCE

Sixth Book of Junior Authors and Illustrators, ed. by Sally Holmes Holtze. Wilson, 1989, pp. 194–196.

Something about the Author, ed. by Anne Commire. Gale, 1981, Vol. 22, pp. 183–184; ed. by Donna Olendorf and Diane Telgen, Gale, 1993, Vol. 70, pp. 156–160.

Rankin, Laura. *The Handmade Alphabet*
Illus. by the author. Dial, 1991, LB (0-8037-0975-7)
Suggested Use Level: Gr. 2–4

Plot Summary

The alphabet is presented as capital letters and by hands demonstrating the letter through the manual alphabet of American Sign Language. Each picture also shows an item that depicts the letter—asparagus, bubbles, a cup, and so on. The hands that shape the manual alphabet letters are multicultural and multigenerational. A baby's hand forms the letter *K* while holding some toy keys. A wrinkled hand, wrapped in a web, forms a *W*. Skin tones vary with shades of pink, beige, and brown. A list of the items depicted is included at the end of the book.

Thematic Material

This alphabet book focuses on the American Sign Language manual alphabet, providing information about other forms of communication and on resources used by hearing-impaired people.

Book Talk Material and Activities

Some alphabet books do more than introduce the letters to preschoolers. In *The Handmade Alphabet,* readers are introduced to another version of the familiar alphabet. The manual alphabet is part of American Sign

Language, which is used by many people with hearing impairments. There are many books that feature sign language, like the *Handtalk* books. After sharing information about the manual alphabet, children could be shown how to sign their own names and sign some simple words or phrases.

As children become more aware of the world around them, they realize there are many people with special needs. A book talk program on physical challenges would provide information and answer questions. Books like *Mom Can't See Me* and *Cindy, A Hearing Ear Dog* relate personal experiences with physical challenges. Many community agencies, such as the United Way, provide speakers who will work with children to explain physical challenges and special needs.

Related Titles

Cindy, a Hearing Ear Dog, by Patricia Curtis. Photographs by David Cupp. Dutton, 1981. Cindy is trained to be the "ears" of a deaf person. When she hears a noise, such as the telephone or the doorbell, she alerts her owner. Information about programs for training these dogs is included.

A Guide Dog Puppy Grows Up, by Caroline Arnold. Photographed by Richard Hewett. Harcourt, 1991. Color photographs show the training of a guide dog, including the pairing of a dog and a blind person.

Handmade ABC: A Manual Alphabet, written and illustrated by Linda Bourke. Addison-Wesley, 1981. Finger-spelling positions for the letters of the alphabet are drawn clearly enough for children to follow.

Hands On, Thumbs Up: Secret Handshakes, Fingerprints, Sign Language, and More Handy Ways to Have Fun with Your Hands, by Camilla Gryski. Illustrated by Pat Cupples. Addison-Wesley, 1990. The subtitle covers the variety of hand and finger activities in this book, including sign language and finger spelling.

Handtalk: An ABC of Finger Spelling and Sign Language, by Remy Charlip, Mary Beth, and George Ancona. Photographs. Four Winds, 1974. Bright, colorful photographs clearly depict the finger spelling for each letter of the alphabet. Other books in this series include *Handtalk Birthday* (Four Winds, 1987), *Handtalk Zoo* (Four Winds, 1989), and *Handtalk School* (Four Winds, 1991).

Mom Can't See Me, by Sally Hobart Alexander. Photographs by George Ancona. Macmillan, 1990. Black-and-white photographs depict the story of the author, who is blind, and her family. The author writes from the point of view of her nine-year-old daughter, describing some of the every-day events in their home, including going for walks, taking tap dancing lessons, riding bikes, baking cookies. Yet these activities are influenced by Mom's blindness and her needs; for example, she rides on a two-seater with Dad, and her spices are marked with Braille labels.

Raschka, Chris. *Charlie Parker played be bop*
Illus. by the author. Orchard, 1992, LB (0-531-08599-6)
Suggested Use Level: Gr. 1–3

Plot Summary

In a rhyming text, the music of jazz great Charlie Parker is described. Repetition and nonsense words (such as "Be bop," "Fisk, fisk," "Boomba, boomba," and Zznnzznn") create a beat that slides, snaps, and pops.

Thematic Material

The staccato rhythm of this text encourages participation through clapping, snapping fingers, and movement. This book could be included in studies of poetry and jazz music.

Book Talk Material and Activities

Choral reading is a great way for children to become involved with language. The rhyme and rhythm of *Charlie Parker played be bop* make it a great choice for reading aloud. In one class of third graders, the children enjoyed deciding how to read the words, snapping their fingers along with some of the words and moving their arms from side to side along with other words. Several children decided to make mouth noises—popping, clicking, hissing, buzzing—as background sounds while their classmates read the book aloud. Everyone joined in on the phrase "Never leave your cat alone." There was a lot of discussion and cooperation as different children made suggestions and tried them out. The author information on the book jacket notes that a recording of "A Night in Tunisia" was the inspiration for this book, and it would be fun to play this to further extend the experience.

Poetry books were also shared with these third graders. They chose poems that promoted participation, like Eloise Greenfield's "Way Down in the Music" from *Honey, I Love* and the raps in *Nathaniel Talking*. They experimented with the poems in *Joyful Noise*. Other books with rhythmic texts were available for these children, including *Nicholas Cricket* and *Mama Don't Allow*. The children enjoyed the rhyming text in *Nicholas Cricket*, and chanted "The music is just so grand." They talked about how both *Nicholas Cricket* and *Charlie Parker played be bop* had phrases that were very easy to remember, phrases that encouraged choral reading. They liked how reading these books was an active, shared experience.

Picture books that had a musical theme were booktalked for this class. Some of these books focused on characters whose enjoyment of music set them apart, like Max in *Musical Max* and Ty in *Ty's One-Man Band*.

Related Titles

Geraldine, the Music Mouse, written and illustrated by Leo Lionni. Pantheon, 1979. Geraldine is enchanted with music. It is a special moment when she discovers she can create her own music.

Honey, I Love and Other Love Poems, by Eloise Greenfield. Illustrated by Diane Dillon and Leo Dillon. Crowell, 1978. There are many poems in this collection that encourage movement and activity. Children have jumped rope to "Rope Rhyme," clapped their hands to "Way Down in the Music," and dramatized "Harriet Tubman."

Joyful Noise: Poems for Two Voices, by Paul Fleischman. Illustrated by Eric Beddows. Harper, 1988. These creative poems focus on insects. The format is designed for two readers. *Joyful Noise* was the Newbery Medal winner in 1989.

Mama Don't Allow: Starring Miles and the Swamp Band, written and illustrated by Thacher Hurd. Harper, 1984. Miles and his band play at the Alligator Ball. At the end of the ball, they use their music to escape from the alligators, who plan to eat them.

Musical Max, by Robert Kraus. Illustrated by Jose Aruego and Ariane Dewey. Simon & Schuster, 1990. Max loves to practice playing music on many instruments. His family and neighbors do not always appreciate his talent. When Max stops playing, though, everyone misses his music.

Nathaniel Talking, by Eloise Greenfield. Illustrated by Jan Spivey Gilchrist. Writers and Readers Publishing, 1988. Nathaniel raps about his life and neighborhood; children enjoy reading and responding to his words.

Nicholas Cricket, by Joyce Maxner. Illustrated by William Joyce. Harper, 1989. This is a toe-tapping, finger-snapping rhyming story about the Bug-a-Wug Cricket Band. Nicholas Cricket is a banjo-playing cricket with some human characteristics, although he does have two legs and four arms.

Something Special for Me, written and illustrated by Vera B. Williams. Greenwillow, 1983. Rosa is looking for just the right thing for her birthday. She finally chooses an accordion. Rosa's story continues in *Music, Music for Everyone* (Greenwillow, 1984).

Ty's One-Man Band, by Mildred Pitts Walter. Illustrated by Margot Tomes. Scholastic, 1980. Ty loves to listen to different sounds. He meets Andro, who promises to show Ty how to be a one-man band. People come out to watch and listen to Andro's performance.

Rockwell, Anne.   *Trains*
Illus. by the author. Dutton, 1988 (0-525-44377-0); pap. (0-525-44888-8)
Suggested Use Level: PreS–Gr. 2

Plot Summary

Beginning with a fox child playing with a toy train, this book presents information about real trains. Real trains run on tracks, with engineers at the helm. Specific types of trains are featured: passenger trains, freight trains, subways, elevated trains, a monorail, and an old-fashioned steam engine. Diesel and electric trains are common now. The characters in this book are all foxes, and at the conclusion, two fox children watch the toy train come out of the tunnel.

Thematic Material

This nonfiction book describes different kinds of trains. *Trains* could be included in a unit on transportation.

Book Talk Material and Activities

Simple informational books are often the focus of preschool and primary grade studies. Young children can learn not only about trains, but also about informational books, by looking at a variety of titles. Anne Rockwell's *Trains* is very brief, featuring simple facts about a few trains. Gail Gibbons's *Trains* has more details, including information about the history of trains. The illustrations depict people and often have captions that highlight specific details, such as the kinds of cars on a passenger train. Anne Rockwell's book would be a good introductory title to share. *Trains* by Gail Gibbons would add more details.

Many other books about trains, both fiction and nonfiction, could be available for children to examine on their own. *Train Whistles* describes how whistles and other noises are used to send messages between trains. Angela Royston's *Trains* (a book in the Eye Openers series) uses photographs and drawings, whereas Diane Siebert's *Train Song* is a poem with information about trains in the rhymes. *Freight Train, The Train to Lulu's,* and *A Regular Rolling Noah* describe specific train experiences, as does *Country Crossing* (elsewhere in this chapter). Having access to many different books introduces children to a variety of approaches to presenting information and stories.

Related Titles

Freight Train, written and illustrated by Donald Crews. Greenwillow, 1978. In this Caldecott Honor book, the cars of the train are different colors: red, orange, yellow, green, blue, purple, and black.

A Regular Rolling Noah, by George Ella Lyon. Illustrated by Stephen Gammell. Bradbury, 1986. A young man helps a family move their farm, including the animals, on the train.

Train Song, by Diane Siebert. Illustrated by Mike Wimmer. Crowell, 1990. The rhyming text describes different features of trains. Names of railroad companies, like Santa Fe and New York Central, are incorporated into the poem.

The Train to Lulu's, by Elizabeth Fitzgerald Howard. Illustrated by Robert Casilla. Bradbury, 1988. Beppy and Babs are taking the train to visit their Great-Aunt Lulu. This book is based on an experience from the author's childhood.

Train Whistles: A Language in Code, revised edition, by Helen Roney Sattler. Illustrated by Giulio Maestro. Lothrop, 1985. Trains often communicate with whistles. Two long, one short, one long is a warning to stop because the train is coming. A list of train whistles follows the text.

Trains, written and illustrated by Gail Gibbons. Holiday, 1987. Details about trains are presented in the text and the illustrations. There is a page of train signs and signals following the text.

Trains, by Angela Royston. Photographs by Dave King. Macmillan,

1992. This is part of the Eye Openers series. Photographs and drawings are accompanied by a very brief text. A Crocodile Train and the Orient Express are two of the unusual trains in this book.

About the Author and Illustrator

ROCKWELL, ANNE

Fifth Book of Junior Authors and Illustrators, ed. by Sally Holmes Holtze. Wilson, 1983, pp. 264–266.

Illustrators of Children's Books: 1967–1976, Vol. IV, comp. by Lee Kingman, Grace Allen Hogarth, and Harriet Quimby. Horn Book, 1978, pp. 6, 154–155, 207.

Something about the Author, ed. by Anne Commire. Gale, 1983, Vol. 33, pp. 170–174; ed. by Diane Telgen, Gale, 1993, Vol. 71, pp. 165–168.

Schwartz, David M. *If You Made a Million*
Illus. by Steven Kellogg. Photographs by George Ancona. Lothrop, 1989, LB (0-688-07018-3)
Suggested Use Level: Gr. 3–4

Plot Summary

As children earn money, Marvelosissimo the Mathematical Magician explains the amounts of money that have been received. First a penny, then a nickel, then a dime, then a quarter, then a dollar are earned. Each amount is depicted with photographs of actual money, and each money total is depicted in different coin combinations. For example, a quarter is also five nickels, two dimes and one nickel, three nickels and one dime, and twenty-five pennies. Spending the money is also described in different combinations of amounts. For example, a dollar could buy 100 penny candies or ten stickers for ten cents each. The concept of putting money in a bank and earning interest is presented. Five-dollar and ten-dollar bills and what they might buy are also discussed, then $100, $1,000, $10,000, $50,000, and finally, $1 million. Also presented is information about paying with checks and having the bank lend you additional money. An author's note follows the text and describes more complex issues, including interest, checking accounts, and income tax.

Thematic Material

This book provides information about different amounts of money and suggests some possible uses for each amount.

Book Talk Material and Activities

By the middle elementary grades, many children receive allowances. They often have opportunities to earn money at home. Many schools have fund-raising activities to support special projects, such as adopting an animal at the local zoo. *If You Made a Million* could be used as a focus book for a discussion of money. This book would also correlate with several math activities. Using play money and working in pairs, children could take some of the amounts described in the book and demonstrate different combinations of denominations to reach that amount. They could share information about the ways they earn money and, using their experiences, devise some simple math problems. For example, if Jamil earns 75 cents for watching his brother for one hour, how much will he earn in two hours? How many hours will he have to work to earn enough to buy a toy that costs $3? Reading stories in which the characters try to earn money, such as *Arthur's Funny Money*, *The Bunnysitters*, and *What's Cooking, Jenny Archer?*, would add to the fun.

Visiting a bank and interviewing some of the employees could be a class trip or a project for a few children. This would extend a study of community services. Before the visit, children could research banks and money, using nonfiction books like *Banks: Where the Money Is* and *Making Cents. How Much Is a Million?* would also help children understand some of the larger numbers discussed in *If You Made a Million*.

Audiovisual Adaptation

If You Made a Million. Library Learning Resources, kit (book/activity cards/yarn/paper), 1990.

Related Titles

Arthur's Funny Money, written and illustrated by Lillian Hoban. Harper, 1981. Arthur the chimp needs to earn money for a team uniform. When he and his sister go into the bike-washing business, they find how much money it costs to earn money.

Banks: Where the Money Is, by David A. Adler. Illustrated by Tom Huffman. Watts, 1985. Describes some of the services offered at a bank, including savings and checking accounts.

The Bunnysitters, by Kate Banks. Illustrated by Blanche Sims. Random, 1991. Nicholas Buchanan needs some money to buy the materials for building a car for the Soapbox Derby. He and his friend Alex agree to watch Mrs. Peach's bunny, but their bunnysitting turns into a disaster. Children enjoy suggesting other, more practical ways the boys could have earned money.

How Much Is a Million?, by David M. Schwartz. Illustrated by Steven Kellogg. Lothrop, 1985. Using familiar items, the author makes very large numbers understandable to children. In one of the comparisons, readers are asked to imagine children standing on each other's shoulders, and then are told how high 1 million children would reach. (Condensed in *Primaryplots,* Bowker, 1989, pp. 114–115.)

Making Cents: Every Kid's Guide to Money, How to Make It, and What to Do with It, by Elizabeth Wilkinson. Illustrated by Martha Weston. Little, Brown, 1989. There are many ways children can earn money, including walking dogs and selling old toys. This book makes creative suggestions for making money.

26 Letters and 99 Cents, written and photographed by Tana Hoban. Greenwillow, 1987. This is actually two books in one. Reading from one direction, the letters of the alphabet are depicted. Turning the book around, numbers are shown (from 1 to 30 and then 35, 40, 45, 50, 60, 70, 80, and 99). Next to the numbers are photographs of coins in combinations that add up to the number being presented. (Condensed in *Primaryplots,* Bowker, 1989, pp. 99–101.)

What's Cooking, Jenny Archer?, written by Ellen Conford. Illustrated by Diana Palmisciano. Little, Brown, 1989. When Jenny's friends see the great lunches she makes for herself, they decide to buy their lunches from her. Let's see . . . if one lunch will cost $1.50, how much will Jenny make for two lunches? Or three? Jenny's plan seems too good to be true, and it is.

About the Author

SCHWARTZ, DAVID M.

Sixth Book of Junior Authors and Illustrators, ed. by Sally Holmes Holtze. Wilson, 1989, pp. 270–272.

Something about the Author, ed. by Anne Commire. Gale, 1990, Vol. 59, pp. 181–183.

About the Illustrators

Ancona, George
Something about the Author, ed. by Anne Commire. Gale, 1977, Vol. 12, pp. 10–12.

Kellogg, Steven
Fourth Book of Junior Authors and Illustrators, ed. by Doris de Montreville and Elizabeth D. Crawford. Wilson, 1978, pp. 208–209.
Illustrators of Children's Books: 1967–1976, Vol. IV, comp. by Lee Kingman, Grace Allen Hogarth, and Harriet Quimby. Horn Book, 1978, pp. 136, 196.
Something about the Author, ed. by Anne Commire. Gale, 1976, Vol. 8, pp. 95–97; Gale, 1989, Vol. 57, pp. 88–97.
Talking with Artists, comp. and ed. by Pat Cummings. Bradbury, 1992, pp. 54–59.

Serfozo, Mary. *Who Said Red?*
Illus. by Keiko Narahashi. McElderry, 1988 (0-689-50455-1); pap., Aladdin (0-689-71592-7); Big Book, Aladdin (0-689-71651-6)
Suggested Use Level: PreS–Gr. 1

Plot Summary
When a girl's young brother says "Red," she tells him about red and several other colors. He insists on saying red until he finds his red kite.

Thematic Material
This book introduces the colors red, green, blue, and yellow by naming items of each color.

Book Talk Material and Activities
Through this story of a young boy looking for his red kite, children learn about other colors. The author lists some items that are red (stop sign) while the illustrator includes other items (fire engine, barn). Children would enjoy adding to the list using familiar items and making lists or pictures of colors not featured in this book. In *Who Said Red?* the illustrations extend the text. The half-title page shows the young boy and his red kite. On the title page, there is a picture of a farm, and the young boy is flying his red kite while his sister does her chores. These two illustrations start the story, making it clear why the boy is insisting on red. Children

develop their knowledge of books through opportunities to examine and discuss them. Focusing on the first two illustrations and asking young children to talk about what is happening encourages young children to see the relationship between the illustrations and the text. Other stories incorporating colors, such as *The Color Box* and *Mr. Rabbit and The Lovely Present*, could be shared for children to sign out.

Related Titles

The Color Box, by Dayle Ann Dodds. Illustrated by Giles Laroche. Little, Brown, 1992. Alexander the monkey climbs into a box and sees colors: black, yellow, orange, blue, red, green, purple, and white. When he leaves the box, he is back in the colorful world. Cut-outs in the pages reveal each new color.

Colors, written and illustrated by Heidi Goennel. Little, Brown, 1990. Although the names of the colors are not mentioned, relationships between items of similar colors are described, such as comparing a bike to a robin's eggs.

I Went Walking, by Sue Williams (elsewhere in this chapter). Illustrated by Julie Vivas. Harcourt, 1989. On a walk, a young boy sees a black cat, a brown horse, a red cow, a green duck, a pink pig, and a yellow dog.

Mr. Rabbit and the Lovely Present, by Charlotte Zolotow. Illustrated by Maurice Sendak. Harper, 1962. Mr. Rabbit helps the little girl choose just the right birthday present for her mother.

My First Look at Colors, photography by Stephen Oliver. Random, 1990. Red, yellow, blue, green, orange, pink, brown, black, and white are featured in this book. For each color there are photographs of several items of that color.

Samuel Todd's Book of Great Colors, written and illustrated by E. L. Konigsburg. Atheneum, 1990. A young boy lists some of the things he associates with different colors.

Tryon, Leslie. *Albert's Alphabet*
Illus. by the author. Atheneum, 1991 (0-689-31642-9)
Suggested Use Level: PreS–Gr. 1

Plot Summary

Albert the goose is the carpenter for Pleasant Valley School. He receives a note from the school principal asking him to build an alphabet by 3:00 P.M. that day. He gathers his materials—wood, nails, glue, and tools. It is 7:00 A.M. as Albert begins, with the letter "A," of course. Using all the materials, including what is left over from each letter, Albert constructs the letters from "A" to "I." He makes "J," "K," "L," "M," and "N" from the box where his wood had been stored. Then, "Oh Oh," as Albert moves on to the letter "O," he finds he is out of materials. He begins to use parts of his house and other resources around him to finish the alphabet. For "O" and "P" he uses the wall of his house; he makes a "Q" out of rocks from the schoolyard. For other letters, he uses lumber, poles, and pipes. He forms a "Y" by trimming the branches of a tree. Finally, he makes a "Z" by rearranging the rooms of his house. At 3:00 P.M., the alphabet is complete and Albert is cleaning his workroom and making a list of needed supplies.

Thematic Material

This book introduces the letters of the alphabet. It also focuses on a character who is very creative.

Book Talk Material and Activities

Albert is a creative carpenter who must use his imagination to build the letters of the alphabet. When he runs out of regular supplies, he looks for other resources. Albert is also a very responsible character, because he completes his alphabet on time. *Albert's Alphabet* could be shared along with other creative alphabet books, such as *Anno's Alphabet* or Suse MacDonald's *Alphabatics*. Like *Albert's Alphabet, Anno's Alphabet* features letters that appear to have been constructed, although the grain of the wood twists and turns in unusual directions. Across from each letter is an item that begins with that letter; for example, a clock is across from "C." In the border around the pages and elsewhere on the page are other items that begin with that letter, such as a clown, a child, and some clover. A guide to some of the hidden items follows the letters. In *Alphabatics,* the letters of the alphabet tumble and twist to create an item that begins with that letter. The "T" sprouts additional branches and becomes a tree. These creative approaches to the alphabet encourage children to play with letters, shapes, and words.

Books with a construction theme could also be featured along with *Albert's Alphabet. Changes, Changes* is a wordless book in which two wooden toys build with blocks. They make a house and then make a fire engine and hose to put out a fire. When *Louise Builds a House,* she designs it to include everything she wants. Children might enjoy reading Douglas Florian's *A Carpenter,* which describes some of the activities involved in working with wood.

Related Titles

Action Alphabet, written and illustrated by Marty Neumeier and Byron Glaser. Greenwillow, 1984. Letters of the alphabet act out the words that illustrate them, including a "D" that is a "Drip" and an "O" that is in "Orbit."

Albert's Play, written and illustrated by Leslie Tryon. Atheneum, 1992. The rhyming text describes the behind-the-scenes preparations by Albert and the students from the Pleasant Valley School for their performance of *The Owl and the Pussycat.*

Alphabatics, written and illustrated by Suse MacDonald. Bradbury, 1986. Each letter of the alphabet makes acrobatic movements to transform itself into an item that begins with that letter. For example, "S" stretches into a swan.

Anno's Alphabet: An Adventure in Imagination, written and illustrated by Mitsumasa Anno. Crowell, 1974. The letters of the alphabet seem to have been built out of wood. Look closely at how these letters are constructed.

A Carpenter, written and illustrated by Douglas Florian. Greenwillow, 1991. In this rhyming text, the activities of a carpenter are presented.

Changes, Changes, written and illustrated by Pat Hutchins. Macmillan, 1971. This is a wordless book in which two wooden toys create items from blocks, including a fire engine, a boat, a truck, and a train.

Louise Builds a House, written and illustrated by Louise Pfanner. Orchard, 1987. Louise plans her house so it has everything she needs.

Weiss, Nicki. *Where Does the Brown Bear Go?*
Illus. by the author. Greenwillow, 1989, LB (0-688-07863-X); pap.,
Puffin (0-14-054181-0)
Suggested Use Level: PreS–Gr. 1

Plot Summary

As night approaches, a white cat, a monkey, a camel, a stray dog, a
seagull, and a brown bear all head for home. They end up as stuffed
animals in the bed of a child who is sleeping.

Thematic Material

This story has a rhythm and a repetitive text that create a quiet mood
for bedtime. It could be included in a bedtime story hour for young
children and their parents.

Book Talk Material and Activities

Libraries and day-care centers often have special evening activities. A
bedtime story hour, where young children come ready for bed, would be
a great time for sharing this book. Children could bring their own stuffed
animals and extend the mood of *Where Does the Brown Bear Go?* by talking
about their own toy friends.

A display of other bedtime books could be featured so children could
select some books for their "at home" bedtime stories. Brief book talks
could highlight some recent titles, including *Asleep, Asleep; While I Sleep;* and
Half a Moon and One Whole Star; as well as more familiar stories such as
Goodnight Moon and *Ten, Nine, Eight.*

Related Titles

Asleep, Asleep, by Mirra Ginsburg. Inspired by a verse by A. Vvedensky.
Illustrated by Nancy Tafuri. Greenwillow, 1992. At night, a mother holds
her young child and talks of all the animals that are already asleep.

Goodnight, Goodnight, written and illustrated by Eve Rice. Greenwillow,
1980. Throughout the city, people say "Goodnight." Even the little kitten
is going to sleep.

Goodnight Moon, by Margaret Wise Brown. Illustrated by Clement Hurd.
Harper, 1947. In this classic bedtime book, a little rabbit looks around the
room and says "Goodnight" to familiar items.

Half a Moon and One Whole Star, by Crescent Dragonwagon. Illustrated by Jerry Pinkney. Macmillan, 1986. The poetic text in this book describes the sounds and activities that occur as a young girl sleeps.

Roll Over! A Counting Book, illustrated by Merle Peek. Clarion, 1981. Different animals are pushed out of bed in this version of the popular counting rhyme. At the end of the book, the animals in the rhyme appear as the decorative border in the child's bedroom.

Ten, Nine, Eight, written and illustrated by Molly Bang. Greenwillow, 1983. As a little girl prepares for bed, she and her father count backward from ten and describe some of the things in her room. (Condensed in *Primaryplots,* Bowker, 1989, pp. 1–3.)

While I Sleep, by Mary Calhoun. Illustrated by Ed Young. Morrow, 1992. This is a poetic description of the activities of animals while a young child sleeps.

About the Author and Illustrator

WEISS, NICKI

Sixth Book of Authors and Illustrators, ed. by Sally Holmes Holtze. Wilson, 1989, pp. 313–315.
Something about the Author, ed. by Anne Commire. Gale, 1983, Vol. 33, pp. 229–230.

Williams, Sue.   *I Went Walking*

Illus. by Julie Vivas. Harcourt, 1989 (0-15-200471-8); pap. (0-15-238011-6); Big Book (0-15-238010-8)

Suggested Use Level: PreS–Gr. 1

Plot Summary

On a walk, a young boy sees a black cat, a brown horse, a red cow, a green duck, a pink pig, and a yellow dog.

Thematic Material

In this book, children can follow the pattern of the text. The concepts of colors and sequencing are presented.

Book Talk Material and Activities

Children in preschools and primary grade classes focus on concepts like colors, numbers, and the alphabet. *I Went Walking* could be shared with young children and compared to Bill Martin, Jr.'s *Brown Bear, Brown Bear What Do You See?* Both books have a patterned text and focus on animals and colors. A chart could be made of the sequence of each book.

I Went Walking	*Brown Bear*
Black cat	Red bird
Brown horse	Yellow duck
Red cow	Blue horse
Green duck	Green frog
Pink pig	Purple cat
Yellow dog	White dog
	Black sheep
	Goldfish
	Mother
	Beautiful children

Many children enjoy making their own books using the pattern of a familiar story. They suggest new items to include and add their own illustrations. Predictable books provide children with support strategies for their reading and writing. As children learn the pattern of the text, they develop fluency and feel success as readers.

Audiovisual Adaptation

I Went Walking. Trumpet Club, cassette/book, 1992.

Related Titles

Brown Bear, Brown Bear What Do You See?, by Bill Martin, Jr. Illustrated by Eric Carle. Holt, 1967. A brown bear sees a red bird, who sees a yellow duck, who sees a blue horse, and so on.

The Color Box, by Dayle Ann Dodds. Illustrated by Giles Laroche. Little, Brown, 1992. Alexander the monkey climbs into a box and sees colors: black, yellow, orange, blue, red, green, purple, and white. When he leaves the box, he is back in the colorful world. Cut-outs in the pages reveal each new color.

Freight Train, written and illustrated by Donald Crews. Greenwillow, 1978. In this Caldecott Honor book, the cars of the train are different colors: red, orange, yellow, green, blue, purple, and black.

I Need a Lunch Box, by Jeannette Caines. Illustrated by Pat Cummings. Harper, 1988. When his older sister gets a new lunch box, a young boy dreams of a different, colorful lunch box for each day of the week.

Mary Wore Her Red Dress and Henry Wore His Green Sneakers, adapted and illustrated by Merle Peek. Clarion, 1985. In this song about clothes, including green shoes, purple pants, and violet ribbons, young children can learn about colors too. The musical arrangement is included.

Polar Bear, Polar Bear What Do You Hear?, by Bill Martin, Jr. Illustrated by Eric Carle. Holt, 1991. The sequence in this book goes from the polar bear, to the lion, to the hippopotamus, to the flamingo, to the zebra, to the boa constrictor, to the elephant, to the leopard, to the peacock, to the walrus, and finally to the zookeeper, who hears children.

Samuel Todd's Book of Great Colors, written and illustrated by E. L. Konigsburg. Atheneum, 1990. A young boy lists many of the things he associates with different colors.

Who Said Red?, by Mary Serfozo (elsewhere in this chapter). Illustrated by Keiko Narahashi. McElderry, 1988. A little girl discusses colors with her young brother, who is searching for his red kite.

4

Finding the Humor
in Picture Books

WHAT makes you laugh? Is it watching sheep shop or bugs play ball? Is it word plays and rhymes, as in *Chicka Chicka Boom Boom*, *Old Mother Hubbard and Her Wonderful Dog*, or *A Hippopotamusn't?* Is it a pig on a picnic or a frog in the library? In this chapter, there are books with imaginary trips, as in *Alphabet Soup* and *Time Train*. There are books about unusual creatures, like *The Grumpalump* and *Bently & Egg*. Children will laugh at the antics of Fox, Jimmy's Boa, and the *Piggies*. Reading and listening to these books will be filled with fun.

Alexander, Lloyd.   *The Fortune-Tellers*
Illus. by Trina Schart Hyman. Dutton, 1992 (0-525-44849-7)
Suggested Use Level: Gr. 2–4

Plot Summary
A young man visits a fortune-teller to learn about his future. The elderly fortune-teller makes many predictions, although each one has a condition with it. For example, when the young man asks if he will be wealthy, the fortune-teller answers that he will be, if he earns lots of money. The young man does not see the duality of these answers, and he leaves the fortune-teller filled with happiness about his promising future. He thinks of more questions and returns to the fortune-teller only to find that he is gone. The landlady enters and mistakenly thinks the fortune-teller has magically transformed himself into this handsome young man. She allows him to stay and demands that he tell her family's fortunes. The young man repeats the words the fortune-teller had shared with him, and the family is delighted. The neighbors come to hear their fortunes, and the young

man obliges, collecting money for repeating the old man's predictions. The young man marries the daughter of his landlady, and they live happily in prosperity. The fate of the real fortune-teller is revealed. He had fallen out of the window into a cart. The cart was pulled far out of the city where more misfortunes occurred, and the fortune-teller was swept down river. The young man thinks of the fortune-teller and is grateful for his accurate predictions.

Thematic Material

This is a humorous story, especially in the fortune-teller's predictions. The illustrations place this story in the West African country of Cameroon.

Book Talk Material and Activities

The young man in this story does not listen to all the information the fortune-teller gives him. As a result, he does not realize the fortune-teller qualifies each prediction: wealth if you get money, fame if you are well-known, true love if you find her, happiness if you are not miserable, and a long life if you do not die soon. The young man's good fortune comes by accident—the fortune-teller falls out the window and is taken away in a cart. The young man is a foolish character who succeeds by luck and circumstance. There are many characters who are more lucky than wise. Some, like the young man in *The Fortune-Tellers* and Ming Lo (in *Ming Lo Moves the Mountain*) are found in original stories, others are in folktales, including *The Three Sillies, Simon Boom Gives a Wedding,* and *The Three Wishes*.

Folktales also include many stories of humble characters who achieve wealth. *Puss in Boots, The Fool of the World and the Flying Ship,* and *Aladdin and the Wonderful Lamp* all feature the "rags to riches" theme. Like the young man in *The Fortune-Teller,* these characters receive a fortune and live in prosperity.

Related Titles

Aladdin and the Wonderful Lamp, by Carol Carrick. Illustrated by Donald Carrick. Scholastic, 1989. An old magician tricks Aladdin into entering the hidden cave and finding the magic lamp. When Aladdin falls in love with the princess, he uses the lamp to try to win her. The old magician steals the lamp from Aladdin, who must regain it if he is to be reunited with the princess.

The Fool of the World and the Flying Ship: A Russian Tale, retold by Arthur Ransome. Illustrated by Uri Shulevitz. Farrar, 1968. The youngest son, who is called the Fool of the World, sets out to win the czar's daughter. On his journey, he befriends several men who help him win his prize. This book received the Caldecott Award in 1969.

Ming Lo Moves the Mountain, written and illustrated by Arnold Lobel. Greenwillow, 1982. The mountain causes Ming Lo nothing but trouble, so he decides he must move the mountain. The wise man gives Ming Lo some suggestions for moving the mountain. Nothing seems to work, until Ming Lo and his wife learn a special dance.

Puss in Boots, by Charles Perrault. Translated by Malcolm Arthur. Illustrated by Fred Marcellino. Farrar, 1990. The cat's cleverness results in good fortune for his master, and the hand of the princess. This book was a Caldecott Honor selection in 1991.

Rum Pum Pum: A Folk Tale from India, retold by Maggie Duff. Illustrated by Jose Aruego and Ariane Dewey. Macmillan, 1978. When the king takes Blackbird's wife, Blackbird makes war on him. On his journey, Blackbird is joined by Cat, the ants, Stick, and River, and when the king tries to destroy Blackbird, his companions come to his rescue.

Simon Boom Gives a Wedding, by Yuri Suhl. Illustrated by Margot Zemach. Four Winds, 1972. Simon Boom will have nothing but the best, even if it does not meet his needs, like a winter hat for summertime. For his daughter's wedding, he serves only water, but it is the very best water.

The Three Sillies, by Joseph Jacobs. Retold and illustrated by Paul Galdone. Clarion, 1981. A young man will not marry his beloved because she is so foolish, but then he meets some even bigger fools.

The Three Wishes: An Old Story, written and illustrated by Margot Zemach. Farrar, 1986. When the woodcutter helps an imp, he is rewarded with three wishes, but he uses them foolishly.

About the Author

ALEXANDER, LLOYD

Something about the Author, ed. by Anne Commire. Gale, 1972, Vol. 3, pp. 7–9; 1987, Vol. 49, pp. 21–35.

Third Book of Junior Authors, ed. by Muriel Fuller. Wilson, 1963, pp. 6–7.

About the Illustrator

HYMAN, TRINA SCHART

Fourth Book of Junior Authors and Illustrators, ed. by Doris de Montreville and Elizabeth D. Crawford. Wilson, 1978, pp. 191–192.

Illustrators of Children's Books, 1957–1966, Vol. III, comp. by Lee Kingman, Grace Allen

Hogarth, and Harriet Quimby. Horn Book, 1968, pp. 125, 224; *1967–1976, Vol. IV*, 1978, pp. 9, 16, 68, 82, 83, 129–130, 176, 194.
Something about the Author, ed. by Anne Commire. Gale, 1975, Vol. 7, pp. 137–139; 1987, Vol. 46, pp. 90–112.

Aylesworth, Jim.   *Old Black Fly*
Illus. by Stephen Gammell. Holt, 1992 (0-8050-1401-2)
Suggested Use Level: Gr. K–2

Plot Summary
In this rhyming alphabet book, the buzzing of an old black fly causes many problems, such as bothering the Baby, licking the Frosting, pestering the Parrot, and sniffing the Salami. "Shoo fly! Shoo fly! Shooo" is repeated after every rhyming pair of letters. After the letter Z, the fly is swatted, and the rhyme says "he won't be bad no more."

Thematic Material
Old Black Fly describes the adventures of a pesty fly from A to Z.

Book Talk Material and Activities
While the alphabet provides the framework for the fly's activities, the focus in *Old Black Fly* is on the humorous situations that result as the fly creates his chaos. The rhyme and repetition in this book automatically involve children as they listen and join in, especially saying "Shoo fly!" At the end of the book, when the fly is swatted, several first graders said it reminded them of *Why Mosquitoes Buzz in People's Ears*. Both books feature insect pests that cause trouble for a group of characters, and there is a sequence of events in both books. *The Napping House* is another book where an insect (a flea) starts a sequence of activities. Songs and rhymes could also be shared with *Old Black Fly*. *Possum Come a-Knockin'* and *Skip to My Lou* have a rollicking country feeling similar to that in *Old Black Fly*. *Skip to My Lou* even has a "Shoo fly shoo" refrain.

Stephen Gammell's illustrations are filled with color and activity. The fly is causing chaos, which is reflected in the splattered, overlapping, dripping colors. The book jacket for *Old Black Fly* includes a quote from Stephen Gammell about his illustrations, indicating that these drawings are a new direction for him. Looking at other books he has illustrated, such as *The Relatives Came* and *Old Henry,* could promote a discussion of the changes. Children could look at his use of lines in *Old Henry.* What is the background like in each book? How do the illustrations reflect the action in the story? Some first graders who heard *Old Black Fly* suggested that the antics of the fly are extended by the spatters and drips in the illustrations.

Audiovisual Adaptation

Old Black Fly. Scholastic, cassette/book, 1993.

Related Titles

A My Name Is Alice, by Jane Bayer. Illustrated by Steven Kellogg. Dial, 1984. This is an alphabet game involving names, occupations, and places. Children like to invent chants using their own names.

The Napping House, by Audrey Wood. Illustrated by Don Wood. Harcourt, 1984. In this sequential story, everyone is sleeping, piled up in the same bed. When the flea bites one of the sleepers, a series of events causes everyone to wake up. (Condensed in *Primaryplots,* Bowker, 1989, pp. 154–156.)

Old Henry, by Joan W. Blos. Illustrated by Stephen Gammell. Morrow, 1987. Old Henry is a man who is different, yet he is comfortable with himself. Gammell's illustrations are whimsical, with wild lines around Henry's house and tightly controlled lines depicting the neighbors.

Possum Come a-Knockin', by Nancy Van Laan. Illustrated by George Booth. Knopf, 1990. When the possum comes to the door, only the little girl hears him knockin' because everyone else is so busy and so loud.

The Relatives Came, by Cynthia Rylant. Illustrated by Stephen Gammell. Bradbury, 1985. One summer, the relatives from Virginia come to visit. Everyone squeezes together and shares the space until the relatives crowd back into their car and return home. Gammell's illustrations are crowded with many different characters, and it is a challenge to find the same relatives on different pages. (Condensed in *Primaryplots,* Bowker, 1989, pp. 31–33.)

She'll Be Comin' Round the Mountain, retold and illustrated by Robert Quackenbush. Lippincott, 1973. A popular folk song in a picture-book format. The characters are part of a Wild West show arriving in town on the railroad.

Skip to My Lou, adapted and illustrated by Nadine Bernard Westcott.

Little, Brown, 1989. When the flies are in the sugar, you say "Shoo fly shoo." This would be a fun song to sing after hearing *Old Black Fly*.

Why Mosquitoes Buzz in People's Ears, retold by Verna Aardema. Illustrated by Leo Dillon and Diane Dillon. Dial, 1975. In this sequential story, a mosquito's silly behavior creates fear in the jungle. Now we know why mosquitoes are such annoying pests.

About the Author

AYLESWORTH, JIM

Something about the Author, ed. by Anne Commire. Gale, 1985, Vol. 38, p. 35.

About the Illustrator

GAMMELL, STEPHEN

Fifth Book of Junior Authors and Illustrators, ed. by Sally Holmes Holtze. Wilson, 1983, pp. 121–122.
Something about the Author, ed. by Anne Commire. Gale, 1988, pp. 50–58.

Banks, Kate. *Alphabet Soup*
Illus. by Peter Sís. Knopf, 1988, LB (0-394-99151-6)
Suggested Use Level: Gr. 1–2

Plot Summary

A boy does not want to eat his alphabet soup for lunch. His mother compares him to a grumpy bear. The boy takes one spoonful of soup, finding the letters B-E-A-R in his spoon, and a bear appears. The boy and the bear begin an adventure. First, they meet an ogre, so the boy takes a spoonful of soup and gets the letters S-W-O-R-D. They come to a lake, and the letters from the soup spell B-O-A-T. When the bear falls out of the boat, the boy uses the letters N-E-T to rescue him. To climb a mountain, the boy takes the letters R-O-P-E from his soup. The boy uses the letters T-R-E-E to impress the wizard. They catch a crow and put it in a C-A-G-E. As night approaches they visit the H-O-U-S-E of an old man and sleep in a B-E-D. Finally, the boy is back at the kitchen table, and he has finished his soup.

Thematic Material

Children enjoy this story about "reading" alphabet soup. Some of the humor in the story comes from the relationship between the story and the illustrations.

Book Talk Material and Activities

As the boy sits at the kitchen table, he will not eat his lunch. In addition to his bowl of soup, there are other items on the table, including a honey container in the shape of a bear, a large mound of pieces of fruit, and a teacup. As the boy becomes bored, he invents a fantasy that involves the letters of his soup and the items on the table. The honey bottle become the bear in the story, the pepper mill becomes the ogre, the teacup is the boat, and so on. As the fantasy continues, children enjoy seeing how the items from the table are incorporated into the story. On the final page, when the boy is back at the table, many children study the table to see which items were used in the story. After sharing this story with a group of second graders, we talked about the relationship between the text and the illustrations in this book. For each page of text, there are as many as seven illustrations, often including several panels of small pictures. There is always a picture of the soup spoon containing the letters the boy brings out from his soup. The children liked the variety of illustrations and the changing details in the panels of smaller drawings. Because many of these children were beginning readers, they liked figuring out the words in the boy's spoon and predicting what would happen next in the story.

As children become more proficient readers, they enjoy books that play with language. The soup-letter words in *Alphabet Soup* involved everyone in this story. Other stories with unusual letter and alphabet activities include *Chicka Chicka Boom Boom* (elsewhere in this chapter), *The Story of Z*, *A My Name Is Alice*, and *Albert B. Cub and Zebra*. *Alligators All Around* and *Aster Aardvark's Alphabet Adventures* are two other books with the alphabet built into a story.

Related Titles

A My Name Is Alice, by Jane Bayer. Illustrated by Steven Kellogg. Dial, 1984. This is an alphabet game involving names, occupations, and places. Children like to invent their own chant using their names.

Albert B. Cub and Zebra: An Alphabet Storybook, written and illustrated by Anne Rockwell. Crowell, 1977. On the first page of this wordless book, Zebra is abducted. Albert B. Cub searches through wordless pages filled with items from A to Z to find him.

Alligators All Around, written and illustrated by Maurice Sendak. Harper, 1962. This is a classic rhyming story in which the alligators are involved in activities in alphabetical order, such as "bursting balloons" and "catching colds."

Aster Aardvark's Alphabet Adventures, written and illustrated by Steven Kellogg. Morrow, 1987. Kellogg tells a story about Aster Aardvark, Bertha Bear, Cyril Capon, and other alliterative animals. Children enjoy the antics of "Hermione, a hefty hyperactive hippo" and "Kenilworth, the kind kangaroo."

The Story of Z, by Jeanne Modesitt. Illustrated by Lonni Sue Johnson. Picture Book Studio, 1990. Z is tired of always being last, so she leaves the alphabet. Imagine a world without Z—"ig-ag," "ebra," and "oo" are some of the words in this story.

About the Illustrator

Sis, Peter

Sixth Book of Junior Authors and Illustrators, ed. by Sally Holmes Holtze. Wilson, 1989, pp. 279–281.

Something about the Author, ed. by Donna Olendorf. Gale, 1992, Vol. 67, pp. 178–185.

Blake, Quentin. *All Join In*
Illus. by the author. Little, Brown, 1990 (0-316-09934-1)
Suggested Use Level: PreS–Gr. 2

Plot Summary

The seven poems in this collection invite participation. In each poem there are phrases or words printed in capital letters, such as "BEEP-BEEP BEEP-BEEP" in "The Hooter Song," and joining in becomes almost automatic. In "Sorting Out the Kitchen Pans," there are "BANGS," "CLANGS," and "BONGS"; a chorus of cats "MIAOW" in "Bedtime Song." Colorful, cartoon-style illustrations show the humorous impact of these noisy poems.

Thematic Material

The poems in *All Join In* invite participation. Children will enjoy the rhythm, rhyme, and sounds of these noisy poems.

Book Talk Material and Activities

There are many books filled with noises that, like *All Join In,* encourage children to be noisy too. These stories and poems provide opportunities for creative dramatics. Children can act like ducks while reciting "Nice

Weather for Ducks." They can be cats during "Bedtime Song." If they want to act like other animals, Jean Marzollo's poems in *Pretend You're a Cat* describe activities of thirteen animals: a cat, a dog, a fish, a bee, a chick, a bird, a squirrel, a pig, a cow, a horse, a seal, a snake, and a bear. *Roar and More* is another book of animals and noises, and there are many noises in *Too Much Noise*. Other poems in *All Join In* could be acted out too. Banging and clanging pots and pans for "Sorting Out the Kitchen Pans" could turn into the sounds of a parade to go with *THUMP, THUMP, Rat-a-Tat-Tat*. *Surprises* and *More Surprises* have more poems with rhyme and repetition that will attract children to poetry.

Related Titles

More Surprises, edited by Lee Bennett Hopkins. Illustrated by Megan Lloyd. Harper, 1987. Whistling, reading, and playing in the water from a fire hydrant are some of the activities captured in these poems.

Pretend You're a Cat, by Jean Marzollo. Illustrated by Jerry Pinkney. Dial, 1990. Animal activities are described in these poems, which encourage young children to jump, buzz, scratch, soar, twirl, snort, munch, slither, and wiggle as they imitate each animal.

Roar and More, written and illustrated by Karla Kuskin. Harper, 1990. A roaring lion, a snarling tiger, and a hissing snake are some of the animals and noises in this rhyming text.

Surprises, edited by Lee Bennett Hopkins. Illustrated by Megan Lloyd. Harper, 1984. In this collection there are poems on topics of everyday interest to children, such as having a pet and admiring a friend's freckles. (Condensed in *Primaryplots*, Bowker, 1989, pp. 103–105.)

THUMP, THUMP, Rat-a-Tat-Tat, by Gene Baer. Illustrated by Lois Ehlert. Harper, 1989. A marching band is on parade. Colors and sound words fill the pages, coming closer and growing louder, then moving away and becoming quieter.

Too Much Noise, by Ann McGovern. Illustrated by Simms Taback. Houghton, 1967. An old man brings farm animals into his noisy house. When he removes these animals, his noisy house seems much less noisy.

About the Author and Illustrator

BLAKE, QUENTIN

Fifth Book of Junior Authors and Illustrators, ed. by Sally Holmes Holtze. Wilson, 1983, pp. 34–35.

Illustrators of Children's Books: 1957–1966, Vol. III, comp. by Lee Kingman, Grace Allen

Hogarth, and Harriet Quimby. Horn Book, 1968, pp. 82, 210; *1967–1976, Vol. IV,* 1978, pp. 20, 22, 36, 38, 101, 180–181.
Something about the Author, ed. by Anne Commire. Gale, 1988, Vol, 52, pp. 10–18.

Cummings, Pat.   *Clean Your Room, Harvey Moon!*
Illus. by the author. Bradbury, 1991 (0-02-725511-5)
Suggested Use Level: PreS–Gr. 1

Plot Summary

A rhyming text describes Harvey Moon's dismay as his mother insists he clean his room before he watches his favorite Saturday morning television programs. Of course, Harvey's room is such a mess that it will take a very long time to really clean it, so he begins to push things under the rug. As he moves things around, Harvey finds lost treasures: his softball, some library books, a caboose. When everything is under the rug, and it is almost 2:00 P.M., Harvey calls his mom to inspect his room. She is "amazed," and Harvey is pleased, thinking he will get to watch television now. But instead, his mom tells him to eat lunch and then they will work on the lumps under the rug. The reader is left wondering if Harvey Moon will get to watch any television that Saturday.

Thematic Material

Helping around the house and doing chores are very familiar experiences. So is having a messy room. The experiences of Harvey Moon, an African-American child, are similar to those of most children.

Book Talk Material and Activities

How messy is your room? What chores do you do around the house? Children enjoy relating book experiences to their own lives. Many can empathize with the antics of Harvey Moon. Harvey never really believes his room needs to be cleaned. He is comfortable with the clutter. In fact, as he cleans, he is distracted by what he finds, stopping to read a dinosaur book and to put on his skates. *Tidy Titch* would be a good choice to contrast with *Clean Your Room, Harvey Moon!* In *Tidy Titch,* Titch's room is very neat, and he offers to help his brother and sister clean their rooms. As they clean, Titch takes their old toys and games to his room and, like Harvey Moon, he ends up with a very cluttered room. *Never Spit on Your Shoes* is another book in which the narrator does not seem to really understand the situation.

Stories focusing on children who try to help others would correlate with *Clean Your Room, Harvey Moon!* Humorous stories like *Two and Too Much* and *Max's Dragon Shirt* (see chapter 1) could be booktalked along with more serious stories like *The Patchwork Quilt* and *Miss Maggie*. Children may talk about what they do to help others, and some classroom activities may feature children as helpers.

Audiovisual Adaptation

Clean Your Room, Harvey Moon! Spoken Arts, cassette/book, 1991; videorecording, 1991.

Related Titles

"Bertie, Bertie" in *Blackberry Ink,* by Eve Merriam. Illustrated by Hans Wilhelm. Morrow, 1985. This poem features a character who will not take a bath. He enjoys being dirty. (Condensed in *Primaryplots,* Bowker, 1989, pp. 108–109.)

Mariana May and Nursey, written and illustrated by Tomie dePaola. Holiday, 1983. Mariana May gets dirty when she plays, until her friends come up with a plan.

Miss Maggie, by Cynthia Rylant. Illustrated by Thomas DiGrazia. Dutton, 1983. Miss Maggie lives alone in an old house. Nat is afraid of her until one day, when she needs his help, he discovers she is lonely and afraid too.

Never Spit on Your Shoes, written and illustrated by Denys Cazet. Orchard, 1990. Arnie describes some of the activities that occur on his first day at school, but there are many things he does not tell.

The Patchwork Quilt, by Valerie Flournoy. Illustrated by Jerry Pinkney. Dial, 1985. When Tanya's grandma becomes ill, Tanya decides to work on the quilt her grandmother had begun. When Grandma feels stronger, she returns to work on the quilt too. (Condensed in *Primaryplots,* Bowker, 1989, pp. 9–11.)

Tidy Titch, written and illustrated by Pat Hutchins. Greenwillow, 1991. Titch's room is very neat, until he helps his brother and sister clean their rooms. He takes all their discarded items, and his room becomes a mess.

Two and Too Much, by Mildred Pitts Walter. Illustrated by Pat Cummings. Bradbury, 1990. When this boy tries to take care of his two-year-old sister, he finds she can do a lot of damage.

About the Author and Illustrator

Cummings, Pat

Sixth Book of Junior Authors and Illustrators, ed. by Sally Holmes Holtze. Wilson, 1989, pp. 68–69.

Something about the Author, ed. by Anne Commire. Gale, 1986, Vol. 46, pp. 60–61; ed. by Diane Telgen, Gale, 1993, Vol. 71, pp. 56–59.

Talking with Artists, ed. by Pat Cummings. Bradbury, 1992, pp. 16–21.

Fleischman, Paul. *Time Train*

Illus. by Claire Ewart. Harper, 1991, LB (0-06-021710-3)
Suggested Use Level: Gr. 1–3

Plot Summary

During spring vacation, Miss Pym and her class have planned a trip to Utah to learn about dinosaurs. However, the ticket seller directs them to a different train. Leaving New York, the train heads toward Philadelphia, but something strange is happening. At each stop, the train seems to have traveled back in time. In Philadelphia, there are horses and wagons; in Pittsburgh, Union soldiers board the train; in Ohio, the train is stopped by buffalo on the track. The train travels through the Ice Age and reaches Utah, where the group gets off to observe and interact with dinosaurs. Miss Pym is dismayed by the unusual events, but the class in delighted with their adventures—cooking a dinosaur egg, riding a stegosaurus, and flying on a pterodactyl. The train returns and transports Miss Pym and the class back to their own place and time.

Thematic Material

Time Train takes readers on a strange and wonderful field trip to Dinosaur National Monument in Utah, where they learn firsthand about dinosaurs. The fantasy element of this journey could spark many creative writing and art activities.

Book Talk Material and Activities

In *Time Train*, Miss Pym and her class were headed for the Dinosaur National Monument. This museum and visitors' center, called Dinosaur Quarry, is in Jensen, Utah, and is featured in the book *Dinosaur Mountain* by Caroline Arnold. One wall of this building is the actual cliff face of the quarry, so visitors can observe the excavation activities. Many children would appreciate hearing some factual information about dinosaurs after the fantasy encounter in *Time Train*. Patricia Lauber's *The News about Dinosaurs* (see chapter 5) highlights some recent information.

The illustrations for *Time Train* extend the text and add humor. Many of the fantasy elements are conveyed only by the pictures; for example, when Miss Pym and some of the students eat dinner on the train, the text reads that it was "surprisingly good." The illustrations show a waiter coming to the table with a giant drumstick. The matter-of-fact tone of the text is offset by the fantastic events in the illustrations. Miss Pym's dismay is shown only in the pictures. Children enjoy talking about the humorous situations they observe as they focus on the pictures.

There are many books in which a fantasy trip occurs, and these could be used as models for students to write and illustrate their own stories. Joanna Cole has written the Magic School Bus books, including *The Magic School Bus inside the Earth*, in which Ms. Frizzle and her class study geology. In *Will's Mammoth*, a young boy goes outside and seems to travel to the Ice Age, where he sees mammoths and prehistoric people. *The Polar Express* describes a trip to the North Pole. Literature often provides children with ideas for their own writing and illustrating. A publishing center might feature specific books and some "What if . . ." suggestions, such as "What if you could travel on a Time Train?" or "What if you could see a mammoth?"

Related Titles

Dinosaur Mountain: Graveyard of the Past, by Caroline Arnold. Photographs by Richard Hewett. Clarion, 1988. Describes the Dinosaur National Monument in Utah, featuring the displays of fossils from the Jurassic period. This is the place that Miss Pym and her class planned to visit.

The Magic School Bus inside the Earth, by Joanna Cole. Illustrated by Bruce Degen. Scholastic, 1987. Ms. Frizzle and her class take a fantasy trip into the earth and learn about geology. This class has taken other fantasy trips, including *The Magic School Bus on the Ocean Floor* (see chapter 6).

Patrick's Dinosaurs, by Carol Carrick. Illustrated by Donald Carrick. Clarion, 1983. Patrick's imagination leads him to see dinosaurs all around him. In *What Happened to Patrick's Dinosaurs?* Patrick uses his imagination again. (Condensed in *Primaryplots*, Bowker, 1989, pp. 165–167.)

The Polar Express, written and illustrated by Chris Van Allsburg. Houghton, 1985. On Christmas Eve, a young boy boards a train that appears outside his house. He is transported to the North Pole, where he meets Santa Claus and receives the first gift of Christmas. This book received the Caldecott Medal in 1986. (Condensed in *Primaryplots*, Bowker, 1989, pp. 277–280.)

Will's Mammoth, by Rafe Martin. Illustrated by Stephen Gammell. Putnam, 1989. Will's room is decorated with drawings, toys, and books featuring woolly mammoths and other prehistoric creatures. When Will goes outside to play in the snow, he encounters many mammoths before returning home for dinner.

About the Author

FLEISCHMAN, PAUL

Fifth Book of Junior Authors and Illustrators, ed. by Sally Holmes Holtze. Wilson, 1983, pp. 114–116.

Something about the Author, ed. by Anne Commire. Gale, 1983, Vol. 32, p. 71; 1985, Vol. 39, pp. 72–73.

Hayes, Sarah. *The Grumpalump*
Illus. by Barbara Firth. Clarion, 1990 (0-89919-871-6)
Suggested Use Level: PreS–Gr. 1

Plot Summary

A pile of colorful fabrics is on the ground. One by one, some animals come over to the lump. First a bear, then a cat, a mole, a dove, a bull, a yak, an armadillo, and finally, a gnu. Each animal is involved in a rhyming action toward the lump, such as "The cat sat." When the gnu fills the lump with air, it becomes a hot air balloon. The gnu climbs into it and flies away.

Thematic Material

This is a humorous book with rhyming words and a predictable sequence.

Book Talk Material and Activities

The Grumpalump is a very unusual creation. At first, it is just a pile of fabric that appears to have a squashed, grumpy face. When the gnu fills the fabric with air, it becomes a balloon with a smiling face. Kindergarten children enjoyed the rhyming words and the humorous ending of this book. They talked about other books with unusual creatures, such as the Skog in *The Island of the Skog* and the many creatures in *What's under My Bed?* Several children thought the skog and the grumpalump were alike because no one knew what they were, at first. Others added that both characters turned out to be friendly.

The rhyming words and repetitive sequence of *The Grumpalump* made it a fun book to read aloud. As each new animal comes to look at the lump, it is added onto the list of animals ("The bear stared, the cat sat, and the mole rolled . . ."). Children quickly joined in and then tried to guess what rhyming activity the next animal would do. After they heard this book, they asked to hear it again so they could join in on everything. *Silly Sally* is another book with repetition these children enjoyed, as are *Shoes* and *Hi Bears, Bye Bears*. Before they can read, many children say the words from memory as they turn the pages. Books with rhyme and repetition support these strategies of beginning readers.

Related Titles

Hi Bears, Bye Bears, by Niki Yektai. Illustrated by Diane deGroat. Orchard, 1990. The simple rhyming text in this book describes bears: "Mom bear, Dad bear; Good bear, Bad bear." Beginning readers find it very easy to learn the words in this book and "read" them.

The Island of the Skog, written and illustrated by Steven Kellogg. Dial, 1971. The mice in this story sail away to find a place that is safe and peaceful. Instead, they meet the skog. The mice must decide how to deal with this creature.

A Mouse in My House, by Nancy Van Laan. Illustrated by Marjorie Priceman. Knopf, 1990. A repeating phrase describes a different animal in the house, but in each case, the animal is really a little boy.

Possum Come a-Knockin' by Nancy Van Laan. Illustrated by George Booth. Knopf, 1990. The amusing antics of a possum are featured in this rhyming text.

Pretend You're a Cat, by Jean Marzollo. Illustrated by Jerry Pinkney. Dial, 1990. The poems in this collection encourage children to act like animals, including a bird, a seal, and a snake.

Shoes, by Elizabeth Winthrop. Illustrated by William Joyce. Harper, 1986. A rhyming text describes many features associated with shoes.

Silly Sally, written and illustrated by Audrey Wood. Harcourt, 1992. As Sally goes to town, she meets many different creatures, who join her. Sally has an unusual way of walking. The rhyme and pattern of this text make it a good choice for beginning readers.

What's under My Bed?, written and illustrated by James Stevenson. Greenwillow, 1983. After hearing a scary story from Grandpa, Mary Ann and Louie go to bed and begin to wonder about the shadows and noises. Grandpa tells them of a similar experience when he was growing up. (Condensed in *Primaryplots*, Bowker, 1989, pp. 152–154.)

Hayes, Sarah.   *This Is the Bear and the Scary Night*
Illus. by Helen Craig. Little, Brown, 1992 (0-316-35250-0)
Suggested Use Level: PreK–Gr. 1

Plot Summary

The rhyming text in this book describes the adventures of a stuffed bear named Fred when he is accidentally left in the park. When night comes, Fred is frightened by an owl, who swoops down and carries him into the sky. The owl drops Fred into a pond, and he is rescued by a man with a trombone, who takes Fred home and cleans him up. The man brings Fred back to the park, where he is reunited with the boy who forgot him.

Thematic Material

Stories about toys and their adventures are very common in picture books for children, and there are many that involve stuffed bears. Toys that seem to talk, at least to their owners and to other toys, are also a familiar part of many stories.

Book Talk Material and Activities

This Is the Bear and the Scary Night continues the adventures of Fred the stuffed bear, who can also be seen in *This Is the Bear* and *This Is the Bear and the Picnic Lunch*. Like *Corduroy*, Fred is involved in several adventures. Also like *Corduroy*, Fred talks to himself about his activities. Children who have enjoyed the stories about Corduroy will have fun reading about Fred.

Bears are a very popular unit in the primary grades. A book talk and display could feature some of the newer books that feature teddy bears, such as the *This Is the Bear* . . . books and books like *Golden Bear* and *My Brown Bear Barney*. Teachers and children will enjoy adding these to their bear activities. In one school, some kindergartners heard three new bear books during a library visit: *This Is the Bear and the Scary Night, Golden Bear,* and *My Brown Bear Barney.* They voted on their favorite "new bear" book, selecting *This Is the Bear and the Scary Night* because, as one child said, "It was scary and the words rhymed." They also liked that it continued the adventures of Fred from the earlier books.

Related Titles

Corduroy, written and illustrated by Don Freeman. Viking, 1968. Corduroy waits in the department store for someone to buy him. After an adventure in the furniture section, Corduroy is returned to the toy department, and Lisa buys him and takes him home. Corduroy's adventures continue in *A Pocket for Corduroy* (Viking, 1978).

Golden Bear, by Ruth Young. Illustrated by Rachel Isadora. Viking, 1992. The rhyming text of this book is also written as a song on the endpapers. The illustrations show an African-American child and a golden teddy bear romping, reading, and playing together.

Ira Sleeps Over, written and illustrated by Bernard Waber. Houghton, 1972. Ira has a problem. He is going to sleep over at Reggie's house but doesn't know if he should bring his stuffed bear.

My Brown Bear Barney, by Dorothy Butler. Illustrated by Elizabeth Fuller. Greenwillow, 1989. A girl lists all the things she will take with her on various trips, always including her teddy bear. When she prepares for school, she does not include Barney on her list, but the illustrations show that Barney is included.

Peabody, written and illustrated by Rosemary Wells. Dial, 1983. Annie gets a new doll, and she ignores her stuffed bear, Peabody. When the doll breaks, she remembers her old friend and goes to him for comfort.

This Is the Bear, by Sarah Hayes. Illustrated by Helen Craig. Lippincott, 1986. In this rhyming story, a stuffed bear named Fred is involved in a series of mishaps. He falls in the trash and is taken away to the dump. His owner searches for him, finds him, and takes him home, where Fred keeps his adventure a secret from the other toys. (Condensed in *Primaryplots,* Bowker, 1989, pp. 95–97.)

This Is the Bear and the Picnic Lunch, by Sarah Hayes. Illustrated by Helen Craig. Little, Brown, 1988. In this rhyming book about Fred the teddy bear, Fred's owner prepares a picnic lunch, only to have the dog take the lunch and Fred.

About the Illustrator

CRAIG, HELEN

Something about the Author, ed. by Anne Commire. Gale, 1987, Vol. 46, p. 56; 1987, Vol. 49, pp. 75–77.

Joyce, William. *Bently & Egg*
Illus. by the author. Harper, 1992, LB (0-06-020386-2)
Suggested Use Level: Gr. K–2

Plot Summary

Bently Hopperton is an artistic frog who becomes responsible for an egg. Bently's friend Kack Kack, a duck, has gone to visit her sister, who has some new ducklings. Kack Kack has left Bently in charge of her own egg, which Bently has resented because it has diverted Kack Kack's attention from Bently and his art. At first, Bently does not accept much responsibility for the egg. He is disdainful of its drab exterior and decorates it, only to have it attract the attention of a little boy. The boy takes the egg, thinking it is an Easter egg. Bently's adventures to retrieve his egg take him on a balloon ride, to a little girl's room, and onto a lady's hat at an Easter egg party. When Bently finally escapes with the egg, its decorations have been washed away, and Bently has come to love the egg for itself, not for his decorations. Worn out from his adventures, Bently falls asleep. When he wakes up, Kack Kack has returned, and the egg has hatched. Kack Kack names her duckling Ben, after Bently.

Thematic Material

Bently is a very self-centered frog who becomes more aware of the needs of others and learns to care about those needs before his own. Bently's adventures as he tries to rescue the egg are very humorous.

Book Talk Material and Activities

In this imaginative fantasy, Bently has become responsible for Kack Kack's egg. Like Horton the elephant in *Horton Hatches the Egg*, Bently makes sacrifices and takes risks to make sure the egg is safe. Many books show characters who take responsibility for smaller creatures. In *Horton Hears a Who!*, Horton the elephant risks his own life to protect the Whos.

The Ernest and Celestine books describe the relationship between a large bear and a dainty childlike mouse.

Much of the humor in *Bently and Egg* is conveyed through the personality of Bently. He is a very selfish and conceited frog. He loves his own singing and drawing; he loves being the center of attention. A group of second graders heard this story read aloud several times. When they were asked to describe Bently, they talked about how he demanded attention and how he pouted when Kack Kack and his other friends ignored him. They liked that Bently is depicted wearing clothes (a white shirt and a pink vest) and small round glasses that sit on his wide frog nose. They enjoyed the light colors and the changing perspectives of the illustrations.

When they were asked to name some other characters that they thought were funny, they suggested *George and Martha*, Miss Viola Swamp in *Miss Nelson Has a Field Day*, Pinkerton, and *The Cat in the Hat*. They especially liked books in which everyday situations were disrupted, as when Pinkerton visited the museum in *Prehistoric Pinkerton* and the Cat in the Hat came into the house.

Related Titles

The Cat in the Hat, written and illustrated by Dr. Seuss. Random, 1957. The cat nearly destroys the house when he comes to visit on a rainy day. Children enjoy the rhyming text and the unexpected events.

Ernest and Celestine, written and illustrated by Gabrielle Vincent. Greenwillow, 1982. Ernest protects and looks after little Celestine. When she loses her toy, he finds a way to replace it. Other books about these two friends include *Bravo, Ernest and Celestine* (Greenwillow, 1982) and *Feel Better, Ernest!* (Greenwillow, 1988).

George and Martha, written and illustrated by James Marshall. Houghton, 1972. This is the first book about these two hippo friends. In this book, George gets his gold tooth. *George and Martha Back in Town* (Houghton, 1984), is condensed in *Primaryplots* (Bowker, 1989), pp. 144–146.

Horton Hatches the Egg, written and illustrated by Dr. Seuss. Random, 1940. Horton promises to watch Maisie's egg while she takes a vacation. When the egg hatches, Horton is rewarded for his dependability.

Horton Hears a Who!, written and illustrated by Dr. Seuss. Random, 1954. Horton protects the Whos, even though they are so small that no one else believes they exist.

Miss Nelson Has a Field Day, written and illustrated by Harry Allard and James Marshall. Houghton, 1985. Is Miss Nelson really Miss Viola

Swamp? For a while, it appears that she is not, but careful observers will figure it out.

Prehistoric Pinkerton, written and illustrated by Steven Kellogg. Dial, 1987. Pinkerton is teething, so it is a big mistake to take him to the exhibit of dinosaur bones at the museum. (Condensed in *Primaryplots,* Bowker, 1989, pp. 137–140.)

About the Author and Illustrator

JOYCE, WILLIAM

Sixth Book of Junior Authors and Illustrators, ed. by Sally Holmes Holtze. Wilson, 1989, pp. 152–153.

Something about the Author, ed. by Anne Commire. Gale, 1987, Vol. 46, p. 122.

Kasza, Keiko.   *The Pigs' Picnic*

Illus. by the author. Putnam, 1988 (0-399-21543-3); pap. (0-399-21883-1)

Suggested Use Level: Gr. K–2

Plot Summary

Mr. Pig is planning a picnic with Miss Pig. To impress her, he is bringing her a flower. On his way to her house, he meets Fox, who gives Mr. Pig his tail. He continues and meets Lion, who gives Mr. Pig his mane. Next, he sees Zebra, who gives Mr. Pig his stripes. When he reaches Miss Pig's house, she opens the door and is frightened by the "monster." Mr. Pig returns all the items to their owners and then goes back to Miss Pig's house. She is relieved to see a familiar face and is delighted to go on a picnic with him.

Thematic Material

This is a humorous story with pigs as the main characters. The theme "Be yourself" applies to this book.

Book Talk Material and Activities

There are many humorous books about pigs. Organizing a program around these books could lead to a discussion about the humor of having animals in human situations. What is funny about a pig, and how does each author capitalize on these elements? One group of first graders felt that pigs were funny because they are fat and because they have snouts. In *The Pig's Picnic*, the author/illustrator added features from other animals, so the pig became even more amusing to look at. The illustrations of the animals who loaned their features to Mr. Pig were also very funny, especially the lion without his mane. In *Pigs in Hiding*, the situation was funny because the pig who was "it" could not find the other pigs, even though they were in view. The books about Pig Pig are also very funny, particularly *Pig Pig Grows Up*, where he will not admit to being too big for his baby things. *The Book of Pigericks* and the books about Piggins (including *Picnic with Piggins*) would also add to this humorous program.

Several books could relate to the theme of "Be yourself" that correlates with *The Pigs' Picnic*. Bill Peet has written some books in which the characters wish to be something they are not. When Scamp becomes *The Whing-dingdilly* he finds he is not happy, and when *Ella* the elephant leaves the circus, she learns different is not always better. Eric Carle's *The Mixed-Up Chameleon* also relates to this theme, as does *Hey, Al!*

Audiovisual Adaptation

The Pigs' Picnic. American School Publishers, cassette/book, 1990; filmstrip/cassette, 1990; videorecording, 1990.

Related Titles

The Book of Pigericks: Pig Limericks, written and illustrated by Arnold Lobel. Harper, 1983. Children like limericks. Lobel's fancy pigs and inventive humor are delightful.

Ella, written and illustrated by Bill Peet. Houghton, 1964. Ella the elephant is the star of the circus. When something at the circus annoys Ella, she hides and is left behind when the circus leaves town. Ella finds her new life is not what she expected.

Hey, Al!, by Arthur Yorinks. Illustrated by Richard Egielski. Farrar, 1986. Al is not happy with his life, but when he is taken to an island in the sky, he realizes that his life was not so bad. This book received the Caldecott Award in 1987.

The Mixed-Up Chameleon, written and illustrated by Eric Carle. Crowell, 1984. At the zoo, the chameleon sees many different animals. He wishes he could have some feature from each animal—and his wishes are granted. Eventually, the chameleon wishes to be himself again.

Picnic with Piggins, by Jane Yolen. Illustrated by Jane Dyer. Harcourt,

1988. Piggins' picnic is very different from Mr. Pig's. It appears that Rexy Reynard, a young fox, has been kit-napped. Will Piggins solve this mystery? Of course!

Pig Pig Grows Up, written and illustrated by David McPhail. Dutton, 1980. In this first book about Pig Pig, he has outgrown his crib, baby clothes, high chair, and stroller, but he insists on being "the baby." It takes a real baby to get Pig Pig to act his age.

Pigs in Hiding, written and illustrated by Arlene Dubanevich. Four Winds, 1983. A group of pigs play a game of hide-and-seek. The pig who is "it" counts to 100 and then begins to look for the other pigs. (Condensed in *Primaryplots,* Bowker, 1989, pp. 123–125.)

The Whingdingdilly, written and illustrated by Bill Peet. Houghton, 1970. Scamp is not happy being a dog. When a witch changes him into a "whingdingdilly," he is even more unhappy. Scamp learns he should have been satisfied being himself.

Kimmel, Eric A.   *I Took My Frog to the Library*
Illus. by Blanche Sims. Viking, 1990 (0-670-82418-6)
Suggested Use Level: PreS–Gr. 1

Plot Summary

Bridgett takes her animal friends to the library, including a frog, a hen, a pelican, a python, a giraffe, a hyena, and an elephant. Each animal causes a problem in some area of the library, such as jumping on the checkout desk or laughing too much during the story. At the end, Bridgett leaves her animals at home, where her elephant reads stories to them.

Thematic Material

This book offers a humorous introduction to the library and its resources.

Book Talk Material and Activities

I Took My Frog to the Library was featured at a special program for preschoolers at the public school library. This program, held in the spring, allowed parents with young children to visit the local elementary school.

The librarian worked with the Parent Teacher Organization to encourage families to get to know the public school. The young children enjoyed the humorous events in *I Took My Frog to the Library*. As a follow-up, the librarian asked if they thought there were really frogs, giraffes or other animals in the library. She took them on a tour of the places mentioned in the book, and there were books displayed at every location—frog books at the checkout desk, books about hens at the card catalog, and so on. The children and their parents got to move around the library and look at some of the other resources that were available.

After sharing *I Took My Frog to the Library*, the librarian showed some other book about experiences at school, including *School Days*, *Spot Goes to School*, and *School Bus*. They talked about some of the supplies they would need for school, such as pencils, paper, a backpack, and a lunch box. The librarian read *I Need a Lunch Box*, in which a young boy dreams about having a different imaginative lunch box for every day of the week, such as a blue whale-shaped lunch box for Wednesday. The children were given paper to draw their own imaginative lunch boxes, which were then displayed in the library. The program ended with the children and their parents singing *The Wheels on the Bus*.

Related Titles

Annabelle Swift, Kindergartner, written and illustrated by Amy Schwartz. Orchard, 1988. Before Annabelle starts school, her older sister, Lucy, coaches her in some school activities. When Annabelle gets to school, she finds Lucy's suggestions are not that helpful.

I Need a Lunch Box, by Jeannette Caines. Illustrated by Pat Cummings. Harper, 1988. When his older sister gets a new lunch box, a young boy dreams of a different, colorful lunch box for each day of the week.

School Bus, written and illustrated by Donald Crews. Greenwillow, 1984. This book describes a typical day for some school buses. (Condensed in *Primaryplots*, Bowker, 1989, pp. 83–85.)

School Days, by B. G. Hennessy. Illustrated by Tracey Campbell Pearson. Viking, 1990. An activity-filled day at school is described in this book.

Spot Goes to School, written and illustrated by Eric Hill. Putnam, 1984. Spot the dog and his animal friends enjoy the many activities at school.

The Wheels on the Bus, written and illustrated by Marilyn Kovalski. Joy Street Books, 1987. This popular song is presented as part of a story about a grandmother and her grandchildren on a shopping trip.

About the Author

KIMMEL, ERIC
Something about the Author, ed. by Anne Commire. Gale, 1978, Vol. 13, pp. 120–121.

Levine, Evan.   *Not the Piano, Mrs. Medley!*

Illus. by S. D. Schindler. Orchard, 1991, LB (0-531-08556-2)
Suggested Use Level: Gr. K–2

Plot Summary

Max is visiting his grandmother, Mrs. Medley, at her new home. She decides they should go to the beach, and she begins organizing their supplies. Max, Mrs. Medley, and her dog, Word, start to walk to the beach when Mrs. Medley decides they might need to be prepared for rain. She heads back home and fetches rain gear. As they start out again, Mrs. Medley thinks they may want toys, so they return to the house for toys, including a Monopoly game and a table and chairs. The next time they start out, they go back for music. As they start for the beach again, Mrs. Medley is ready to go back for something else, but Max has had enough. He insists they continue. This time, they reach the beach, and Mrs. Medley is enchanted. Max tries to get her to use some of the items they have brought, but she is fascinated by the sights, sounds, smell, and feel of the beach. She admits they did not need everything they brought, and she promises that she will not pack so much for their trip to the park.

Thematic Material

In this humorous story, Mrs. Medley's need to be prepared almost keeps her from enjoying the beach with her grandson.

Book Talk Material and Activities

Is it a good idea to be organized? Is it a good idea to plan ahead? A group of first graders felt that organization and planning are important. After hearing *Not the Piano, Mrs. Medley!* they decided you could have too much of a good thing. One girl said, "You have to just pick what you really need." Another girl felt Mrs. Medley had "too many ideas." Several children mentioned *Curious George,* who has problems because he is too curious. As an activity, the children looked at a list of all the things Mrs.

Medley took to the beach. They suggested which ones were really needed. *At the Beach* and *On Our Vacation* added some realistic ideas for what might be taken.

In this book, Mrs. Medley takes too much with her. Children enjoyed choosing some other books in which characters decide what they need, like *My Brown Bear Barney* and *Now We Can Go*. The alphabet game, *I Unpacked My Grandmother's Trunk*, could also be correlated with *Not the Piano, Mrs. Medley!*

Related Titles

At the Beach, written and illustrated by Anne Rockwell and Harlow Rockwell. Macmillan, 1987. A young girl tells about her day at the beach, including what she takes and her activities.

Curious George, written and illustrated by H. A. Rey. Houghton, 1941. When the man with the yellow hat brings George to the city, George finds it difficult to stay out of trouble.

I Unpacked My Grandmother's Trunk: A Picture Book Game, written and illustrated by Susan Ramsey Hoguet. Dutton, 1983. This is an illustrated version of the popular alphabet game. As the trunk is unpacked, each new item that is shown begins with the next letter of the alphabet. (Condensed in *Primaryplots,* Bowker, 1989, pp. 101–103.)

My Brown Bear Barney, by Dorothy Butler. Illustrated by Elizabeth Fuller. Greenwillow, 1988. A little girl lists all the things she takes with her when she goes on outings, always including her stuffed bear.

Now We Can Go, written and illustrated by Ann Jonas. Greenwillow, 1986. For this trip, a child takes all the toys from the toy box. Look carefully at the illustrations and see what will be chosen next.

On Our Vacation, written and illustrated by Anne Rockwell. Dutton, 1989. The bear family plans their trip to the island. They take a lot with them too.

About the Illustrator

SCHINDLER, S. D.
Something about the Author, ed. by Anne Commire. Gale, 1988, Vol. 50, p. 188.

Lewis, J. Patrick. *A Hippopotamusn't and Other Animal Verses*
Illus. by Victoria Chess. Dial, 1990, LB (0-8037-0519-0)
Suggested Use Level: Gr. 1–4

Plot Summary

Thirty-five humorous poems depict a variety of animals. Included are poems about mammals (tomcat, giraffe, elephant, camel, yak, wolf, whale), birds (owl, pelican, hummingbird, rooster, robin), reptiles (snake, turtle), sea creatures (eel, oyster), and insects (praying mantis, dragonfly). Many of the poems rhyme and have a rhythmic pattern, but some use different poetic devices and structures. The poem about the flamingo is a concrete poem; "Penguins" is written in free verse; "How to Tell a Camel" creatively uses the layout of the type; "River-Lovers" describes a variety of river creatures with hyphenated or compound words.

Thematic Material

The humorous poems in this book feature a variety of poetic styles. This book could be featured in a poetry unit or could be enjoyed as children learn about animals.

Book Talk Material and Activities

Recently, several books have been published that feature animal poetry and word play. A book talk program could promote these books. Children enjoy joining in on the rhyme, rhythm, and repetition of poetry. They like to clap to the beat and chant the refrain. Often, they remember part of a poem after hearing it once. Reading some of the poems in *A Hippopotamusn't* would encourage children to look at the images other poets have used. Compare Lewis's description of a giraffe to the poem by Geoffrey Dearmer in *A Zooful of Animals* or to the one by Patricia Hubbell in *To the Zoo*. Or look at the pelican poem in *A Hippopotamusn't* and in Aileen Fisher's *Feathered Ones and Furry*. *To the Zoo*, Eric Carle's *Animals Animals*, and *A Hippopotamusn't* have poems about camels—what words are used to describe this animal in each poem?

In one fourth-grade class, the children worked in pairs to find poems on a similar topic. Some used the *Index to Poetry for Children and Young People,* while others just browsed through the collection. The librarian had pulled some poetry books from the shelves and placed them around the room. Among the poetry books about animals there was *A Hippopotamusn't, Eric Carle's Animals Animals,* and *To the Zoo.* After the partners found some poems, they practiced reading them aloud and then shared them with the class.

Related Titles

Animals Galore!, written and illustrated by Patricia McCarthy. Dial, 1989. Descriptive words gather animals into groups, like "a colony of penguins."

Eric Carle's Animals Animals, collected by Laura Whipple. Illustrated by Eric Carle. Philomel, 1989. The poems about animals in this book are illustrated with colorful collages by Eric Carle. Many students recognize his art from having enjoyed his picture book stories.

Feathered Ones and Furry, by Aileen Fisher. Illustrated by Eric Carle. Crowell, 1971. These poems are about animals, including the pelican, squirrel, robin, duck, and raccoon.

Herds of Words, written and illustrated by Patricia McCarthy. Dial, 1991. Creative descriptions of groups of animals, peoples, and habitats are presented in this book, including "a stand of flamingos" and "a cloud of flies."

Index to Poetry for Children and Young People, 1982–1987: A Title, Subject, Author, and First Line Index to Poetry in Collections for Children and Young People, compiled by G. Meredith Blackburn III. Wilson, 1989. Children find the subject groupings of poems especially helpful when they are looking for poems to correlate with topics they are studying.

On the Farm: Poems, selected by Lee Bennett Hopkins. Illustrated by Laurel Molk. Little, Brown, 1991. This collection of poems about the farm include some about animals (cow, rooster, pig, foal) and also some about life on the farm, including David McCord's "The Pickety Fence" and William Carlos Williams's "The Red Wheelbarrow."

To the Zoo: Animal Poems, selected by Lee Bennett Hopkins. Illustrated by John Wallner. Little, Brown, 1992. The nineteen poems in this collection highlight animals at the zoo, including the camel, giraffe, seal, and hippo.

A Zooful of Animals, selected by William Cole. Illustrated by Lynn Munsinger. Houghton, 1992. Forty-five poems describe different animals, including the giraffe, the chameleon, seals, and the raccoon.

About the Author

LEWIS, J. PATRICK
Something about the Author, ed. by Donna Olendorf. Gale, 1992, Vol. 69, pp. 135–136.

About the Illustrator

CHESS, VICTORIA
Illustrators of Children's Books: 1967–1976, Vol. IV, comp. by Lee Kingman, Grace Allen
    Hogarth, and Harriet Quimby. Horn Book, 1978, pp. 107, 183.
Sixth Book of Junior Authors and Illustrators, ed. by Sally Holmes Holtze. Wilson, 1989, pp.
    55–56.
Something about the Author, ed. by Anne Commire. Gale, 1983, Vol. 33, pp. 48–50.
Talking with Artists, ed. by Pat Cummings. Bradbury, 1992, pp. 10–15.

Marshall, James.   *Fox Outfoxed*
   Illus. by the author. Dial, 1992, LB (0-8037-1037-2)
   Suggested Use Level: Gr. 1–3

Plot Summary

There are three stories in this book, and each one shows Fox being too clever for his own good. In "A Faster Fox," Fox decides to enter the car race, and he wins, until the official finds out why Fox's car was so fast. Fox loses some of his favorite comic books in "Comic Fox." "Fox Outfoxed" takes place on Halloween. Fox's sister, Louise, tricks Fox into thinking she has turned into a pumpkin.

Thematic Material

The books about Fox and his family and friends are filled with humor. Fox often ends up in foolish situations.

Book Talk Material and Activities

Children love to read the beginning reader books about Fox. *Fox Outfoxed* is a recent entry in this series, which includes *Fox All Week, Fox Be Nimble, Fox on Wheels,* and the first book about Fox, *Fox and His Friends.* The format for all these books is similar. There are several vignettes in each book. The chapter format and large, well-spaced print make these books accessible to beginning readers.

These humorous stories about Fox provide a perfect opportunity to look at the books by James Marshall and to talk about what makes a book funny. Marshall wrote and illustrated the delightful George and Martha books, as well as the series about Lolly, Spider, and Sam (beginning with *Three by the Sea*). He retold and illustrated several familiar folktales (receiving a Caldecott Honor award for *Goldilocks and the Three Bears*—see chapter 8). He wrote several books, including *Space Case* and some of the Fox books, under the name Edward Marshall. After examining many of Marshall's books, children begin to recognize some common elements. His characters often end up in zany situations; their clothing is unusual; they often make expressive exclamations. For example, Fox says "Rats!" and "Hot dog!" while his sister, Louise, says "Tra la!" When children look closely at an author's style, they frequently begin to incorporate similar features into their own writing. Studying James Marshall's books could lead children to experiment with humorous expressions and foolish situations.

Related Titles

Fox All Week, by Edward Marshall. Illustrated by James Marshall. Dial, 1984. There are seven short stories in this book, one for each day of the week. Librarians will enjoy "Wednesday Evening at the Library."

Fox and His Friends, by Edward Marshall. Illustrated by James Marshall. Dial, 1982. In one story, Fox is supposed to watch his sister, Louise. Another story shows Fox working as a traffic patrol guard.

Fox Be Nimble, written and illustrated by James Marshall. Dial, 1990. Fox loves to show off. In the last story, "Fox on Parade," the illustrations depict many familiar James Marshall characters, including chickens, who carry the band's banner, and marching cats and dogs.

Fox on Wheels, by Edward Marshall. Illustrated by James Marshall. Dial, 1983. The story "Fox and the Grapes" would be great to read along with the Aesop's fable.

George and Martha, written and illustrated by James Marshall. Houghton, 1972. In this first book in the series about these two hippo friends, there are five stories. The illustrations add to the humor. For example, in "The Tub," Martha stops George from peeking in when she is in the bathtub. The text does not say how, but the illustration shows George with a bathtub on his head. Children can find other examples in which the illustrations expand the text. *George and Martha Back in Town* (Houghton, 1984) is condensed in *Primaryplots* (Bowker, 1989), pp. 144–146.

Space Case, by Edward Marshall. Illustrated by James Marshall. Dial, 1980. It is Halloween, and a spaceship has landed on Earth. As everyone is in costume, no one pays any attention to it. Children can look at the picture at the breakfast table and see some funny details.

Three by the Sea, by Edward Marshall. Illustrated by James Marshall. Dial, 1981. Lolly, Spider, and Sam tell stories using the simplified vocabulary from their reading book. There are more adventures with these three friends in *Three up a Tree,* written and illustrated by James Marshall. Dial, 1986.

About the Author and Illustrator

MARSHALL, JAMES

Fourth Book of Junior Authors and Illustrators, ed. by Doris de Montreville and Elizabeth D. Crawford. Wilson, 1978, pp. 253–254.

Illustrators of Children's Books, 1967–1976, Vol. IV, comp. by Lee Kingman, Grace Allen Hogarth, and Harriet Quimby. Horn Book, 1978, pp. 5, 144, 201.

Something about the Author, ed. by Anne Commire. Gale, 1974, Vol. 6, pp. 160–161; 1988, Vol. 51, pp. 109–121.

Martin, Bill, Jr., and Archambault, John.   *Chicka Chicka Boom Boom*

Illus. by Lois Ehlert. Simon & Schuster, 1989 (0-671-67949-X); Big Book, DLM, 1989 (155924576-X)

Suggested Use Level: PreS–Gr. 1

Plot Summary

The lower-case letters of the alphabet are climbing the coconut tree. Each letter climbs in order, but when they are all in the tree, it is too crowded, and they fall out. The capital letters of the alphabet come to comfort the injured lower-case letters. The title, *Chicka Chicka Boom Boom,* is repeated throughout the text along with other rhythmic nonsense phrases.

Thematic Material

The humorous adventures of the lower-case letters are extended by the use of repetitive nonsense words. *Chicka Chicka Boom Boom* is a playful romp with the letters of the alphabet.

Book Talk Material and Activities

After hearing this story one time, young children chant "Chicka chicka boom boom." They demand that the book be read again and again. Soon they are joining in on other repeated phrases. Many children find they are reading much of the text from memory. This story is available as a Big Book and as a tape read by Ray Charles, which enhances its use with a large group. On the other side of the tape, John Archambault sings the words to the book and then talks about writing the book.

Books with repetition and rhyme are excellent choices for beginning readers. Children become familiar with the pattern of the words and join in from memory. Some children even memorize the complete text. For many children, this is an early experience with books and reading; it is one that allows them to behave like readers. *Mary Wore Her Red Dress and Henry Wore His Green Sneakers, Roll Over!,* and *Cat Goes Fiddle-i-Fee* are songs presented in picture books. *A Dark, Dark Tale* and *Hattie and the Fox* use repetition within the story. In *My Brown Bear Barney,* a girl lists items (shown in the illustrations) that she will take with her, including her teddy bear. In the text and illustrations, these books provide support for beginning readers.

Audiovisual Adaptation

Chicka Chicka Boom Boom, Simon & Schuster, cassette/book, 1991.

Related Titles

Cat Goes Fiddle-i-Fee, adapted and illustrated by Paul Galdone. Clarion, 1985. The rhyme is also a song, in which animals appear in sequence and make noises. Some are familiar, such as the dog's "Bow-wow"; others, such as the goose's "Swishy, swashy," are not so familiar. Many children like to follow the pattern of the rhyme.

A Dark, Dark Tale, written and illustrated by Ruth Brown. Dial, 1981. There are many spooky images in the dark, sinister pictures and text of this familiar story.

Hattie and the Fox, by Mem Fox. Illustrated by Patricia Mullins. Bradbury, 1987. Hattie the hen sees something suspicious in the bushes, and she tries to warn her barnyard friends. Their unconcerned responses are repeated after each new warning from Hattie. (Condensed in *Primaryplots,* Bowker, 1989, pp. 126–127.)

Mary Wore Her Red Dress and Henry Wore His Green Sneakers, adapted and illustrated by Merle Peek. Clarion, 1985. In this song about clothes, including green shoes, purple pants, and violet ribbons, young children can learn about colors too. The musical arrangement is included.

My Brown Bear Barney, by Dorothy Butler. Illustrated by Elizabeth Fuller. Greenwillow, 1989. A girl lists the items that she will take with her, always including Barney, her teddy bear.

Roll Over!, written and illustrated by Mordicai Gerstein. Crown, 1984. In this story, a little boy keeps pushing animals out of his bed. The pattern of this story is easy to remember. Children enjoy opening the folded pages to see who falls out of the bed.

THUMP, THUMP, Rat-a-Tat-Tat, by Gene Baer. Illustrated by Lois Ehlert. Harper, 1989. A marching band is on parade. Colors and sound words fill the pages, coming closer and growing louder, then moving away and becoming quieter. This book could correlate with units on shapes and colors.

About the Authors

ARCHAMBAULT, JOHN

Sixth Book of Junior Authors and Illustrators, ed. by Sally Holmes Holtze. Wilson, 1989, pp. 19–20.

MARTIN, BILL, JR. (WILLIAM IVAN MARTIN)

Sixth Book of Junior Authors and Illustrators, ed. by Sally Holmes Holtze. Wilson, 1989, pp. 188–189.

Something about the Author, ed. by Anne Commire. Gale, 1985, Vol. 40, p. 128; ed. by Donna Olendorf, Gale, 1992, Vol. 67, pp. 120–125.

About the Illustrator

EHLERT, LOIS

Illustrators of Children's Books: 1957–1966, comp. by Lee Kingman, Grace Allen Hogarth, and Harriet Quimby. Horn Book, 1968, pp. 103, 203, 216; *1967–1976, Vol. IV,* 1978, pp. 116, 187.

Something about the Author, ed. by Anne Commire. Gale, 1984, Vol. 35, pp. 97–98; ed. by Donna Olendorf, Gale, 1992, Vol. 69, pp. 50–53.

Talking with Artists, comp. and ed. by Pat Cummings. Bradbury, 1992, pp. 36–41.

Martin, Sarah Catherine. *Old Mother Hubbard and Her Wonderful Dog*

Illus. by James Marshall. Farrar, 1991 (0-374-35621-1)
Suggested Use Level: PreS–Gr. 1

Plot Summary

The familiar nursery rhyme about Old Mother Hubbard looking for items for her dog is illustrated with humorous cartoon-style drawings by James Marshall.

Thematic Material

Nursery rhymes are a familiar experience for many young children. The illustrations for this version of *Old Mother Hubbard and Her Wonderful Dog* are filled with humorous details.

Book Talk Material and Activities

This version of the familiar nursery rhyme is a great choice to compare with other versions. Comparing several versions works well as an activity for a small group of children. The rhyming text is very memorable, and even students who are not yet able to read can remember some of the text and follow along, especially with the help of their classmates. One group of first graders listed the Old Mother Hubbard's locations and activities in four of the books.

Comparisons of *Old Mother Hubbard*
What is alike and what is different?

Marshall	*dePaola*	*Lobel*	*Galdone*
cupboard	cupboard	cupboard	cupboard
baker's	baker's	baker's	baker's
undertaker's	undertaker's	undertaker's	joiner's
clean dish	clean dish	clean dish	clean dish
fishmonger's	fishmonger's	fishmonger's	fishmonger's
———	———	———	alehouse
tavern	tavern	tavern	tavern
fruiterer's	fruiterer's	fruiterer's	hatter's
tailor's	tailor's	tailor's	barber's
hatter's	hatter's	hatter's	fruiterer's
barber's	barber's	barber's	tailor's
cobbler's	cobbler's	cobbler's	cobbler's
seamstress	seamstress	seamstress	sempstress
hosier's	hosier's	hosier's	hosier's

They looked at the different ways each illustrator depicted the dog: James Marshall drew a gruff bulldog, Tomie dePaola drew a bright orange poodle, Arnold Lobel drew a very little white dog, and Paul Galdone drew a shaggy gray mutt. They even voted on their favorite version, picking Lobel's version because, as one child said, "The dog is little and he is smiling." They enjoyed some of the other features in these books, including the humorous details in James Marshall's illustrations and the stage setting and other nursery rhyme characters in Tomie dePaola's version. These children looked for other versions of this rhyme and also looked at other books of other nursery rhymes. Their familiarity with many of the rhymes made it possible for them to read these books.

Related Titles

The Comic Adventures of Old Mother Hubbard and Her Dog, illustrated by Tomie dePaola. Harcourt, 1981. An orange poodle and Old Mother Hubbard put on a play of this rhyme. In the audience are other nursery rhyme characters, including Mother Goose.

The Comic Adventures of Old Mother Hubbard and Her Dog, illustrated by Arnold Lobel. Bradbury, 1968. Lobel's illustrations and the small size of this book make this version of the familiar rhyme a good one to share with small groups.

James Marshall's Mother Goose, illustrated by James Marshall. Farrar, 1979. The first verse of "Old Mother Hubbard" is illustrated here. How does it compare to James Marshall's picture book of this rhyme?

Old Mother Hubbard, illustrated by Alice Provensen and Martin Provensen. Random, 1977. This book features a hound dog, and the illustrations have many humorous details. Children could add this to their chart of other versions of this rhyme.

Old Mother Hubbard and Her Dog, illustrated by Paul Galdone. McGraw-Hill, 1960. There is an old-fashioned feeling to the words and pictures in this book. In the comparison, this book has several differences.

Old Mother Hubbard and Her Dog, illustrated by Eveline Ness. Holt, 1972. Another version of this rhyme in format of a picture book. In this book, the dog is a large, shaggy sheep dog.

The Random House Book of Mother Goose, selected and illustrated by Arnold Lobel. Random, 1986. Arnold Lobel has different illustrations for this version of "Old Mother Hubbard." Compare these to the drawings for the picture book version.

About the Illustrator

MARSHALL, JAMES

Fourth Book of Junior Authors and Illustrators, ed. by Doris de Montreville and Elizabeth D. Crawford. Wilson, 1978, pp. 253–254.

Illustrators of Children's Books, 1967–1976, Vol. IV, comp. by Lee Kingman, Grace Allen Hogarth, and Harriet Quimby. Horn Book, 1978, pp. 5, 144, 201.

Something about the Author, ed. by Anne Commire. Gale, 1974, Vol. 6, pp. 160–161; 1988, Vol. 51, pp. 109–121.

McKissack, Patricia C.   *A Million Fish . . . More or Less*
Illus. by Dena Schutzer. Knopf, 1992, LB (0-679-90692-4)
Suggested Use Level: Gr. 2–4

Plot Summary

On the Bayou Clapateaux, young Hugh Thomas is fishing. Papa-Daddy and Elder Abbajon come by and begin to tell him some wild tales of their adventures in the Bayou. One time they caught a turkey that weighed five hundred pounds. Carrying it home, they found a lamp from 1542—still burning. Then they met a snake with legs and were attacked by giant mosquitoes. They got away, but they lost the turkey and the lamp. After the two men leave, Hugh Thomas catches some fish—a million of them. He plans to take them home, but Atoo the alligator demands his share, so Hugh gives him half. Then Hugh meets an army of raccoons and their leader, Mosley. Again, he loses half his fish, even though he wins a jumping contest. As he nears his home, more of his fish are taken, first by some fish crows, then by some cats. Back home, he only has three fish left, but they are just enough for dinner. He begins to tell his story to Papa-Daddy and Elder Abbajon, realizing that he now has his own tall tale about the Bayou.

Thematic Material

Telling stories, especially exaggerated tales, is featured in *A Million Fish . . . More or Less*. It could spark a discussion of tall tales and encourage children to create their own unusual stories.

Book Talk Material and Activities

Many children enjoy learning and telling favorite stories. They enjoy dramatizing characters and exaggerating events. *A Million Fish . . . More or Less* would fit into a program on telling stories. The Bayou Clapateaux is described as a strange place where unusual things happen. The stories the characters tell could be as a result of the Bayou, or the characters could be exaggerating what is happening, trying to tell the best story. Hugh Thomas seems to be following the tradition of creating outlandish stories like those he has heard from Papa-Daddy and Elder Abbajon. Other stories of the Bayou and swamp, like *Mama Don't Allow* and *Wiley and the Hairy Man*, build on this tradition.

Telling stories is a part of many books, often showing a respect for the past. In *Knots on a Counting Rope*, a young Native American boy listens to the stories his grandfather tells him and prepares to be a storyteller himself. The little girl in *Tell Me a Story, Mama*, demands to hear stories about when her mother was growing up. *A Story, A Story*, an African folktale, begins with Ananse as the storyteller describing how he earned the Sky God's stories. It answers a question about how stories came to Earth. Books about telling stories would be fun to booktalk along with *A Million Fish . . . More or Less*.

The exaggerations in *A Million Fish . . . More or Less* lead naturally to a look at tall tales. *Larger Than Life* and *American Tall Tales* are two recent collection of tall tales that "stretch the truth." Children enjoy creating their own stories. It is fun to have them start with a simple premise, such as a child going home from school—like Marco in *And to Think That I Saw It on Mulberry Street*—and then add outlandish details. Many children enjoy telling exaggerated stories about themselves after reading some tall tales.

Related Titles

American Tall Tales, by Mary Pope Osborne. Illustrated by Michael McCurdy. Knopf, 1991. Tall tale characters, including Pecos Bill and Paul Bunyan, are featured, along with some real people, such as Johnny Appleseed.

And to Think That I Saw It on Mulberry Street, written and illustrated by Dr. Seuss. Vanguard, 1937. Marco's trip to school is uneventful. His story about his trip is fantastic.

Knots on a Counting Rope, by Bill Martin, Jr., and John Archambault. Illustrated by Ted Rand. Holt, 1987. Boy-Strength-of-Blue-Horses sits with his grandfather and asks for the story about himself. The boy and his grandfather remember and celebrate the past. (Condensed in *Primaryplots*, Bowker, 1989, pp. 61–63.)

Larger Than Life: The Adventures of American Legendary Heroes, by Robert D. San Souci. Illustrated by Andrew Glass. Doubleday, 1991. Five stories are included: "John Henry," "Old Stormalong," "Slue-Foot Sue and Pecos Bill," "Strap Buckner," and "Paul Bunyan and Babe the Blue Ox."

Mama Don't Allow: Starring Miles and the Swamp Band, written and illustrated by Thacher Hurd. Harper, 1984. Miles and his pals play music for the Alligator Ball, and they almost become the dinner at the Alligator Ball too.

A Story, A Story, retold and illustrated by Gail E. Haley. Atheneum, 1970. Ananse, a storyteller, tells about how he won his stories from the Sky God.

Tell Me a Story, Mama, by Angela Johnson. Illustrated by David Soman. Orchard, 1989. A girl wants to hear stories about when her mother was young, including a story about a mean old lady and a story about finding a puppy. Children could think about some of their own stories after hearing these.

Wiley and the Hairy Man, adapted from an American folktale and illustrated by Molly Bang. Macmillan, 1976. Wiley and his mother must outwit the Hairy Man. This story has the feel of life in the Deep South.

About the Author

McKissack, Patricia C.
Something about the Author, ed. by Anne Commire. Gale, 1988, Vol. 51, p. 122.

Noble, Trinka Hakes.   *Jimmy's Boa and the Big Splash Birthday Bash*
Illus. by Steven Kellogg. Dial, 1989, LB (0-8037-0540-9)
Suggested Use Level: Gr. K–2

Plot Summary

When Meggie returns home from a trip to SeaLand, her mother wonders why she is wet. Meggie calmly tells her about being in a whale's mouth, hiding from sharks, diving into the big water tank to look for Jimmy's goldfish and to rescue Jimmy's mother, getting bumped by seals, and playing with penguins. Jimmy, Meggie, and all their friends end up at a birthday party at Jimmy's house with lots of new goldfish, an octopus, and, of course, Jimmy's boa.

Thematic Material

The improbable events that happen to Jimmy and his boa add to the humor of this story. This book could also be included in a program featuring birthdays.

Book Talk Material and Activities

Like other books about Jimmy and his boa, this book uses exaggeration and slapstick adventures to add to the humor. Having Meggie, one of Jimmy's friends, tell the story bit by bit makes the antics of Jimmy and his friends even more amusing. Meggie's mother reacts to each new bit of information with increasing alarm and disbelief. Meggie tells the story somewhat out of sequence, and children could list the events in the story and try to put them into a more logical sequence. Children would also enjoy telling or writing their own exaggerated stories. After sharing *Jimmy's Boa and the Big Splash Birthday Bash*, librarians and teachers may want to booktalk *If You Give a Mouse a Cookie* and *If You Give a Moose a Muffin*, two books that describe the humorous sequence of events that result from some simple gestures of friendship. Reeve Lindbergh's *The Day the Goose Got Loose* is another story of improbable events. And the books by James Stevenson about Grandpa, Louie, and Mary Ann, such as *What's Under My Bed?* are filled with exaggerated humor.

Librarians and teachers could read or booktalk the other "Jimmy's Boa" books (*The Day Jimmy's Boa Ate the Wash* and *Jimmy's Boat Bounces Back*). These books could be used to introduce book series in which the same characters appear in different books. Many children feel comfortable reading books about familiar characters, and they enjoy finding out there are other books available.

Related Titles

Arthur's Birthday, written and illustrated by Marc Brown. Little, Brown, 1989. Arthur's friends have a problem. Should they go to Arthur's party or to Muffy's?

The Day Jimmy's Boa Ate the Wash, by Trinka Hakes Noble. Illustrated by Steven Kellogg. Dial, 1980. This is the first book about Jimmy and his boa.

Jimmy's friend Meggie describes the havoc that occurs on a class trip to the farm.

The Day the Goose Got Loose, by Reeve Lindbergh. Illustrated by Steven Kellogg. Dial, 1990. In this rhyming text, a runaway goose causes consternation on the farm.

If You Give a Moose a Muffin, by Laura Joffe Numeroff. Illustrated by Felicia Bond. Harper, 1991. After the moose gets a muffin, he wants jam. When there is no more jam, he wants to go to the store, which leads to a series of surprising activities.

If You Give a Mouse a Cookie, by Laura Joffe Numeroff. Illustrated by Felicia Bond. Harper, 1985. Things seem to get out of hand just because a mouse wanted a cookie.

Jimmy's Boa Bounces Back, by Trinka Hakes Noble. Illustrated by Steven Kellogg. Dial, 1984. Meggie's mother wears Jimmy's boa to the garden club party. The ladies are not amused, but young readers will be.

What's Under My Bed?, written and illustrated by James Stevenson. Greenwillow, 1983. After hearing a scary story from Grandpa, Mary Ann and Louie go to bed and wonder about the shadows and noises. (Condensed in *Primaryplots,* Bowker, 1989, pp. 152–154.)

About the Author

NOBLE, TRINKA HAKES

Sixth Book of Junior Authors and Illustrators, ed. by Sally Holmes Holtze. Wilson, 1989, pp. 209–210.
Something about the Author, ed. by Anne Commire. Gale, 1985, Vol. 37, p. 144.

About the Illustrator

KELLOGG, STEVEN

Fourth Book of Junior Authors and Illustrators, ed. by Doris de Montreville and Elizabeth D. Crawford. Wilson, 1978, pp. 208–209.
Illustrators of Children's Books: 1967–1976, Vol. IV, comp. by Lee Kingman, Grace Allen Hogarth, and Harriet Quimby. Horn Book, 1978, pp. 136, 196.
Something about the Author, ed. by Anne Commire. Gale, 1976, Vol. 8, pp. 95–97; Gale, 1989, Vol. 57, pp. 88–97.
Talking with Artists, comp. and ed. by Pat Cummings. Bradbury, 1992, pp. 54–59.

Rosen, Michael, reteller. *We're Going on a Bear Hunt*
Illus. by Helen Oxenbury. McElderry, 1989 (0-689-50476-4); pap.,
Aladdin (0-689-71653-2)
Suggested Use Level: PreS–Gr. 1

Plot Summary
The familiar Bear Hunt adventure is expanded as four children and
their father go through the grass, the river, the mud, the forest, a snowstorm, and finally through a cave, where they meet a bear. The bear
chases them back through all these places until the family is safe at home
under the covers. As the family passes through each area, words are
chanted to imitate the sounds of their movements, like "swishy swashy"
through the grass and "squelch squerch" through the mud.

Thematic Material
Children enjoy playing games. This book encourages participation in a
new version of a familiar activity.

Book Talk Material and Activities
Young children enjoy active participation with books. *We're Going on a
Bear Hunt* provides a familiar game in a book format. Many children will
join in with the very first book sharing. They will chant along with the
repeated phrases and act out the rhymes. They can suggest other places
the family could go and other sounds they might hear. By dramatizing this
book, children develop a familiarity with the sequence of events. Rosen's
creative use of sound words encourages children to experiment with words
and sounds. Quentin Blake's *All Join In* (elsewhere in this chapter) could
be shared as part of a book talk program on books that invite participation,
as could *A My Name Is Alice* by Jane Bayer. Other activity books, such as
Marc Brown's *Finger Rhymes*, Tom Glazer's finger-play books, and the play
rhymes collected by Joanna Cole and Stephanie Calmenson in *Pat-a-Cake*,
could be displayed.

Related Titles
A My Name Is Alice, by Jane Bayer. Illustrated by Steven Kellogg. Dial,
1984. This popular game encourages readers to invent their own names,
places, and occupations for each letter of the alphabet.

All Join In, written and illustrated by Quentin Blake. The seven poems in this collection invite participation. The rhymes and repetition focus on sounds like "beep-beep" and "quack quack quack" (elsewhere in this chapter).

Do Your Ears Hang Low? Fifty More Musical Fingerplays, by Tom Glazer. Illustrated by Mila Lazarevich. Doubleday, 1980. Fifty finger plays and rhymes set to music. This is a companion to *Eye Winker, Tom Tinker, Chin Chopper.*

Eye Winker, Tom Tinker, Chin Chopper: Fifty Musical Fingerplays, by Tom Glazer. Illustrated by Ronald Himler. Doubleday, 1973. Clear illustrations and musical arrangements for finger plays, action poems, and songs are provided.

Finger Rhymes, collected and illustrated by Marc Brown. Dutton, 1980. A clearly presented collection of fun and familiar finger plays.

Pat-a-Cake and Other Play Rhymes, compiled by Joanna Cole and Stephanie Calmenson. Illustrated by Alan Tiegreen. Morrow, 1992. These rhymes encourage active participation. Included are some well-known finger rhymes and hand rhymes as well as sections entitled "Face Rhymes" and "Tickling Rhymes."

Roar and More, written and illustrated by Karla Kuskin. Harper, 1990. Animals and their sounds are featured in the poems in this book. Included are a lion, an elephant, a tiger, a snake, two kangaroos, some fish, a cat, some dogs, a bee, a mouse, and a giraffe.

About the Author

ROSEN, MICHAEL

Something about the Author, ed. by Anne Commire. Gale, 1985, Vol. 40, p. 192; Gale, 1987, Vol. 48, pp. 196–198.

About the Illustrator

OXENBURY, HELEN

Illustrators of Children's Books: 1967–1976, Vol. IV, comp. by Lee Kingman, Grace Allen Hogarth, and Harriet Quimby. Horn Book, 1978, pp. 20, 36, 37, 38, 148–149, 203.

Something about the Author, ed. by Anne Commire. Gale, 1972, Vol. 3, pp. 150–152; ed. by Donna Olendorf, Gale, 1992, Vol. 68, pp. 173–177.

Third Book of Junior Authors, ed. by Doris de Montreville and Donna Hill. Wilson, 1972, pp. 217–218.

Shaw, Nancy. *Sheep in a Shop*
Illus. by Margot Apple. Houghton, 1991 (0-395-53681-2)
Suggested Use Level: PreS–Gr. 2

Plot Summary

Five sheep shop for a birthday gift. The rhyming text describes what they see in the country store, including blocks and clocks, trains and planes. Choosing to buy a beach ball, the sheep knock over the display. When they try to pay for their beach ball, the sheep do not have enough money. Using their wits and their wool, they trade their fleeces (three bags full) for the ball. Back home, the sheep celebrate at a birthday picnic for another sheep.

Thematic Material

The adventures of these sheep are very funny. There is humor in the rhymes and in the illustrations.

Book Talk Material and Activities

This is the third book about these sheep, and all three are full of fun. In *Sheep in a Shop*, the sheep blunder inside the country store. They create chaos as they try out possible gifts, including tennis rackets. The illustrations have many humorous details. On the title page, two of the sheep look through baskets of woolen goods, perhaps checking the finished work that started with their fleeces. In the shop, there are some alphabet blocks that sometimes spell out messages like "HI" and "OOPS." On the shearing page, one sheep checks the trim with a hand-held mirror. In *Sheep on a Ship*, there is humor in the incongruity of seeing sheep dressed as pirates trying (unsuccessfully) to sail a ship. *Sheep in a Jeep* is the first book that places these six sheep in an unexpected, and humorous, setting. A new book, *Sheep Out to Eat*, follows the sheep to out to tea.

Sheep in a Shop could also be included in a program featuring birthday stories, including *Aunt Nina and Her Nephews and Nieces, Happy Birthday, Sam,* and *Jimmy's Boa and the Big Splash Birthday Bash* (elsewhere in this chapter).

Related Titles

Aunt Nina and Her Nephews and Nieces, by Franz Brandenberg. Illustrated by Aliki. Greenwillow, 1983. When visiting Aunt Nina for a birthday party, her nieces and nephews are surprised to celebrate six new birth-days—kittens!

Happy Birthday, Sam, written and illustrated by Pat Hutchins. Greenwillow, 1978. On his birthday, Sam does not feel older, but a special present from his grandfather shows that Grandpa understands what Sam needs.

Sheep in a Jeep, by Nancy Shaw. Illustrated by Margot Apple. Houghton, 1986. In this rhyming story, five sheep go for an eventful ride. Their jeep breaks down, they get stuck in the mud, and they run into a tree.

Sheep on a Ship, by Nancy Shaw. Illustrated by Margot Apple. Houghton, 1989. In this book, the sheep try to sail a ship, with disastrous results.

Sheep Out to Eat, by Nancy Shaw. Illustrated by Margot Apple. Houghton, 1992. Five sheep go for tea and create a catastrophe. As in the other books, there is a rhyming text, and the illustrations capture the humor of the antics of these sheep.

About the Author

SHAW, NANCY

Something about the Author, ed. by Diane Telgen. Gale, 1993, Vol. 71, pp. 174–176.

About the Illustrator

APPLE, MARGOT

Something about the Author, ed. by Anne Commire. Gale, 1986, Vol. 42, p. 30; 1991, Vol. 64, pp. 20–28.

Teague, Mark. *The Field beyond the Outfield*
Illus. by the author. Scholastic, 1992 (0-590-45173-1)
Suggested Use Level: Gr. 1–3

Plot Summary

Ludlow Grebe worries that there are monsters in the closet and also outside his house. To distract him, his parents put him on a baseball team, where he sits on the bench and watches others play. The day comes when Ludlow is allowed to play the outfield, but he plays so far back that he encounters another baseball field. The players on this field are all creatures, including oversized insects, dogs, pigs, and chickens. Ludlow joins their game, overcoming his fear, and hits a home run. The creatures cheer his success. Ludlow returns to his own game, and after the game, he goes home with his parents. In his room that night, Ludlow does not worry about monsters any more.

Thematic Material

This humorous fantasy features unusual creatures involved in a baseball game. Ludlow's success in the creatures' baseball game helps him overcome his fear and develop confidence. The theme of facing your fears is a focus in *The Field beyond the Outfield*.

Book Talk Material and Activities

A spring program featuring baseball stories included *The Field beyond the Outfield*. Children in a second grade class loved the unusual creatures, especially the six-legged insect pitcher who could use two arms when pitching. After they heard this story, the librarian showed them a book version of *Take Me Out to the Ball Game*, and the class sang the familiar song. *Frank and Ernest Play Ball* and *Casey at the Bat* were also available at this program, as well as a selection of nonfiction books about baseball.

Many children enjoy the fantasy situation in this book as Ludlow interacts with the creatures. They like how the illustrations show the creatures sitting in the stadium holding pennants and eating hot dogs. They look at the insects on the field in their uniforms, noticing there are four sleeves in the shirts. Other books in which creatures are accepted in ordinary situations were displayed, including *Dinosaur Bob and His Adventures with the Family Lazardo*, *Nicholas Cricket*, and *What Happened to Patrick's Dinosaurs?*

Related Titles

Casey at the Bat: A Ballad of the Republic Sung in the Year 1888, by Ernest Lawrence Thayer. With additional text and illustrations by Patricia Polacco. Putnam, 1988. Casey is almost late for the game between the Mudville Meadowlarks and the Williamston Hornets. In this familiar poem, even though Casey gets the last at-bat, his team does not win.

Dinosaur Bob and His Adventures with the Family Lazardo, written and illustrated by William Joyce. Harper, 1988. The Lazardo family returns from their trip to Africa with a dinosaur they have named Bob, after a favorite uncle. Bob rides the train; he scares away burglars; he plays baseball.

Frank and Ernest Play Ball, written and illustrated by Alexandra Day.

Scholastic, 1990. Frank the bear and Ernest the elephant take over as managers for the Elmville Mudcats. As they learn about baseball, they explain some of the terms of the game, such as "in the cellar," playing "pepper," and "bullpen."

Nicholas Cricket, by Joyce Maxner. Illustrated by William Joyce. Harper, 1989. The unusual characters in this book are insects and animals. Nicholas Cricket plays the banjo in the Bug-a-Wug Cricket Band.

Take Me Out to the Ball Game, written and illustrated by Marilyn Kovalski. Scholastic, 1992. Two girls enjoy going to a baseball game with their grandmother and singing this familiar song.

What Happened to Patrick's Dinosaurs?, by Carol Carrick. Illustrated by Donald Carrick. Clarion, 1986. Patrick suggests a fantastic explanation of how dinosaurs and people once shared the earth: When the dinosaurs became tired of being responsible for everything, they built a spaceship and left. (Condensed in *Primaryplots*, Bowker, 1989, pp. 165–167.)

About the Author and Illustrator

TEAGUE, MARK
Something about the Author, ed. by Donna Olendorf. Gale, 1992, Vol. 68, pp. 227–228.

Winthrop, Elizabeth. *Bear and Mrs. Duck*
Illus. by Patience Brewster. Holiday, 1988 (0-8234-0687-3); pap. (0-8234-0843-4)
Suggested Use Level: PreS–Gr. 1

Plot Summary

Nora loves her stuffed bear, named Bear. When Nora has to go to the store and Bear is not feeling well, Mrs. Duck comes to watch Bear. At first Bear feels awkward with Mrs. Duck. He misses Nora, so he pouts and is uncooperative. But Mrs. Duck is an experienced sitter. She cajoles Bear into drawing a picture of Nora. She reads Bear a story, she plays ball with him, they play hide-and-seek, and they float boats in the bathtub. As a duck, Mrs. Duck has special abilities that help her as a sitter. For example, she can fly to the top shelf of the bookcase for Bear's favorite book, and she can swim after boats that are floating too far away. When Nora returns home, Bear is happy to see her. As Mrs. Duck waddles away, Bear tells Nora about the fun they had together, but how glad he is to be with his best friend.

Thematic Material

Young children understand that this is a fantasy story of talking toys and baby-sitting ducks. They enjoy the theme of toys as friends.

Book Talk Material and Activities

Mrs. Duck is a wonderful baby-sitter. As a duck, she is able to do special things, such as fly and swim. What other animals would be good baby-sitters? Why? One group of preschoolers thought a bear would be a good choice, because it would be warm and would hug them. A dog would be good for playing games like catch. This group also enjoyed hearing *What Kind of Baby-Sitter Is This?*, in which Kevin's baby-sitter wins his affection with her love of baseball. They also liked *Who's Going to Take Care of Me?*, in which Eric has to go to the day-care center by himself after his sister goes to school. All the characters in these books learn to adjust to new situations.

Bear and Mrs. Duck could also be part of a book talk or display of books about toy bears. *Brunus and the New Bear* is a lovely story of a toy bear who resents a new little bear that comes into his house. In *My Brown Bear, Barney*, a young girl will not make any plans that do not include her toy bear. *This Is the Bear and the Scary Night* (elsewhere in this chapter), *Peabody*, and the stories about *Old Bear* could also be included.

Related Titles

Brunus and the New Bear, written and illustrated by Ellen Stoll Walsh. Doubleday, 1979. When Benjamin gets a new stuffed bear, Brunus, his old toy, is jealous. Brunus learns that the more love is shared, the more it grows.

My Brown Bear, Barney, by Dorothy Butler. Illustrated by Elizabeth Fuller. Greenwillow, 1989. A girl lists all the things she will take with her on various trips, always including her teddy bear. When she prepares for school, she does not include Barney on her list, but the illustrations show that he is included.

Old Bear, written and illustrated by Jane Hissey. Philomel, 1986. The toys work together to rescue a stuffed bear who has been stored in the attic and forgotten. The adventures of these toys continue in *Old Bear Tales* (Philomel, 1988).

Peabody, written and illustrated by Rosemary Wells. Dial, 1983. Annie gets a new doll and ignores her toy bear, Peabody. When the doll breaks, she remembers her old friend and goes to him for comfort.

What Kind of Baby-Sitter Is This?, written and illustrated by Dolores Johnson. Macmillan, 1991. Kevin does not want his mother to leave, and he does not want to like Mrs. Lovey Pritchard, his baby-sitter. Mrs. Pritchard's love of baseball wins Kevin's friendship.

Who's Going to Take Care of Me?, by Michelle Magorian. Illustrated by James Graham Hale. Harper, 1990. Eric has always had his older sister, Karin, with him at day care. Now that Karin is in school, Eric is worried about being alone.

About the Author

WINTHROP, ELIZABETH

Fifth Book of Junior Authors and Illustrators, ed. by Sally Holmes Holtze. Wilson, 1983, pp. 330–331.
Something about the Author, ed. by Anne Commire. Gale, 1976, Vol. 6, p. 125.

About the Illustrator

BREWSTER, PATIENCE

Something about the Author, ed. by Anne Commire. Gale, 1988, Vol. 51, pp. 19–21.

Wood, Don, and Wood, Audrey. *Piggies*
Illus. by Don Wood. Harcourt, 1991 (0-15-256341-5)
Suggested Use Level: PreS–Gr. 1

Plot Summary

Two hands, left and right, display their digits. Fat, pink piggies romp on the thumb and fingers. The piggies are fat, smart, long, silly, and wee. The hands then illustrate hot, cold, clean, dirty, and good. Finally, after the piggies on the fingers have danced on the toes, both hands come together, the piggies kiss, and it is time for sleep.

Thematic Material

This book is filled with humor and playfulness. It provides opportunities for hand and finger-play activities.

Book Talk Material and Activities

After enjoying the book *Piggies,* one group of children wanted to make drawings of their hands. They traced their hands and then suggested some descriptive words like those in the book: fat, smart, long, silly, wee. They illustrated their hand pictures with a variety of creatures and then participated in some finger rhymes and hand games. Marc Brown's *Finger Rhymes* and *Hand Rhymes* and Tom Glazer's *Do Your Ears Hang Low?* and *Eye Winker, Tom Tinker* are some good sources of activity songs and rhymes.

At the end of *Piggies,* the hands (and their owner) are ready for bed. The bright-yellow daytime palette of the beginning of the book changes to dark-brown and blue shades of night as the hands are folded together and the piggies are ready for bed. In *The Napping House,* another bedtime story by Audrey and Don Wood, blue and yellow shades are used as night becomes morning. By studying illustrations, children become more aware of the contribution of the artist. In *Piggies,* much of the humor is conveyed through the zany antics of the fat little pigs on each finger. They are reading, eating, diving, and dancing. Looking more closely at the pictures shows that these piggies have personality. The piggie on the thumb of the right hand is usually eating fruit from a basket; the piggie on the index finger of the right hand is reading—even in the bathtub and in the mud. The closer children look, the more humorous details are revealed.

Related Titles

Clap Your Hands: Finger Rhymes, chosen by Sarah Hayes. Illustrated by Toni Goffe. Lothrop, 1988. Clear diagrams show how to do the activities in this book.

Do Your Ears Hang Low? Fifty More Musical Fingerplays, by Tom Glazer. Illustrated by Mila Lazarevich. Doubleday, 1980. Fifty finger plays and rhymes set to music. This is a companion to *Eye Winker, Tom Tinker, Chin Chopper.*

Eye Winker, Tom Tinker, Chin Chopper: Fifty Musical Fingerplays, by Tom Glazer. Illustrated by Ronald Himler. Doubleday, 1973. Clear illustrations and musical arrangements for finger plays, action poems, and songs.

Finger Rhymes, collected and illustrated by Marc Brown. Dutton, 1980.

"Where Is Thumbkin?" and "The Eensy, Weensy Spider" are two of the rhymes in this collection.

Hand Rhymes, collected and illustrated by Marc Brown. Dutton, 1985. Hand movements are depicted to accompany simple rhymes with topics including goblins, monkeys, babies, and kittens.

If You're Happy and You Know It: Eighteen Story Songs Set to Pictures, by Nicki Weiss. Music arranged by John Krumich. Greenwillow, 1987. These songs, like the title song, encourage clapping, dancing, and other movements.

My Hands, revised edition, written and illustrated by Aliki. Crowell, 1990. Fingers, palms, fingernails, and thumbs are all parts of hands. Hands help with many everyday tasks, including carrying, waving, and buttoning.

The Napping House, by Audrey Wood. Illustrated by Don Wood. Harcourt, 1984. In this sequential story, everyone is sleeping. Granny is in her bed and other characters join her there, ending with a flea, who bites the mouse, setting off a chain of events that wakes everyone up. (Condensed in *Primaryplots,* Bowker, 1989, pp. 154–156.)

Play Rhymes, collected and illustrated by Marc Brown. Dutton, 1987. Many of these rhymes are very familiar, such as "Do Your Ears Hang Low?" and "I'm a Little Teapot." Musical notations are included for six of the rhymes.

About the Author and Illustrator

WOOD, AUDREY

Sixth Book of Junior Authors and Illustrators, ed. by Sally Holmes Holtze. Wilson, 1989, pp. 320–321.

Something about the Author, ed. by Anne Commire. Gale, 1986, Vol. 44, p. 214; 1988, Vol. 50, pp. 218–224.

WOOD, DON

Sixth Book of Junior Authors and Illustrators, ed. by Sally Holmes Holtze. Wilson, 1989, pp. 322–323.

Something about the Author, ed. by Anne Commire. Gale, 1986, Vol. 44, p. 214; 1988, Vol. 50, pp. 224–231.

5

Exploring the Past

READING about the past experiences of others, children can make connections between life long ago and their own lives. In this chapter, there are books about dinosaurs and a minotaur. There are books featuring historical figures, including Charles Lindbergh, Dr. Martin Luther King, Jr., and Paul Revere. Sharing these books will help children understand the contributions and accomplishments of people from earlier times.

Adler, David A.   *A Picture Book of Martin Luther King, Jr.*
Illus. by Robert Casilla. Holiday, 1989 (0-8234-0770-5); pap. (0-8234-0847-7)
Suggested Use Level: Gr. 1–3

Plot Summary
Martin Luther King, Jr., was a prominent civil rights leader in the 1960s. Born in Atlanta, Georgia, Martin and his brother and sister spent a lot of time in their father's church. He experienced prejudice, from his friends and within his community. In the area where Martin lived there were many instances of segregation. Blacks were excluded from restaurants, hotels, jobs, and other daily activities. Education was important in Martin's life. He graduated from high school early and went on to college, eventually receiving a doctorate and becoming a minister. He served as a minister in Montgomery, Alabama, and helped organize the bus boycott in response to the actions of Rosa Parks. Dr. King continued to face

prejudice, even threats, yet he continued his efforts for equality. Dr. King received worldwide recognition for his work, including the Nobel Peace Prize in 1964. Martin Luther King, Jr., was assassinated on April 4, 1968, in Memphis, Tennessee. This biography ends with a list of important dates in the life of Dr. King.

Thematic Material

This book presents historical information about the life and times of Dr. Martin Luther King, Jr. This biography is part of the "Picture Book of" series about famous people.

Book Talk Material and Activities

Biographies provide information about important people and the time when they lived. Martin Luther King, Jr., lived during a time of great social change, and his contributions to the civil rights movement are celebrated by children today. Young children often have a limited under-standing of the past, and they need to have opportunities to learn about some well-known people. The "Picture Book of" introductory biographies focus on events that young children can understand. *A Picture Book of Helen Keller, A Picture Book of Eleanor Roosevelt, A Picture Book of Thomas Jefferson*, and *A Picture Book of John F. Kennedy* are some of the titles in this series. More are listed in Related Titles. Books on Frederick Douglass and Anne Frank are planned for 1993. After reading one of these biographies, children could meet in pairs or small groups to discuss the person in their book. They could read the book together and then list a few facts they would like to share with the group. As a class project, the children could create a timeline of the people being studied.

Martin Luther King, Jr., Day is recognized in many schools and librar-ies. In addition to *A Picture Book of Martin Luther King, Jr.*, some other resources would meet the needs of younger children, including *Happy Birthday, Martin Luther King* and *My First Martin Luther King Book.*

Audiovisual Adaptation

A Picture Book of Martin Luther King, Jr. Live Oak Media, cassette/book, 1990; filmstrip/cassette, 1990; videocassette, 1990.

Related Titles

Happy Birthday, Martin Luther King, by Jean Marzollo. Illustrated by J. Brian Pinkney. Scholastic, 1993. Scratchboard illustrations depict the life and times of Dr. Martin Luther King, Jr. The text describes his work as a minister and his commitment to nonviolent change.

Martin Luther King, Jr.: Man of Peace, by Patricia McKissack and Frederick McKissack. Illustrated by Ned O. Enslow, 1991. In addition to drawings, there are photographs of Dr. King and important people and places in his life. A table of contents and index are included, along with a list, "Words to Know." This book is part of the Great African Americans series.

Martin Luther King, Jr.: A Man Who Changed Things, by Carol Greene. Illustrated with photographs. Childrens Pr., 1989. Five chapters focus on Dr. King and the civil rights movement. A table of contents and index provide reference aids for research.

My First Martin Luther King Book, by Dee Lillegard. Illustrated by Helen Endres. Childrens Pr., 1987. Poems tell about the life of Dr. King, including his love of books, his wife, and his commitment to equality.

Books in the "Picture Book of" series of biographies by David A. Adler include:

A Picture Book of Abraham Lincoln. Illustrated by John Wallner and Alexandra Wallner. Holiday, 1989.

A Picture Book of Benjamin Franklin. Illustrated by John Wallner and Alexandra Wallner. Holiday, 1990.

A Picture Book of Christopher Columbus. Illustrated by John Wallner and Alexandra Wallner. Holiday, 1991.

A Picture Book of Eleanor Roosevelt. Illustrated by Robert Casilla. Holiday, 1991.

A Picture Book of Florence Nightingale. Illustrated by John Wallner and Alexandra Wallner. Holiday, 1992.

A Picture Book of George Washington. Illustrated by John Wallner and Alexandra Wallner. Holiday, 1989.

A Picture Book of Harriet Tubman. Illustrated by Samuel Byrd. Holiday, 1992.

A Picture Book of Helen Keller. Illustrated by John Wallner and Alexandra Wallner. Holiday, 1990.

A Picture Book of Jesse Owens. Illustrated by Robert Casilla. Holiday, 1992.

A Picture Book of John F. Kennedy. Illustrated by Robert Casilla. Holiday, 1991.

A Picture Book of Simon Bolivar. Illustrated by Robert Casilla. Holiday, 1992.

A Picture Book of Thomas Jefferson. Illustrated by John Wallner and Alexandra Wallner. Holiday, 1990.

About the Author

ADLER, DAVID A.

Sixth Book of Junior Authors and Illustrators, ed. by Sally Holmes Holtze. Wilson, 1989, pp. 6–7.
Something about the Author, ed. by Anne Commire. Gale, 1978, Vol. 14, pp. 2–3; ed. by
    Donna Olendorf and Diane Telgen, Gale, 1993, Vol. 70, pp. 1–4.

Barton, Byron.   *Bones, Bones, Dinosaur Bones*
Illus. by the author. Crowell, 1990, LB (0-690-04827-0)
Suggested Use Level: PreS–Gr. 1

Plot Summary
    A line of people carrying shovels and pick axes are looking for bones. They search for dinosaur bones, dig them up, and take them to the natural history museum. There, they study the bones and assemble them into the skeleton of a dinosaur. It is Tyrannosaurus rex. Then they march off, looking for more bones.

Thematic Material
    This book provides an opportunity to discuss dinosaurs and museums.

Book Talk Material and Activities
    Dinosaurs are very popular with children. Before many children learn to read, they are identifying dinosaurs and saying their names. They "read" Tyrannosaurus rex, Apatosaurus, Stegosaurus, and Triceratops. After hearing *Bones, Bones, Dinosaur Bones,* many children ask for dinosaur books. A book talk program featuring fiction and nonfiction titles capitalizes on this interest. It also provides an opportunity to introduce different areas of the library.
    In many libraries, children become familiar with the picture story books, often learning to find books on their own by looking for the last name of the author. Showing several dinosaur stories would reinforce this concept. Find *Bones, Bones, Dinosaur Bones* under B for Barton; find *What Happened to Patrick's Dinosaurs?* under C for Carrick; find *Prehistoric Pinkerton* under K for Kellogg. Using the alphabetical arrangement of the picture book section builds on children's knowledge of the alphabet, giving them the opportunity to apply their knowledge. They are encouraged to develop independence in the library. Presenting nonfiction dinosaur books ex-

pands that independence. At first, many children just learn where the "dinosaur shelf" is. Showing them dinosaur nonfiction in the 560s (like *My Visit to the Dinosaurs* and *New Questions and Answers about Dinosaurs*) and dinosaur poetry (like *Tyrannosaurus Was a Beast* and *Dinosaurs: Poems*) in the 811s expands their awareness of different kinds of books and the places where they can be found in the library.

Related Titles

Dinosaurs: Poems, edited by Lee Bennett Hopkins. Illustrated by Murray Tinkelman. Harcourt, 1987. In this collection, there are 18 poems about dinosaurs, fossils, paleontology, and other related topics. (Condensed in *Primaryplots*, Bowker, 1989, pp. 175–176.)

My Visit to the Dinosaurs, revised edition, written and illustrated by Aliki. Harper, 1985. Going to the natural history museum provides information about archaeology and paleontology as well as facts about several dinosaurs.

New Questions and Answers about Dinosaurs, by Seymour Simon. Illustrated by Jennifer Dewey. Morrow, 1990. The question-and-answer format of this book fits very well with the kinds of information many children want to know about dinosaurs.

Prehistoric Pinkerton, written and illustrated by Steven Kellogg. Dial, 1987. The little girl who owns Pinkerton is studying dinosaurs in school. She takes the big dog on a class trip to the museum. (Condensed in *Primaryplots*, Bowker, 1989, pp. 137–140.)

Tyrannosaurus Was a Beast: Dinosaur Poems, by Jack Prelutsky. Illustrated by Arnold Lobel. Greenwillow, 1988. Fourteen dinosaurs are featured in these poems, including the stegosaurus, triceratops, and allosaurus.

What Happened to Patrick's Dinosaurs?, by Carol Carrick. Illustrated by Donald Carrick. Clarion, 1986. While raking leaves, Patrick stops and talks to his brother about dinosaurs. Patrick creates a fantasy about what might have happened to the dinosaurs. (Condensed in *Primaryplots*, Bowker, 1989, pp. 165–167.)

About the Author and Illustrator

BARTON, BYRON

Fifth Book of Junior Authors and Illustrators, ed. by Sally Holmes Holtze. Wilson, 1983, pp. 21–23.

Something about the Author, ed. by Anne Commire. Gale, 1976, Vol. 9, p. 17.

Burleigh, Robert. *Flight: The Journey of Charles Lindbergh*
Illus. by Mike Wimmer. Philomel, 1991 (0-399-22272-3)
Suggested Use Level: Gr. 2–4

Plot Summary

On the morning of May 20, 1927, Charles Lindbergh began his historic flight from New York to Paris, France. Boarding the *Spirit of St. Louis* alone, he started the engine. Adjustments had been made for such a long journey—there was an extra fuel tank, but to reduce the weight, there was no radio or parachute. At 7:52 A.M., Lindbergh began his flight. He kept the plane along the coastline, knowing he had to stay on course to have enough fuel to make the journey. He also kept a journal of his flight, noting the icebergs and, later, recording his thoughts about navigating over water and staying awake. He flew through night, dense fog, and turbulence. Although he wanted to sleep, he could not; his life depended on staying awake. When morning came, Lindbergh could see a porpoise, some seagulls, and fishing boats. He reached the coast of Ireland and then flew over England. After nearly thirty-four hours in the air, Lindbergh reached Paris. When he landed, he was given a hero's welcome. Charles Lindbergh made the first solo flight across the Atlantic without stopping.

Thematic Material

Flight describes the dramatic adventure of Charles Lindbergh, one of the pioneers of flight. It could be included in units on technology as well as in studies of famous Americans.

Book Talk Material and Activities

In Jean Fritz's introduction to *Flight*, she notes that Charles Lindbergh was twenty-five years old when he made this historic flight. Like Louis Blériot in *The Glorious Flight*, Lindbergh had the courage to take risks and the spirit to succeed. Comparing *Flight* with *The Glorious Flight* could be part of a study of technology. Lindbergh's nonstop flight across the Atlantic was in 1927. Blériot's nonstop flight across the English Channel was in 1909. Lindbergh flew for nearly thirty-four hours; Blériot's flight took thirty-six minutes. Charting this on a timeline could lead to researching other historic flights, like Neil Armstrong reaching the moon in 1969. How long did it take for Neil Armstrong to reach the moon? Children could even add their own first flights and how long they took to the chart.

A book talk program featuring titles about historic achievements would extend this experience. Sally Ride's *To Space and Back* brings the story of pioneers of flight into today's world. *The Day We Walked on the Moon* provides information about the achievements that led to putting a human being on the moon and to the Space Shuttle program. Children are also interested in the space camp program, described in the book *Space Camp*. A related activity would be to make paper airplanes and have a flying contest. Seymour Simon's *The Paper Airplane Book* has many designs.

Related Titles

Amazing Flying Machines, by Robin Kerrod. Photographed by Mike Dunning. Knopf, 1992. This Eyewitness Juniors book looks at the history of flight including balloons, early planes, gliders, and jets.

The Day We Walked on the Moon: A Photo History of Space Exploration, by George Sullivan. Illustrated with photographs. Scholastic, 1990. Newspaper clippings and photographs add to the drama of the exploration of outer space, including famous "firsts," such as the first spacewalk. Included is information about astronaut training.

The Glorious Flight: Across the Channel with Louis Blériot, July 25, 1909, written and illustrated by Alice Provensen and Martin Provensen. Viking, 1983. Louis Blériot was a pioneer in the development of the airplane. He won a contest and piloted his plane across the English Channel. (Condensed in *Primaryplots,* Bowker, 1989, pp. 185–188.)

The Paper Airplane Book, by Seymour Simon. Illustrated by Byron Barton. Viking, 1971. Clear instructions and illustrations for making paper airplanes.

Planes, by Angela Royston. Photographed by Tim Ridley. Macmillan, 1992. Photographs of model planes are used to introduce different types of planes, such as the passenger plane and the glider. Small drawings highlight special features of the planes, such as the rudder and the canopy of the glider.

Space Camp: The Great Adventure for NASA Hopefuls, by Anne Baird. Photographs by Robert Koropp. Morrow, 1992. Follows the experiences of 12 young people as they attend the NASA Space Camp and experience a simulated shuttle mission.

To Space and Back, by Sally Ride with Susan Okie. Lothrop, 1986. Sally Ride gives a personal account of her experiences in space in this beautifully illustrated photoessay.

The Wright Brothers: How They Invented the Airplane, by Russell Freedman.

Illustrated. Holiday, 1991. Archival photographs add to the drama of this biography of these pioneers of flight. This was a Newbery Honor book in 1992.

About the Author

BURLEIGH, ROBERT

Something about the Author, ed. by Anne Commire. Gale, 1989, Vol. 55, p. 20.

About the Illustrator

WIMMER, MIKE

Something about the Author, ed. by Donna Olendorf and Diane Telgen. Gale, 1993, Vol. 70, p. 238.

Fisher, Leonard Everett. *Theseus and the Minotaur*

Illus. by the author. Holiday, 1988 (0-8234-0703-9); pap. (0-8234-0954-6)

Suggested Use Level: Gr. 3–4

Plot Summary

In this version of the Greek myth, Theseus, the son of King Aegus of Athens, is raised by his mother, Aethra. As a child, he is told of a task his father had set for him. To be acknowledged as Aegus' heir, Theseus must move the stone that covers the king's sword and sandals. When Theseus performs the task, he travels to Athens. King Aegus' new wife tries to keep Theseus from his father, but the two are reunited. The king talks about his kingdom, telling Theseus about the punishment King Minos of Crete demands each year. Each year, fourteen Atheneans, seven men and seven women, must be sent to the labyrinth of the Minotaur, where they are destroyed by the hideous half-man, half-bull. Theseus volunteers to go to the labyrinth with the next group and to kill the Minotaur. In Crete, Theseus is taken to the dungeon, but he is seen by Ariadne, the daughter of King Minos. She comes to his cell, gives him his sword, and tells him how to find his way out of the labyrinth. Unwinding the silk thread she has given him, Theseus enters the labyrinth and confronts and kills the Minotaur. He returns to Ariadne, and they escape from Crete. On their return to Athens, Theseus dreams that the god Dionysus demands Ariadne, so

Theseus returns to Athens alone. In his grief, Theseus forgets to display the white sail that tells of his triumph. Believing Theseus has failed, King Aegus jumps from a cliff into the sea. Theseus briefly becomes the ruler of Athens, only to give his kingdom to his people.

Thematic Material

Studying the Greek myths is included in the Ancient Greece unit in many social studies programs. This book could also be included in language arts activities in which similar versions of stories and myths are analyzed.

Book Talk Material and Activities

In a social studies class, one group of fourth graders focused on Greek mythology. Their teacher had selected several recent picture book versions of Greek myths, including *Theseus and the Minotaur, King Midas and the Golden Touch,* and *Wings.* Children worked in small groups to develop skits on these myths. After dramatizing the stories for their classmates, many students wanted to continue looking at Greek myths, both in picture books and in collections.

In the library, books of Greek mythology were on display, and the librarian booktalked two new books—*Cyclops* and *The Race of the Golden Apples.* An overview of the subject heading and library location for mythology was also given. Some children even selected Roman and Norse myths for their recreational reading.

This activity involved the teacher and librarian in a collaborative experience. Working with the librarian, the teacher selected some mythology books to use in the classroom. Then the classroom activity sparked an interest, which was supported by a library visit and lesson. As a result, children became enthusiastically involved in reading Greek mythology.

Related Titles

Cyclops, written and illustrated by Leonard Everett Fisher. Holiday, 1991. Odysseus and his men are on their way home from fighting in Troy when a storm takes their ship to the island of Polyphemus, a huge creature with one eye. The creature begins to eat the men from the ship, and Odysseus must find a way to save them.

Jason and the Golden Fleece, written and illustrated by Leonard Everett Fisher. Holiday, 1990. This myth is filled with fantastic creatures, violent encounters, and heroic adventures.

King Midas and the Golden Touch, by Nathaniel Hawthorne. Retold and illustrated by Kathryn Hewitt. Harcourt, 1987. In this familiar myth, King Midas wants to have even more wealth. His greed nearly leads to disaster.

The Macmillan Book of Greek Gods and Heroes, by Alice Low. Illustrated by Arvis Stewart. Macmillan, 1985. Familiar stories about Zeus, Pandora, Echo, Atalanta, Theseus, and other characters from Greek mythology are included in this book.

Pandora's Box, retold and illustrated by Lisl Weil. Atheneum, 1986. When Zeus and the other gods of Mount Olympus created Pandora and sent her to earth, they wanted to make the people of earth appreciate the gifts of the gods.

The Race of the Golden Apples, by Claire Martin. Illustrated by Leo Dillon and Diane Dillon. Dial, 1991. Atalanta was raised by Diana, Goddess of the Hunt. When she returns to her father's kingdom, she is stronger and faster than any man who would marry her, until Hippomenes finds a way to win the race.

Theseus and the Minotaur, retold and illustrated by Warwick Hutton. McElderry, 1989. Compare this version of the myth with the one by Leonard Everett Fisher. What parts of the story are emphasized? How does the art work add to the presentation?

Wings, by Jane Yolen. Illustrated by Dennis Nolan. Harcourt, 1991. Daedalus is exiled from Athens and travels to Crete. There, he builds the labyrinth for King Minos. In this story, he helps Ariadne and Theseus master the maze and kill the Minotaur. King Minos imprisons Daedalus and his son, Icarus.

About the Author and Illustrator

FISHER, LEONARD EVERETT

Illustrators of Children's Books: 1946–1956, Vol. II, comp. by Lee Kingman, Grace Allen Hogarth, and Harriet Quimby. Horn Book, 1978, pp. 111, 223; *1957–1966, Vol. III,* 1968, pp. 5, 15, 108, 200, 218; *1967–1976, Vol. IV,* 1978, pp. 66, 118, 188.

Something about the Author, ed. by Anne Commire. Gale, 1973, Vol. 4, pp. 84–87; 1984, Vol. 34, pp. 87–98.

Third Book of Junior Authors, ed. by Doris de Montreville and Donna Hill. Wilson, 1972, pp. 84–85.

Houston, Gloria. *My Great-Aunt Arizona*
Illus. by Susan Condie Lamb. Harper, 1992, LB (0-06-022607-2)
Suggested Use Level: Gr. 2–4

Plot Summary

Arizona grew up in a cabin in the Blue Ridge Mountains. Her brother suggested her name after seeing the beautiful land out west. Arizona liked many things, including reading, singing, and dancing. She played with her brother, did chores, and went to school. After the death of her mother, Arizona had to leave school and care for her family until her father remarried. Then Arizona left home to attend another school. When she returned, she taught in the one-room school she had attended. She married, had children, and taught school. She taught her classes about the world around them and the world far away. She taught for fifty-seven years and lived to be ninety-three.

Thematic Material

This story is based on the author's recollections of her great-aunt. It captures the feelings and experiences of a woman who lived in the late nineteenth and early twentieth centuries.

Book Talk Material and Activities

In this book, the author remembers the life and times of one of her favorite relatives, her great-aunt. This book could be shared with children in third and fourth grades as part of a family history study. After hearing the story, each child could interview older relatives (for example, parents, aunts, uncles, and grandparents) to put together a story about his or her own family. Or children could share some of their own favorite memories about childhood. At this age, children are becoming better at "looking back" and reflecting on their early experiences. Some children would enjoy asking for old family photographs and creating a display with them.

When I Was Young in the Mountains, The Best Town in the World, In Coal Country, and *My Prairie Year* are other reminiscences that could correlate with this activity. After sharing some of these stories, the teacher or librarian could lead a discussion about the feelings each author conveys. What memories were important in each book? How did the authors describe their relatives? What specific experiences were included? How does each author feel about the people and places he or she is describing? Looking carefully at the details an author includes helps children become more aware of writing styles.

Related Titles

The Best Town in the World, by Byrd Baylor. Illustrated by Ronald Himler. Scribner, 1983. Father shared his memories of growing up in a small Texas town, always finding something very special about that place. The people all seemed to know each other. There was always something interesting to do, like enjoy a town celebration. As his children and grandchildren hear about the town, they hope they will find a place like that some day. (Condensed in *Primaryplots*, Bowker, 1989, pp. 162–164.)

Eight Hands Round: A Patchwork Alphabet, by Ann Whitford Paul. Illustrated by Jeanette Winter. Harper, 1991. An alphabet of quilt designs provides information about rural life in America. The country setting of *My Great-Aunt Arizona* could spark an interest in different rural activities, like quilting.

In Coal Country, by Judith Hendershot. Illustrated by Thomas B. Allen. Knopf, 1987. In this memoir, a girl recalls her father and his work in the coal mines of Ohio. The presence of the coal mines was felt and seen everywhere, but the girl remembers the warmth of her father's smile, the care and attention of her mother, and the happiness of playing with friends. (Condensed in *Primaryplots*, Bowker, 1989, pp. 172–174.)

Miss Rumphius, written and illustrated by Barbara Cooney. Viking, 1982. Miss Rumphius lives her life exactly the way she chooses. She shares her happiness by planting lupines and making the world more beautiful.

My Prairie Year: Based on the Diary of Elenore Plaisted, by Brett Harvey. Illustrated by Deborah Kogan Ray. Holiday, 1986. Brett Harvey describes the life of her grandmother, who lived on the prairie in the Dakotas in the late 1800s and early 1900s.

When I Was Young in the Mountains, by Cynthia Rylant. Illustrated by Diane Goode. Dutton, 1982. This book focuses on the strength and love shared by this family in West Virginia. The illustrations for this memoir received a Caldecott Honor award in 1983.

Jonas, Ann. *Aardvarks, Disembark!*
Illus. by the author. Greenwillow, 1990, LB (0-688-07207-0)
Suggested Use Level: PreS–Gr. 2

Plot Summary
After the Great Flood, and with his ark on top of a mountain, Noah sent a dove to find land. When the dove returned, Noah knew the waters had receded. He called out the names of animals, from aardvarks to zebras, but there were many animals still on the ark. Noah ordered them off the ark, and then hurried down the mountain, passing many of the animals, from zebus and zorils to addaxes and aoudads. At the bottom of the mountain, Noah and his family and all the animals settled around the world. Following the story is a list of the 132 unusual animals that Noah followed down the mountains. Many of these animals are now endangered or extinct.

Thematic Material
Using the story of Noah's Ark as a framework, this book presents a variety of unusual animals in reverse alphabetical order.

Book Talk Material and Activities
Aardvarks, Disembark! would be a great resource in schools or libraries that use many religious books. It could be included in a comparison activity with other books on Noah and the ark, including Peter Spier's wordless *Noah's Ark*, which received the Caldecott Award in 1978. Songs and spirituals of Bible stories could also be featured, including *Climbing Jacob's Ladder*.

While focusing on the story of the Great Flood and the ark, this book also presents an overview of many unusual animals. The list of animals that follows the story also gives a brief description of the animal. Symbols indicate endangered or extinct animals. This list of animals would provide a beginning resource for children who are studying animals and who are interested in less-familiar animals.

Related Titles
Climbing Jacob's Ladder: Heroes of the Bible in African-American Spirituals, selected and edited by John Langstaff. Illustrated by Ashley Bryan. Piano arrangements by John Andrew Ross. Macmillan, 1991. The spiritual

"Didn't It Rain?" describes the experiences of Noah on the ark. Some other songs are "Rock-a My Soul," "Go Down, Moses," and "Ezekiel Saw the Wheel."

Noah and the Ark, retold and illustrated by Tomie dePaola. Winston Press, 1983. Tomie dePaola's illustrations are a delightful feature of this retelling.

Noah's Ark, by Linda Hayward. Illustrated by Freire Wright. Random, 1987. This version of the Bible story is retold for beginning readers. Large print and a controlled vocabulary make this more accessible for children to read on their own.

Noah's Ark, illustrated by Nonny Hogrogian. Knopf, 1986. When the people of the earth disappointed the Lord, he sent a flood. The endpapers of this book show a cross-section of the ark.

Noah's Ark, written and illustrated by Peter Spier. Doubleday, 1977. Detailed drawings show the activities on the ark. The format includes large pictures and smaller, cartoon-style panels. This book received the Caldecott Medal in 1978.

Tomie dePaola's Book of Bible Stories, New International Version, retold and illustrated by Tomie dePaola. Putnam, 1989. The story of the Great Flood is included along with other stories from the Old and New Testaments.

About the Author and Illustrator

JONAS, ANN
Something about the Author, ed. by Anne Commire. Gale, 1986, Vol. 42, p. 122; 1988, Vol. 50, pp. 106–109.

Lauber, Patricia. *The News about Dinosaurs*
Illus. by John Gurche, et al. Bradbury, 1989 (0-02-754520-2)
Suggested Use Level: Gr. 2–4

Plot Summary

How can there be any news about dinosaurs? Patricia Lauber highlights some of the recent information scientists have discovered about these creatures from the past. Beginning with a pronunciation guide to the names of dinosaurs, Lauber then features ten "The News Is" sections. For example, four new kinds of dinosaurs have been discovered, and they are briefly described in the text and drawings. The news about matching the correct skull to Apatosaurus is presented, along with an explanation of why this is now the more appropriate name for Brontosaurus. Some previous beliefs about dinosaurs have been revised based on recent information. For example, although reptiles of today do not live in groups, fossil footprints indicate that some dinosaurs may have hunted and lived in groups. Lauber concludes by reminding readers that discoveries will continue to be made about dinosaurs. An index follows the text.

Thematic Material

Dinosaurs are very popular with children. This book contains accurate scientific information about dinosaurs. It highlights recent findings about these creatures of the past.

Book Talk Material and Activities

Children need access to many materials that present information on similar topics. Patricia Lauber's *The News about Dinosaurs* could be featured in a discussion focusing on books about dinosaurs and highlighting some more recent titles. Many children are surprised that information about dinosaurs could change and that books would need to be updated. After hearing some of the information in *The News about Dinosaurs*, some third graders looked at other dinosaur books. They focused on the use of the word *Apatosaurus* instead of the more general *Brontosaurus*. Lauber notes that *Brontosaurus* is not wrong; however, its use may indicate the information is not as up-to-date as in other books. The children checked several books and found some using the more recent term, while others still used *Brontosaurus*. *Dinosaur Time* was a book these children had used when they first became interested in dinosaurs. They found that it was published in 1974 and used the word *Brontosaurus*. *The News about Dinosaurs* was published in 1989, and *New Questions and Answers about Dinosaurs* in 1990. Both these books discuss the name change of this dinosaur.

By looking at different books on the same topic, these third graders became more aware of when the books were published. The librarian asked them to suggest some topics that would need to have very up-to-date information and some topics whose information could be used for many years without changing. Cars, jets, outer space, and sports were some subjects they felt should be up-to-date. One child said drawing books could probably be used for several years. Another felt that books about pets might not need to be changed that often. As they selected books to sign out, many dinosaur books were chosen to compare to *The News about Dinosaurs*.

Related Titles

Digging Up Dinosaurs, revised edition, written and illustrated by Aliki. Crowell, 1988. This revision does refer to the Apatosaurus as it describes the work of archaeologists, geologists, and other fossil hunters and preservers.

Dinosaur Time, by Peggy Parish. Illustrated by Arnold Lobel. Harper, 1974. The information about dinosaurs is presented in an easy-to-read format of large print and wide spaces between lines. Many children find this is the first dinosaur book they can read on their own.

Dinosaurs, by Angela Royston. Photographed by Colin Keates. Macmillan, 1991. Eight dinosaurs are featured in this book: Stegosaurus, Tyrannosaurus rex, Triceratops, Hypsilophodus, Diplodocus, Deinonychus, Scolosaurus, and Gallimimus. This book is part of the Eye Openers series of books.

The Largest Dinosaurs, by Seymour Simon. Illustrated by Pamela Carroll. Macmillan, 1986. Includes the recent information about Apatosaurus. Simon's *The Smallest Dinosaurs* (Crown, 1982) is a companion book.

New Questions and Answers about Dinosaurs, by Seymour Simon. Illustrated by Jennifer Dewey. Morrow, 1990. The chapter titles for this book are in the form of questions such as, "What Are Dinosaurs?" and "How Are Dinosaurs Named?" There is an index and a pronunciation guide.

What Happened to the Dinosaurs?, by Franklyn M. Branley. Illustrated by Marc Simont. Crowell, 1989. Different possibilities for what happened to the dinosaurs are presented here. This would be a good book to compare to the fiction book, *What Happened to Patrick's Dinosaurs?* by Carol Carrick (Clarion, 1986), which is condensed in *Primaryplots* (Bowker, 1989, pp. 165–167).

About the Author and Illustrator

LAUBER, PATRICIA

Something about the Author, ed. by Anne Commire. Gale, 1971, Vol. 1, pp. 138–139; 1983, Vol. 33, pp. 124–127.

Third Book of Junior Authors, ed. by Doris de Montreville and Donna Hill. Wilson, 1972, pp. 173–174.

Longfellow, Henry Wadsworth. *Paul Revere's Ride*
Illus. by Ted Rand. Dutton, 1990 (0-525-44610-9)
Suggested Use Level: Gr. 2–4

Plot Summary
Longfellow's classic poem is presented as a picture book. Appended is additional information about Paul Revere. The endpapers are a map of the route Paul Revere followed on April 18–19, 1775.

Thematic Material
This narrative poem celebrates a historical event and could be included in social studies units on the American Revolution. It could also be the focus of a unit on poetry.

Book Talk Material and Activities
In many social studies programs, students are introduced to narrative poems that focus on historical events. Poetry can capture the emotion of real-life experiences. The language, rhythm, pacing, and rhyme create a variety of moods. In Longfellow's poem, historical facts are woven into the narrative. Ted Rand's illustrations, with their use of shadows and reflected light, create a sense of drama and danger. Children should hear this poem read aloud several times, listening for the details and appreciating the rhythm and rhyme. They could look at another illustrated version of this poem. How do Nancy Winslow Parker's illustrations compare to Ted Rand's? What details from the poem does each illustrator include in the illustrations? What additional features are provided in each book, such as maps, historical notes, and so forth? Children could select other historical poems and illustrate them.

In classes where poetry receives regular attention, children would enjoy seeing many illustrated versions of poems. They could listen to poems read aloud and discuss what they would expect to see in the illustrations. What details would they include? What colors might be used? Looking at the illustrated version would provide them with one artist's interpretation of the poet's vision.

Librarians could feature other picture book versions of poems, including *Stopping by Woods on a Snowy Evening* and *Birches,* by Robert Frost; and *Block City* and *My Shadow,* by Robert Louis Stevenson.

Related Titles

Birches, by Robert Frost. Illustrated by Ed Young. Holt, 1988. Winter scenes in shades of brown, gold, yellow, and beige capture the images of Robert Frost's poem.

Block City, by Robert Louis Stevenson. Illustrated by Ashley Wolff. Dutton, 1988. Stevenson's poem presents the imaginative play that can come from simple blocks. Ashley Wolff's illustrations begin with realistic scenes of a child playing with blocks; then they depict the imaginary city that is created.

Casey at the Bat: A Ballad of the Republic Sung in the Year 1888, by Ernest Lawrence Thayer. With additional text and illustrations by Patricia Polacco. Putnam, 1988. This well-known poem is set into the story of a Little League game. Casey is reminded about the important game by his sister, Connie. After the game, Casey and Connie walk home with the umpire, who is their father.

My Shadow, by Robert Louis Stevenson. Illustrated by Ted Rand. Putnam, 1990. Ted Rand's illustrations depict scenes from around the world as children play with their shadows. Most of the pictures are in bright sunlight, but the final picture shows two children making shadow shapes with their hands with a candle as the source of light.

Paul Revere's Ride, by Henry Wadsworth Longfellow. Illustrated by Nancy Winslow Parker. Greenwillow, 1985. Here is another illustrated version of this well-known poem.

Stopping by Woods on a Snowy Evening, by Robert Frost. Illustrated by Susan Jeffers. Dutton, 1978. The illustrations for this poem are dominated by gray and white with a few touches of color.

About the Author

LONGFELLOW, HENRY WADSWORTH

Something about the Author, ed. by Anne Commire. Gale, 1980, Vol. 19, pp. 181–204.

About the Illustrator

RAND, TED

Sixth Book of Junior Authors and Illustrators, ed. by Sally Holmes Holtze. Wilson, 1989, pp. 238–239.

Lyon, George Ella.   *Who Came Down That Road?*
Illus. by Peter Catalanotto. Orchard, 1992, LB (0-531-08587-2)
Suggested Use Level: Gr. 1–4

Plot Summary

A boy asks his mother to tell him about the people who have traveled down the old road. She tells him about farmers, like her own great-grandparents, who came to clear the land and build a home. Before them, there were soldiers on the road, and before them there were the settlers who came when the land was a wilderness. Before them, there were Native American peoples from different groups, including Shawnee, Cherokee, Wyandot, and Chippewa. Even before there were people, there were animals on the road: buffalo, bear, and elk; before that, there were mastadons and mammoths. Before these animals, the land was covered with water, and sea creatures filled the water. The boy and his mother continue their walk, pondering all that has passed this way before them.

Thematic Material

This is a book about a child's wonder at the world around him and the lives that have gone before him. In this story, the mother makes a connection between the present and the past as she describes different groups of people and animals that might have traveled the old road.

Book Talk Material and Activities

For many children, the past is yesterday or, perhaps, last week. This book lets children think about the many events that have taken place in the past. It would be an excellent book to focus on before a study of fossils and prehistoric creatures, or it could accompany a social studies archaeology unit. *Fossils Tell of Long Ago* describes some of the work of archaeologists, as do *Digging Up Dinosaurs* and *My Visit to the Dinosaurs*. Byrd Baylor's books about the artifacts of Native Americans *(Before You Came This Way* and *When Clay Sings)* would extend the theme of *Who Came Down That Road?*

Lynne Cherry's *A River Ran Wild* would be an excellent companion book for *Who Came Down That Road?* In Cherry's book, the focus is a river. The Nashua River in Massachusetts and New Hampshire is described from early times, when Indian peoples lived near the river, through the mid-1800s when the river was polluted by industries, to the recent decades when the river was revitalized. Children could relate these books to their own geographical areas. They could speculate about the events that occurred in their region and then research them. *Brother Eagle, Sister Sky* focuses on the importance of caring for the earth, portraying the earth as a gift from the peoples from earlier generations.

Related Titles

Before You Came This Way, by Byrd Baylor. Illustrated by Tom Bahti. Dutton, 1969. Baylor writes about the ancient drawings that can still be seen on canyon walls. These messages from the past tell of another time and another people. Bahti's illustrations evoke the images of prehistoric cave paintings.

Brother Eagle, Sister Sky: A Message from Chief Seattle. Illustrated by Susan Jeffers. Dial, 1991. A powerful message about caring for the earth and for each other is presented in this book. This book conveys a sense of the earth as a legacy from the people of past generations and cultures.

Digging Up Dinosaurs, revised edition, written and illustrated by Aliki. Crowell, 1988. The work of paleontologists and archaeologists is described, including how scientists prepare the dinosaur bones for museum displays.

Fossils Tell of Long Ago, revised edition, written and illustrated by Aliki. Harper, 1990. This book describes the formation of fossils. It also discusses how scientists learn about life long ago by studying fossils. Information is given about making an imprint of your hand.

My Visit to the Dinosaurs, revised edition, written and illustrated by Aliki. Crowell, 1985. Visiting the natural history museum and viewing fossils and bones leads to a discussion of different dinosaurs.

A River Ran Wild: An Environmental History, written and illustrated by Lynne Cherry. Harcourt, 1992. Focusing on the Nashua River in Massachusetts and New Hampshire, the author describes the changes in the river, beginning around 7000 years ago.

When Clay Sings, by Byrd Baylor. Illustrated by Tom Bahti. Scribner, 1972. The images that remain on fragments of clay pots used by the desert people of long ago provide information about their lives. To interpret Baylor's poetic text, Bahti has based his drawings on the images on the pottery of prehistoric Native Americans.

About the Author

Lyon, George Ella
Something about the Author, ed. by Donna Olendorf. Gale, 1992, Vol. 68, pp. 150–152.

About the Illustrator

Catalanotto, Peter
Something about the Author, ed. by Donna Olendorf and Diane Telgen. Gale, 1993, Vol. 70, pp. 21–24.

MacLachlan, Patricia.   *Three Names*
Illus. by Alexander Pertzoff. Harper, 1991, LB (0-06-024036-9)
Suggested Use Level: Gr. 2–4

Plot Summary
Great-Grandfather describes his relationship with his dog on the prairie in the early 1900s. Each person in the family had a name for the dog, so he had three different names. Great-Grandfather called him Three Names, even though that was a fourth name. Three Names would ride in the wagon with the children to the schoolhouse. Great-Grandfather was with his friends, Rachel, Matty, and William, traveling across the prairie, seeing the plants and animals. At the one-room schoolhouse, Three Names came inside, sometimes sitting by the wood stove, sometimes sitting with Great-Grandfather. The children shared their food with Three Names before they played their games, like fox-and-geese and marbles. In the winter, the teacher, Mr. Beckett, had a party at the school and Three Names joined in the program, howling when Martha played her fiddle. Winter snowstorms raced across the prairie, then spring came, with more windy weather, including tornadoes. At the beginning of summer, the school year was over. Great-Grandfather and Three Names both missed school and the time they spent together.

Thematic Material
This is a realistic story of the relationship between a boy and his dog. *Three Names* is written as a reminiscence and is set in the past, including some details about life on the prairie in the early 1900s.

Book Talk Material and Activities

As she did in *Sarah, Plain and Tall,* Patricia MacLachlan has written a story of everyday life on the American prairie in the early part of this century. Woven into this reminiscence are details about the land, the weather, the plants and animals, and the experiences of a family. Children who hear this story often talk about the concepts of "then and now," focusing on the descriptions of the school, the games, and the daily activities. Other books about experiences on the prairie, such as *My Prairie Year* or *Dakota Dugout,* could be correlated with *Three Names.*

Three Names is a realistic animal story focusing on a dog. Older children who hear this story may want to investigate some of their own family stories. One fourth-grade teacher had the children in her class talk with their families about their favorite memories of a pet. Another group of third graders looked at some other realistic dog stories, particularly those by Carol Carrick about Christopher and his family. *Ben and the Porcupine* and *The Foundling* were two books they read. Some of these children then interviewed their classmates about their pets, focusing on the feelings they shared with their pets. Other novels about dogs, such as *Wanted . . . Mud Blossom* and *Shiloh,* could also be booktalked along with *Three Names.*

Related Titles

Ben and the Porcupine, by Carol Carrick. Illustrated by Donald Carrick. Houghton, 1981. Christopher's new dog, Ben, finds a porcupine in the woods and will not leave it alone. When Ben comes home with quills in his nose, Christopher is upset. He worries that Ben will not be safe on the island, but he later realizes Ben must learn to adjust to this new situation.

Dakota Dugout, by Ann Turner. Illustrated by Ronald Himler. Macmillan, 1985. A woman remembers her life in a sod house on the prairie.

The Foundling, by Carol Carrick. Illustrated by Donald Carrick. Clarion, 1977. Ever since his dog, Bodger, was killed, Christopher's parents have wondered if he might want another dog. His father takes him to the animal shelter, but Christopher cannot accept another dog. Back at their house, Christopher notices a puppy that has strayed over from the neighbor's house. When Christopher takes the dog to his neighbor, he finds that the puppy does not belong there. Christopher decides to keep the puppy and names him Ben.

My Prairie Year: Based on the Diary of Elenore Plaisted, by Brett Harvey. Illustrated by Deborah Kogan Ray. Holiday, 1986. Brett Harvey describes the life of her grandmother, who lived on the prairie in the Dakotas in the late 1800s and early 1900s.

Sarah, Plain and Tall, by Patricia MacLachlan. Harper, 1985. This 1986 Newbery Medal—winning book tells of Anna and Caleb and their life on the American prairie. The arrival of Sarah, who has been corresponding with their father, changes their lives.

Shiloh, by Phyllis Reynolds Naylor. Atheneum, 1991. Marty finds a dog that has been mistreated. He is disturbed when he must return the dog to his owner. Marty's relationship with the dog he calls Shiloh helps him make some important decisions.

Stories about Rosie, by Cynthia Voigt. Illustrated by Dennis Kendrick. Atheneum, 1986. Rosie the dog knows what she is supposed to do, such as play in the house and yard and bark at strangers. She knows what her people are supposed to do too. There are four stories in this book.

Wanted . . . Mud Blossom, by Betsy Byars. Illustrated by Jacqueline Rogers. Delacorte, 1991. This is the fourth book about the Blossom family; it focuses on Pap's dog, Mud.

About the Author

MacLachlan, Patricia

Sixth Book of Junior Authors and Illustrators, ed. by Sally Holmes Holtze. Wilson, 1989, pp. 183–184.

Something about the Author, ed. by Anne Commire. Gale, 1986, Vol. 42, p. 146; 1990, Vol. 62, pp. 115–112.

Van Allsburg, Chris.   *The Widow's Broom*
Illus. by the author. Houghton, 1992 (0-395-64051-2)
Suggested Use Level: Gr. 2–4

Plot Summary

When a witch's broom loses its power, the witch and the broom crash into Minna Shaw's garden. Minna helps the witch, who contacts a colleague and flies off with her. The witch's broom is left behind and Minna, a widow, begins to use it, only to discover that it still has some powers. The broom becomes Minna's helper and companion. It loves to sweep and learns to do other chores too. It even learns to pick out tunes on the piano. When the neighbors hear of Minna's unusual broom, there are mixed reactions. The men are fearful of the unusual broom; the women appreciate how helpful it is. When the Spivey children tease the broom, it attacks them. Mr. Spivey and the other men demand it be destroyed. Minna agrees, and the broom is burned. However, a ghost broom returns, haunting the Spivey family until they become so frightened they move away. Minna stays in her home, content with her friendly and helpful broom, which she has painted white.

Thematic Material

This story is set in the past, perhaps in the time of witch trials. Like many books by Chris Van Allsburg, there are unusual events and mysterious circumstances.

Book Talk Material and Activities

The Widow's Broom arrived just in time to be incorporated into a unit on the books of Chris Van Allsburg. In third grade, children had focused on the works of this author/illustrator, so they were very familiar with his work. As fourth graders, they were excited to see some of his newer books, including *The Wretched Stone* and *The Widow's Broom*. In the library, they were introduced to *The Widow's Broom*. Before reading the book, they were asked what they expected this book to be about. Based on their familiarity with Van Allsburg's other books, almost everyone had something to contribute: "There should be magic and a mystery." "Strange things will happen." "I think there will be a murder." "You'll be surprised at the end. He won't do what you think." "There will be a dog in the story." "This book will be a surprise." After listing their comments on the chalkboard, the librarian read the book. The children nodded and smiled as some of their expectations were confirmed.

Although this is not specifically a Halloween story, the images of witches and pumpkins make this perfect for sharing with other scary stories, particularly with older children. *The Boy and the Ghost* and *The Magic Wood* describe suspenseful situations. The poems in *Halloween ABC* are sinister, haunting, and even somewhat gruesome, as are the stories collected by Alvin Schwartz. Older children often ask for scary books, and *The Widow's Broom* could lead them to other stories of suspense.

Related Titles

The Boy and the Ghost, by Robert D. San Souci. Illustrated by J. Brian Pinkney. Simon & Schuster, 1989. A boy spends the night in a haunted house, facing the ghost that lives there.

Halloween ABC, by Eve Merriam. Illustrated by Lane Smith. Macmillan, 1987. There are twenty-six poems in this book—one for each letter of the alphabet. Each poem highlights some aspect of Halloween. There are poems of fear, suspense, and even some humor. (Condensed in *Primaryplots*, Bowker, 1989, pp. 109–111.)

The Magic Wood: A Poem, by Henry Treece. Illustrated by Barry Moser. Harper, 1992. A child enters the wood at night and encounters a mysterious man who encourages the child to go deeper into the wood. The repeated verse is a warning to avoid the wood at night.

The Moonbow of Mr. B. Bones, by J. Patrick Lewis. Illustrated by Dirk Zimmer. Knopf, 1992. When Mr. B. Bones brings his wagon into the Gap, all the children hurry to buy his magic jars. The jars are treasured, but never opened, until Tommy Morgan comes to town.

The Mysteries of Harris Burdick, written and illustrated by Chris Van Allsburg. Houghton, 1984. Van Allsburg's inventive premise is that an artist left his portfolio containing some black-and-white drawings and suggested chapter titles and captions with a publisher and then never returned. The rest of the story is left to the reader's imagination. Each drawing has a slight twist, sometimes sinister, sometimes magical. This book is often used to start creative-writing projects.

Nightmares: Poems to Trouble Your Sleep, by Jack Prelutsky. Illustrated by Arnold Lobel. Greenwillow, 1976. There are some gruesome, sinister, and very scary poems in this collection. *The Headless Horseman Rides Tonight* (Greenwillow, 1980) offers more haunting images from Prelutsky and Lobel.

Scary Stories 3: More Tales to Chill Your Bones, collected from folklore and retold by Alvin Schwartz. Illustrated by Stephen Gammell. Harper, 1991. Haunted houses, mysterious events, gruesome ghosts, and other strange occurrences are featured in this book.

Witch Hazel, by Alice Schertle. Illustrated by Margot Tomes. Harper, 1991. Johnny makes a scarecrow from the branches of a witch hazel bush. One windy night, Johnny and his scarecrow have an unusual adventure.

The Wretched Stone, written and illustrated by Chris Van Allsburg. Houghton, 1991. When an unusual stone is brought onto the ship, it changes the crew from men to monkeys.

About the Author and Illustrator

VAN ALLSBURG, CHRIS

Fifth Book of Junior Authors and Illustrators, ed. by Sally Holmes Holtze. Wilson, 1983, pp. 316–317.

Something about the Author, ed. by Anne Commire. Gale, 1985, Vol. 37, pp. 204–207; 1988, Vol. 53, pp. 160–172.

Winter, Jeanette. *Follow the Drinking Gourd*
Illus. by the author. Knopf, 1988, LB (0-394-99694-1); pap. (0-679-81997-5)
Suggested Use Level: Gr. 2–4

Plot Summary

Peg Leg Joe worked on a plantation that used slaves. He helped the slaves escape by teaching them a song to follow the drinking gourd. After teaching the song, Joe went to work on another plantation and taught those slaves the song. Two slaves, Molly and James, remembered Joe's song. They saw the stars of the Big Dipper in the sky and they ran away from the plantation, taking others with them. For weeks, they walked across fields and streams, they hid from those who hunted them, and they followed the drinking gourd—the stars of the Big Dipper. The words of Joe's song told them the path to follow, and Joe met them at the Ohio River and rowed them across. Joe told them of the safe houses on the way to freedom in Canada. The escaping slaves still hid from those who hunted them, but they were helped by many along the way to Lake Erie, then to Canada, then to freedom. The music and verses for the song follow the text. An introductory note describes the Underground Railroad and the origin of the song "Follow the Drinking Gourd."

Thematic Material

Set prior to the Civil War, this story focuses on historical events. Many slaves escaped by following the North Star; they were helped by many along the Underground Railroad. The experience of African Americans during this period is an important part of U.S. history.

Book Talk Material and Activities

Follow the Drinking Gourd describes a time before the Civil War, when slavery was an accepted practice by many landowners. During Black History Month in February, one fourth grade class put on a play using *Follow the Drinking Gourd.* One student read the text while others dramatized the events. After the play, other students in the class read brief biographical sketches of famous African Americans, including Harriet Tubman, Sojourner Truth, Frederick Douglass, James Weldon Johnson, and Martin Luther King, Jr. They used many other biographies from the library to prepare their reports.

The class concluded its program with choral readings of poems, including Eloise Greenfield's "Harriet Tubman" in *Honey, I Love* and Myra Cohn Livingston's "Martin Luther King" in *The Random House Book of Poetry for Children.*

These fourth graders also prepared a timeline featuring the people they had studied. Their work was displayed in the hall outside their classroom. History and historical fiction books introduce children to events in the past. These books often lead to a discussion of how people lived, what they ate, what they wore, and how they traveled. Children also learn of the hardships that many people have endured throughout history.

Audiovisual Adaptation

Follow the Drinking Gourd. American School Publishers, cassette/book, 1990.

Related Titles

Aunt Harriet's Underground Railroad in the Sky, written and illustrated by Faith Ringgold. Crown, 1992. While flying, Cassie and Be Be meet Harriet Tubman. Be Be rides on the train in the sky, and Cassie follows the route to freedom on the ground.

The Big Dipper, by Franklyn M. Branley. Illustrated by Molly Coxe. Harper, 1991. This Let's-Read-and-Find-Out Science book tells about the constellations of the Big and Little Dippers. Although no reference is made to the North Star as it related to the freedom of slaves, this book does provide information about finding the Big Dipper.

The Drinking Gourd, by F. N. Monjo. Illustrated by Fred Brenner. Harper, 1970. Tommy and his family become involved in helping some runaway slaves escape to Canada. This historical fiction book is accessible to younger readers.

Honey, I Love, and Other Love Poems, by Eloise Greenfield. Illustrated by Leo Dillon and Diane Dillon. Crowell, 1972. The poem "Harriet Tubman" incorporates many historical details into the rhythmic language.

A Picture Book of Harriet Tubman, by David A. Adler. Illustrated by Samuel Byrd. Holiday, 1992. Tells of the life of Harriet Tubman, who was born into slavery, escaped, and then led many others to freedom. A list of important dates follows the text.

The Random House Book of Poetry for Children, selected and introduced by Jack Prelutsky. Illustrated by Arnold Lobel. Random, 1983. One section of this book includes poems on seasons and celebrations, including a poem about Martin Luther King, Jr.

6

Learning about the World Around You

CHILDREN are naturally curious about the world around them. They observe changes in weather and seasons. They wonder about plants, animals, and places. In this chapter, there are books about the ocean, the forest, the desert, and outer space. There are project and activity books that promote hands-on experiences with nature and encourage children to investigate. There are nonfiction and picture books about animals and places. Teachers and librarians can correlate many of these books with activities in the sciences and social studies.

Arnosky, Jim. *In the Forest: A Portfolio of Paintings*
   Illus. by the author. Lothrop, 1989, LB (0-688-09138-5)
   Suggested Use Level: Gr. 2–4

Plot Summary
   The portfolio of oil paintings in this book depict many different aspects of the forest. A stand of firs, a clearing, a beaver pond, and a great white pine are some of the views Jim Arnosky has painted. Accompanying each painting is a description of the scene and of the artist's impressions of each image. For the fir stand, Arnosky describes the land beneath the trees. "Clearing" tells of an encounter with a doe during the preliminary work for the painting. Together, the paintings and text describe the variety of life and habitats in a forest, as well as the perspective of the artist/naturalist.

Thematic Material
   In the Forest celebrates the beauty of the forest. The artist/naturalist conveys a deep respect and appreciation for the natural world.

Book Talk Material and Activities

After reading *In the Forest,* a group of children visited a nature center and looked for examples of the areas Jim Arnosky portrayed. They used his terms, such as copse and clearing, as they described their observations. They wrote about their impressions of nature, the sounds and the quiet, the movement and the stillness. *In the Forest* encouraged these children to be observant. They looked at a familiar setting and realized there were things in it they had never seen. After returning from this nature walk, the children looked at other books about the forest. They added more terms to their descriptive vocabularies. They looked at the illustrations of other artists. They also read Jim Arnosky's *Near the Sea,* studying his paintings and descriptions of coastal Maine.

Teachers and librarians who are incorporating more literature into the science curriculum will want to include *In the Forest* as well as other books about trees and the forest, including *A Tree in a Forest* and *The Big Tree.* Each book provides different images in words and pictures, so children find additional information with each title. They learn that research is a process that involves many resources and that information can be presented in many ways.

Related Titles

The Big Tree, written and illustrated by Bruce Hiscock. Atheneum, 1991. For more than two hundred years, this maple tree has been growing. A timeline shows events that have occurred during the life of the tree, from the American Revolution to the launching of space rockets. Descriptions of the tree through the seasons are included.

Discover My World: Forest, by Ron Hirschi. Illustrated by Barbara Bash. Bantam, 1991. Simple facts about life in the forest are presented through a series of questions that relate to the illustration on the opposite page. At the back of the book is information that answers each question.

How the Forest Grew, by William Jaspersohn. Illustrated by Chuck Eckart. Greenwillow, 1980. The growth of a forest is described, including the animals that live there, the process of succession, and the layers of a full-grown forest.

Mighty Tree, written and illustrated by Dick Gackenbach. Harcourt, 1992. Some trees provide products that people use, like paper, boxes, and books. Some are used for decorations at Christmastime. And some trees are the home for woodland animals. This book describes three trees and the purposes they serve.

Near the Sea: A Portfolio of Paintings, written and illustrated by Jim Arnosky. Lothrop, 1990. The focus of these paintings is an island in Maine. Gulls, the tidal pool, the coastal marsh at low tide, and the surf are some of the areas depicted.

A Tree in a Forest, written and illustrated by Jan Thornhill. Simon & Schuster, 1991. The growth of a maple tree, through seasons and centuries, is described. The color illustrations show the animals and people who depend on the forest.

About the Author and Illustrator

ARNOSKY, JIM

Fifth Book of Junior Authors and Illustrators, ed. by Sally Holmes Holtze. Wilson, 1983, pp. 12–13.

Something about the Author, ed. by Anne Commire. Gale, 1981, Vol. 22, pp. 19–21; ed. by Donna Olendorf and Diane Telgen, Gale, 1993, Vol. 70, pp. 8–12.

Barton, Byron.   *I Want to Be an Astronaut*
Illus. by the author. Crowell, 1988, LB (0-690-04744-4); pap., Trophy (0-06-443280-7)
Suggested Use Level: PreS–Gr. 1

Plot Summary

A child who wants to be an astronaut describes the events on a space shuttle. Once in space, there is a mission to complete, special meals to eat, and weightlessness to experience. Wearing a space suit and working in space on a satellite and an orbiting factory are part of this trip. After all the work is completed, the shuttle returns to earth.

Thematic Material

This book focuses on a young child's fascination with space.

Book Talk Material and Activities

Like many young children, the main character in *I Want to Be an Astronaut* has a general understanding of the responsibilites of an astronaut. Teachers and librarians could expand on this interest with a book talk program featuring other books about space. In a discussion with a group of children, ask "What do you know about space?" and "What does an astronaut do?" After the children write down their responses, books could be presented that provide additional information. Informational books illustrated with photographs build on what children know and extend their experiences. *I Can Be an Astronaut* is an excellent companion book to *I Want to Be an Astronaut*.

I Want to Be an Astronaut suggests some of the experiences that would occur on a trip into space. *The Magic School Bus Lost in the Solar System* adds another perspective—and some humor—to the same premise. Ms. Frizzle takes her class on a trip to the planetarium, only to find that it is closed. As the school bus heads back to school, rockets in the back of the bus send it into space. The class visits the moon, the sun, and all the planets before finally returning to earth. After hearing *I Want to Be an Astronaut*, young children will enjoy the antics of Ms. Frizzle and her class in *The Magic School Bus Lost in the Solar System*.

Related Titles

Astronauts, by N. S. Barrett. Illustrated with photographs. Watts, 1985. Photographs show astronauts performing many routine tasks in space, including taking a shower. The table of contents and index help make the information more accessible to young researchers.

I Can Be an Astronaut, by June Behrens. Illustrated with photographs and drawings. Childrens Pr., 1984. Some of the qualifications and preparation needed to be an astronaut are described, as are some of the tasks that might be performed on a space flight.

The Magic School Bus Lost in the Solar System, by Joanna Cole. Illustrated by Bruce Degen. Scholastic, 1990. Ms. Frizzle takes her class on a trip to the moon, the sun, and the planets. Along the way, Ms. Frizzle is lost in an asteroid belt.

My Place in Space, by Robin Hirst and Sally Hirst. Illustrated by Roland Harvey and Joe Levine. Orchard, 1990. When the bus driver asks Henry where he lives, Henry describes the street, town, country, hemisphere, planet, solar system, solar neighborhood, galaxy, supercluster, and universe.

The Planets in Our Solar System, by Franklyn M. Branley. Illustrated by Don Madden. Crowell, 1987. In addition to facts about the planets, directions are included for a mobile of the nine planets as well as a wall model of the relative distance of each planet from the sun.

About the Author and Illustrator

BARTON, BYRON

Fifth Book of Junior Authors and Illustrators, ed. by Sally Holmes Holtze. Wilson, 1983, pp. 21–23.

Something about the Author, ed. by Anne Commire. Gale, 1976, Vol. 9, p. 17.

Bash, Barbara. *Desert Giant: The World of the Saguaro Cactus*
Illus. by the author. Little, Brown, 1989 (0-316-08301-1)
Suggested Use Level: Gr. 2–4

Plot Summary

The saguaro cactus grows in the desert in the southwestern United States and in northern Mexico. It provides shelter and food for many animals, including the Gila woodpecker, the elf owl, Harris's hawk, long-nosed bats, and other birds, insects, and animals. The Tohono O'odham Indians harvest the fruit of the saguaro and make jams, syrups, and other sweets from it. Even after the saguaro begins to decompose, it is a resource for desert creatures, including termites, spiders, centipedes, lizards, beetles, and scorpions. Saguaros grow slowly, producing flowers and fruit after fifty years; they can survive in the desert for more than one hundred and fifty years.

Thematic Material

The life cycle of a saguaro cactus is the focus of *Desert Giant*. Plants, animals, and people of the desert are featured. This book relates to science units on the ecology of the desert.

Book Talk Material and Activities

Many teachers and librarians have implemented the whole-language philosophy in their classrooms and libraries. Reading, writing, and language arts were the initial focus of whole-language activities, but many educators are applying this philosophy to other curriculum areas as well. One way this is done is by expanding the use of trade books in science and social studies. *Desert Giant* could be a focus book for groups studying the desert. Woven into the text and illustrations are details about life in the desert. After sharing this book, children could list what animals are mentioned and then look for additional information in other library books and resources. *Cactus Hotel* would add additional details to the information gathered in *Desert Giant,* as would Carol Lerner's *Cactus.*

Learning that many resources are available on similar topics allows children to develop research strategies. They may read all of one book, like *Desert Giant,* but use the index in another, like *Cactus,* to look for specific information about how a cactus collects water or where cacti grow. They may decide to focus on one creature that depends on the cactus and use the library for encyclopedias, other books, and audiovisual materials. By sharing trade books with children, librarians and teachers can model some research strategies and can expose children to quality informational literature.

Audiovisual Adaptation

Desert Giant. "Reading Rainbow." Great Plains National Instructional Television Library, videorecording, 1989.

Related Titles

Cactus, written and illustrated by Carol Lerner. Morrow, 1992. This book provides a detailed look at cacti, including how and where they grow. A table of contents, glossary, and index are additional research aids.

Cactus Hotel, by Brenda Z. Guiberson. Illustrated by Megan Lloyd. Holt, 1991. The giant cactus provides a home and food for many desert animals. The jackrabbit chews on the cactus. The Gila woodpecker builds a home in the cactus and eats the insects that also feed on the cactus. Even after the cactus falls to the ground, it is used by the desert animals.

Cactus in the Desert, by Phyllis S. Busch. Illustrated by Harriett Barton. Crowell, 1979. This is a Let's-Read-and-Find-Out Science book. Several kinds of cactus plants are described, and there is information about how the cactus collects and stores water.

A Desert Year, written and illustrated by Carol Lerner. Morrow, 1991. For each of the four seasons, information is provided about mammals, birds, reptiles and amphibians, arthropods, and plants.

Deserts, by Seymour Simon. Morrow, 1990. Four deserts of North America are featured in this book: the Great Basin, the Mojave, the Sonoran, and the Chihuahuan. Physical conditions, plants, and animals are described.

Deserts, by Lynn M. Stone. Rourke, 1989. Illustrated with photographs. One chapter describes plants of the desert, including the cactus and other succulents.

The Hidden Life of the Desert, written and illustrated by Thomas Wiewandt. Crown, 1990. Color photographs and a brief text introduce readers to some of the plants and animals of the desert.

A Night and Day in the Desert, written and illustrated by Jennifer Owings Dewey. Little, Brown, 1991. Animals and plants of the desert are described in a narrative text that describes one night and day.

One Day in the Desert, by Jean Craighead George. Illustrated by Fred Brenner. Crowell, 1983. The people and animals of the Sonoran Desert of Arizona are described in this book. Information about desert plants, including the cactus, is presented.

Berger, Fredericka. *Robots: What They Are, What They Do*
Illus. by Tom Huffman. Greenwillow, 1992, LB (0-688-09864-9)
Suggested Use Level: Gr. 1–3

Plot Summary

The simple text in this book is divided into sections. The introduction provides some background information about robots. Chapter 1, "Myth and Story," describes some of the early fictional accounts of robots, including Frankenstein. Chapter 2, "Myth Becomes Reality," explains the development of some early automatic machines. Chapter 3, "Today's Robots," describes some of the components of robots and the functions they can perform. This chapter also focuses on the computer programming that provides the robot with instructions. Chapter 4, "How We Use Robots," looks at industrial, agricultural, medical, and recreational applications for robotics. The Conclusion looks at the relationship between robots and humans. A glossary follows the text.

Thematic Material

This nonfiction book describes robots and some of the ways they are used. It could be included in a science study of technology.

Book Talk Material and Activities

Stories and poetry are the focus of many classroom and library activities, but there are excellent nonfiction books for reading aloud. *Robots: What They Are, What They Do* is a nonfiction book in the format of a beginning reader. The text is printed in large type, and the sentences are fairly simple. The lines of text have ample space between them, allowing readers to focus on the text more easily. There is a table of contents and a glossary to assist young researchers.

Before reading this book aloud to a group of third graders, the librarian asked the children to listen for two or three facts that interested them. They all had paper and pencils and were encouraged to jot down some key words. After hearing the story, the children shared their facts, which were copied by the librarian onto a transparency. Sometimes the page in the book was reread to check the information. During another visit, the class heard *Get Ready for Robots!*, and a similar activity followed. The children then looked at the information they learned from each book. They discussed how some facts were in both books, but that each book had some specialized information. Learning to read for information can be modeled with children so that they are better prepared to use nonfiction materials. *Robots: What They Are, What They Do* and *Get Ready for Robots!* are two titles that work very well for modeling strategies for obtaining information. Other robot and technology books were available in the library for additional reading, including *Robots: Your High-Tech World.*

These children were reading *My Robot Buddy* in their classroom. They used the information they had found in nonfiction books to talk about robots. If they could have a robot, as Jack does in the book, what would they want it to do? What name would they give it? How would they want their robot to look? Many children wanted a robot that would do their chores, particularly the dishes. Some children made model robots (from shoeboxes); others made drawings of their robots. They made a list of characteristics they would like a robot/friend to have. Using the informational books about robots enhanced their discussion of *My Robot Buddy.*

Related Titles

Almost the Real Thing: Simulation in Your High-Tech World, by Gloria Skurzynski, with photographs chosen and arranged by the author. Bradbury, 1991. Simulations involve creating situations to test possibilities. Robots have been used in simulations, particularly involving activities in space.

Get Ready for Robots!, by Patricia Lauber. Illustrated by True Kelley. Crowell, 1987. This book describes some of the uses for robots—at home, in a factory, even in the forest cutting trees. Some future uses for robots are suggested, including exploring under the sea and in space.

My Robot Buddy, by Alfred Slote. Illustrated by Joel Schick. Lippincott, 1975. Jack's parents get him a robot, Danny One, to be his friend and to help keep an eye on him. Jack and Danny have many adventures together.

Robots: Your High-Tech World, by Gloria Skurzynski. Illustrated with photographs. Bradbury, 1990. Color photographs of many different robots extend the text, which focuses on present-day robots as well as some future possibilities.

Voyager: An Adventure to the Edge of the Solar System, by Sally Ride and Tam O'Shaughnessy. Illustrated with photographs. Crown, 1992. *Voyager 1* and *Voyager 2* were designed to travel to the outer regions of the solar system. They were controlled from earth and contained complex computer systems that directed their travel and functions.

Voyagers 1 and 2: Robots in Space, by Ruth Radlauer and Carolynn Young. Illustrated with photographs. Childrens Pr., 1987. Describes the Voyager space project and highlights some of the information that was received from it.

About the Illustrator

HUFFMAN, TOM
Something about the Author, ed. by Anne Commire. Gale, 1981, Vol. 24, pp. 131–132.

Branley, Franklyn M. *Shooting Stars*
Illus. by Holly Keller. Crowell, 1989, LB (0-690-04703-7); pap., Trophy (0-06-445103-8)
Suggested Use Level: Gr. K–2

Plot Summary

Looking into the night sky, you can see "shooting stars." These are not really stars, they are bits of ash or rock. Meteors, meteoroids, and meteorites are described. Many meteoroids fall to earth, but they are too small to be noticed. Some large meteorites can be seen in museums, and a crater from a meteorite can be seen in Arizona. There are meteorite craters on the moon, Mercury, and Mars. Sometimes there are many meteorites, and they can be found on the ground after they land.

Thematic Material

This is a nonfiction science book about shooting stars. It is part of the Let's-Read-and-Find-Out Science series of books and is designed as an introductory nonfiction book for beginning readers.

Book Talk Material and Activities

Before a trip to the planetarium, a first grade class did some research in the library. This class had been learning about finding books in the library. They knew the fiction books were arranged alphabetically by the author's last name. They also knew there were different areas of fiction in this library, such as picture books and beginning readers. To prepare them for using some nonfiction books, the librarian showed them *Shooting Stars* and several other books about stars, including *The Sky Is Full of Stars* and *The Big Dipper*. As each book was displayed, the librarian asked a child to read the numbers on the spine. The number for each book began with 523, and the children were shown where other books with that number would be found in the library. They noticed that all the books near that shelf were about outer space, and they talked about how that would be helpful for them when they were doing their research, because if they knew the number for one book, they could find other similar books nearby.

Shooting Stars was then read aloud to this group. Some children noticed there were drawings and photographs in the book. Other children remembered specific facts that they heard. Often, what one child remembered would help another child think of an interesting fact. For example, one boy said, "Shooting stars are not stars." His classmate added, "Yes, they're just dust and rocks." Other children added their recollections about what they had heard. By sharing information, the children helped each other focus on facts. They also asked to see the page that had the information they wanted, and they checked the text to verify their memories. Many of these children selected space books when it was time to choose books. Not only were they interested in the topic, they knew where to find it in the nonfiction section of the library.

Related Titles

The Big Dipper, revised edition, by Franklyn M. Branley. Illustrated by Molly Coxe. Harper, 1991. Describes the stars that form the constellation the Big Dipper, also called Ursa Major. Tells how to find the Big Dipper using a compass.

The Sky Is Full of Stars, by Franklyn M. Branley. Illustrated by Felicia

Bond. Crowell, 1981. Provides an overview of how to look at stars, including how stars move through the day and through the seasons. Also describes some simple constellations.

Stars, by Seymour Simon. Illustrated with photographs and drawings. Morrow, 1986. Gives more detailed information about stars, focusing on types of stars, including variable stars, red giant stars, and dwarf stars.

The Sun, by Seymour Simon. Illustrated with photographs and drawings. Morrow, 1986. The sun is a star that is the center of our solar system. This book tells what it is like inside the sun and explains that the sun's light and heat are from explosions of hydrogen.

The Sun: Our Nearest Star, by Franklyn M. Branley. Illustrated by Don Madden. Crowell, 1988. This book provides simple facts about the sun, including what it is made of and why it shines. A simple experiment is included to show how the sun helps things grow.

About the Author

BRANLEY, FRANKLYN M.

More Junior Authors, ed. by Muriel Fuller. Wilson, 1963, pp. 24–25.

Something about the Author, ed. by Anne Commire. Gale, 1973, Vol. 4, pp. 32–34; ed. by Donna Olendorf, Gale, 1992, Vol. 68, pp. 34–38.

About the Illustrator

KELLER, HOLLY

Something about the Author, ed. by Anne Commire. Gale, 1986, Vol. 42, p. 123.

Cherry, Lynne. *The Great Kapok Tree: A Tale of the Amazon Rain Forest*

Illus. by the author. Harcourt, 1990 (0-15-200520-X)
Suggested Use Level: Gr. 2–4

Plot Summary

While chopping down a kapok tree in the rain forest, a man stops to rest. As he sleeps, he is visited by different creatures, who give him messages. A boa constrictor tells of the tree's age, a bee talks of his hive in the tree, and monkeys describe how the tree protects the soil from erosion. Tropical birds tell of other, burned-out forests they have seen. A tree frog warns of the creatures that will be without a home if the tree is destroyed, while a jaguar worries that without these creatures, he will find it difficult to find food. Porcupines, anteaters, a sloth, and a child add their warnings about the impact of the man's plan to destroy the tree. Awakening, the man sees the child and the animals. He leaves his axe and walks out of the forest. The endpapers depict tropical rain forests in the world and are bordered by drawings of some of the animals of the rain forest and an illustration of the layers of the forest.

Thematic Material

Ecology and caring for the environment are related themes in this book. This book could be included in studies of the rain forest and endangered environments and species.

Book Talk Material and Activities

The message in *The Great Kapok Tree* could be a springboard to nonfiction books about the rain forest. Children could learn more about the conditions in the rain forest. They could research individual plants and animals. *The Great Kapok Tree* is a persuasive text. Are there other issues to consider? Beginning with one point of view, children could research different perspectives on the issues associated with the rain forest. Their research could expand to other ecological issues. Chris Van Allsburg's *Just a Dream* provides another look at a possible future.

The endpapers provide a model for a mural on the rain forest, or on other biomes. As children research plants and animals, they could illustrate their research and provide brief captions. Incorporating written information into the visual display adds to the shared information. Children could contact some of the organizations that provide information about the rain forest (there is a list of organizations and addresses in *Rain Forest Secrets*) or visit a rain forest display at a zoo or museum.

Related Titles

Just a Dream, written and illustrated by Chris Van Allsburg. Houghton, 1990. Walter is very careless about the environment, until he falls asleep and dreams about some of the problems the world may face in the future.

One Day in the Tropical Rain Forest, by Jean Craighead George. Illustrated by Gary Allen. Crowell, 1990. A young Indian boy observes the struggle between supporters of preserving the environment and developers who wish to bring technological advances to the rain forest.

Rain Forest, written and illustrated by Helen Cowcher. Farrar, 1988. This book also carries a message about preserving and protecting the rain forest. The animals in *Rain Forest* express emotions about the encroaching machines that are destroying their habitat.

Rain Forest Secrets, written and illustrated by Arthur Dorros. Scholastic, 1990. Plants and animals in the rain forest are featured in this book. The layers of the forest (canopy, understory, forest floor) are described. Included is a list of names and addresses of rain forest organizations.

Rainforest Animals, by Michael Chinery. Illustrated by David Holmes and Bernard Robinson. Random, 1991. Many unusual creatures are featured in this book, including the tarsier, the tailorbird, the kinkajou, and arrow-poison frogs. For each animal, there is a fact box and a special "Do You Know" feature.

What Do You Know about Rainforests?, by Brian J. Knapp. Illustrated with photographs. Simon & Schuster, 1991. Presents facts about the rain forests, including geographical locations and forest crops.

About the Author and Illustrator

CHERRY, LYNNE
Something about the Author, ed. by Anne Commire. Gale, 1984, Vol. 34, pp. 51–52.

Cole, Joanna.   *The Magic School Bus on the Ocean Floor*
Illus. by Bruce Degen. Scholastic, 1992 (0-590-41430-5)
Suggested Use Level: Gr. K–2

Plot Summary

When the class is studying oceans, its teacher, Ms. Frizzle, plans a field trip to the ocean. The students plan for a day at the beach, but in the Magic School Bus, Ms. Frizzle takes them to the ocean floor instead. As the bus travels under the water, the children (and a lifeguard who unexpectedly joins the class) learn about the continental shelf, tides, sea plants and creatures, and the floor of the ocean. They visit a coral reef and surf on giant waves. On their return to school, the class works on a mural of some of the sights of the trip. Displayed throughout the book are examples of student reports and projects. Jokes and other humorous remarks are included, usually in the comments of the characters.

Thematic Material

There is a blend of fact and fantasy in *The Magic School Bus on the Ocean Floor*. It is an informational picture book with a creative format and a humorous tone.

Book Talk Material and Activities

Children love the adventures of Ms. Frizzle and her students. They laugh at the jokes and puns, and at Ms. Frizzle's outfits, while they learn information about the waterworks, the body, the solar system, the earth, and now, the ocean. They use the inventive format to meet different needs, sometimes reading the student reports for information and sometimes reading the jokes for fun. Many children model their own reports and projects after the ones they see in these books. Knowing that Ms. Frizzle's shoes, clothes, and accessories often signal the next area of study for her class, they try to guess the next destination for the Magic School Bus. (At the end of the ocean unit, Ms. Frizzle is wearing an ensemble featuring prehistoric images.) They create outfits for Ms. Frizzle to accompany new areas of study.

The Magic School Bus on the Ocean Floor could be a springboard to other informational books on the ocean. A book talk program could feature books that expand the areas studied by the students in Ms. Frizzle's class, including tides, the ocean floor, and sea creatures.

Related Titles

The Desert beneath the Sea, by Ann McGovern and Eugenie Clark. Illustrated by Craig Phillips. Scholastic, 1991. Descriptions of sea creatures that are based on observations are featured in this book.

The Magic School Bus at the Waterworks, by Joanna Cole. Illustrated by Bruce Degen. Scholastic, 1986. Where does water come from? How does it travel into homes and other buildings? Ms. Frizzle takes her class right into the raindrops and follows the process of water purification back to their school.

The Magic School Bus inside the Earth, by Joanna Cole. Illustrated by Bruce

Degen. Scholastic, 1987. The class travels into the earth to observe fossils, volcanoes, and caves.

The Magic School Bus inside the Human Body, by Joanna Cole. Illustrated by Bruce Degen. Scholastic, 1989. Arnold swallows the Magic School Bus and Ms. Frizzle, and the class learns about the functions of the human body, only to be released when Arnold sneezes.

The Magic School Bus Lost in the Solar System, by Joanna Cole. Illustrated by Bruce Degen. Scholastic, 1990. Ms. Frizzle takes the class to the sun and then to all the planets. In the asteroid belt, Ms. Frizzle is separated from the bus. Is this the end of the class's adventures?

Oceans, by Seymour Simon. Illustrated with photographs and drawings. Morrow, 1990. There is information about the ocean floor, tides, currents, and waves in this well-written book.

Oceans, by Lawrence Williams. Illustrated with photographs and drawings. Marshall Cavendish, 1990. Chapters feature information about the ocean basins, currents, waves and tides, resources of the oceans, and other facts that would extend children's knowledge of the ocean. A table of contents, glossary, and index will help children as they do research.

Sunken Treasure, written and illustrated by Gail Gibbons. Crowell, 1988. Children are fascinated by stories of finding treasures. This book describes the work of archaeologists and divers as they recover and document the contents of a Spanish ship.

Under the Sea from A to Z, by Anne Doubilet. Photographed by David Doubilet. Crown, 1991. From anemones to zebrafish, this book presents a variety of sea creatures and plants.

About the Author

COLE, JOANNA

Fifth Book of Junior Authors and Illustrators, ed. by Sally Holmes Holtze. Wilson, 1983, pp. 77–78.

Something about the Author, ed. by Anne Commire. Gale, 1985, Vol. 37, p. 50; 1987, Vol. 49, pp. 68–74.

About the Illustrator

DEGEN, BRUCE

Sixth Book of Junior Authors and Illustrators, ed. by Sally Holmes Holtze. Wilson, 1989, pp. 74–76.

Something about the Author, ed. by Anne Commire. Gale, 1987, Vol. 47, p. 73; 1989, Vol. 57, pp. 27–30.

Dorros, Arthur. *Feel the Wind*

Illus. by the author. Crowell, 1989, LB (0-690-04741-X); pap., Harper (0-06-445095-3)

Suggested Use Level: Gr. 1–3

Plot Summary

What is wind? It is moving air. You can feel it, hear it, and see the things it moves. How wind is formed is described: the sun heats the air, the warm air rises, and cooler air moves to take its place. Examples are given using experiences that would be familiar to many children—for example, the sidewalk usually gets warmer than grass and dirt. As the warm air above the sidewalk rises, cooler air moves in. Some of the uses of wind-powered machines are described, including for irrigation and grinding grain. Directions for making a weather vane are provided.

Thematic Material

This nonfiction book presents information about the wind. It is part of the Let's-Read-and-Find-Out Science series and provides introductory science information for beginning readers.

Book Talk Material and Activities

Young children need many "hands-on" experiences as they investigate scientific principles. Learning about wind could lead to a discussion of related topics, such as weather and air. Beginning with the weather vane activity described in this book, children could look at books with other science experiments using air. Neil Ardley's *The Science Book of Air* suggests some simple activities.

In the classroom or library, a science station could be set up with the materials that would be used for experiments with air: a wool glove and a bowl of water to show how air is trapped in clothes; books and a balloon to demonstrate how air can lift objects. This could become a class project involving writing and using science books from the library. Children could look for other experiments, write them onto cards, gather the materials, and add them to the science station. Working in groups, other children could do the activities and report on the results. Some children may want to do a demonstration of the experiment. These "hands-on" activities involve children in using the library to research experiments, discussing the results, and writing or presenting their findings.

Related Titles

Air, by Angela Webb. Photography by Chris Fairclough. Watts, 1986. The photographs and text of this book encourage young children to investigate some of the properties of air. Questions are posed ("What happens when you fan yourself?"), and the young children in the photographs act out the principles being introduced.

Air Is All around You, revised edition, by Franklyn M. Branley. Illustrated by Holly Keller. Crowell, 1986. Simple facts about air are explained using familiar experiences and easy-to-do experiments.

The Science Book of Air, by Neil Ardley. Photography by Clive Streeter. Harcourt, 1991. These simple experiments with air demonstrate that air has space and weight; air pressure can make a bottle collapse and a paper plane fly.

The Science Book of Weather, by Neil Ardley. Photographed by Dave King. Harcourt, 1992. Simple activities are provided, including directions for making a weather vane and an anemometer and for creating a cloud in a bottle.

Weather Experiments, by Vera Webster. Illustrated with photographs. Childrens Pr., 1986. There are several experiments related to wind and air, including making a weather vane and a barometer.

Weather Words and What They Mean, written and illustrated by Gail Gibbons. Holiday, 1990. Some basic terms used to describe the weather are presented in this book, including explanations of air pressure and wind. The colorful illustrations enhance the explanation of the concepts.

Ehlert, Lois.   *Feathers for Lunch*
Illus. by the author. Harcourt, 1990 (0-15-230550-5)
Suggested Use Level: PreS–Gr. 1

Plot Summary

The cat has escaped from the house and is looking at the birds in the yard. It sees a robin, a blue jay, a cardinal, some wrens, a woodpecker, a blackbird, an oriole, some doves, some flickers, a hummingbird, a sparrow, and a goldfinch. The birds all hear the cat because there is a bell attached to its collar. The cat may get close to the birds, but the birds do not become the cat's lunch. Appended to the rhyming text is some information about each bird, including its size, food, home, and the area where it can be found.

Thematic Material

Cats and birds are part of the everyday experiences of many children. The factual information at the end of *Feathers for Lunch* could be a springboard to the study of birds.

Book Talk Material and Activities

The rhyming text in *Feathers for Lunch* make it a fun book to read aloud. It could be included in a program on cats and expanded to include other pets. Children could share information about their pets, perhaps charting the types of pet, their names, and one favorite activity. Other stories about cats or other pets could be presented for children to select and sign out.

The facts about the birds that are included extend the story, encouraging children to look for birds in their neighborhoods. Stories, poetry, and nonfiction books about birds could be booktalked, including *A Year of Birds, Amazing Birds,* and *Bird Watch.*

Related Titles

Amazing Birds, by Alexandra Parsons. Photographed by Jerry Young. Knopf, 1990. Color photographs are accompanied by captions and a brief text to focus on interesting birds, including the vulture and the hummingbird. This is part of the Eyewitness Juniors series.

Bird Watch: A Book of Poetry, by Jane Yolen. Illustrated by Ted Lewin.

Philomel, 1990. Images of birds are captured in poetic words and colorful illustrations.

Cookie's Week, by Cindy Ward. Illustrated by Tomie dePaola. Putnam, 1988. Beginning with Monday, the daily adventures of Cookie the cat are described.

Feathered Ones and Furry, by Aileen Fisher. Illustrated by Eric Carle. Crowell, 1971. These poems are about animals, including the pelican, squirrel, robin, duck, and raccoon.

Kitten, by Angela Royston. Photographed by Jane Burton. Dutton, 1991. Newborn kittens cuddle with their mother, who lets them explore and play. Color photographs show the offspring up to ten weeks old.

Only the Cat Saw, written and illustrated by Ashley Wolff. Dodd, Mead, 1985. As the sun is setting, the cat begins to prowl around the countryside. Parallel information shows what is happening inside the house and what the cat observes outside.

A Year of Birds, written and illustrated by Ashley Wolff. Dodd, Mead, 1984. A young girl watches the birds that visit her house throughout the year. (Condensed in *Primaryplots,* Bowker, 1989, pp. 284–286.)

About the Author and Illustrator

EHLERT, LOIS

Illustrators of Children's Books: 1957–1966, comp. by Lee Kingman, Grace Allen Hogarth, and Harriet Quimby. Horn Book, 1968, pp. 103, 203, 216; *1967–1976, Vol. IV,* 1978, pp. 116, 187.

Something about the Author, ed. by Anne Commire. Gale, 1984, Vol. 35, pp. 97–98; ed. by Donna Olendorf, Gale, 1992, Vol. 69, pp. 50–53.

Talking with Artists, comp. and ed. by Pat Cummings. Bradbury, 1992, pp. 36–41.

George, William T. *Box Turtle at Long Pond*
Illus. by Lindsay Barrett George. Greenwillow, 1989, LB (0-688-08185-1)
Suggested Use Level: Gr. 1–3

Plot Summary

In the morning, a box turtle leaves the rotting log where he has spent the night. He moves slowly toward the pond to drink some water. Box turtles cannot swim, so he walks away to look for food. While looking for some wild grapes, he sees a chipmunk. Now that the sun is out, the box turtle finds a rock and basks in the sun, but when it begins to rain he moves under an apple tree. After the rain, the turtle eats some worms. He pulls into his shell to escape the inquisitive attentions of a young raccoon. As evening comes, the turtle is still looking for food and returns to the wild grapes. Some birds have been feeding there, and there are now many grapes on the ground. After eating, the turtle nestles in some pine needles for the night.

Thematic Material

This nature story follows the activities of a box turtle on one day. The information about the pond and surrounding area could be included in science units on habitats.

Book Talk Material and Activities

The four books in the Long Pond series describe activities in nature. Focusing on one location, the books describe what happens during the day *(Box Turtle at Long Pond)* and night *(Beaver at Long Pond)*. Seasons are also presented, including winter *(Christmas at Long Pond)* and spring *(Fishing at Long Pond)*. These books could be booktalked prior to a class visit to a pond or nature center along with other pond books, like *The Hidden Life of the Pond.*

Children could extend these books by reading other books that feature animals, including *The Goodnight Circle, Large as Life: Nighttime Animals,* and *Large as Life: Daytime Animals.* A related activity would be to chart daytime and nighttime animals. Making a mural of Long Pond and the animals that live there would encourage children to reread these books and to focus on details in each book.

Audiovisual Adaptation

Box Turtle at Long Pond. Soundprints, cassette/book, 1989.

Related Titles

Beaver at Long Pond, by William T. George and Lindsay Barrett George. Illustrations by Lindsay Barrett George. Greenwillow, 1988. At dusk, the beaver leaves his lodge and searches for food. He chews on the trunk of a black birch tree and, when it falls, eats the bark and some branches. At dawn, he encounters a boy with his dog. The beaver hurries back to the safety of his lodge.

Christmas at Long Pond, by William T. George. Illustrations by Lindsay Barrett George. Greenwillow, 1992. When a father and son and their dog come to Long Pond in the winter to look for their Christmas tree, there are many animals, some they see and some they do not. A snowshoe hare is chased by a great horned owl. A doe and two fawns are disturbed by the people. The boy and his father walk across the frozen pond, looking at the beaver lodge.

Fishing at Long Pond, by William T. George. Illustrated by Lindsay Barrett George. Greenwillow, 1991. Katie and Grampy are fishing for bass on Long Pond. At the pond, there are many plants, including wild irises, swamp azaleas, and blueberry bushes. Animals include deer, a Canada goose, and an osprey, which swoops down and catches a perch. Katie catches a bass, which they take home for dinner.

The Goodnight Circle, by Carolyn Lesser. Illustrated by Lorinda Bryan Cauley. Harcourt, 1984. Deer, foxes, turtles, and frogs all prepare to sleep, but owls, beavers, opossums, and raccoons are busy throughout the night.

The Hidden Life of the Pond, by David M. Schwartz. Photographed by Dwight Kuhn. Crown, 1988. Bullfrog, salamander, mallard ducks, crayfish, raccoon, water strider, and the star-nosed mole are some of the animals featured in the color photos and descriptive text.

Large as Life: Daytime Animals, by Joanna Cole. Illustrated by Kenneth Lilly. Knopf, 1985. The illustrations in this oversized book are life-size depictions of several animals, including the erimin, the common tree frog, and the eastern chipmunk. A brief text describes each animal.

Large as Life: Nighttime Animals, by Joanna Cole. Illustrated by Kenneth Lilly. Knopf, 1985. The elf owl, chinchilla, and giant toad are among the nighttime animals described in this book.

Hoban, Tana.   *All about Where*
Photographs by the author. Greenwillow, 1991, LB (0-688-09698-0)
Suggested Use Level: PreS–Gr. 1

Plot Summary
Twenty-six color photographs illustrate words that show locations. The photographs are printed on pages that are approximately ¾ the size of the rest of the pages in the books. The photography pages are "framed" by full-sized pages that list fifteen location words: above, on, behind, under, out, against, across, between, in, through, beside, among, below, over, and around. Scenes in the photographs show children jumping rope, a boat in a bottle, ladders leaning on a house, and other images that could lead to discussions of what is happening and where it is taking place.

Thematic Material
All about Where encourages observations and discussions about locations.

Book Talk Material and Activities
Tana Hoban has created many books of photographs illustrating concepts. Her books offer opportunities for language experience activities as children examine the pictures and create their own descriptions. Preschool and kindergarten children could work with older children for a cooperative learning experience that crosses grade levels. Young children could dictate their descriptions to older children, thus having an opportunity to see their words in print. Children could discuss different words that apply to the locations in *All about Where*. For example, a picture of a child blowing a bubble could be described as saying the child is *behind* the bubble or that the child is looking *through* the large bubble-maker or that the bubbles are floating *in* the air. By discussing many words, children improve both their vocabulary and their social skills.

Other Tana Hoban photographic concept books could be looked at for locations. The everyday scenes in *Is It Red? Is It Yellow? Is It Blue?*, *Look! Look! Look!*, and *Shapes, Shapes, Shapes* could provide opportunities to talk about above, below, between, and the other location words in *All about Where*. Stories like *Rosie's Walk* and *Bear Hunt* incorporate location words into the plot; *We're Going on a Bear Hunt* (see chapter 4) is another book to use. Other books in which characters look for something missing (such as *Where's Spot?* and *Where Can It Be?*) could promote more discussions of locations.

Related Titles

Bear Hunt, by Margaret Siewert and Kathleen Savage. Illustrated by Leonard Shortall. Prentice-Hall, 1976. This is a popular game involving locations such as over and under. Children enjoy seeing familiar activities in a book.

Is It Red? Is It Yellow? Is It Blue? An Adventure in Color, written and photographed by Tana Hoban. Greenwillow, 1978. As they look for red, yellow, and blue, children will find many colors in these photographs of everyday places.

Look! Look! Look!, written and photographed by Tana Hoban. Greenwillow, 1988. A square is cut in the middle of a black page, revealing a small portion of the photograph on the next page. Turning the page shows the full photograph. Some of the items include a dog, yarn, a flower, and a pumpkin.

Rosie's Walk, written and illustrated by Pat Hutchins. Macmillan, 1968. As Rosie the hen goes for a walk, a fox follows her. Rosie goes across, around, over, past, through, and under. The illustrations show all the disasters that befall the fox while Rosie calmly continues her walk.

Shapes, Shapes, Shapes, written and photographed by Tana Hoban. Greenwillow, 1986. This book begins with a list of eleven shapes and a picture of each shape. Color photographs of everyday scenes and items follow, and children are encouraged to look for many different shapes. (Condensed in *Primaryplots,* Bowker, 1989, pp. 97–99.)

Where Can It Be?, written and illustrated by Ann Jonas. Greenwillow, 1986. As a little girl searches for her blanket, children lift pages that seem to open doors, pull down blankets, and lift up tablecloths.

Where's Spot?, written and illustrated by Eric Hill. Putnam, 1980. Spot's mother is looking for him. Children lift the flap on each page to see if Spot is there. Words like behind, inside, and under are used in the search for Spot.

About the Author and Illustrator

HOBAN, TANA

Fourth Book of Junior Authors and Illustrators, edited by Doris de Montreville and Elizabeth D. Crawford. Wilson, 1978, pp. 178–179.

Illustrators of Children's Books: 1967–1976, Vol. IV, comp. by Lee Kingman, Grace Allen Hogarth, and Harriet Quimby. Horn Book, 1978, p. 176.

Something about the Author, ed. by Anne Commire. Gale, 1981, Vol. 22, pp. 158–159; ed. by Donna Olendorf and Diane Telgen, Gale, 1993, Vol. 70, pp. 87–91.

Joseph, Lynn. *Coconut Kind of Day: Island Poems*
Illus. by Sandra Speidel. Lothrop, 1990, LB (0-688-09120-2); pap.,
Puffin (0-14-054527-X)
Suggested Use Level: Gr. 1-3

Plot Summary
Tropical colors—aqua water, pink and blue sky, and faces in shades of brown—depict the experiences of a young girl in Trinidad. From early morning, to family experiences, to time at school with friends, these are poems about the daily life on a tropical island. Boys play cricket, vendors sell coconuts and mangoes, scarlet birds fly into the orange sky. There's a musical beat in some of the poems, and there are unusual sounds from island creatures. There are thirteen poems describing island experiences from morning to night.

Thematic Material
Poetry captures the rhythm and mood of many people and places. In *Coconut Kind of Day,* children are introduced to some of the experiences of the people of Trinidad.

Book Talk Material and Activities
Learning about other cultures helps children become more aware of the variety of ways of life in the world. Poetry, music, and stories show children how people live, work, and play. The poems in *Coconut Kind of Day* describe some daily experiences in Trinidad. "Miss Teacher" and "Snail Race" tell about being at school and with friends. "All Star Boys" describes how girls are excluded from this game of cricket. The lilt of the island language is captured in this poem and in several others. Eloise Greenfield's *Under the Sunday Tree* contains poems about another area of the Caribbean—the Bahamas. There are many similar images. For example, both books include poems about people carrying things on their heads. And fishing is featured in both books. *Caribbean Carnival* features songs of the West Indies, like "Day-O" and "Yellow Bird." Several stories would also correlate with a study of the Caribbean, including *Baby-O, Island Baby,* and the folktales in *A Wave in Her Pocket.* All these would help children develop a better understanding of this area.

Related Titles

Baby-O, by Nancy White Carlstrom. Illustrated by Suçie Stevenson. Little, Brown, 1992. The lively rhythm and repeated words tell about a baby, brother, sister, mama, papa, grandfather, and grandmother who board the jitney bus to the market. The family's activities include fishing and collecting mangoes, which could be correlated with poems in *Coconut Kind of Day.*

The Calypso Alphabet, by John Agard. Illustrated by Jennifer Bent. Holt, 1989. Letters of the alphabet feature the life and language of the Caribbean, including "O for Okra" and "S for Sugarcane."

Caribbean Carnival: Songs of the West Indies, by Irving Burgie. Illustrated by Frané Lessac. Tambourine, 1992. Popular songs of this region, including "Jamaica Farewell" and "Day-O," provide images of everyday experiences. There are notes about the songs that describe their roots and focus on calypso.

Island Baby, written and illustrated by Holly Keller. Greenwillow, 1992. Simon's grandfather cares for injured birds. With his grandfather's help, Simon rescues a wounded flamingo and nurses it back to health. When it is time to release the bird, Simon has mixed feelings.

Under the Sunday Tree: Poems, by Eloise Greenfield. Illustrated by Amos Ferguson. Harper, 1988. There are twenty poems focusing on different experiences in the Bahamas, including fishing and watching the tourists.

A Wave in Her Pocket: Stories from Trinidad, by Lynn Joseph. Illustrated by J. Brian Pinkney. Clarion, 1991. Six stories are related here, some part of the folklore of Trinidad, some reflecting the heritage of Africa.

Lyon, George Ella. *A B Cedar: An Alphabet of Trees*
Illus. by Tom Parker. Orchard, 1989, LB (0-531-08395-0)
Suggested Use Level: Gr. 2–4

Plot Summary

Framed by a brief rhyme, twenty-six trees are presented, from Aspen to Zebrawood. All the capital letters of the alphabet are printed in black across each double-page spread, while the letters for the trees featured on that page are printed in a rust color. For example, J and K are printed in a rust color on the pages featuring Juniper and Kumquat. The illustrations provide additional information about each tree. Placed at the bottom of each page is a small black silhouette of each tree. Under the tree silhouette are silhouettes of people, to provide a reference for the size of the tree. Large hands reach across each page, sometimes holding a leaf or the fruit/nut of the tree. These hands have the skin tones of many peoples, thus providing multicultural images.

Thematic Material

A B Cedar presents the capital letters of the alphabet and names a tree to correlate with each letter. This book could be included in science curriculum units on observation and nature.

Book Talk Material and Activities

The alphabet is a seemingly simple concept that is introduced to young children. In *A B Cedar*, however, the alphabet is used as the structure for presenting information. Classrooms studying leaves and trees have used this book as a model for their own tree projects. Children have researched the size, leaf shape, and fruit/nut of other trees. They drew an outline of their own hands on a paper and gave their information in the style of *A B Cedar*. Some created collages using leaves, twigs, and other materials they collected.

An informational alphabet book like *A B Cedar* can also serve as a springboard for writing projects on other subjects. In some classrooms, students made their own alphabet books on astronomy, animals, geographical landmarks and locations, or other topics of interest. They studied other theme-based alphabet books, like *Animal Alphabet, Under the Sea from A to Z, Astronaut to Zodiac,* and *Antler, Bear, Canoe.* They looked at books with unusual formats, like David Pelham's pop-up *A Is for Animals.* Their finished projects were very creative in content and format.

Related Titles

A Is for Animals: An Animal ABC, written and illustrated by David Pelham. Simon & Schuster, 1991. Readers lift the flaps in this book, and animals pop out. The creative format of this book inspires children to try their own pop-up projects.

Animal Alphabet, written and illustrated by Bert Kitchen. Dial, 1984. In this oversized alphabet book, each letter of the alphabet is illustrated by an animal, from armadillo to zebra. (Condensed in *Primaryplots,* Bowker, 1989, pp. 105–106.)

Antler, Bear, Canoe: A Northwoods Alphabet Year, written and illustrated by Betsy Bowen. Little, Brown, 1991. Woodcut illustrations are used to depict the habitats and changing seasons in the northern woods.

Astronaut to Zodiac: A Young Stargazer's Alphabet, by Roger Ressmeyer. Illustrated with photographs. Crown, 1992. An alphabet of information about space and explorations.

Under the Sea from A to Z, by Anne Doubilet. Photographed by David Doubilet. Crown, 1991. From anemones to zebrafish, this book presents a variety of sea creatures and plants.

About the Author

Lyon, George Ella
Something about the Author, ed. by Donna Olendorf. Gale, 1992, Vol. 68, pp. 150–152.

Maass, Robert. *When Autumn Comes*
Photographs by the author. Holt, 1990 (0-8050-1259-1); pap. (0-8050-2349-6)
Suggested Use Level: PreS–Gr. 1

Plot Summary

In *When Autumn Comes*, the text describes activities associated with fall: the harvest, returning to school, Halloween, falling leaves. People prepare for the coming of winter by cutting wood, cleaning chimneys, and doing repairs. The farmer prepares the fields for the snow; animals store food. With the coming of Thanksgiving, there is cold and snow. Clear color photographs depict these events, ending with the arrival of winter.

Thematic Material

This nonfiction photoessay provides some introductory information about what happens in autumn.

Book Talk Material and Activities

Books about autumn, both fiction and nonfiction, could be featured at a story program in a school or public library. Included could be books about fall activities, like going back to school and celebrating Halloween.

The photographic images in *When Autumn Comes* focus on a New England community. What is fall like in other areas? What experiences are featured in your neighborhood? Football games, cornstalks, and sunny beaches may be familiar images. The school or public library might want to display children's photographs or drawings that relate to fall.

A book talk or display could feature many seasonal titles, including the photoessays for each season by Ron Hirschi and Thomas D. Mangelsen. Marjorie N. Allen and Shelley Rotner feature changes that occur in nature in the book *Changes*. And Ann Schweninger has three seasonal books that include activities for different times of the year *(Summertime, Autumn Days,* and *Wintertime)*. Seasonal poetry, like *In for Winter, Out for Spring* and *The Sky Is Full of Song* could also be featured.

Related Titles

Autumn Days, written and illustrated by Ann Schweninger. Viking, 1991. A community of dogs describe some activities they enjoy in the autumn, including planting bulbs, making a wreath of leaves, and celebrating Halloween and Thanksgiving.

Caps, Hats, Socks, and Mittens: A Book about the Four Seasons, by Louise Borden. Illustrated by Lillian Hoban. Scholastic, 1989. Activities and items associated with each season are presented after a patterned phrase—for instance, "Winter is . . . ," "Spring is . . . ," etc. Children could make their own list of things they associate with each season.

Changes, by Marjorie N. Allen and Shelley Rotner. Photographs by Shelley Rotner. Macmillan, 1991. Color photographs capture changes in nature, from bud to bloom, egg to bird, baby to toddler to child.

Fall, by Ron Hirschi. Photographs by Thomas D. Mangelsen. Dutton, 1991. Color photographs and a poetic text depict some of the images of fall: flocks of birds, falling leaves, salmon returning, frost on the ground.

In for Winter, Out for Spring, by Arnold Adoff. Illustrated by Jerry Pinkney. Harcourt, 1991. Playing in the snow, finding the first flower, going barefoot, and collecting walnuts are some of the activities featured in these poems.

School, written and illustrated by Emily Arnold McCully. Harper, 1987. In this wordless book, it is fall and the mouse children are returning to school. The littlest mouse decides to go to the school too.

The Sky Is Full of Song, edited by Lee Bennett Hopkins. Illustrated by Dirk Zimmer. Harper, 1983. The 38 poems in this collection celebrate the seasons. Included are poems from many well-known poets, such as Aileen Fisher, Lilian Moore, David McCord, and Gwendolyn Brooks. (Condensed in *Primaryplots,* Bowker, 1989, pp. 219–221.)

Spring, by Ron Hirschi. Photographs by Thomas D. Mangelsen. Dutton, 1990. Color photographs of spring flowers and of birds and animals are described in a brief, poetic text.

Summer, by Ron Hirschi. Photographs by Thomas D. Mangelsen. Dutton, 1991. Summer is described as a time for plants and animals to grow. Color photographs show birds, bears, caribou, and moose.

Summertime, written and illustrated by Ann Schweninger. Viking, 1992. In the summer, these dogs learn about flowers, thunderstorms, and gardens. They enjoy making ice pops and sleeping outside.

Winter, by Ron Hirschi. Photographs by Thomas D. Mangelsen. Dutton, 1990. Scenes of snow and ice and of the plants, animals, and birds that survive in the winter are described in the color photographs and brief text.

Wintertime, written and illustrated by Ann Schweninger. Viking, 1990. When the cold weather comes, these dogs are ready. They know to dress warmly, and they enjoy looking for animal tracks. They even describe how to make a bird feeder.

McDonald, Megan.   *Is This a House for Hermit Crab?*
Illus. by S. D. Schindler. Orchard, 1990, LB (0-531-08455-8)
Suggested Use Level: Gr. K–2

Plot Summary

Hermit Crab has grown too big for the shell where he has been living. As he scrambles across the sand, he searches for a new home. He finds a rock, but it will not be a suitable house. Nor will an old can, or a piece of driftwood, or a plastic pail, or the hole of a fiddler crab, or a fishing net. There does not seem to be any house for Hermit Crab. When he is swept into the sea, he must hurry to escape a hungry fish. As he scurries across the ocean floor, he finds a sea snail—but the shell is empty. Hermit Crab pulls himself into the shell and is safe from the hungry fish. Finally, Hermit Crab has a new house.

Thematic Material

This nonfiction picture book presents factual information about hermit crabs by focusing on the adventures of one hermit crab who needs a larger house.

Book Talk Material and Activities

Is This a House for Hermit Crab? could be read along with Eric Carle's *A House for Hermit Crab.* Some second graders were surprised that these books had titles that are so similar. They read the books carefully to find where the stories and illustrations were the same and where they were different. Both books describe how the hermit crab uses abandoned shells from other creatures for its "house." There is also a sequence of events in each book. In *Is This a House for Hermit Crab?*, the crab looks at a rock, an old can, a piece of driftwood, a plastic pail, the house of a fiddler crab, and a fishing net before finding another shell for his home. At the end of Megan McDonald's book, Hermit Crab is happy to have found a home. In *A House for Hermit Crab,* the crab finds a shell for a home right away, but then he wants to decorate it. He adds a sea anemone, a starfish, a coral, a snail, a sea urchin, and a lanternfish before he builds a wall of pebbles around his shell. At the end of Eric Carle's book, a year has passed (the months of the year are incorporated into the story), and Hermit Crab needs a new home. He gives his decorated shell to a young hermit crab. The children felt that *Is This a House for Hermit Crab?* was more realistic, while *A House for Hermit Crab* had some fanciful elements. Several children looked at informational books about animal homes for more facts about hermit crabs.

After looking at these books, many children wrote stories using a sequence of characters. They looked for other books that used a sequence of events, like *Chicken Little, One Fine Day,* and *Why Mosquitoes Buzz in People's Ears.*

Related Titles

Animals and Their Hiding Places, by Jane R. McCauley. Illustrated with photographs. National Geographic Society, 1986. Only one photograph and a brief bit of text discuss the hermit crab; in the section entitled "More about Animals and Their Hiding Places," however, there is information about having a land hermit crab as a pet.

Animal Homes, by Thomas Rowland Entwistle. Illustrated by Graham Allen, Mike Atkinson, Roy Coombs, and Susan Neale. Random, 1987. The hermit crab is discussed in the section called "Borrowers and Sharers." As in Eric Carle's *A House for Hermit Crab,* this crab has a sea anemone on its shell.

Chicken Little, retold and illustrated by Steven Kellogg. Morrow, 1985. When an acorn hits Chicken Little on the head, she hurries to tell other animals, including Henny Penny, Ducky Lucky, Goosey Loosey, Gosling Gilbert, and Turkey Lurkey.

A House for Hermit Crab, written and illustrated by Eric Carle. Picture Book, 1991. Beginning in January, a hermit crab searches for a larger house. When he finds it, he continues searching for ways to make it more decorative. After a year has passed, the crab has outgrown his house and begins to look for another.

One Fine Day, retold and illustrated by Nonny Hogrogian. Macmillan, 1971. After drinking the old woman's milk, the fox loses his tail. He must find a way to repay the old woman so she will sew his tail back in place. He asks the grass for help, but the grass wants water. He asks the water for help, but the water wants a jug. Everything he asks wants something in return.

Why Mosquitoes Buzz in People's Ears, retold by Verna Aardema. Illustrated by Leo Dillon and Diane Dillon. Dial, 1975. The events in this story happen in a sequence, as the mosquito bothers the iguana, who frightens the python, who worries the rabbit, who alerts the crow, who upsets the monkey. The monkey hurries through the trees and breaks a branch that falls and kills a baby owl.

About the Author

McDONALD, MEGAN
Something about the Author, ed. by Donna Olendorf. Gale, 1992, Vol. 67, p. 135.

About the Illustrator

SCHINDLER, S. D.
Something about the Author, ed. by Anne Commire. Gale, 1988, Vol. 50, p. 188.

Morris, Ann. *Bread Bread Bread*
Photographs by Ken Heyman. Lothrop, 1989, LB (0-688-06335-7); pap., Mulberry (0-688-12275-2)
Suggested Use Level: PreS–Gr. 2

Plot Summary
Throughout the world, people make, share, and enjoy bread. The text of this book describes different types and shapes of bread. The color

photographs extend the text, showing the importance of bread in many cultures. An index is included, telling the location of each picture and providing additional information. Included are scenes from Israel, the United States, Peru, Ghana, England, Indonesia, France, Portugal, India, Germany, Sicily, Greece, Italy, Mexico, Ecuador, Hong Kong, and Guatemala.

Thematic Material

Focusing on the importance of bread, this book provides insight into world cultures.

Book Talk Material and Activities

Young children need opportunities to learn about other people and other ways of living. Their self-centered view of the world is expanded by reading about and discussing different experiences. The books by Ann Morris focus on very familiar topics: bread *(Bread Bread Bread)*, hats *(Hats Hats Hats)*, and families *(Loving)*. Ken Heyman's photographs depict images from many countries and help young children see that something that is familiar to them is familiar to many children and their families. The index pages, which cite the locations of each photograph, emphasize the international impact of the experiences. Other books could be included that feature the activities of children around the world, like going to school *(This Is the Way We Go to School)* and playing games *(Hopscotch around the World)*.

A story program focusing on *Bread Bread Bread* and the other collaborations between Ann Morris and Ken Heyman could lead to a discussion of nonfiction books that describe cultures and countries. James Haskins's Count Your Way Through . . . books, such as *Count Your Way through the Arab World*, provides information about numerals and the world where they are used. Leonard Everett Fisher's *Alphabet Art* and *Number Art* provide some information about cultures within the framework of a presentation about alphabets and numbers. The Take a Trip to . . . series from Watts and the Families the World Over series (entitled "A Family in . . .") from Lerner Publications provide introductory information about countries that could be shared with primary grade children.

Related Titles

Alphabet Art: Thirteen ABCs from around the World, written and illustrated by Leonard Everett Fisher. Four Winds, 1985. Provides brief facts about thirteen alphabets, including Chinese, Greek, Hebrew, and Japanese.

Count Your Way through the Arab World, by James Haskins. Illustrated by Dana Gustafson. Carolrhoda, 1987. Arabic numerals from one to ten are introduced, along with details about life in the Arab world.

A Family in Italy, by Penny Hubley and John Hubley. Illustrated with photographs. Lerner Publications, 1987. This book focuses on the everyday activities of one family in Italy. Other books in the series focus on families in Mexico, Egypt, Morocco, and other countries.

Hats Hats Hats, by Ann Morris. Illustrated by Ken Heyman. Lothrop, 1989. As in *Bread Bread Bread,* this book depicts many cultures, focusing on different varieties of hats. An index of the locations is included.

Hopscotch around the World, by Mary D. Lankford. Illustrated by Karen Milone. Morrow, 1992. Many versions of hopscotch are played around the world, including Pele, which is played in Aruba, and Ta Galagala, which is played in Nigeria. In addition to the descriptions of nineteen hopscotch games in this book, there is a map of the locations and a bibliography of the research sources.

Loving, by Ann Morris. Photographs by Ken Heyman. Lothrop, 1990. Color photographs and a brief text focus on caring relationships in families around the world. An index of the locations is included. The locations are also indicated on an outline map of the world.

Number Art: Thirteen 1 2 3s from around the World, written and illustrated by Leonard Everett Fisher. Four Winds, 1982. Includes information about thirteen numerical systems, including Egyptian, Roman, and Mayan.

Take a Trip to Morocco, by Keith Lye. Illustrated with photographs. Watts, 1988. Describes the people, geography, culture, and history of Morocco. Some of the other books in this series feature Israel, Syria, and Turkey.

This Is the Way We Go to School: A Book about Children around the World, by Edith Baer. Illustrated by Steven Björkman. Scholastic, 1990. A rhyming text describes the ways many children go to school. After the story, there is a list of where each child lives and a map showing the locations.

About the Illustrator

HEYMAN, KEN
Something about the Author, ed. by Anne Commire. Gale, 1984, Vol. 34, pp. 112–114.

Peters, Lisa Westberg. *Water's Way*
Illus. by Ted Rand. Little, Brown, 1991 (1-55970-062-9)
Suggested Use Level: Gr. K–2

Plot Summary

In Tony's house, water changes the environment. Steam from a pot on the stove fogs the kitchen window and drips down the glass. Water is changing the environment outside Tony's house too. Moist air from the sea cools and forms clouds. Rain falls from the clouds forming puddles, which evaporate in the warmth of the afternoon sun. Inside, Tony takes a bath, mixing bath soap into the water. Outside, streams flow into rivers and then mix into the water of the sea. The water inside and out churns and bubbles. As night comes, the clouds again drop water, this time as snow, and Tony scratches his name in the frost on his window. In the morning, Tony takes his new sled out into the snow, enjoying the way the water has changed.

Thematic Material

Scientific concepts are part of the everyday life of children. Information about water and weather is included in many science curriculum units.

Book Talk Material and Activities

Young children can see science in their own homes. Like Tony in *Water's Way,* they may have seen water boil or heard steam hissing from a tea kettle. They may have written on steamy windows. Teachers and librarians can build on these personal experiences by discussing the scientific principles that are being demonstrated. Simple experiments can be set up around the classroom or library. Children can be introduced to the science sections in the library, focusing on books with experiments, like the "Science Book of" series.

Water's Way could also spark an interest in weather and forecasting. Children enjoy monitoring the weather and keeping charts. They could use resources from the library to learn more about meteorology, perhaps even visiting a local television station to observe the preparation for a broadcast. *Weather Forecasting* and *What Will the Weather Be?* would be good resource books for children.

Related Titles

Amy Loves the Rain, by Julia Hoban. Illustrated by Lillian Hoban. Harper, 1989. On a rainy day, Amy rides in the car with her mom. Together they enjoy the sights and sounds of the rain.

Anna's Rain, by Fred Burstein. Illustrated by Harvey Stevenson. Orchard, 1990. A young girl and her father go out into the rain to make sure there is food for the birds.

The Cloud Book, written and illustrated by Tomie dePaola. Holiday, 1975. Information about specific clouds and the weather conditions they indicate is featured in this book.

Rain and Hail, by Franklyn M. Branley. Illustrated by Harriett Barton. Harper, 1983. Types of clouds, water vapor, and condensation are described, as well as the difference between rain and hail. This is a Let's-Read-and-Find-Out Science book.

The Science Book of Water, by Neil Ardley. Photographed by Clive Streeter. Harcourt, 1991. The experiments in this book provide examples of buoyancy, displacement, density, and other properties of water.

The Science Book of Weather, by Neil Ardley. Photographed by Dave King. Harcourt, 1992. Simple activities are provided, including directions for making a weather vane and an anemometer and for creating a cloud in a bottle.

Snow Is Falling, revised edition, by Franklyn M. Branley. Illustrated by Holly Keller. Crowell, 1986. This Let's-Read-and-Find-Out Science book provides factual information about snow, including why snow is useful and how it can be harmful.

The Sun, the Wind and the Rain, by Lisa Westberg Peters. Illustrated by Ted Rand. Holt, 1988. Elizabeth is at the beach making a mountain of sand. As she creates her mountain, the formation of another mountain is described. This mountain was formed of hot rock that shifted and cooled over millions of years.

Weather Forecasting, written and illustrated by Gail Gibbons. Four Winds, 1987. Weather for each of the four seasons is described, as are some of the techniques and instruments used to forecast the weather. Weather terms are defined.

Weather Words and What They Mean, written and illustrated by Gail Gibbons. Holiday, 1990. Some basic terms used to describe the weather are presented, including explanations of air pressure and wind. The colorful illustrations enhance the explanation of the concepts.

What Will the Weather Be?, by Lynda DeWitt. Illustrated by Carolyn Croll. Harper, 1991. Some basic concepts of the weather are explained, including how a cold front may produce rain or snow and how meteorologists use many measurements to predict the weather.

About the Illustrator

RAND, TED

Sixth Book of Junior Authors and Illustrators, ed. by Sally Holmes Holtze. Wilson, 1989, pp. 238–239.

Rockwell, Anne.   *Apples and Pumpkins*
Illus. by Lizzy Rockwell. Macmillan, 1989 (0-02-777270-5)
Suggested Use Level: PreS–Gr. 1

Plot Summary

In the fall, a father, mother, and young girl visit a farm and pick apples from the orchard. Before they leave, the little girl selects one pumpkin, and her father cuts it off the vine. At home, the pumpkin becomes a jack-o'-lantern for Halloween.

Thematic Material

Apples and Pumpkins gives simple information about farms and orchards. This book could also be included in programs for Halloween.

Book Talk Material and Activities

Even though this book focuses on a family trip to a farm, it could be read before a class or day-care center field trip. Children could discuss some of the things they expect to see or do on the trip. After they return, a class book could be made describing the experience.

Many schools are incorporating more field trips and hands-on experiences into the curriculum for young children. Children sometimes visit the same place at different times in the year and observe the changing seasons. *Apples and Pumpkins* could be read before a trip in the fall. Books like *The Seasons of Arnold's Apple Tree* and *The Life and Times of the Apple* could provide children with information about the other seasons. Stories about Johnny Appleseed would add to the enjoyment.

Children may want to plant pumpkin seeds and watch them grow, documenting changes like those photographed in *The Pumpkin Patch.*

Related Titles

An Apple a Day: From Orchard to You, by Dorothy Hinshaw Patent. Photographs by William Muñoz. Dutton, 1990. There is a description of how apples grow, how they are marketed, and products that are made with apples in this book. Color photographs highlight the text.

Apple Tree, written and illustrated by Peter Parnall. Macmillan, 1987. This book focuses on what the apple tree provides for other creatures, including pollen for bees, a nesting place for birds, and food for woodland animals.

Apple Tree, written and illustrated by Barrie Watts. Silver Burdett, 1986. Color photographs and a simple text present information about apples, from bud to fruit.

An Apple Tree through the Year, by Claudia Schnieper. Photographs by Othmar Baumli. Carolrhoda, 1987. This book provides more detailed information than Watts's *Apple Tree* and would be useful for students doing reports.

How Do Apples Grow?, by Betsy Maestro. Illustrated by Giulio Maestro. Harper, 1992. Text and illustrations describe how apples grow, including information about pollination and different varieties of apples. This book is part of the Let's-Read-and-Find-Out Science series.

Johnny Appleseed: A Tall Tale, retold and illustrated by Steven Kellogg. Morrow, 1988. Kellogg's biography of John Chapman's life is lively and full of fun.

The Life and Times of the Apple, written and illustrated by Charles Micucci. Orchard, 1992. This book is filled with apple facts. From information about planting seeds to cut-away drawings of an apple flower to varieties of apples to Johnny Appleseed, this is a super book to use before visiting an orchard or cider mill.

The Pumpkin Patch, written and photographed by Elizabeth King. Dutton, 1990. Color photographs present the development of a pumpkin from seed to flowering plant to fruit.

The Seasons of Arnold's Apple Tree, written and illustrated by Gail Gibbons. Harcourt, 1984. Arnold's apple tree is his own secret place, and throughout the year, he enjoys his tree—climbing, watching bees, picking blossoms, building a tree house, picking apples, and hanging food for winter birds.

About the Author

ROCKWELL, ANNE

Fifth Book of Junior Authors and Illustrators, ed. by Sally Holmes Holtze. Wilson, 1983, pp. 264–266.

Illustrators of Children's Books: 1967–1976, Vol. IV, comp. by Lee Kingman, Grace Allen Hogarth, and Harriet Quimby, Horn Book, 1978, pp. 6, 154–155, 207.

Something about the Author, ed. by Anne Commire. Gale, 1983, Vol. 33, pp. 170–174; ed. by Diane Telgen, Gale, 1993, Vol. 71, pp. 165–168.

Rotner, Shelley, and Kreisler, Ken. *Nature Spy*

Photographs by Shelley Rotner. Macmillan, 1992 (0-02-777885-1)
Suggested Use Level: PreS–Gr. 1

Plot Summary

A little girl leaves her house and observes her neighborhood. She looks at flowers and leaves, often studying the details of these items. Color photographs provide close-up images of acorns, seeds, feathers, and even the eye of a frog. Shapes, patterns, colors, and sizes are emphasized as the little girl encourages readers to observe their world.

Thematic Material

Nature Spy encourages children to observe the world around them. The close-up color photography in this book focuses on looking at details.

Book Talk Material and Activities

Preschools, libraries, and day-care centers often take advantage of regional parks and nature centers for trips. Children are encouraged to look closely at leaves, flowers, rocks, rivers, and animals. Reading *Nature Spy* before a trip would help prepare children for their experience. The photographs in *Nature Spy* correlate with the text to encourage young children to develop their observations skills, to look more closely at ordinary things. Arthur Dorros's *Animal Tracks* is another book that alerts young readers to nature "clues" that they might observe, specifically the tracks of animals, like the raccoon, frog, robin, black bear, beaver, dog, and human. *The Listening Walk* would be another good choice to include in a story program on developing an awareness of the world around us.

After sharing books and then taking an observation walk, children could work on some nature projects. In *Animal Tracks,* there are instructions for making plaster casts of tracks as well as for making tracings or drawings. *My First Nature Book* has more suggestions for activities. *Nature All Year Long* and Ann Schweninger's series on the seasons *(Summertime, Autumn Days,* and *Wintertime)* incorporate stories and projects that relate to different times during the year.

Related Titles

Animal Tracks, written and illustrated by Arthur Dorros. Scholastic, 1991. A question-and-answer format introduces children to the tracks that are made by some common animals, including a porcupine, deer, and some ducks. The endpapers depict the tracks of more than twenty animals.

Autumn Days, written and illustrated by Ann Schweninger. Viking, 1991. A community of dogs describe some activities they enjoy in the autumn, including planting bulbs, making a wreath of leaves, and celebrating Halloween and Thanksgiving.

The Listening Walk, by Paul Showers. Illustrated by Aliki. Harper, 1991. On a walk with her father and their dog, a girl listens carefully and hears the dog's toenails on the sidewalk, a lawn mower, a baby crying, a wood-pecker, and other everyday sounds.

Look! Look! Look!, written and photographed by Tana Hoban. Greenwillow, 1988. A die-cut square shows one part of the photograph on the next page, encouraging the reader to suggest possibilities for what is depicted. For example, through the square there are curved pink layers. The next page reveals a pink rose.

My First Nature Book, by Angela Wilkes. Photographs by Dave King. Knopf, 1990. Very clear descriptions and photographs encourage children to explore their world. Simple nature activities are included, such as collecting seeds, making bird feeders, and pressing flowers.

Nature All Year Long, written and illustrated by Clare Walker Leslie. Greenwillow, 1991. Information and activities are presented for each month of the year. Included are animal tracks, rain projects, suggestions for drawing birds, seacoast activities, and leaf identifications.

Summertime, written and illustrated by Ann Schweninger. Viking, 1992. In the summer, these dogs learn about flowers, thunderstorms, and gardens. They enjoy making ice pops and sleeping outside.

Wintertime, written and illustrated by Ann Schweninger. Viking, 1990. When the cold weather comes, these dogs are ready. They know to dress warmly, and they enjoy looking for animal tracks. They even describe how to make a bird feeder.

Royston, Angela. *Duck*

Photographs by Barrie Watts. Dutton, 1991 (0-525-67346-6)
Suggested Use Level: PreS–Gr. 2

Plot Summary

A mother duck sits on a nest. Color photographs show the sequence of an egg hatching. The baby duck pushes out of the shell. The young duck learns to swim, looks for things to eat, grows new feathers, and becomes a full-grown duck.

Thematic Material

The factual information in this book introduces young children to ducks and how they grow.

Book Talk Material and Activities

Duck is part of the See How They Grow series of books, which includes *Kitten*, *Frog*, and *Chick*. These books feature color photographs and a brief text to present information to beginning readers. The photographs are placed on a white background to minimize clutter. Young children who are learning to read can follow the sequence of events through the photographs. The text is clear and direct, suitable for beginning readers. Children enjoy making their own See How I Grow stories, using photographs from when they were babies, toddlers, and preschoolers.

When small animals are cared for in schools and libraries, an information center can be created. Children can gather resource materials, like *Duck* and *Ducks Don't Get Wet*. They can chart the growth and changes of the animal. They can monitor the chores, including feeding and cleaning. When they write stories and poems about the animal or draw pictures, these can be included in the display, along with stories like *Have You Seen My Duckling?*, *Make Way for Ducklings*, and *The Chick and the Duckling*.

Related Titles

Chick, by Angela Royston. Photographed by Jane Burton. Dutton, 1991. Color photographs show a chick from hatching to eight weeks old.

The Chick and the Duckling, translated and adapted by Mirra Ginsburg. Illustrated by Jose Aruego and Ariane Dewey. Macmillan, 1972. The chick tries to imitate the duckling, until the duckling goes for a swim.

Ducks Don't Get Wet, by Augusta Goldin. Illustrated by Leonard Kessler. Crowell, 1989. Ducks cover their feathers with oil so that when they get wet, the water beads up on the feathers and can be shaken off.

Egg Story, written and illustrated by Anca Hariton. Dutton, 1992. As the hen sits on her eggs, cut-away drawings show the internal development of an egg. Finally, the eggs hatch and the hen takes the chicks out into the farmyard.

Frog, by Angela Royston. Photographed by Kim Taylor and Jane Burton. Dutton, 1991. From egg to tadpole to frog, color photographs and captions describe the growth cycle of a frog.

Have You Seen My Duckling?, written and illustrated by Nancy Tafuri. Greenwillow, 1984. One duckling wanders off, and the mother duck tries to find it.

Kitten, by Angela Royston. Photographed by Jane Burton. Dutton, 1991. Newborn kittens cuddle with their mother, who lets them explore and play. Color photographs show the kitten up to ten weeks old.

Make Way for Ducklings, written and illustrated by Robert McCloskey. Viking, 1941. After the ducklings are born, Mrs. Mallard wants to take them from the Charles River to the pond in the Public Garden in Boston. Their walk across Boston attracts lots of attention.

Schoenherr, John. *Bear*
Illus. by the author. Philomel, 1991 (0-399-22177-8)
Suggested Use Level: Gr. 1–3

Plot Summary

A young bear awakens to find that he has become separated from his mother. He begins to forage for food, eating some berries and bulbs. A lemming bites him, and he runs toward the forest. Alone and hungry, he wanders for several days over mountains and across cold, barren snowfields. One night, he climbs a tree to escape another bear. In the morning, he hurries down from the tree, rushing into the icy water of a stream filled with salmon. His first efforts to catch a salmon are frustrating, but he continues, finally succeeding. He stays at the stream for weeks, eating fish, growing larger, and even chasing an old bear away. He is able to survive on his own.

Thematic Material

Bear is a realistic picture book story. It focuses on some of the situations that one young bear might experience in the wild.

Book Talk Material and Activities

In many books for children, animals are depicted as carefree and friendly. Many are shown living as humans—wearing clothes, sleeping in beds, going to school. Reading *Bear* would be a contrast to these animal fantasy books. In *Bear*, the bear must survive on his own, often at the expense of other animals. His life depends on his ability to defend himself and adapt to his environment. The bear in this book is not described in terms of human emotions. He is "alone," but not "lonely"; he faces dangers but he is not "afraid." The author's careful use of language does not anthropomorphize this bear. The bear's behaviors reflect his instinctive need to face the often harsh realities of his world and survive. In *The Barn*, John Schoenherr presents another realistic view of the natural world, this time describing the experiences of a skunk. Jane Yolen's *Owl Moon* describes the experiences of a young girl and her father as they look for an owl on a winter night. Schoenherr's realistic water color paintings for *Owl Moon* received the Caldecott Medal in 1988.

Researching bears would be a natural follow-up to reading or booktalking *Bear*. How do naturalists work with bears? How is information gathered about the life of bears in the wilderness? *Bearman* describes the black bear but also presents details about how bears are studied. Other realistic nature stories could be highlighted, including *Tigress* and *Raccoons and Ripe Corn*.

Audiovisual Adaptations

Bear. Soundprints, cassette/book, 1991.

Related Titles

The Barn, written and illustrated by John Schoenherr. Little, Brown, 1968. As a skunk searches for food, he becomes the target of a hungry owl in this realistic story of predator and prey.

Bearman: Exploring the World of Black Bears, by Laurence Pringle. Photographs by Lynn Rogers. Scribner, 1989. In this nonfiction photoessay, Pringle describes the work of photographer Lynn Rogers, a biologist who has spent many years observing black bears in Minnesota.

Bears, by Lynn M. Stone. Illustrated with photographs. Rourke, 1990.

This introductory nonfiction book describes how and where bears live, what they look like, and how they interact with people.

Black Bears, by Caroline Greenland. Illustrated with photographs. Grolier, 1986. This nonfiction book would provide information for middle-grade students. The table of contents, glossary, and index provide reference assistance. This book is part of the Nature's Children series, which also includes *Grizzly Bears,* by Caroline Greenland (Grolier, 1986).

Owl Moon, by Jane Yolen. Illustrated by John Schoenherr. Philomel, 1987. A young girl and her father go owling together for the first time on a winter's night. John Schoenherr received the Caldecott Medal in 1988 for his watercolor illustrations. (Condensed in *Primaryplots,* Bowker, 1989, pp. 240–243.)

Raccoons and Ripe Corn, written and illustrated by Jim Arnosky. Lothrop, 1987. During the night, a family of raccoons comes into the cornfield and eats the corn. As morning comes, they hurry back to the woods.

Tigress, written and illustrated by Helen Cowcher. Farrar, 1991. This picture book presents a realistic situation. Three tigers (a tigress and two cubs) leave their own area to search for food in the sanctuary. The herdsmen and ranger want to protect themselves and their animals without destroying the tigers.

Watching Foxes, written and illustrated by Jim Arnosky. Lothrop, 1985. Colorful, realistic illustrations depict the antics of four fox cubs.

About the Author and Illustrator

SCHOENHERR, JOHN

Fourth Book of Junior Authors and Illustrators, ed. by Doris de Montreville and Elizabeth D. Crawford. Wilson, 1978, pp. 306–308.

Illustrators of Children's Books: 1957–1966, Vol. III, comp. by Lee Kingman, Grace Allen Hogarth and Harriet Quimby. Horn Book, 1978, pp. 170, 239; *1967–1976, Vol. IV,* 1978, pp. 61, 157, 208.

Something about the Author, ed. by Anne Commire. Gale, 1985, Vol. 37, pp. 166–170; ed. by Donna Olendorf, Gale, 1991, Vol. 66, pp. 194–198.

Simon, Seymour. *Mercury*
Illus. with photographs and drawings. Morrow, 1992, LB (0-688-10545-9)
Suggested Use Level: Gr. 1–4

Plot Summary
The planet Mercury is closest to the sun. It is visible from Earth at dusk and dawn. It has no moons and is smaller than the moons of several larger planets. Mercury is a heavy, dense planet. Its core is molten iron, followed by a layer of molten rock, and topped with a rocky crust. The surface of Mercury is similar to the surface of Earth's moon, with craters from meteorites or asteroids. Mercury has almost no atmosphere, so it is strongly affected by the sun. During the day, the temperature is over 750 degrees Fahrenheit, while at night, the temperature can reach −300 degrees Fahrenheit. There has been only one space probe that studied Mercury, *Mariner 10* in the mid-1970s, so scientists still have many questions about this planet.

Thematic Material
This nonfiction photoessay features the planet nearest to the sun, Mercury.

Book Talk Material and Activities
Seymour Simon has written a book about almost every planet in our solar system. He has a book about the sun, stars, galaxies, and Earth's moon. He has also written an overview, called *Our Solar System*. Each book features clearly written information and excellent photographs and drawings. The format of the books is slightly oversized with a photograph on the cover, making them very appealing. These books have become the nucleus of our "Seymour Simon Space Station." The books are on display (multiple copies make it possible to keep the display fairly complete), and there are writing materials nearby for children to take notes. When children complete reports or projects, their work is often added to the display. One child made a chart of the relative positions and sizes of the planets. Another child made a diorama of the moon circling the Earth while both

circled the sun. There are mobiles and models of the planets, stars, and comets.

Seymour Simon includes similar information in each of the books about the planets. He relates the information to children's familiar experiences on Earth. For example, in each book, Simon uses Earth as a frame of reference for the size of the planet being discussed. In *Mercury,* Simon notes that eighteen planets the size of Mercury could fit into the planet Earth. Working in pairs or small groups, children could chart this information from each book, and look for other information that is in each book, such as: What is it like on the surface of Mercury? (Answer: It is cratered, like the surface of Earth's moon.) Similar information could be listed for the other planets.

Related Titles

Earth: Our Planet in Space, by Seymour Simon. Illustrated with photographs and drawings. Four Winds, 1984. Simon describes the planet Earth, its position in space, its atmosphere, and its structure. This is a good book to share at the beginning of a study of Simon's books about other planets, most of which make some reference to Earth.

Galaxies, by Seymour Simon. Illustrated with photographs. Morrow, 1988. Focusing on the Milky Way galaxy, Simon describes the size, shape, and formation of galaxies, and also includes information about supernovas and magnetic clouds.

Jupiter, by Seymour Simon. Illustrated with photographs and drawings. Morrow, 1985. How many planet Earths could fit into the planet Jupiter? (Answer: More than 1,300.) What is is like on the surface of Jupiter? (Answer: It is an ocean of liquid hydrogen.) These are among the facts presented in this fascinating book.

Mars, by Seymour Simon. Illustrated with photographs and drawings. Morrow, 1987. How many planets the size of Mars could fit into the planet Earth? (Answer: Seven.) What is it like on the surface of Mars? (Answer: It is dusty and there are violent storms.) Color photographs from the *Mariner* and *Viking* spacecrafts enhance Simon's description of Earth's neighbor.

The Moon, by Seymour Simon. Illustrated with photographs and drawings. Morrow, 1984. Black-and-white photographs from lunar explorations, including photos of astronauts on the moon, add to the drama of this book. Earth's only natural satellite is described in detail.

Neptune, by Seymour Simon. Illustrated with photographs and drawings. Morrow, 1991. How many planet Earths could fit inside Neptune? (Answer: Forty-two.) What is it like on the surface of Neptune? (Answer: There are winds and hurricanes and clouds of methane-ice.) Much of the information in this book is from the *Voyager 2* spacecraft voyage from 1989.

Our Solar System, by Seymour Simon. Illustrated with photographs and drawings. Morrow, 1992. This overview of the solar system includes information about each planet, as well as information about comets, asteroids, and meteors. It includes information that is contained in the other books about the solar system.

Saturn, by Seymour Simon. Illustrated with photographs and drawings. Morrow, 1985. Facts about the size, length of day, and gravity of Saturn are explained in terms of experiences on Earth. Detailed information about Saturn's rings is accompanied by photographs and drawings. How many planet Earths could fit into Saturn? (Answer: 750.) What is it like on the surface of Saturn? (Answer: It is cold with very strong winds.) (Condensed in *Primaryplots,* Bowker, 1989, pp. 234–237.)

Stars, by Seymour Simon. Illustrated with photographs and drawings. Morrow, 1986. Children could read this book along with Simon's *The Sun* to find out the similarities and differences between these huge, hot balls.

The Sun, by Seymour Simon. Illustrated with photographs and drawings. Morrow, 1986. How many planet Earths could fit inside the sun? (Answer: 1.3 million.) What is it like on the surface of the sun? (Answer: It is a continuous series of nuclear explosions.) This book will encourage children's fascination with the sun.

Uranus, by Seymour Simon. Illustrated with photographs and drawings. Morrow, 1987. How many planet Earths could fit inside Uranus? (Answer: Fifty.) What is it like on the surface of Uranus? (Answer: Scientists think Uranus has a hot, watery atmosphere.) Uranus's rings are also described, with an explanation of how scientists found out about them.

Venus, by Seymour Simon. Illustrated with photographs and drawings. Morrow, 1992. Venus and Earth are similar in size. What is it like on the surface of Venus? (Answer: It is very hot on Venus, and there is very little water.) Information is included from the *Magellan* spacecraft in 1990.

About the Author

SIMON, SEYMOUR

Fifth Book of Junior Authors and Illustrators, ed. by Sally Holmes Holtze. Wilson, 1983, pp. 292–294.

Something about the Author, ed. by Anne Commire. Gale, Vol. 4, pp. 191–192.

Simon, Seymour. *Snakes*
Illus. with photographs. Harper, 1992, LB (0-06-022530-0)
Suggested Use Level: Gr. 2–4

Plot Summary

Snakes are fascinating creatures. Most are basically harmless to humans, even some of the snakes that have poisonous venom. Snakes can be found on most continents of the world. Snakes have the features of other reptiles. Their internal organs are described as well as their ability to bend their bodies. Snakes are very strong, using much of their strength as they move. Snakes move in different ways, including looping along the ground and sidewinding. Snakes grow quickly and they usually eat animals, which they catch by waiting quietly, catching the animal in their powerful jaws, and then swallowing the animal. The senses of sight, smell, and hearing are different for snakes. Some snakes are hatched from eggs, others are live at birth. Enemies to the snake include frogs, foxes, badgers, coyotes, birds, and even other snakes. Humans are also a great threat to snakes. Some harmless snakes are discussed, followed by giant snakes and poisonous snakes.

Thematic Material

In this photoessay, factual information about snakes is presented.

Book Talk Material and Activities

When a class of fourth graders came to the library, the librarian had three recent books about snakes on display: *Snakes* by Seymour Simon, *Take a Look at Snakes* by Betsy Maestro, and *Amazing Snakes* by Alexandra Parsons. The library activity focused on evaluating these nonfiction books. The children were asked to suggest some criteria to apply to these books, and the librarian wrote their ideas on the chalkboard. Some of their suggestions included "The book should be about the topic—snakes," "There should be information about different snakes," "It should tell about poisonous snakes," "It should tell how snakes move," and "It should show their fangs." When asked about illustrations, one student said, "Snakes are real, so the pictures should be real too. And in color." Many other children supported this expectation of having color photographs.

The librarian reminded them that these were nonfiction books, ones they might use for reports. She asked them about other features that would help them, like a table of contents, an index, and a glossary. Most students felt that an index would be important, especially if they were interested in just one kind of snake. The librarian then went through each book, looking for the features that were suggested. *Amazing Snakes* has color photographs of snakes and was arranged by topics, such as "What is a snake?," "The deadly cobra," and "How snakes move." It has a table of contents and an index. The students liked that there were several photographs and drawings on each double-paged spread and that there was information in the captions for the pictures. *Take a Look at Snakes* is illustrated with detailed color drawings, and there are no reference aids. There are several drawings on each page and captions that explain the drawings. The drawings often show a close-up view of what is being described, like the pit on a pit viper. Even though these students had asked for color photographs, they liked the drawings in this book. They felt that the drawings showed things that might not have been easy to photograph, like a snake swallowing a fish. *Snakes* has a larger format than the other two books. There are color photographs, one per page. The photographs are not captioned, but the snake that is shown is referred to in the text on the page across from it. The photographs are very sharp and often dramatic, like a yellow rat snake swallowing a rodent. There are no reference aids.

After seeing each book, the class started to talk about which one was "the best." Everyone felt that Seymour Simon's *Snakes* was the most dramatic. The cover, with a photograph of a young green tree python wrapped around a stick, was very enticing. (There was a note explaining that this yellow snake would turn green as an adult, hence the name.) The librarian read them some of the information aloud, and most of the fourth graders felt they would read it on their own. Even though there was no contents or index, the students said the book looked so interesting, they would just read it all. One girl said, "I've read lots of Seymour Simon books. He always tells me what I want to know." The children felt that *Amazing Snakes* would be useful too. They were familiar with other books in this series, and they liked to browse through the tidbits of information. *Take a Look at Snakes* also received a positive vote from this class. One girl said, "At first, I didn't like that there were no photographs, but I really thought the drawings were good." The librarian read aloud from this book, and the children found the facts interesting and easy to understand.

Seeing three different nonfiction books encouraged these children to think about different formats for informational books. It let them describe what they felt would be useful and then apply their criteria to specific books. Even when the book did not end up meeting their criteria, they realized it could still be a book they would use and enjoy. This information helped them see the importance of having many materials in the library on similar topics. It also helped them when they were selecting informational books, and many students found other snake books that interested them.

Related Titles

Amazing Snakes, by Alexandra Parsons. Photographs by Jerry Young. Knopf, 1990. The information in this book is presented on double-page spreads. Specific snakes are featured, including the cobra, rattlesnake, and milk snake. Much of the information in this book is presented in the captions that accompany the color photographs and drawings.

Discovering Snakes and Lizards, by Neil Curtis. Illustrated with photographs. Bookwright, 1986. Information is divided into chapters describing what snakes and lizards look like, where they live, what they eat, reproduction, and how they survive. Color photographs accompany the text, and there is a table of contents, a glossary, a bibliography, and an index.

Poisonous Snakes, by Seymour Simon. Illustrated by William R. Downey. Four Winds, 1981. Cobras, sea snakes, vipers, and rattlesnakes are featured in this book. Information about fangs and venom is included, as well as a chapter called "How Dangerous Are Poisonous Snakes?" There are black-and-white drawings, a table of contents, a bibliography, and an index.

Snake, by Caroline Arnold. Photographs by Richard Hewett. Morrow, 1991. Rosy is a boa at the Los Angeles Zoo. She is used in the zoo's educational program. After describing Rosy, the text provides information about other snakes. This book has color photographs and an index.

Take a Look at Snakes, by Betsy Maestro. Illustrated by Giulio Maestro. Scholastic, 1992. Illustrated with drawings, this book provides an overview of snakes, including where they live, how they move, and what they eat. Specific snakes are not featured, but there is information about many different snakes.

About the Author

SIMON, SEYMOUR

Fifth Book of Junior Authors and Illustrators, ed. by Sally Holmes Holtze. Wilson, 1983, pp. 292–294.

Something about the Author, ed. by Anne Commire. Gale, Vol. 4, pp. 191–192.

Stock, Catherine. *Armien's Fishing Trip*
Illus. by the author. Morrow, 1990, LB (0-688-08396-X)
Suggested Use Level: Gr. 1–3

Plot Summary
Armien is visiting his Aunt Amelia and Uncle Faried in Kalk Bay, on the southern tip of Africa. This is where Armien used to live, and he misses being by the water and with his friends. As he fishes with his friends, they tease him about having moved inland. To show off, Armien brags that his uncle is taking him fishing the next day, even though that is not true. Early the next morning, Armien sneaks out of the house and onto his uncle's boat. When the boat is out at sea, Armien leaves his hiding place. He sees an old fisherman, Sam, cutting bait, but then a wave crashes into the boat, sweeping Sam overboard. Armien calls for help, alerting the other fishermen. Uncle Faried rescues Sam. Back in the harbor, Armien is a hero, and everyone celebrates his bravery.

Thematic Material
Armien's Fishing Trip is set in South Africa, and details about the community and its way of life are woven into the story and illustrations. This story of Armien's adventures could be included in social studies units on families around the world.

Book Talk Material and Activities
Through stories like *Armien's Fishing Trip*, children learn about other people and the way they live. Set in a fishing village in South Africa, this book focuses on a very familiar experience—bragging to your friends. Within the story, there are details about Kalk Bay, such as the kind of fish that are caught and how the people come to the jetty to buy the fresh fish, using *rands* and *bobs* for payment. Armien's aunt makes him a *samoosa* to eat. A note at the beginning of the book discusses how this area was settled by "Filipino fishermen, European sailors, and freed slaves from Malaya and Java." This diversity is reflected in the illustrations. For example, Armien is depicted with light-brown skin, and his friends include a white boy and two boys with darker brown skin.

Sharing other books set in this area of Africa offers more opportunities to discuss the diversity of experiences. In *Over the Green Hills*, Zolani leaves the seacoast and travels inland, passing through a village and seeing monkeys, pigs, and an ostrich. He plays with a pet mongoose at his grandmother's house, called a *rondavel*. *Not So Fast, Songololo* describes the experiences of a young boy on a trip to the city, while *Charlie's House* describes a family living in a shelter in a South African city. The details in these stories could be compared and contrasted with those in *Armien's Fishing Trip*. Children could also relate the experiences of these South African families to their own activities.

Related Titles

Charlie's House, by Reviva Schermbrucker. Illustrated by Niki Daly. Viking, 1991. Charlie lives in a shelter made of sheets of iron. In the mud around his home, Charlie creates a home for himself and his family. Charlie's imagination lets him dream about leaving the shelter home one day.

Galimoto, by Karen Lynn Williams. Illustrated by Catherine Stock. Lothrop, 1990. Kondi makes a toy car, a *galimoto,* out of some wire he has collected. This story is set in Malawi, a country in southeast Africa. Compare Kondi's village and activities with those of the characters in the other stories.

Jafta, by Hugh Lewin. Illustrated by Lisa Kopper. Carolrhoda, 1981. In this first book in a series about Jafta and his family, aspects of Jafta's lively personality are compared with animals that are a familiar part of his South African home.

Not So Fast, Songololo, written and illustrated by Niki Daly. Atheneum, 1985. Malusi lives with his family near a big city in South Africa. On a trip into the city, Malusi helps his grandmother, and she buys him a new pair of shoes (called "tackies"). (Condensed in *Primaryplots,* Bowker, 1989, pp. 212–214.)

Over the Green Hills, written and illustrated by Rachel Isadora. Greenwillow, 1992. Zolani lives in a village by the sea on the east coast of South Africa. He and his mother travel inland to visit Zolani's grandmother. There are many details about the animals and way of life in the Transkei homeland of South Africa in this story.

About the Author and Illustrator

STOCK, CATHERINE

Something about the Author, ed. by Donna Olendorf. Gale, 1991, Vol. 65, pp. 197–199.

Wilkes, Angela. *My First Green Book*
Photographs by Dave King and Mike Dunning. Knopf, 1991, LB
(0-679-91780-2)
Suggested Use Level: Gr. 1–4

Plot Summary

This nonfiction book, part of a series of My First books, features projects
and activities to involve children in preserving and protecting the environment. Many of the activities encourage observation; others are simple
experiments. Air pollution, acid rain, dirty water, water filtration, decom-
position, and recycling are some of the environmental issues presented.
Activities include "green shopping," creating a window box of wildflowers
and plants, growing plants that provide food for animals, and planting
trees. Suggestions for campaigning for environmental concerns, such as
protecting the rain forest, are given. One example is to organize a group
committed to environmental issues, complete with membership cards,
posters, and badges.

Thematic Material

Using this book, children will learn about environmental issues and be
introduced to ways to participate in conservation activities.

Book Talk Material and Activities

The My First books involve children in a variety of activities, including
science, nature, and cooking. The environmental focus of *My First Green
Book* correlates with many school and library programs on ecology and
conservation. Many children participate in recycling activities at home
and in school. They take newspapers, plastics, glass, and cans to collection
centers. They reuse paper. They begin to learn about packaging that is
environmentally friendly. Research projects often focus on environmental
issues, like the destruction of the rain forest (see *The Great Kapok Tree*,
elsewhere in this chapter), landfills *(Trash!)*, and disasters *(Spill! The Story of
the Exxon Valdez)*.

Many classrooms become involved in environmental projects, and they
use the resources of the library for suggested activities. Booktalking books
that present projects and activities capitalizes on the interest of children
and teachers. *Going Green, 50 Simple Things You Can Do to Save the Earth,*

Dinosaurs to the Rescue, and *Recycle!* would extend the introductory activities in *My First Green Book.*

Related Titles

Dinosaurs to the Rescue: A Guide to Protecting Our Planet, written and illustrated by Laurene Krasny Brown and Marc Brown. Little, Brown, 1992. Most of the dinosaurs in this community are working to improve the environment. Only Slobosaurus won't recycle, reuse, or reduce waste. Finally, some young dinosaurs get him involved in pitching in.

50 Simple Things You Can Do to Save the Earth, by the Earth Works Group. Earthworks Press, 1989. This collection of suggestions for recycling, carpooling, and conserving encourages readers to make a difference in the way the earth's resources are used.

Going Green: A Kid's Handbook to Saving the Planet, by John Elkington, Julia Hailes, Douglas Hill, and Joel Makower. Illustrated by Tony Ross. Puffin, 1990. Chapters describe various environmental concerns, like acid rain, the greenhouse effect, and water pollution. Activities and projects are included in an A to Z list, such as "Bike instead of ride" and "Don't buy aerosols."

My First Cook Book, by Angela Wilkes. Photographed by David Johnson. Knopf, 1989. Fun food projects—like pizzas with faces and designs—are attractively presented. Color photographs show the finished projects. Part of the series of My First books.

My First Nature Book, by Angela Wilkes. Photographed by Dave King. Knopf, 1990. Very clear descriptions and photographs prepare children for exploring the world around them. Activities include collecting seeds, making bird feeders, and pressing flowers. Some guidelines for enjoying nature are included. Part of the series of My First books.

My First Science Book, by Angela Wilkes. Illustrated with photographs by Dave King. Knopf, 1990. Simple activities are provided that illustrate some basic principles of science. Layering liquids, casting shadows, and creating gliders are some of the projects. Part of the series of My First books.

Recycle! A Handbook for Kids, written and illustrated by Gail Gibbons. Little, Brown, 1992. After a brief introduction, Gibbons presents information about recycling paper, glass, cans, and plastic. Information about polystyrene is also included. At the end of the book are facts about trash and suggestions for activities.

Spill! The Story of the Exxon Valdez, by Terry Carr. Illustrated with photographs and drawings. Watts, 1991. Color photographs show the devastation caused by the wreck of the *Exxon Valdez*. Particular attention is given to the wildlife that was destroyed and to the efforts to rescue animals.

Trash!, by Charlotte Wilcox. Photographed by Jerry Pushey. Carolrhoda, 1988. A variety of approaches to disposing of trash are explained, along with some suggestions for recycling.

7

Analyzing Illustrations

Pɪᴄᴛᴜʀᴇ books feature a wide variety of illustration techniques. The creativity of the artist often enhances the story, adding details and extending the meaning. Scratchboard, collage, watercolor, even handmade paper are some of the techniques used in the books in this chapter. Compare Leo Lionni's collages in *Six Crows: A Fable* to Eric Carle's art in *The Very Quiet Cricket*. Examine the nature paintings in *Keep Looking!* and those in *Turtle in July*. Look at Denise Fleming's paper art in *In the Tall, Tall Grass* and David Wisniewski's cut paper in *The Warrior and the Wise Man*. Children can become involved in examining illustrations and, thus, develop an appreciation for the contributions of the artists.

Carle, Eric. *The Very Quiet Cricket*
Illus. by the author. Philomel, 1990 (0-399-21885-8)
Suggested Use Level: PreS–Gr. 1

Plot Summary
A cricket is greeted by a variety of creatures. A large cricket, a locust, a praying mantis, a worm, a spittlebug, a cicada, a bumblebee, a dragonfly, and some mosquitioes all welcome him. When the cricket tries to answer, by rubbing his wings together, he does not make a sound. A luna moth flies past, and the cricket sees another cricket. She greets him and this time, when he rubs his wings together, he chirps his greeting to her. A sound chip on the last page of the book reproduces a chirping sound, and the cricket succeeds in communicating.

Thematic Material
This book uses creative book engineering to enhance the predictable, repetitive text. Eric Carle's collage illustrations and creative use of language tell a story of perseverence and success.

Book Talk Material and Activities

Eric Carle has written and/or illustrated some of the most popular books for children. Young children have learned about days of the week, colors, and counting while hearing *The Very Hungry Caterpillar*. They have used his illustrations for *Brown Bear, Brown Bear, What Do You See?* and *Polar Bear, Polar Bear, What Do You Hear?* to join in on the sequence and learn about patterns. They have learned about counting and the zoo in *1, 2, 3 to the Zoo*. His books often have unusual formats, like the fold-out pages in *Papa, Please Get the Moon for Me* and the raised web, spider, and fly in *The Very Busy Spider*. After hearing *The Very Quiet Cricket*, they become more aware of descriptive language and creative book-making. One group of first graders heard and discussed three Eric Carle books: *The Very Hungry Caterpillar, The Very Busy Spider,* and *The Very Quiet Cricket*. They looked at the patterned text and discussed how the special feature in each book really extended the story: the caterpillar's holes, the spider's web, and the cricket's chirp. After the discussion, one girl said, "That Eric Carle, he makes every book so special."

After reading many books by Eric Carle and talking about his illustrations, one teacher had her class make different kinds of textured paper. They made sponge paintings, they experimented with printing techniques, and they made designs with tissue paper. The pictures were then cut into random shapes to be used for collages, and children were encouraged to experiment with the different shapes and textures. The children in this class became familiar with the sequencing in many of Carle's books by charting the days of the week and the foods in *The Very Hungry Caterpillar*, the farm animals and sounds in *The Very Busy Spider*, and the insects and worm in *The Very Quiet Cricket*. The patterns in Carle's books (such as the days of the week or the sequence of colors) became a part of the art and stories the children were creating.

Related Titles

Brown Bear, Brown Bear, What Do You See?, by Bill Martin, Jr. Illustrated by Eric Carle. Holt, 1967. A brown bear sees a red bird who sees a yellow duck who sees a blue horse, and so on. Each animal is depicted with bright colors on a double-page spread, making this a fine book to share with a group of children.

Do Bears Have Mothers, Too?, written by Aileen Fisher. Illustrated by Eric Carle. Cromwell, 1973. These poems about baby animals are illustrated with large, colorful pictures of the animals and their mothers. Like *Brown Bear,* it is great to share with a group of children. Compare the pictures of the bears on the covers of these two books.

Draw Me a Star, written and illustrated by Eric Carle. Philomel, 1992. A young boy draws a star and then continues to draw throughout his life. He enjoys his own art and the appreciation it has brought him. A diagram for drawing a star follows the text.

Feathered Ones and Furry, by Aileen Fisher. Illustrated by Eric Carle. Crowell, 1971. These poems about animals are illustrated with linoleum cuts, some filling a page and some adding a small detail. Page 36 shows another bear to compare to other Carle pictures.

1, 2, 3 to the Zoo, written and illustrated by Eric Carle. Philomel, 1968. In this wordless book, a train chugs by carrying animals for the zoo. Each car carries one more animal than the car before it, beginning with one elephant and ending with ten birds. The last page folds out to show all the animals in the zoo. As with other books by Eric Carle, there is an extra feature. A miniature picture of the train appears at the bottom of the page and shows all the cars that have been presented.

Papa, Please Get the Moon for Me, written and illustrated by Eric Carle. Picture Book, 1986. A little girl asks her papa for the moon, and he climbs a ladder and brings it to her. The pictures in this book fold out, becoming larger and larger until the full moon is pictured and then decreasing in size as the moon wanes.

Polar Bear, Polar Bear, What Do You Hear?, by Bill Martin, Jr. Illustrated by Eric Carle. Holt, 1991. The sequence in this book goes from the polar bear, to the lion, to the hippopotamus, to the flamingo, to the zebra, to the boa constrictor, to the elephant, to the leopard, to the peacock, to the walrus, and finally to the zookeeper, who hears children.

The Very Busy Spider, written and illustrated by Eric Carle. Philomel, 1984. As a spider is spinning her web in the farmyard, farm animals come to talk to her. Each animal asks the spider to leave her work, but she will not. The spider finishes her web and catches a fly. The spider, her web, and the fly are printed on the pages with raised lines so they can be felt. (Condensed in *Primaryplots,* Bowker, 1989, pp. 254–256.)

The Very Hungry Caterpillar, written and illustrated by Eric Carle. Collins-World, 1969. The little caterpillar eats and eats until he is full, then he builds a cocoon and rests before becoming a butterfly. The die-cut holes in this book are perfect for showing the caterpillar's progress through the food he eats.

About the Author and Illustrator

CARLE, ERIC

Fourth Book of Junior Authors and Illustrators, ed. by Doris de Montreville and Elizabeth D. Crawford. Wilson, 1978, pp. 68–69.

Illustrators of Children's Books: 1967–1976, Vol. IV, comp. by Lee Kingman, Grace Allen Hogarth, and Harriet Quimby. Horn Book, 1978, pp. 11, 105–106, 183.

Something about the Author, ed. by Anne Commire. Gale, 1973, Vol. 4, pp. 41–43; ed. by Donna Olendorf, Gale, 1991, Vol. 65, pp. 30–36.

Ehlert, Lois. *Color Zoo*
   Illus. by the author. Lippincott, 1989, LB (0-397-32260-7)
   Suggested Use Level: PreS–Gr. 1

Plot Summary
   In this concept book, colors and die-cut shapes are used to create nine zoo animals. Included are a tiger, a mouse, a fox, an ox, a monkey, a deer, a lion, a goat, and a snake. The shapes are a square, a triangle, a circle, a rectangle, an oval, a heart, a diamond, an octagon, and a hexagon. The designs for the animals are done in layers of the shapes and colors; for example, the ox is formed from a rectangle, an oval, and a heart. A chart of shapes (including the star that outlines the title), colors, and animals appears at the end of the book.

Thematic Material
   Unusual illustrations, using layers of colors and shapes, make this an intriguing book for young children. *Color Zoo* was a Caldecott Honor book in 1990.

Book Talk Material and Activities
   The die-cut shapes in this book are combined with bright colors to imaginatively depict some familiar zoo animals. Children who see this book, and the companion *Color Farm*, are fascinated by the design of the book. They feel the shapes and often "read" the book in reverse order, adding shapes to create another animal. They are attracted by the bright colors of both *Color Zoo* and *Color Farm*. Some children enjoy taking shapes

and trying to make their own pictures. They also look at other books of shapes and colors to compare the way these concepts are presented, including books by Tana Hoban, like *Shapes, Shapes, Shapes,* and Bruce McMillan's *Fire Engine Shapes* (see chapter 3).

The books by Lois Ehlert are often the focus in classes where authors and illustrators are studied. She has illustrated several concept books, including an alphabet book *(Eating the Alphabet)* and several books featuring colors *(Color Farm, Color Zoo,* and *Planting a Rainbow)* and shapes *(Color Farm, Color Zoo)*. She uses collage for her illustrations, and she incorporates creative book design features, like die-cut and partial pages. In some books, the pages are bright colors (as in *Chicka Chicka Boom Boom*—see chapter 4), while others effectively use color and white space (as in *Feathers for Lunch* in chapter 6). Many children enjoy the variety and creativity of Lois Ehlert's books.

Related Titles

Circus, written and illustrated by Lois Ehlert. Harper, 1992. Bright-colored shapes on a black background create the excitement of a circus. An orange elephant, a blue bear, a green goat, and multicolored snakes are all part of the show.

Color Farm, written and illustrated by Lois Ehlert. Lippincott, 1990. Die-cut shapes and colors are layered to create farm animals, including a chicken, duck, sheep, pig, and cow.

Eating the Alphabet: Fruits and Vegetables from A to Z, written and illustrated by Lois Ehlert (see chapter 3). Harcourt, 1989. Collage illustrations show fruits and vegetables, both familiar (apples, lettuce, tomato) and less well known (gooseberry, jicama, ugli fruit).

Fish Eyes: A Book You Can Count On, written and illustrated by Lois Ehlert. Harcourt, 1990. A rhyming text introduces the sequence of numbers from one to ten in this book. Die-cut holes show the eyes of the fish. There is some simple addition in this book, as a small fish appears on each page and is added on to the number on that page.

Is It Red? Is It Yellow? Is It Blue? An Adventure in Color, written and illustrated by Tana Hoban. Greenwillow, 1978. Color photographs of everyday scenes are provided for readers to search for the colors red, yellow, and blue. Other language experience activities could be correlated with this book, like discussing shapes or describing what is happening.

My First Look at Shapes. Photography by Stephen Oliver. Random, 1990.

Color photographs of simple shapes are clearly labeled for young children to "point and say" the item and the shape.

1, 2, 3 to the Zoo, written and illustrated by Eric Carle. Philomel, 1968. In this wordless book, a train chugs by carrying animals to the zoo. Each car carries one more animal than the car before it, beginning with one elephant and ending with ten birds. The last page folds out to show all the animals in the zoo.

Planting a Rainbow, written and illustrated by Lois Ehlert. Harcourt, 1988. Flowers from every color of the rainbow are planted. Captions label the many plants.

Red Leaf, Yellow Leaf, written and illustrated by Lois Ehlert. Harcourt, 1991. Collage illustrations using materials of various textures depict the growth of a maple tree. Facts about the sugar maple are included after the text, along with information about planting a tree. Studying the illustrations, children will see actual seeds, sticks, and roots along with fabric, twine, and other materials.

Shapes, Shapes, Shapes, written and illustrated by Tana Hoban. Greenwillow, 1986. This book begins with a list of eleven shapes and a picture of each shape. Color photographs of everyday scenes and items follow, encouraging the reader to look for many different shapes and develop observation skills. (Condensed in *Primaryplots,* Bowker, 1989, pp. 97–99.)

THUMP, THUMP, Rat-a-Tat-Tat, by Gene Baer. Illustrated by Lois Ehlert. Harper, 1989. The sounds and excitement of a marching band are captured in the rhythm of the words and the bright colors and design of the illustrations.

About the Author and Illustrator

EHLERT, LOIS

Illustrators of Children's Books: 1957–1966, comp. by Lee Kingman, Grace Allen Hogarth, and Harriet Quimby. Horn Book, 1968, pp. 103, 203, 216; *1967–1976, Vol. IV,* 1978, pp. 116, 187.

Something about the Author, ed. by Anne Commire. Gale, 1984, Vol. 35, pp. 97–98; ed. by Donna Olendorf, Gale, 1992, Vol. 69, pp. 50–53.

Talking with Artists, comp. and ed. by Pat Cummings. Bradbury, 1992, pp. 36–41.

Fleming, Denise. *In the Tall, Tall Grass*
Illus. by the author. Holt, 1991 (0-8050-1635-X)
Suggested Use Level: PreS–Gr. 1

Plot Summary

A young child bends low and peeks into the grass, finding caterpillars, hummingbirds, bees, birds, ants, snakes, moles, beetles, frogs, rabbits, fireflies, and, as night falls, bats. Each creature is presented with descriptive words, many of which rhyme ("crunch, munch") or are onomatopoetic ("rich, ratch").

Thematic Material

In the Tall, Tall Grass is an adventure in observing nature and playing with language. The colorful illustrations could be featured in a study of picture books that creatively use papermaking and paper design techniques.

Book Talk Material and Activities

Exploring the natural world, even the simple world in the backyard, provides opportunities for young children to observe. *In the Tall, Tall Grass* could precede a neighborhood nature walk. This would be a super opportunity for some cooperative learning activities across grade levels. Young children could be paired with some older children. They could walk together and observe, with the older child taking notes and recording some of the observations. *Nature Spy* in chapter 6 would also correlate with this activity, as would *Nature Walk*.

The illustrations for *In the Tall, Tall Grass* are made using paper pulp. The book jacket notes that the author/illustrator "poured colored cotton pulp through hand-cut stencils. The result—handmade paper!" Children who have read and discussed many books would enjoy looking at the works of other artists who creatively use paper for their illustrations, including Leo Lionni (see *Six Crows*, elsewhere in this chapter), Eric Carle (see *The Very Quiet Cricket*, elsewhere in this chapter), and Ezra Jack Keats (for example, *The Snowy Day* and *Goggles*). One group of children became very interested in picture book art and looked for some other recent books with collage illustrations, adding Lois Ehlert (see *Color Zoo*, elsewhere in this chapter) and Patricia Mullins (for example, *Crocodile Beat* and *Shoes from*

Grandpa) to their list of artists. In their discussions, they noticed the variety of materials used, including tissue paper, sticks, twine, and paper that the artist painted or created. Many children began to experiment with using found materials in their own art projects.

Audiovisual Adaptation
In the Tall, Tall Grass. Spoken Arts, cassette/book, 1992.

Related Titles
Crocodile Beat, by Gail Jorgensen. Illustrated by Patricia Mullins. Bradbury, 1989. Tissue paper collage illustrations show the adventures of the jungle animals.

Goggles, written and illustrated by Ezra Jack Keats. Macmillan, 1969. Peter and Archie find some goggles and get chased by some older boys. Keats's collages use paint and different kinds of paper, including newspaper.

Nature Walk, written and illustrated by Douglas Florian. Greenwillow, 1989. The rhyming text of this book takes the reader on a walk through the forest.

Shoes from Grandpa, by Mem Fox. Illustrated by Patricia Mullins. Orchard, 1990. Collage illustrations using tissue paper, fabric, yarn, and other materials depict the gifts Jessie gets from her family.

The Snowy Day, written and illustrated by Ezra Jack Keats. Viking, 1962. A little boy named Peter enjoys his day in the snow, making a snowman and snow angels. Collage illustrations create a very stylized urban environment.

Kimmel, Eric A.　*Hershel and the Hanukkah Goblins*
Illus. by Trina Schart Hyman. Holiday, 1989 (0-8234-0769-1)
Suggested Use Level: Gr. 2–4

Plot Summary
On the first night of Hanukkah, Hershel walks through the winter night toward a village. He is surprised the village is so dark and wonders why the Hanukkah candles are not glowing. The villagers tell him of goblins that have haunted their synagogue, and they explain how to get rid of the goblins. Someone must spend eight nights in the synagogue, lighting the

Hanukkah candles each night, and making the king of the goblins light the candles on the last night. Hershel agrees to try to get rid of the goblins, and he enters the synagogue. As he lights one candle on the menorah, a small goblin appears. Hershel tricks the goblin into leaving him alone. On each of the next five nights, a goblin appears, each more frightening than the one before it. Hershel tricks them all, continuing to light the Hanukkah candles. He even tricks one goblin into playing a dreidel game and losing his gold to Hershel. On the seventh night, no goblin appears, but the voice of the king of the goblins warns Hershel that he is coming. The king appears on the eighth night, but Hershel has a plan. He sits in the dark and ignores the king. The goblin king is so angry at Hershel's lack of fear that he demands Hershel look at him closely. Claiming it is too dark, Hershel tricks the king of the goblins into lighting all the Hanukkah candles, thus breaking the power the goblins have over the town. A note about Hanukkah follows the text.

Thematic Material

Details about the celebration of Hanukkah are incorporated into this story of bravery and monsters. This was a Caldecott Honor book in 1990.

Book Talk Material and Activities

Hershel and the Hanukkah Goblins could be included in a program on monsters and scary stories, as well as in a holiday program for Hanukkah. Many children enjoy this story of goblins and how Hershel outwits them. They think of other books in which the characters must use their wits to get the best of some creature, like *Wiley and the Hairy Man* and *Do Not Open*. Children may want to know more about Hanukkah, and booktalking David A. Adler's *A Picture Book of Hanukkah* and Miriam Chaikin's *Hanukkah* would build on this interest. Eric Kimmel has written some other stories that feature this holiday season, including *The Chanukkah Tree* and *The Chanukkah Guest*, which could also be presented at a holiday program.

Trina Schart Hyman received a Caldecott Honor award for the illustrations in *Hershel and the Hanukkah Goblins*. The illustrations are very dark and shadowy, except for the glow from Hershel's candles. The goblins are wonderful. Each goblin is different. The first goblin is small and has wings. The second goblin is green and fat—and Hershel uses this goblin's greed against him. The third goblin is red, with a tail that ends in the head of a snake. Although the goblins are a bit frightening, children see the humorous elements in them too. The king of the goblins is never seen directly. His shadow fills the door to the synagogue, then his bony hand holds the Hanukkah candle, then his spirit floats into the night. After looking at the illustrations for these creatures, many children ask for other "monster" stories. They enjoy the illustrations of the creature in *Do Not Open* as well as James Stevenson's creatures in *What's under My Bed?* A display of these and other creepy-creature books adds to the enjoyment of *Hershel and the Hanukkah Goblins*.

Related Titles

The Chanukkah Guest, by Eric A. Kimmel. Illustrated by Giora Carmi. Holiday, 1990. Bubba Brayna is old, and she does not see or hear as well as she did when she was younger. When a bear comes into her house, she believes he is the rabbi and lets him eat all her potato latkes.

The Chanukkah Tree, by Eric A. Kimmel. Illustrated by Giora Carmi. Holiday, 1987. Claiming it is a "Chanukkah tree," a peddler sells a leftover Christmas tree to some Jewish townspeople. When they realize they have been tricked, the people are very sad, but something happens that brings joy back to them.

Do Not Open, written and illustrated by Brinton Turkle. Dutton, 1981. Miss Moody opens a bottle she finds on the beach and releases a frightening creature. Now she must find a way to destroy the creature.

Hanukkah, by Miriam Chaikin. Illustrated by Ellen Weiss. Holiday, 1990. After the temple in Jerusalem was reclaimed, there was only enough oil to burn for one day, but the flames burned for eight days. Includes information about how the holiday is celebrated today.

A Picture Book of Hanukkah, by David A. Adler. Illustrated by Linda Heller. Holiday, 1982. When Judah and the Maccabees beat the soldiers of Antiochus, they celebrated by lighting the candles in the temple. The remembrance of this historical event is part of the celebration of Hanukkah. Details about holiday activities are also given.

What's under My Bed?, written and illustrated by James Stevenson. Greenwillow, 1983. Grandpa's bedtime story scares Louie and Mary Ann. Grandpa tells them another story about how he was chased by witches, dragons, and other creatures. (Condensed in *Primaryplots,* Bowker, 1989, pp. 152–154.)

Wiley and the Hairy Man, adapted from an American folktale and illustrated by Molly Bang. Macmillan, 1976. The Hairy Man wants Wiley. If Wiley and his mother can outwit the Hairy Man three times, he will not bother Wiley again. Like Hershel, Wiley and his mother have a plan.

About the Author

KIMMEL, ERIC A.
Something about the Author, ed. by Anne Commire. Gale, 1978, Vol. 13, pp. 120–121.

About the Illustrator

HYMAN, TRINA SCHART
Fourth Book of Junior Authors and Illustrators, ed. by Doris de Montreville and Elizabeth D. Crawford. Wilson, 1978, pp. 191–192.
Illustrators of Children's Books, 1957–1966, Vol. III, comp. by Lee Kingman, Grace Allen Hogarth, and Harriet Quimby. Horn Book, 1968, pp. 125, 224; *1967–1976, Vol. IV,* 1978, pp. 9, 16, 68, 82, 83, 129–130, 176, 194.
Something about the Author, ed. by Anne Commire. Gale, 1975, Vol. 7, pp. 137–139; 1987, Vol. 46, pp. 90–112.

Lionni, Leo.   *Six Crows: A Fable*
Illus. by the author. Knopf, 1988, LB (0-394-99572-4)
Suggested Use Level: Gr. 1–4

Plot Summary

Six crows are eating the wheat in the farmer's field. At first, the farmer tries to chase them off, but then he builds a scarecrow. Frightened, the crows discuss their plans to deal with the scarecrow. They decide to scare the scarecrow with a huge kite shaped like a bird. Of course, the scarecrow is not bothered, but the farmer is frightened, and he decides to make another, more fearful scarecrow. The crows respond with a larger kite. Observing the escalating enmity, an owl intervenes, counseling the farmer to talk to the crows and telling the crows to meet with the farmer. The farmer and the crows talk; they realize they are friends. They search for the owl to thank her and find her with the large scarecrow. Its fierce frown has become a smile.

Thematic Material

Six Crows is a fable that stresses the importance of solving disagreements through discussion instead of conflict. The collage illustrations are similar to those in other books by Leo Lionni.

Book Talk Material and Activities

Leo Lionni has written and illustrated many books for children. His collage style of illustration is the focus of study in many schools and libraries. One first-grade class heard and read many books by Leo Lionni. They looked at the different textures of materials used in his collages, including tissue paper and paper with patterns and designs. The children discussed how sometimes the paper was cut for the picture, but other times it was torn; sometimes it was layered. They noticed that the illustrations in most of his books are placed on a clean, white background. After examining and discussing many books, children can experiment with collage, collecting different kinds of paper, fabric, and other materials and trying to make their own designs.

A group of third-grade children studied some of Lionni's fables. They read several books: *It's Mine; Cornelius; Frederick; Tillie and the Wall; Six Crows; Nicolas, Where Have You Been?;* and *Matthew's Dream* (see chapter 2). They discussed the themes they saw: peaceful discussion and mediation instead of conflict; a willingness to take risks, often in the form of journeys to unknown worlds; the value of thoughtful, creative behavior. They talked about the "lesson" that is a part of fables and wrote some of their own "morals" to go with these books. They also looked at some of the original *Fables* and their morals by Arnold Lobel and at some Native American fables in *Doctor Coyote* as well as some Aesop's fables *(Borrowed Feathers)*.

Audiovisual Adaptation

Six Crows. Random/Miller Brody, cassette/book, 1989.

Related Titles

Borrowed Feathers and Other Fables, edited by Bryna Stevens. Illustrated by Freire Wright and Michael Forman. Random, 1977. Here are seven fables from Aesop, each with a clearly stated moral.

Cornelius: A Fable, written and illustrated by Leo Lionni. Pantheon, 1983. Cornelius feels left out because the other crocodiles don't appreciate his special skills. Children could write their own moral to this story.

Doctor Coyote: A Native American Aesop's Fables, retold by John Bierhorst. Illustrated by Wendy Watson. Macmillan, 1987. These Aztec stories focus on Coyote, who is a tricky character in the stories of many Native American people. Like other fables, the stories are short, and the moral lesson is stated at the end.

Fables, written and illustrated by Arnold Lobel. Harper, 1980. There are twenty original fables in this collection. Animals are depicted in human situations and present important lessons about behavior.

Frederick, written and illustrated by Leo Lionni. Pantheon, 1967. While the other mice are getting ready for winter, Frederick appears to be doing nothing. Yet on the coldest, darkest winter days, Frederick's supplies prove to be very valuable.

It's Mine! A Fable, written and illustrated by Leo Lionni. Knopf, 1986. Three frogs quarrel and fight. A toad lectures them about their behavior, but they continue to be disagreeable. When it begins to storm, the frogs find they are comforted by being together. After the storm, they continue to behave kindly and find peace and contentment. (Condensed in *Primaryplots,* Bowker, 1989, pp. 266–268.)

Nicolas, Where Have You Been?, written and illustrated by Leo Lionni. Knopf, 1987. When Nicolas, a mouse, is grabbed by a bird, he fears for his life. After he escapes, he is befriended by some birds. He realizes not all birds are bad. Nicolas learns a lesson about prejudice, and he shares his understanding with his mouse friends.

Tillie and the Wall, written and illustrated by Leo Lionni. Knopf, 1989. Tillie and her mouse friends live on one side of a wall. Tillie wonders about life on the other side. She finally finds a way to get to the other side of the wall, where she meets more mice, just like herself and her friends.

About the Author and Illustrator

LIONNI, LEO

Illustrators of Children's Books: 1957–1966, Vol. III, comp. by Lee Kingman, Grace Allen Hogarth, and Harriet Quimby. Horn Book, 1968, pp. 3, 16, 140, 229; *1967–1976, Vol. IV,* 1978, pp. 7, 11, 139–140, 198.

Something about the Author, ed. by Anne Commire. Gale, 1976, Vol. 8, pp. 114–115.

Third Book of Junior Authors, ed. by Muriel Fuller, Wilson, 1963, pp. 179–180.

Macaulay, David.   *Black and White*
Illus. by the author. Houghton, 1990 (0-395-52151-3)
Suggested Use Level: Gr. 1–3

Plot Summary

There seem to be four stories in this book, perhaps with some connecting elements. The stories are presented simultaneously on the double-page spreads. The illustrations are divided into quadrants. The stories are called "Seeing Things," "Problem Parents," "A Waiting Game," and "Udder Chaos." In "Seeing Things," a boy is traveling on a train. He shares his compartment with a woman in an unusual outfit ("she" is wearing a mask). The train is stopped when there are cows on the track. When the boy opens the window, he thinks he sees snow and hears singing. The snow is really bits of newspaper. As the train continues the journey, the boy falls asleep. He wakes up as the train reaches the station. His parents are there to greet him. In "Problem Parents," a girl discusses her parents, who have come home dressed in newspapers and are singing. They make newspaper outfits for the girl and her brother. On the television, there is an image of a masked man; the pattern on the black-and-white dog makes it appear to have a mask too. When the girl gives the daily mail to her father, he tears it up and throws it into the air. The family, in ordinary clothes, goes out to dinner, eating fish and chips wrapped in newspapers. Back home, the girl's parents check on her homework. "A Waiting Game" is a story with very few words in which people are reading newspapers as they wait for their train. The only words are the announcements that the train is delayed. As the people wait, one woman folds her newspaper into a hat, and pretty soon, everyone is wearing newspaper outfits. They appear to be singing and throwing bits of newspaper like confetti. It looks like a snowstorm of newspaper. The train arrives, and the people go on their ways. A masked man remains on the platform. In "Udder Chaos," a masked man in a black-and-white-striped shirt is climbing down a rope made of sheets (that carries over from the title page). He is in a field of black-and-white cows, and his black-and-white outfit blends in with the pattern of the cows. The cows go to a choir festival, where they blend in with the black-and-white robes of the singers. They cross a railroad track and return home.

Thematic Material

The creative format of *Black and White* fascinates children. They are intrigued by the four stories and try to determine how to read and look at this book. This would be a great book to share in a program on Caldecott books.

Book Talk Material and Activities

After looking at many Caldecott books, a group of first graders was shown *Black and White*. Instead of reading it aloud, the librarian just showed them the pages. She asked the group to look for unusual features and to look for any images that seemed to appear over and over again. She went through the book twice, keeping the focus on unusual features and recurring images. After seeing the book, children could not wait to comment. They noticed there were four sections of illustrations on every two pages. Several commented that the illustrations were very colorful, but the title of the book was *Black and White*. They saw the robber, the cows, and the newspapers in each story. They noticed that the things that seemed to recur were black and white. The librarian read them the warning statement from the first page, which alerts the reader to the variety of possibilities for interpreting the book. Some children met in groups to discuss what they thought was happening in the book. They enjoyed the opportunity to look at the different artistic presentations, identifying the use of watercolors and poster paints. Instead of reading any of the four stories aloud, the librarian signed out copies of *Black and White* for the classrooms, where it was a very popular free-choice reading book.

After looking at the artistic creativity in *Black and White*, several other books were displayed that have unusual and challenging designs. *Round Trip* and *Reflections* by Ann Jonas present their stories in a traditional manner but then are turned around for the story to continue. *Reflections* is in color, while *Round Trip* is in black and white. Anthony Browne's books, like *Changes* and *Piggybook*, challenge the imagination and encourage visual creativity.

Related Titles

Changes, written and illustrated by Anthony Browne. Knopf, 1991. When a boy is told to expect some changes, he wonders what will happen. Will the teapot change into a cat? Will the chair become a gorilla? The illustrations depict these unusual possibilities. The change turns out to be a baby sister.

If at First You Do Not See, written and illustrated by Ruth Brown. Holt, 1982. Turn this book around and see the unusual creatures the caterpillar meets in the vegetables, the ice cream, even the hamburgers.

Piggybook, written and illustrated by Anthony Browne. Knopf, 1986. When Mrs. Piggott leaves the house, her husband and son become pigs, first in their behavior, but eventually in appearance as well. Other familiar items are transformed into pig shapes and pig shadows. (Condensed in *Primaryplots*, Bowker, 1989, pp. 251–253.)

Reflections, written and illustrated by Ann Jonas. Greenwillow, 1987. A young girl describes her day, beginning with watching the sun rise. She goes on a journey, and when she reaches the forest, the book is turned upside down. The girl returns home and goes to bed. (Condensed in *Primaryplots*, Bowker, 1989, pp. 260–262.)

Round Trip, written and illustrated by Ann Jonas. Greenwillow, 1983. Black-and-white illustrations create a "turn around" story that challenges the imagination. This book describes a trip to the city and back home again.

About the Author and Illustrator

MACAULAY, DAVID

Fifth Book of Junior Authors and Illustrators, ed. by Sally Holmes Holtze. Wilson, 1983, pp. 199–201.

Illustrators of Children's Books: 1967–1976, Vol. IV, comp. by Lee Kingman, Grace Allen Hogarth, and Harriet Quimby. Horn Book, 1978, pp. 6, 7, 77, 78, 141, 199.

Something about the Author, ed. by Anne Commire. Gale, 1982, Vol. 27, p. 144; 1987, Vol. 46, pp. 138–151.

San Souci, Robert D. *Sukey and the Mermaid*
Illus. by J. Brian Pinkney. Four Winds, 1992 (0-02-778141-0)
Suggested Use Level: Gr. 2–4

Plot Summary

Sukey lives with her mother and her stepfather. Her step-pa, Mister Jones, is a mean-spirited man who makes sure Sukey works very hard. Sometimes Sukey leaves her work and goes down to the sea. Sitting and singing, Sukey calls forth a mermaid, Mama Jo, who gives her a gold coin. Her ma and step-pa take the coin from Sukey and tell her to keep going to the seashore to look for more coins. Sukey and the mermaid become friends, and Sukey takes another coin home each day. One day, Sukey's ma sees the mermaid and tells Mr. Jones. They plan to catch the mermaid and sell her. Mama Jo evades their net, but she does not come to the seashore to see Sukey anymore. When Sukey becomes ill, Mama Jo visits her in a dream. Sukey is able to travel to the seashore, where Mama Jo takes her under the water to live. Sukey recovers her health and enjoys her time with Mama Jo, but, after a while, she longs to return to her own people. Much time has passed in the world above the sea. When Sukey returns, she is wealthy from the treasures in the sea. She is courted by many men and chooses a fisherman named Dembo. But her step-pa, Mister Jones, steals Sukey's treasure and kills Dembo. Sukey runs to the sea and calls for Mama Jo, who gives her a pearl that will restore life to Dembo. Mister Jones is accused of Dembo's murder. As Mister Jones tries to escape with Sukey's treasure in a canoe, a storm appears around him and he is lost. Sukey and Dembo marry and find the treasure on the seashore. Having helped her friend, Mama Jo will not come to Sukey again.

Thematic Material

Unusual beings, like Mama Jo the mermaid, often appear in folktales. As in many traditional stories, in *Sukey and the Mermaid* a worthy character is assisted by this unusual being. The illustrations for this book were done with scratchboards.

Book Talk Material and Activities

Brian Pinkney is a young illustrator who has received much critical attention. His first book, *The Boy and the Ghost*, was published in 1989. He has received many awards, including having *Sukey and the Mermaid* selected as a Notable Book by the Association for Library Service to Children, a *Horn Book* Blue Ribbon Book for 1992, a Teachers' Choice book from the International Reading Association, and a *School Library Journal* Best Book for 1992. *Sukey and the Mermaid* also received a Coretta Scott King Honor Book award for illustration. For *The Boy and the Ghost*, Brian Pinkney used line drawings and watercolors, reminiscent of the work of his father, Jerry Pinkney. For his more recent books, including *Sukey and the Mermaid*, Brian Pinkney has used scratchboards.

For scratchboard illustrations, a white board is covered with black ink, which is then scratched off with a sharp, pointed instrument. The scratchboard can then be covered with paint, like watercolor or oil pastels, some of which can then be wiped or scratched away too. At a children's literature conference in Ohio, Brian Pinkney said he painted the sky in *Sukey and the Mermaid*, rather than scratch it all away. As a result, the sky is a more solid background for the detailed images of Sukey, Dembo, the mermaid, and the other characters. Like many recent books, there is information about the illustrations included on the page with the copyright information. When this is pointed out to children, they begin to look for this information in other books. It makes them more aware of the people who create books and their creative process.

Brian Pinkney has illustrated many books that reflect his African-American heritage, including *Happy Birthday, Martin Luther King; The Ballad of Belle Dorcas;* and *The Dark Thirty.*

Related Titles

The Ballad of Belle Dorcas, by William H. Hooks. Illustrated by J. Brian Pinkney. Knopf, 1990. Belle Dorcas, a free black woman, loves and marries Joshua, a slave. When Joshua is to be sold, Belle seeks the advice of Granny Lizard, a woman famous for spells and conjuring. Compare the scratchboard sky in this book to the painted sky in *Sukey and the Mermaid.*

The Boy and the Ghost, by Robert D. San Souci. Illustrated by J. Brian Pinkney. Simon & Schuster, 1989. A boy spends the night in a haunted house, facing the ghost that lives there. The illustrations for this book are line and watercolor drawings.

The Dark Thirty: Southern Tales of the Supernatural, by Patricia C. McKissack. Illustrated by J. Brian Pinkney. Knopf, 1992. Black-and-white scratchboard illustrations capture the mood of the ten spooky stories in this collection.

Happy Birthday, Martin Luther King, by Jean Marzollo. Illustrated by J. Brian Pinkney. Scholastic, 1993. Scratchboard illustrations depict the life and times of Dr. Martin Luther King, Jr. The text describes his work as a minister and his commitment to nonviolent change.

Where Does the Trail Lead?, by Burton Albert. Illustrated by J. Brian Pinkney. Simon & Schuster, 1991. After enjoying a day on the beach, a young boy returns to his family and a campfire where dinner is cooking. Oil pastels were used to add the colors to these scratchboard illustrations.

About the Author

SAN SOUCI, ROBERT D.
Something about the Author, ed. by Anne Commire. Gale, 1985, Vol. 40, pp. 220–221.

Selsam, Millicent, and Hunt, Joyce. *Keep Looking!*
Illus. by Normand Chartier. Macmillan, 1989 (0-02-781840-3)
Suggested Use Level: PreS–Gr. 2

Plot Summary

At a house in the country, there are many animals to observe. A chickadee, a bluejay, and other birds are near the bird feeder in the lilac bush. A squirrel and a chipmunk are also about. A mouse is living in the birdhouse, and a rabbit is in the blueberry bushes. Underground, there is a woodchuck, a box turtle, and some ants. Under some rocks, there are garter snakes. A cocoon and spider eggs are under the back steps. At night, racoons get into the trash, and an owl looks for food. At night, there are skunks and bats. In the morning, there are deer. On the last page of the book, several animals are shown in the illustration, and the reader is encouraged to find them. After the text, there is a list headed "Animals in This Book and the Pages Where They Appear."

Thematic Material

Keep Looking! encourages readers to be nature observers. Some of the illustrations include details for children to find and discuss.

Book Talk Material and Activities

At first, the illustrations in *Keep Looking!* directly match the text. The birds near the lilac bush are illustrated. The squirrel is shown "stealing seed from the bird feeder" and the chipmunk is in "its nest in the wood-pile." As the text continues, there are additional details for children to observe. Animals are included in the illustrations that are not mentioned in the words. When the text describes "a loud noise," a careful observer will see the racoons by the trash cans. They will notice the skunk walking beneath the flying bats. They will enjoy looking for the animals on the last page of the book.

Puzzle and game books are very popular with children. *Keep Looking!* encourages children to be observers, not only of nature, but also of books. The illustrations in this book first match, then extend the text. Children who examine this book realize there is information in both the text and the pictures. Other books could build on this. In *Look!* and *Look Again!* there are pairs of illustrations, but one has twelve differences for children to find. *Find Demi's Baby Animals* encourages the reader to find one specific animal from a group of other, similar animals. Children also enjoy the nature mazes in *Animaze!* In all these books, the focus is on animals and on the illustrations.

Related Titles

The Animal Atlas, by Barbara Taylor. Illustrated by Kenneth Lilly. Knopf, 1992. Visual skills are very important when using an atlas. Children learn to use symbols and maps as they learn about animals in this book.

Animaze! A Collection of Amazing Nature Mazes, by Wendy Madgwick. Illustrated by Lorna Hussey. Knopf, 1992. A variety of habitats are featured in this book, including the jungle and the outback. Each illustration has a maze that must be followed—for example, to take the zebra to the water hole.

Find Demi's Baby Animals, written and illustrated by Demi. Grosset, 1990. An animal is featured on each page. There is one large drawing of the animal, then there are many smaller drawings of the animal. Readers are asked to find one specific animal from among the smaller drawings.

Look! The Ultimate Spot-the-Difference Book. Nature notes by A. J. Wood. Illustrated by April Wilson. Dial, 1990. Twelve pairs of pictures—each of a different habitat—are presented. Although the picture pairs may seem identical, there are twelve differences between each pair of pictures. Habitats include the rain forests of the Amazon and the volcanic springs of Japan. A guide to the differences is included.

Look Again! The Second Ultimate Spot-the-Difference Book. Nature notes by A. J. Wood. Illustrated by April Wilson. Dial, 1992. Twelve more picture pairs feature settings like the jungles of Central Africa and the floor of the European deciduous forest.

About the Authors

SELSAM, MILLICENT

More Junior Authors, ed. by Muriel Fuller. Wilson, 1963, pp. 180–181.
Something about the Author, ed. by Anne Commire. Gale, 1971, Vol. 1, pp. 188–189; 1982, Vol. 29, pp. 173–175.

HUNT, JOYCE

Something about the Author, ed. by Anne Commire. Gale, 1983, Vol. 31, pp. 91–92.

About the Illustrator

CHARTIER, NORMAND

Something about the Author, ed. by Donna Olendorf. Gale, 1991, Vol. 66, pp. 39–41.

Singer, Marilyn. *Turtle in July*
Illus. by Jerry Pinkney. Macmillan, 1989 (0-02-782881-6)
Suggested Use Level: Gr. 2–4

Plot Summary

The seventeen poems in this collection celebrate animals and the seasons. Four poems describe a bullhead (a freshwater catfish) during each season. Each of the remaining poems features an animal at a particular time of year. In "Barn Owl," the owl's movements are presented in parenthesis, "(sweep)" and "(search sweep)." The images in "March Bear" convey the bear's confusion after a winter of sleep. "Cow" uses words like *approve, June, food,* and *chew;* saying these words slowly sounds like cows mooing on a hot day in June, although the word *moo* is not used in the poem. "Timber Rattlesnake" uses rhyming words and words that begin with S to convey the sounds of rattles and hisses. "Cat" ends the book, as a very particular cat stays warm in December by staying inside. Jerry Pinkney's illustrations are very detailed, usually providing a close-up image of the animal being featured in the poem.

Thematic Material

These poems could be correlated with studies of animals and seasons. This book could also be a focus book for looking at the illustrations of Jerry Pinkney.

Book Talk Material and Activities

Librarians and teachers who work with children regularly focus on the changing seasons. The poems in *Turtle in July* would be a great resource for this activity. The language in these poems makes them wonderful to read aloud. Most of the poems are in free verse. There is often an internal rhyme or a repeating sound that captures the essence of the animal being featured. In "Barn Owl," the owl sweeps through the cold February night, searching for mice. For most of the lines of this poem, there is only a word or two, conveying a sense of the owl's focus on his search. On the opposite page is the poem "Deer Mouse," which repeats the word *get* as the mouse scurries across the snowy field, perhaps hoping to escape the attention of the barn owl. Other collections of poetry about the seasons could be booktalked along with *Turtle in July,* including *The Sky Is Full of Song* and *In for Winter, Out for Spring.*

Jerry Pinkney's illustrations for *Turtle in July* are filled with activity. The animals often seem to be caught in the act of moving, like the jumping dog in "April Is a Dog's Dream" and the building beaver in "Beavers in November." Even the cow, standing still in the heat of a June day, seems just about to blink and chew. The cat in the final poem, however, is not going to move off the chair. In the video, *Meet the Caldecott Illustrator: Jerry Pinkney,* the artist discusses his technique, describing how he uses pencils to create detailed line drawings and then adds color, usually with watercolors and colored pencils. He works for two to three days on each illustration, and it takes eight to twelve weeks to finish a book. Children could look at his illustrations in two books about the seasons, *Turtle in July* and *In for Winter, Out for Spring.* Although a family is the focus of *In for Winter, Out for Spring,* both books include animals. Children might notice the birds, mice, dogs, and insects in both books. They could then look at the animals and children Pinkney illustrated in *Pretend You're a Cat* and discuss similarities and differences.

Many of the books Jerry Pinkney has illustrated feature African-American children and their families, as in *Wild Wild Sunflower Child Anna* and *In for Winter, Out for Spring.* In the video, Jerry Pinkney talks about using himself and his family as models for some of his books. He also discusses his educational background, emphasizing that his success has been earned through training and hard work. After seeing this video, many children look for other books Jerry Pinkney has illustrated. One art teacher correlates some of her units with children's books. She features books illustrated by Jerry Pinkney when she prepares children to work with watercolors.

Related Titles

In for Winter, Out for Spring, by Arnold Adoff. Illustrated by Jerry Pinkney. Harcourt, 1991. Playing in the snow, finding the first flower, going barefoot, and collecting walnuts are some of the activities featured in these poems. Rebecca, a young African-American girl, and her family are the focus of these poems.

Meet the Caldecott Illustrator: Jerry Pinkney. American School Publishers, videorecording, 1991. This twenty-one-minute video features Jerry Pinkney talking about his work as an illustrator of children's books, including the Caldecott Honor books *Mirandy and Brother Wind* and *The Talking Eggs* (see chapter 8).

Mirandy and Brother Wind, by Patricia C. McKissack. Illustrated by Jerry

Pinkney. Knopf, 1988. Mirandy wants the best partner for the cake walk, so she tries to catch Brother Wind. This was a Caldecott Honor book in 1989.

Pretend You're a Cat, by Jean Marzollo. Illustrated by Jerry Pinkney. Dial, 1990. The poems in this collection encourage children to act like animals, including a bird, a seal, and a snake. Compare Jerry Pinkney's illustrations of the cows in this book to those in *Turtle in July.*

The Sky Is Full of Song, edited by Lee Bennett Hopkins. Illustrated by Dirk Zimmer. Harper, 1983. The thirty-eight poems in this collection celebrate the seasons. Included are poems from many well-known poets, such as Aileen Fisher, Lilian Moore, David McCord, Gwendolyn Brooks, and Dorothy Aldis. (Condensed in *Primaryplots,* Bowker, 1989, pp. 219–221.)

Wild Wild Sunflower Child Anna, by Nancy White Calstrom. Illustrated by Jerry Pinkney. Macmillan, 1987. Anna enjoys being outdoors on a sunny day. She sees flowers, berries, frogs, and insects as she romps through the fields. In many of the illustrations in this book, the pencil lines are very clear, particularly in the details of the folds of Anna's dress. This is a good book to look at after seeing the *Meet the Caldecott Illustrator* video.

About the Author

SINGER, MARILYN

Sixth Book of Junior Authors and Illustrators, ed. by Sally Holmes Holtze. Wilson, 1989, pp. 278–279.

Something about the Author, ed. by Anne Commire. Gale, 1985, Vol. 38, p. 195; 1987, Vol. 48, pp. 202–206.

About the Illustrator

PINKNEY, JERRY

Illustrators of Children's Books: 1957–1966, Vol. III, comp. by Lee Kingman, Grace Allen Hogarth, and Harriet Quimby. Horn Book, 1978, pp. 158, 235; *Vol. IV, 1967–76,* 1978, pp. 151, 205.

Sixth Book of Junior Authors and Illustrators, ed. by Sally Holmes Holtze. Wilson, 1989, pp. 225–227.

Something about the Author, ed. by Anne Commire. Gale, 1983, Vol. 41, pp. 164–174.

Talking with Artists, comp. and ed. by Pat Cummings. Bradbury, 1992, pp. 60–65.

Van Allsburg, Chris. *Two Bad Ants*

Illus. by the author. Houghton, 1988 (0-395-48668-8)
Suggested Use Level: Gr. 1–3

Plot Summary

When a scout returns to the ant world with a delicious sweet crystal, the ant queen sends other ants out into the night to bring back more crystals. The journey is dangerous, through forests filled with predators and over a brick mountain. When they arrive at their destination, most of the ants take the crystals and depart. However, two ants decide to stay and enjoy the crystals themselves. The crystals are really sugar, and the ants are in a kitchen. They gorge on sugar crystals and fall asleep. In the morning, they are scooped up in a spoon of sugar and mixed into some coffee. They are almost swallowed but escape into some muffins, only to be put into the toaster. When they pop out of the toaster, they hurry to the sink for some water, and they are washed into the garbage disposal. They climb out, enter an electrical outlet, and are thrown out after receiving a shock. When night comes again, they wait for the other ants and hurry back to their ant world.

Thematic Material

This story is told from the point of view of the two ants. Readers must use the words and pictures to relate what is happening to their own lives.

Book Talk Material and Activities

The illustrations in *Two Bad Ants* give the reader an ant's-eye view of this story. The title page shows the ants climbing on the saucer of a coffee cup. They are dwarfed by the large size of the cup. As the story begins, the reader travels into the tunnels, entering the underground world of the ants. The ants move through "the woods," which is really grass. The light from a firefly shines on the ants as the moon shines on a forest. The reader looks up at the brick exterior of the house and then up at the kitchen window. As children become more involved in the story of these ants and their point of view, they often talk about the shifting perspectives in the illustrations. Children especially like the pictures looking at the man's face and being inside the toaster.

After sharing *Two Bad Ants,* children want to look at other books in which the illustrations have an unusual perspective. In *Ben's Dream,* Ben visits the locations he had been studying for his geography test. *Chipmunk Song* describes a child whose imaginative play involves spending a day with a chipmunk. Bruce McMillan's *Mouse Views* follows an escaped class pet around a school, showing what the mouse encounters on this adventure. All these books encourage children to consider different points of view.

Related Titles

Ben's Dream, written and illustrated by Chris Van Allsburg. Houghton, 1982. While studying for his social studies test, Ben falls asleep and dreams he is visiting all the places he has been studying. The shifts in perspective provide a challenge to children as they try to identify where Ben is.

Chipmunk Song, by Joanne Ryder. Illustrated by Lynne Cherry. Dutton, 1987. What would you see and do if you were a chipmunk? A child pretends to follow a chipmunk through a day of activities.

George Shrinks, written and illustrated by William Joyce. Harper, 1985. After dreaming he has shrunk, George wakes up to find his dream has come true. It is difficult for the diminutive George to do his daily tasks. (Condensed in *Primaryplots,* Bowker, 1989, pp. 134–135.)

Mouse Views: What the Class Pet Saw, written and photographed by Bruce McMillan. Holiday, 1993. Provides a mouse's-eye view of common school objects—like scissors and crayons.

The Napping House, by Audrey Wood. Illustrated by Don Wood. Harcourt, 1984. In this sequential story, everyone is sleeping. Granny is in her bed, and the other characters join her there. When the flea bites the mouse, everyone wakes up. (Condensed in *Primaryplots,* Bowker, 1989, pp. 154–156.)

Once a Mouse: A Fable Cut in Wood, written and illustrated by Marcia Brown. Scribers, 1972. A hermit puts a mouse through several transformations. When the mouse becomes a tiger, he is too proud to allow the hermit to remember his humble beginnings. The hermit changes the tiger back into a mouse.

The Quilt, written and illustrated by Ann Jonas. Greenwillow, 1984. As the little girl sleeps, she dreams that the patches on her quilt are places she can visit. She imagines she is looking for her missing stuffed dog, only to wake up and find the dog on the floor.

About the Author and Illustrator

VAN ALLSBURG, CHRIS

Fifth Book of Junior Authors and Illustrators, ed. by Sally Holmes Holtze. Wilson, 1983, pp. 316–317.

Something about the Author, ed. by Anne Commire. Gale, 1985, Vol. 37, pp. 204–207; 1988, Vol. 53, pp. 160–172.

Wiesner, David. *Tuesday*

Illus. by the author. Clarion, 1991 (0-395-55113-7)
Suggested Use Level: PreS–Gr. 4

Plot Summary

This book is virtually wordless as it depicts the antics of some frogs one Tuesday evening. Double-page spreads show frogs flying on lily pads. Inset panels detail the adventures of several frogs with some birds and the laundry. Horizontal boxes depict the sequence of an encounter with a dog. After the frogs return to the pond, baffled police study the lily pads left scattered across the town. The final pages indicate that it is Tuesday again, and the illustrations depict flying pigs.

Thematic Material

The humorous details in this almost wordless book encourage "readers" to tell their own stories. *Tuesday* received the Caldecott Medal in 1992.

Book Talk Material and Activities

Tuesday is a wonderful book for encouraging creative writing. After looking at the pictures, many children want to tell or write their version of what they see is happening and what might be happening in other parts of the town. They are especially eager to tell about what may happen when the pigs fly over town, and what adventure will occur on the next Tuesday. Children study the illustrations for details, laughing at the humorous moments like the frogs wearing capes from the laundry and the frog zapping the television remote control with his tongue.

Tuesday could also be booktalked along with other "unusual" Caldecott Medal and Honor books, including wordless, concept, and creative format books. Wiesner's wordless *Free Fall* was an Honor book in 1989, and

Nancy Tafuri's nearly wordless *Have You Seen My Duckling* was an Honor book in 1985. Lois Ehlert used die-cut shapes and bright colors to design the animals in *Color Zoo* (an Honor book in 1990). David Macaulay won the 1991 Caldecott Medal for *Black and White*, a book with pages divided into quadrants that may or may not be telling parts of the same story. Suse MacDonald stretched the letters of the alphabet into shapes and objects in the book *Alphabatics* (an Honor book in 1987). *Ten, Nine, Eight* is a rhyming counting book that was an Honor book in 1984. By seeing the variety of illustrations in these books, children become more involved in examining illustrations and develop an appreciation for the creative contributions of the artists.

Related Titles

Alphabatics, written and illustrated by Suse MacDonald. Bradbury, 1986. The letters of the alphabet acrobatically stretch into items that represent each letter—for example, M stretches into a mustache and S becomes a swan.

Black and White, written and illustrated by David Macaulay. Houghton, 1990. The four quadrants on each page are illustrated in different styles and seem to be telling different stories. As the reader becomes involved in each story, characters and plot elements from other quadrants intervene (elsewhere in this chapter).

Color Zoo, written and illustrated by Lois Ehlert. Lippincott, 1989. Colors and die-cut shapes are used to create nine zoo animals, including a mouse, a monkey, and a lion. This 1990 Caldecott Honor book uses creative book engineering to present the concepts of shapes and colors (elsewhere in this chapter).

Free Fall, written and illustrated by David Wiesner. Lothrop, 1988. A young boy is sleeping. Objects in his room become part of his dream, including a chess set that becomes characters he meets and an atlas that becomes the place he visits.

Have You Seen My Duckling, written and illustrated by Nancy Tafuri. Greenwillow, 1984. A mother duck tries to find her missing duckling, whose antics are visible on each page.

Ten, Nine, Eight, written and illustrated by Molly Bang. Greenwillow, 1983. As a little girl gets ready for bed, she and her father count backward from ten and describe some of the things in her room. (Condensed in *Primaryplots*, Bowker, 1989, pp. 1–3.)

About the Author and Illustrator

WIESNER, DAVID

Talking with Artists, comp. and ed. by Pat Cummings. Bradbury, 1992, pp. 84–89.

Wisniewski, David. *The Warrior and the Wise Man*
Illus. by the author. Lothrop, 1989, LB (0-688-07890-7)
Suggested Use Level: Gr. 2–4

Plot Summary

In Japan, many years ago, an emperor has twin sons, Tozaemon and Toemon. Tozaemon is a brave warrior, and Toemon is a wise man. To decide which son should succeed him, the emperor challenges his sons to bring him all five elements: earth, water, fire, wind, and cloud. Each element is guarded by a fierce demon. The brothers begin their search. Tozaemon uses his strength to take some earth from the demon, but when Toemon arrives at the Earth Demon's garden, he helps restore the damage his brother had done. For a reward, the demon gives Toemon a box of earth. At the well of the Water Demon, Tozaemon has used force to take the water, and Toemon uses the earth he has been given to help repair the damage his brother has done. Toemon is given some water as a reward for helping the Water Demon. At the cave of the Fire Demon, it is the same. Tozaemon has taken some fire; Toemon uses his gift of water to restore order, and he receives a gift of fire. At the castle of the Wind Demon, Tozaemon steals a fan, and Toemon uses his fire to provide light for the Wind Demon, receiving a gift of wind. At the mountain of the Cloud Demon, Toemon uses his wind to blow away the chaos of clouds his brother's theft has caused, and he is given a gift of clouds. Back at the court of the emperor, Tozaemon is triumphant, but the kingdom is being attacked by the elements. Using his clouds, Toemon shields the castle. Then, using the elements his brother has taken, Toemon defeats the armies of the elements. For his wisdom, Toemon is chosen to be the next emperor.

Thematic Material

Although there are some elements from folktales, this is an original story. Wisdom is rewarded over strength as Toemon saves the empire. The cut-paper illustrations include several elements of Japanese decorative arts, which the author/illustrator explains in a note following the story.

Book Talk Material and Activities

David Wisniewski used cut-paper illustrations for *The Warrior and the Wise Man* and for two other books, *Elfwyn's Saga* and *Rain Player*. Children are fascinated by these intricate cuttings. They look at the silhouette cuttings of the people and feel the drama of the story. David Wisniewski includes a note about his research, including studying textile designs and *ikebana*—floral arrangements. In addition to his research, Wisniewski describes his technique for cutting the drawings, noting, "More than eight hundred blades were used to produce the illustrations for this book." After looking at these illustrations, many children experiment with paper-cutting, creating designs with layers of paper and colors. *The Paper Crane* by Molly Bang also has unusual illustrations using cut and folded paper.

In many schools, conflict resolution behaviors are taught to children. Peer mediation and cooperative discipline programs have been incorporated into many schools and classrooms. *The Warrior and the Wise Man* could be included in a program on problem-solving techniques. In this book, Tozaemon's forceful behaviors almost destroy the empire, whereas Toemon uses his wisdom to find a peaceful solution. *King of the Playground* is a contemporary story of solving problems, while Leo Lionni's books, such as *Nicolas, Where Have You Been?* and *Six Crows*, present characters who challenge the views of others.

Related Titles

Elfwyn's Saga, written and illustrated by David Wisniewski. Lothrop, 1990. Elfwyn's family has been cursed by Gorm, and she must find a way to destroy the crystal he has given her father. Intricate cut-paper illustrations capture the symbols and geography of this original tale of the Vikings. Children study the layers of paper, which create a feeling of distance and depth.

King of the Playground, by Phyllis Reynolds Naylor. Illustrated by Nola Langner Malone. Atheneum, 1991. When Sammy threatens Kevin, Kevin leaves the playground and goes home. Kevin's father helps him talk about his problem and think of some solutions. Kevin decides to stand up to Sammy, and together they build a sand fort.

Nicolas, Where Have You Been?, written and illustrated by Leo Lionni. Knopf, 1987. When Nicolas, a mouse, is grabbed by a bird, he fears for his life. After he escapes, he is befriended by some birds and realizes that not all birds are bad. Nicolas learns a lesson about prejudice and shares his understanding with his mouse friends.

The Paper Crane, written and illustrated by Molly Bang. Greenwillow, 1985. In this blend of reality and fantasy, the kindness of the restaurant owner is magically rewarded by a stranger. The three-dimensional paper cutouts that illustrate the book create a feeling of shadowy depth.

Rain Player, written and illustrated by David Wisniewski. Clarion, 1991. In this original Mayan tale, Chac, the god of rain, is displeased with Pik. To earn Chac's forgiveness, Pik challenges him to play *pok-a-tok,* a ball game. If Pik wins, he will be forgiven, and his people will receive rain. The bright colors of these cut-paper illustrations capture the art and geography of the Mayans.

Six Crows: A Fable, written and illustrated by Leo Lionni (elsewhere in this chapter). Knopf, 1988. A farmer and some crows battle over a field of wheat. They succeed in scaring each other and nearly ruin the wheat. An owl helps them realize they would do better as friends than as enemies.

8

Focusing on Folktales

FOLKTALES represent the cultural heritage of many different people. With origins in the oral tradition, folktales are especially effective when told or read aloud. The cadence of the language, with repeated phrases and chants, helps make them memorable. In this chapter, there are stories from Zaire, the Ukraine, Peru, China, and the United States. There is even a takeoff on a familiar folktale *(The True Story of the 3 Little Pigs by A. Wolf)*. Characters defeat giants, climb to the moon, and outwit a wolf. There are lazy characters, brave characters, and tricksters. There is magic, suspense, and wonder. These stories are frightening and funny. Reading them will introduce children to some of the traditional literature that is shared around the world.

Aardema, Verna, reteller.   *Traveling to Tondo: A Tale of the Nkundo of Zaire*
   Illus. by Will Hillenbrand. Knopf, 1991, LB (0-679-90081-0)
   Suggested Use Level: Gr. 2–4

Plot Summary

Bowane, a civet cat, has chosen his bride. She lives in Tondo, a nearby village. Her father has set the marriage price and Bowane has agreed to pay, so he returns home to fetch the demanded items. On his return trip to Tondo, Bowane meets his friend Embenga the pigeon, who joins him on the trip. They are joined by Nguma the python and Ulu the tortoise. The four friends travel to Tondo. At the waterhole, Bowane needs his own dish for water, so he returns home to fetch it. At the palm tree, Embenga finds that the nuts are not ripe, so they wait for them to ripen. When

Nguma swallows an antelope, the friends wait for him to digest it before continuing their journey. In the forest, there is a fallen tree blocking the path, so they wait for the tree to rot so Ulu can walk over it. When they finally arrive in Tondo, many years have passed. The civet cat Bowane had chosen for his bride has married another. Her husband frightens Bowane and his friends, and they hurry home.

Thematic Material

Traveling to Tondo is a folktale with cumulative elements, repetition, and foolish characters. The story ends with a suggestion that sometimes it is necessary to disagree with your friends and say "N-YEH" to their foolish suggestions.

Book Talk Material and Activities

Traveling to Tondo is an excellent choice for a play or puppet activity. The cumulative sequence of the story encourages children to focus on details in the text, like the order of the characters and the dilemmas they face. *Traveling to Tondo* is filled with repeated words that encourage creative interpretation and participation. As each animal travels to Bowane's wedding, there is a sound associated with his movement, for example, "Embenga flapping, *bwa-wa, bwa-wa, bwa-wa.*" These sounds are repeated every time the animals continue the journey, providing lots of opportunities for dramatic interpretations. A glossary and guide to pronunciation provides assistance for storytellers.

Many teachers are eager to involve children in active learning experiences. Sequential stories, like *Traveling to Tondo,* are especially good choices for children to dramatize. A "drama corner" could be a classroom activity center, and *Traveling to Tondo* could be in this area with a stick puppet for each main character. Working on a creative dramatics project allows children to develop cooperative behaviors while they use their language abilities of reading, listening, and speaking.

Children would enjoy looking for other books to add to the "drama corner." In *Toad Is the Uncle of Heaven,* Toad is joined by the Bees, a Rooster, and a Tiger on his journey to the King of Heaven. Blackbird is joined by other creatures when he travels to the king in *Rum Pum Pum. Chicken Little* and *The Gingerbread Boy* are other stories with a journey and characters that appear in sequential order which could be dramatized.

Related Titles

Chicken Little, retold and illustrated by Steven Kellogg. Morrow, 1985. When Chicken Little is hit on the head, she tells other animals, "The sky is falling." Henny Penny, Ducky Lucky, and other well-known figures are almost captured by Foxy Loxy because they listen to Chicken Little.

The Gingerbread Boy, retold and illustrated by Paul Galdone. Seabury, 1975. After he is baked, this gingerbread boy runs away and is chased by many characters. At the end, he trusts the Fox, and he is eaten.

One Fine Day, written and illustrated by Nonny Hogrogian. Macmillan, 1971. When a thirsty fox comes out of the forest and drinks the old woman's milk, she cuts off his tail and will not sew it back on until he replaces her milk. Each character that the fox asks for help demands something in return.

Rum Pum Pum: A Folk Tale from India, retold by Maggie Duff. Illustrated by Jose Aruego and Ariane Dewey. Macmillan, 1978. When the king takes Blackbird's wife, Blackbird makes war on him. On his journey, Blackbird is joined by Cat, the ants, Stick, and River, and when the king tries to destroy Blackbird, his companions come to his rescue.

Toad Is the Uncle of Heaven: A Vietnamese Folk Tale, retold and illustrated by Jeanne M. Lee. Holt, 1985. When there is a drought on earth, Toad journeys to the King of Heaven to ask for rain. With the help of his friends, he is able to convince the king to send rain. (Condensed in *Primaryplots*, Bowker, 1989, pp. 306–308.)

About the Author

AARDEMA, VERNA

Fifth Book of Junior Authors and Illustrators, ed. by Sally Holmes Holtze. Wilson, 1983, pp. 1–2.
Something about the Author, ed. by Anne Commire. Gale, 1973, Vol. 4, pp. 1–3; ed. by Donna Olendorf, Gale, 1992, Vol. 68, pp. 1–4.

Brett, Jan, adapter. *The Mitten: A Ukrainian Folktale*
Illus. by the adapter. Putnam, 1989 (0-399-21920-X)
Suggested Use Level: Gr. K–2

Plot Summary

Nicki's grandmother has made him a new pair of white mittens. When
he goes out to play in the snow, he loses one mitten, which becomes a cozy
haven for a mole, a rabbit, a hedgehog, an owl, a badger, a fox, a bear,
and a mouse. When the bear sneezes, all the animals are pushed out of the
mitten. Nicki finds the mitten and returns home to show his grandmother
that he is safe and still has both mittens, although one is now much larger.

Thematic Material

Brett's illustrations for *The Mitten* are colorful and use designs in the
borders to encourage prediction. Like many other folktales, this Ukrainian
story has events that follow a sequence.

Book Talk Material and Activities

Jan Brett's adaptation of *The Mitten* provides an opportunity to compare
and contrast this folktale with Alvin Tresselt's 1964 version, illustrated by
Yaroslava. A Venn diagram comparison could focus on the plot, charac-

Chart 5

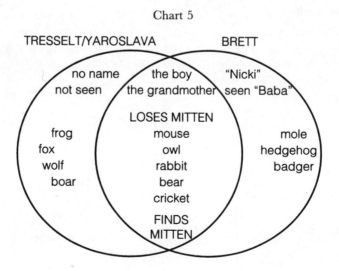

TRESSELT/YAROSLAVA — BRETT

| no name | the boy | "Nicki" |
| not seen | the grandmother | seen "Baba" |

LOSES MITTEN

frog	mouse	mole
fox	owl	hedgehog
wolf	rabbit	badger
boar	bear	
	cricket	

FINDS MITTEN

ters, and illustrations. After each book is shared with children, groups of three or four could meet to chart the sequence. Their results could be compiled into a Venn diagram on a transparency or on chart paper. Returning to each book, children would find additional similarities and differences to add to the group project—for example, looking at the illustrations:

Chart 6

Tresselt/Yaroslava	Brett

Illustrations:
  No borders
  Less colorful
	Illustrations:
	  Borders/designs
	  Colorful
	  Predict action

Brett's illustrations for *The Mitten* have some similarities with her illustrations for other books, particularly in her use of detailed borders. In *The Mitten,* there is a mitten-shaped window in the border, and the next animal in the crowding sequence appears in this window. After examining other books with her illustrations, such as *Annie and the Wild Animals* and *Goldilocks and the Three Bears,* children may want to experiment with using borders in their illustrations.

Audiovisual Adaptation
The Mitten. Scholastic, cassette/book, 1990.

Related Titles
Annie and the Wild Animals, written and illustrated by Jan Brett. Houghton, 1985. Annie cannot find her cat, Taffy. The food Annie leaves out for Taffy attracts many woodland animals instead. The borders that surround the illustrations depict the activities of the animals.

Goldilocks and the Three Bears, retold and illustrated by Jan Brett. Dodd, 1987. For this familiar folktale, Brett includes many details, particularly in the clothes the bears wear. Compare these illustrations to those in *The Mitten.* (Condensed in *Primaryplots,* Bowker, 1989, pp. 292–294.)

It Could Always Be Worse: A Yiddish Folktale, retold and illustrated by Margot Zemach. Farrar, 1976. A peasant is upset by the noise in his crowded house. Chart how many characters crowd into his house and compare the result to the situation in *It's Too Noisy* and *The Mitten.*

It's Too Noisy, by Joanna Cole. Illustrated by Kate Duke. Crowell, 1989. The farmer thinks his house is too noisy, so he visits the Wise Man. The Wise Man tells him first to bring in the farmyard animals and then to take them out. The house is not so noisy now.

The Mitten: An Old Ukrainian Folktale, retold by Alvin Tresselt. Illustrated by Yaroslava. Lothrop, 1964. Animals crowd into a little boy's mitten to try to keep warm.

Too Much Noise, by Ann McGovern. Illustrated by Simms Taback. Houghton, 1967. An old man brings farm animals into his noisy house. When he removes them, his noisy house seems much less noisy.

Who Sank the Boat?, written and illustrated by Pamela Allen. Coward, 1982. A cow, a donkey, a sheep, a pig, and a mouse crowd into a boat and it sinks.

About the Author and Illustrator

BRETT, JAN

Sixth Book of Junior Authors and Illustrators, ed. by Sally Holmes Holtze. Wilson, 1980, pp. 41–42.

Something about the Author, ed. by Anne Commire. Gale, 1986, Vol. 42, pp. 38–39; ed. by Diane Tengen. Gale, 1993, Vol. 71, pp. 29–32.

Ehlert, Lois.   *Moon Rope: A Peruvian Folktale/Un lazo a la luna: Una leyenda peruana*

Illus. by the author. Harcourt, 1992 (0-15-255343-6)
Suggested Use Level: Gr. 1–3

Plot Summary

Mole and Fox are friends. Mole's wants are very simple, but Fox wants to go to the moon. Fox's plan is to make a rope of grass. He will hang the rope on the crescent of the moon and then climb up it. With the help of some birds, Fox and Mole secure the rope and climb toward the moon. Unfortunately, Mole slips off the rope and falls to earth. All the creatures who see him fall laugh at him. To this day, Mole likes to stay hidden from other animals and come out of his hole at night. Fox did make it to the moon, where, when the moon is full, his face can be seen.

Thematic Material

Moon Rope is a *pourquoi* folktale from Peru. Told in English and Spanish, it features animals as the main characters and explains some natural phenomena.

Book Talk Material and Activities

When children read many folktales, they begin to recognize some recurring elements in these stories. In some folktales, there is magic or an enchantment. Many characters take journeys, like Fox and Mole's attempted journey to the moon. Some folktales answer questions, such as, why is the moon in the sky, and why do cats purr? These *pourquoi* tales reflect a need to explain the natural world. *Moon Rope* explains why the moon seems to have a face. It also suggests a reason for why moles stay underground most of the time. *Moon Rope* could be featured in a program on *pourquoi* folktales. *Why Mosquitoes Buzz in People's Ears* and *The Cat's Purr* could also be included. Other moon stories could be featured, like *Anansi the Spider* and *Why the Sun and the Moon Live in the Sky*.

The cut-paper illustrations for this book are spectacular, particularly the silver of the fox and the printed silver image on the full moon. The stylized designs are, according to a note by Lois Ehlert, derived from the images she found when researching Peruvian textiles, jewelry, and other artifacts. Her choice of silver as a dominant color in this book comes from her research into the use of silver in pre-Columbian art.

Related Titles

Anansi the Spider: A Tale from the Ashanti, adapted and illustrated by Gerald McDermott. Holt, 1972. After Anansi's sons rescue him, they find a beautiful globe of light. They cannot decide who should have the light, so the god who lives in the sky takes it, and it becomes the moon.

The Cat's Purr, by Ashley Bryan. Illustrated by the author. Atheneum, 1985. Cat and Rat live happily as friends and neighbors. After the friends fight over Cat's drum, Cat chases Rat, who pushes the drum into Cat's mouth. Cat's drum is inside Cat, which explains why cats purr. (Condensed in *Primaryplots,* Bowker, 1989, pp. 294–296.)

Her Seven Brothers, written and illustrated by Paul Goble. Bradbury, 1988. This Cheyenne legend tells of the stars in the Big Dipper. The illustrations incorporate colors and designs of the Cheyenne.

Moon Song, by Byrd Baylor. Illustrated by Ronald Himler. Scribner,

1982. Coyote sees the moon and cries out for his mother. The story explains why coyotes howl at the moon.

Moon Stories, written and illustrated by William Wiesner. Seabury, 1973. Three folktales that feature the moon. In "The Tidy King," a story from Persia, the king tries to clean the smudges off the moon. Compare this to *Moon Rope,* in which Fox's face is seen in the moon.

Why Mosquitoes Buzz in People's Ears, retold by Verna Aardema. Illustrated by Leo Dillon and Diane Dillon. Dial, 1975. In this sequential story, a mosquito's silly behavior creates fear in the jungle. Now we know why mosquitoes are such annoying pests.

Why the Sun and the Moon Live in the Sky: An African Folktale, retold by Elphinstone Dayrell. Illustrated by Blair Lent. Houghton, 1968. When the Sun and the Moon invite everyone to their home, they find they must jump into the sky to make room for their guests.

About the Author and Illustrator

EHLERT, LOIS

Illustrators of Children's Books: 1957–1966, comp. by Lee Kingman, Grace Allen Hogarth, and Harriet Quimby. Horn Book, 1968, pp. 103, 203, 216; *1967–1976, Vol. IV,* 1978, pp. 116, 187.

Something about the Author, ed. by Anne Commire. Gale, 1984, Vol. 35, pp. 97–98; ed. by Donna Olendorf, Gale, 1992, Vol. 69, pp. 50–53.

Talking with Artists, comp. and ed. by Pat Cummings. Bradbury, 1992, pp. 36–41.

Goble, Paul, reteller. *Iktomi and the Boulder: A Plains Indian Story*
Illus. by the reteller. Orchard, 1988, LB (0-531-08360-8); pap. (0-531-07023-9)
Suggested Use Level: Gr. 2–4

Plot Summary

Iktomi is going for a visit. He is dressed in his finest feathers and carrying his best fan, blanket, and tobacco bag. He revels in his own appearance (while the animals of the plains laugh behind his back). As he walks to the next village, Iktomi becomes hot. He stops and rests in the shade of a large boulder, and he leaves his blanket as a gift for the boulder when he continues his journey (although he is really just too hot to carry it). When it begins to rain, Iktomi hurries back and takes his blanket from the boulder. He lies, saying he did not really mean it as a gift. The angry boulder begins to follow Iktomi. It chases him across the plain, finally rolling onto his legs and trapping him. Iktomi is angry, but he cannot free himself. Some animals come to help him, but they cannot move the boulder. Iktomi tricks the bats into flying into the boulder, chipping it away until it is destroyed. Iktomi continues on his way, still conceited and ready to cause new problems.

Thematic Material

This story from the Plains Indians has several elements common to folktales, including a main character who is a "trickster" and a resolution that explains a natural phenomenon (why bats have flat faces and why there are small rocks across the Great Plains).

Book Talk Material and Activities

Iktomi is a vain and self-centered character. He tricks other characters into helping him. He has links to other troublemakers in folktales, including Coyote (Native American), Anansi (Africa), Brer Rabbit (United States), Jack (England), and Loki (Norse mythology). A study of these characters could lead to many activities. Children could compare and contrast the characteristics of each trickster. They could look for other stories with tricky main characters. Children could make "wanted" posters listing the problems the character has caused.

There are three other Iktomi stories, *Iktomi and the Berries, Iktomi and the Ducks,* and *Iktomi and the Buffalo Skull.* These could be incorporated into a book talk program on Native American stories, which could feature stories from different groups. *Quail Song* is a story from the Pueblo Indians, as is *Arrow to the Sun; Her Seven Brothers* retells a legend of the Cheyenne Indians. *Thirteen Moons on Turtle's Back* is a collection of legends from different Native American peoples that describe the changing seasons. By focusing on stories from many peoples, children are introduced to the variety of experiences of Native Americans.

Related Titles

Arrow to the Sun: A Pueblo Indian Tale, adapted and illustrated by Gerald McDermott. Viking, 1974. A boy must survive four tests to prove his identity and find his father. This book received the Caldecott Medal in 1975.

Doctor Coyote: A Native American Aesop's Fables, retold by John Bierhorst. Illustrated by Wendy Watson. Macmillan, 1987. These Aztec stories focus on Coyote, who is a tricky character in the stories of many Native American people. Like other fables, the stories are short, and the moral lesson is stated at the end.

Her Seven Brothers, written and illustrated by Paul Goble. Bradbury, 1988. This legend describes the origin of the Big Dipper. The illustrations incorporate colors and designs of the Cheyenne.

Iktomi and the Berries: A Plains Indian Story, retold and illustrated by Paul Goble. Orchard, 1989. In this story, Iktomi tries to pick berries from their reflection. Iktomi almost drowns because of his own foolishness.

Iktomi and the Buffalo Skull: A Plains Indian Story, retold and illustrated by Paul Goble. Orchard, 1991. When Iktomi gets his head stuck in a buffalo skull, the people think he is a spirit. His wife knows he is Iktomi, and she uses her stone hammer to remove the skull from her foolish husband's head.

Iktomi and the Ducks: A Plains Indian Story, retold and illustrated by Paul Goble. Orchard, 1990. Iktomi tricks some ducks and prepares to eat them. While they are cooking, he gets stuck in a tree. Coyote eats the roasted ducks, but he leaves a surprise for Iktomi.

Moon Song, by Byrd Baylor. Illustrated by Ronald Himler. Scribner, 1982. Coyote is the child of the moon, and he misses her. At night, he howls for his mother. This story is from Pima Indians.

Quail Song: A Pueblo Indian Tale, adapted by Valerie Scho Carey. Illustrated by Ivan Barnett. Putnam, 1990. Quail uses her wits to trick Coyote.

Thirteen Moons on Turtle's Back: A Native American Year of Moons, by Joseph Bruchac and Jonathan London. Illustrated by Thomas Locker. Philomel, 1992. Legends from many peoples, including the Huron, the Cherokee, and the Lakota Sioux, describe the seasons.

About the Author and Illustrator

GOBLE, PAUL

Fourth Book of Junior Authors and Illustrators, ed. by Doris de Montreville and Elizabeth D. Crawford. Wilson, 1978, pp. 150–151.

Illustrators of Children's Books: 1967–1976, Vol. IV, comp. by Lee Kingman, Grace Allen Hogarth, and Harriet Quimby. Horn Book, 1978, pp. 122, 190.

Something about the Author, ed. by Anne Commire. Gale, 1981, Vol. 25, pp. 120–122; ed. by Donna Olendorf, Gale, 1992, Vol. 69, pp. 66–70.

Kellogg, Steven, reteller. *Jack and the Beanstalk*
Illus. by the reteller. Morrow, 1991, LB (0-688-10251-4)
Suggested Use Level: Gr. 2–4

Plot Summary

Jack lives with his mother and their cow, Milky-white. When Mother sends Jack to sell Milky-white, Jack returns with five magical beans. His mother is angry, calling him "a dolt" and "an idiot." She throws the beans out the window, where, in the night, they grow to be a huge beanstalk. When Jack awakens, he climbs the beanstalk to the sky. He walks to a castle, where he meets the wife of an ogre. Jack asks her for breakfast, and she obliges him, until the ogre returns, chanting the familiar "Fee-fi-fo-fum!" rhyme. He looks for "an Englishman" but does not find Jack, so he eats his breakfast, counts some gold, and falls asleep. Jack takes a bag of gold and runs away, climbing down the beanstalk to his home. When the gold is gone, Jack goes back up the beanstalk and again asks the ogre's wife for some food. Jack hides when the ogre returns. The ogre eats his breakfast and brings out his hen that lays golden eggs. After the ogre falls asleep, Jack takes the hen and goes home. After some time, Jack goes back up the beanstalk. He sneaks past the ogre's wife and hides. Neither the ogre nor his wife can find Jack, although they smell him. Once again, the ogre eats, brings out his golden harp, and falls asleep. Jack takes the harp, which calls out to the ogre. As Jack runs for the beanstalk, the ogre chases him. At the bottom of the beanstalk, Jack chops it down, and the ogre falls to the ground. Using the hen and the harp, Jack and his mother live in prosperity.

Thematic Material

Steven Kellogg's version of the well-known English folktale includes many familiar elements from this story. It could be included in an activity on comparing and contrasting versions of folktales.

Book Talk Material and Activities

Although many children are familiar with the story of *Jack and the Beanstalk*, they might not realize how many other stories and rhymes they know about Jack. When one group of third graders, who were very familiar with folktales, heard Steven Kellogg's *Jack and the Beanstalk*, it led to a list of other stories about Jack:

"JACK" STORIES AND RHYMES

Jack and the Beanstalk
Jack and the Bean Tree
"Jack Be Nimble"
"Jack and Jill"
"Lazy Jack"
"Little Jack Horner"
"Jack Sprat"

After working on the list, the librarian shared some other traditional stories and poems in which Jack appears, such as "The House That Jack Built" and *The Jack Tales* by Richard Chase. Some students selected these books while others looked at nursery rhyme collections for more rhymes about Jack.

Children who are familiar with other "Jack and the Beanstalk" stories will enjoy talking about the differences in Steven Kellogg's version. There are many books about Jack that children could examine, and they could decide on some of the areas to compare. For example, how does Jack get the beans? Is the giant's chant the same in each book? Does Jack bring back the same treasures? Their information could be assembled on a chart or just discussed in a group sharing session. Children also might notice some special features in Steven Kellogg's illustrations, including characters from other books by Steven Kellogg, most noticeably Pinkerton.

Related Titles

The History of Mother Twaddle and the Marvelous Achievements of Her Son, Jack, retold and illustrated by Paul Galdone. Seabury, 1974. In this rhyming version of the story, Jack makes only one trip up the beanstalk and kills the giant by cutting off his head.

"The House That Jack Built" and "Lazy Jack" in *The Three Bears and 15 Other Stories,* selected and illustrated by Anne Rockwell. Crowell, 1975. There are some very familiar folktales in this collection, including these two stories with Jack.

Jack and the Bean Tree, retold and illustrated by Gail E. Haley. Crown, 1986. This is an Appalachian version of "Jack and the Beanstalk." Jack climbs the bean tree and meets the giant, Ephidophilus. Jack makes three trips to the giant's home before chopping down the bean tree and killing the giant (condensed in *Primaryplots,* Bowker, 1989, pp. 303–306).

Jack and the Beanstalk, retold and illustrated by Lorinda Bryan Cauley. Putnam, 1983. This would be an especially good choice for a beginning comparison activity, because there are enough differences to discuss without being confusing.

The Jack Tales, edited by Richard Chase. Illustrated by Berkeley Williams, Jr. Houghton, 1943. The preface to this book gives some fascinating background information on the origin of these stories. There is a version of "Jack and the Bean Tree" in this book.

Jim and the Beanstalk, written and illustrated by Raymond Briggs. Coward, 1970. A helpful boy named Jim climbs a strange plant and meets an even stranger giant. In this story, instead of stealing from the giant, Jim gives the giant three presents.

The Random House Book of Mother Goose, selected and illustrated by Arnold Lobel. Random, 1986. This is a good collection to begin looking for nursery rhymes about Jack.

About the Author and Illustrator

KELLOGG, STEVEN

Fourth Book of Junior Authors and Illustrators, ed. by Doris de Montreville and Elizabeth D. Crawford. Wilson, 1978, pp. 208–209.

Illustrators of Children's Books: 1967–1976, Vol. IV, comp. by Lee Kingman, Grace Allen Hogarth, and Harriet Quimby. Horn Book, 1978, pp. 136, 196.

Something about the Author, ed by Anne Commire. Gale, 1976, Vol. 8, pp. 95–97; Gale, 1989, Vol. 57, pp. 88–97.

Talking with Artists, comp. and ed. by Pat Cummings. Bradbury, 1992, pp. 54–59.

Marshall, James, reteller. *Goldilocks and the Three Bears*
Illus. by the reteller. Dial, 1988, LB (0-8037-0543-3)
Suggested Use Level: Gr. K–2

Plot Summary

The folktale of the Three Bears is humorously retold by James Marshall. The basic structure of the story is the same. Goldilocks is sent to buy some muffins and decides to take the shortcut, even though she has been warned against it. In the forest, three bears live in a charming house. While waiting for their porridge to cool, the bears go for a ride on a bicycle. Goldilocks finds their empty house and enters it, tasting their porridge, sitting in their chairs, and resting in their beds. She makes a mess of everything she touches. When she rests in Baby Bear's bed, she falls asleep. The bears return home and find the mess Goldilocks has made. When the bears find Goldilocks in Baby Bear's bed, she wakes up and runs away, and the bears never see her again.

Thematic Material

James Marshall's retelling of this well-known folktale has many humorous details in the illustrations and in the expressions of the characters. The illustrations for this book received a Caldecott Honor award in 1989.

Book Talk Material and Activities

Many children are familiar with some version of *Goldilocks and the Three Bears*. Librarians and teachers might want to read this book and other books about the Three Bears to allow children to make predictions. Before reading *Goldilocks and the Three Bears,* ask children to retell the story. Write their version of the story on the chalkboard or on chart paper. One group said there should always be three bears and that they should be big, medium, and small. After some discussion, the group decided the bears should be called Papa Bear, Mama Bear, and Baby Bear. Everything they have should be big, medium, and small, including their voices, their bowls, their chairs, and their beds. The children felt that Goldilocks should always have long blond hair. When the bears leave the house and Goldilocks comes, she should spoil their food and mess up their chairs and beds. She should break everything that belongs to Baby Bear. The group expected there would be a pattern to what the bears say when they return home—for example, "Somebody's been sitting in my chair." After the children discussed their expectations, they heard several Three Bears stories and compared them with their predictions. They focused on two aspects of the story, what the bears were called and what they said when they found their bowls, chairs, and beds. The children were interested in how the stories had been adapted by the author and were pleased that, for the most part, their predictions were confirmed.

When comparing illustrated versions of the same story, children can discuss what details the illustrator chose to include, and they can decide which illustrated versions they find the most appealing. In James Marshall's version of *Goldilocks and the Three Bears,* Goldilocks is described as "one of those naughty little girls." She disobeys her mother and goes into the forest. In many of the illustrations, her eyes are looking off to the side, giving her a sly, sneaky appearance. She sticks her tongue out, she sits upside down, and she pouts. The illustrations have many humorous details, particularly in the descriptions of the bears' house. And they are filled with details many children will recognize from other James Marshall books, like the inclusion of some cats and a chicken. The bears in this book are very well dressed. Mama Bear wears a large flowered hat; Baby Bear wears a sailor outfit. The bears make humorous exclamations, like "Patooie!" and "Egads!" In Jan Brett's illustrations for *Goldilocks and the Three Bears*, the bears wear patterned tunics. In Janet Stevens's version, they wear clothes; in Galdone's version, they do not wear clothes. Children can decide which presentation they prefer and why.

Once children have seen many versions of this story, they enjoy looking at books that tell the story a bit differently. *Deep in the Forest* is a wordless book that describes what happens when a bear enters a deserted house. *Somebody and the Three Blairs* tells about a visit from a bear named Somebody, which is convenient when the characters (whose family name is Blair) say "Somebody's been eating my Crunchies." Because children know the original Three Bears story, they find these different tellings even more enjoyable.

Audiovisual Adaptation
  Goldilocks and the Three Bears. Weston Woods, cassette/book, 1991.

Related Titles
  Deep in the Forest, written and illustrated by Brinton Turkle. Dutton, 1976. This wordless book depicts the familiar Three Bears story but with a twist. A baby bear goes into a log cabin and wreaks havoc on the food, chairs, and beds of a Papa, a Mama, and a Baby. When the three settlers return to their cabin, they find the bear cub in the little girl's bed and chase him out into the woods.

  Goldilocks and the Three Bears, retold and illustrated by Jan Brett. Dodd, 1987. These three bears live in a very comfortable house. This retelling follows the traditional patterns. At the end, Goldilocks runs off into the woods. (Condensed in *Primaryplots*, Bowker, 1989, pp. 292–294.)

  Goldilocks and the Three Bears, retold and illustrated by Lorinda Bryan Cauley. Putnam, 1981. The story of the Three Bears is familiar, but details in the illustrations add humor to the book. The bears in this book lead a comfortable life in a lovely home. Father smokes his pipe and reads while Mother works on her embroidery and drinks tea. The baby bear sits in a wicker chair, reading a book and drinking a glass of milk.

  Goldilocks and the Three Bears, retold and illustrated by Janet Stevens. Holiday, 1986. The bears in this version of the Three Bears live in a cozy house and have comfortable clothing and furniture. Stevens has used many different patterns and colors on the fabrics in the bears' house.

  Somebody and the Three Blairs, by Marilyn Tolhurst. Illustrated by Simone

Abel. Orchard, 1990. When the Blair family goes to the park, a bear named Somebody enters their house. He eats their food, sits in their chairs, plays some games, enjoys the water in the bathroom, and takes a nap.

The Three Bears, written and illustrated by Byron Barton. Harper, 1991. This is a very recent version of this story, but it keeps the traditional elements, like porridge and the repeated phrases.

The Three Bears, written and illustrated by Paul Galdone. Seabury, 1972. Galdone's bears are very bearlike—large and furry. Goldilocks is missing a front tooth and looks mischievous. When the bears speak, the size of the print reflects the size of the bear—for example, large letters for the Great Big Bear.

The Three Bears, illustrated by Robin Spowart. Knopf, 1987. The soft colors in these illustrations give a feeling of warmth. The bears' home is a little cottage decorated with simple country furnishings.

About the Author and Illustrator

MARSHALL, JAMES

Fourth Book of Junior Authors and Illustrators, ed. by Doris de Montreville and Elizabeth D. Crawford. Wilson, 1978, pp. 253–254.

Illustrators of Children's Books, 1967–1976, Vol. IV, comp. by Lee Kingman, Grace Allen Hogarth, and Harriet Quimby. Horn Book, 1978, pp. 5, 144, 201.

Something about the Author, ed. by Anne Commire. Gale, 1974, Vol. 6, pp. 160–161; 1988, Vol. 51, pp. 109–121.

San Souci, Robert D., reteller. *The Talking Eggs: A Folktale from the American South*

Illus. by Jerry Pinkney. Dial, 1989, LB (0-8037-0620-0)
Suggested Use Level: Gr. 3–4

Plot Summary

Long ago, in the rural South, a mother lives with her two daughters, Rose and Blanche. Mother and Rose are both lazy and mean; they harass Blanche and make her do all the work. When Blanche runs away, she is befriended by an old woman, who takes her to a rundown shack deep in the woods. Blanche has promised not to laugh at the woman or her home, and she keeps her promise even though she sees many strange things: a two-headed cow, multilegged chickens, dancing rabbits, and talking eggs. Blanche is rewarded for being honest and helpful. She is given permission to take some talking eggs, which open to reveal jewels, dresses, and other treasures. At home, Blanche tells her mother about her experiences. The greedy woman sends Rose out to find the old woman and get more riches. At the old woman's shack, Rose laughs at all the strange creatures, and she refuses to help. On her way home, Rose opens the talking eggs, releasing snakes, toads, and a wolf, which chases Rose and her mother off into the woods. Blanche moves to the city and lives happily, while her mother and sister bitterly search for the old woman and her talking eggs.

Thematic Material

The Talking Eggs has elements from several folktales, including Cinderella. It could be shared as part of a unit in which children learn about different folktales. *The Talking Eggs* was a Caldecott Honor book in 1990.

Book Talk Material and Activities

Before reading this book to children, ask them what they expect to hear in a Cinderella story. Several fourth-grade classes responded by suggesting these elements:

> A girl who does all the work
> A stepmother and stepsisters
> Animals that talk
> A fairy godmother
> Magic
> A ball or a dance
> A prince (and the girl should marry him)
> A glass slipper
> A happy ending

After listening to *The Talking Eggs*, children reviewed their expectations and discussed similarities and differences. They looked at other Cinderella stories, including *Cinderella* by Charles Perrault, *Yeh-Shen* retold by Ai-Ling Louie, *Mufaro's Beautiful Daughters* by John Steptoe, and *Princess Furball* retold by Charlotte Huck.

Several children commented that they recognized elements from other folktales in *The Talking Eggs*. When Blanche makes rice for the old woman, she uses only one grain of rice, reminding children of *The Funny Little Woman*. When the mother sends Rose back out to get more riches, one student thought of *The Month-Brothers*. After hearing *The Talking Eggs*, many children hurried to select folktales and look for other connections.

Audiovisual Adaptation

The Talking Eggs. American School Publishers, cassette/book, 1991.

Related Titles

Cinderella, or The Little Glass Slipper, by Charles Perrault. Translated and illustrated by Marcia Brown. Scribner, 1954. This is the well-known French version of Cinderella. Marcia Brown's illustrations capture details of court life in France. They received the Caldecott Medal in 1955.

The Funny Little Woman, retold by Arlene Mosel. Illustrated by Blair Lent. Dutton, 1972. A woman makes a rice dumpling that rolls away from her. When she chases it, she ends up a prisoner of the oni and is given a magic rice paddle that turns one grain into enough for all the oni. Blair Lent received the Caldecott Medal in 1973.

The Month-Brothers: A Slavic Tale, retold by Samuel Marshak. Illustrated by Diane Stanley. Morrow, 1983. A young girl lives with her stepmother and stepsister, both of whom are cruel to her. They make impossible demands of her, but she receives help from the Month-Brothers. (Condensed in *Primaryplots*, Bowker, 1989, pp. 308–310.)

Mufaro's Beautiful Daughters: An African Tale, by John Steptoe. Illustrated by the author. Lothrop, 1987. Mufaro has two beautiful daughters, Manyara and Nyasha. Nyasha is kind and considerate. Manyara is vain, proud, and bad-tempered. Compare their behavior to Blanche and Rose in *The Talking Eggs*. (Condensed in *Primaryplots*, Bowker, 1989, pp. 318–321.)

Princess Furball, retold by Charlotte Huck. Illustrated by Anita Lobel. Greenwillow, 1989. This clever princess is able to escape her selfish father and an ogre. She becomes a servant in the castle of another king, working in the kitchen and sweeping the ashes. She keeps her true identity hidden while she attends three balls, where she tests the young king, who comes to admire her for her beauty and her cleverness.

Yeh-Shen: A Cinderella Story from China, retold by Ai-Ling Louie. Illustrated by Ed Young. Philomel, 1982. The cruelty of Yeh-Shen's stepmother and stepsister is punished with death after Yeh-Shen is chosen to marry the king.

About the Author

SAN SOUCI, ROBERT D.

Something about the Author, ed. by Anne Commire. Gale, 1985, Vol. 40, pp. 220–231.

About the Illustrator

PINKNEY, JERRY

Illustrators of Children's Books: 1957–1966, Vol. III, comp. by Lee Kingman, Grace Allen
    Hogarth, and Harriet Quimby. Horn Book, 1978, pp. 158, 235; *Vol. IV, 1967–1976,*
    1978, pp. 151, 205.
Sixth Book of Junior Authors and Illustrators, ed. by Sally Holmes Holtze. Wilson, 1989, pp.
    225–227.
Something about the Author, ed. by Anne Commire. Gale, 1983, Vol. 41, pp. 164–174.
Talking with Artists, comp. and ed. by Pat Cummings. Bradbury, 1992, pp. 60–65.

Schwartz, Alvin, reteller.   *Ghosts! Ghostly Tales from Folklore*
Illus. by Victoria Chess. Harper, 1991, LB (0-06-021797-9)
Suggested Use Level: Gr. 1–2

Plot Summary

There are seven ghost stories in this easy-to-read collection. In "The
Haunted House," a ghost makes a surprise appearance; in "The Um-
brella," some ghosts make a surprise disappearance. "Susie" is the story
of a ghost cat. "The Green Bottle" holds the ghost of a bad-tempered girl.
Versions of two well-known ghost stories, "Three Little Ghosts" and "The
Teeny-Tiny Woman," are included, along with a rhyme for getting rid of
a ghost called "Ghost, Get Lost." A brief explanation of the sources for the
stories is given at the end of the book.

Thematic Material

Being afraid of noises, shadows, the dark, and ghosts is a familiar feeling
for many children. Although this is not a collection of Halloween stories,
this book could be incorporated into a program of scary stories for Halloween.

Book Talk Material and Activities

The stories in this book would be fun to share at a spooky story time.
Several of the stories are available in other versions, and they could be

compared. In "The Teeny-Tiny Woman" story, the old woman finds a set of teeth, which she decides to use. This could be compared to the versions by Paul Galdone and Jane O'Connor. In "The Green Bottle," there are links to several other stories. The ghost in this story is tricked into making herself small, which also happens in *Wiley and the Hairy Man*. The ghost is then put into a bottle, and the reader is warned not to open it. In Brinton Turkle's *Do Not Open*, an old lady finds a bottle on the beach and opens it. Linking stories with similar themes or motifs introduces children to some of the conventions that are used in folklore.

The stories in *Ghosts!* are presented in an easy-to-read format. Large print and wide spaces between the lines aid beginning readers as they focus on the text. Illustrations provide details that support the text. *In a Dark, Dark Room, Thump, Thump, Thump, Wiley and the Hairy Man*, and O'Connor's *The Teeny Tiny Woman* are some other slightly scary books that are designed to be accessible to beginning readers.

Related Titles

A Dark, Dark Tale, written and illustrated by Ruth Brown. Dial, 1981. Children can discuss the spooky images in the dark, sinister pictures and text of this familiar story.

Do Not Open, written and illustrated by Brinton Turkle. Dutton, 1981. Miss Moody opens the bottle marked "Do Not Open" and a very frightening monster appears. The conclusion is safe and satisfying.

In a Dark, Dark Room and Other Scary Stories, retold by Alvin Schwartz. Illustrated by Dirk Zimmer. Harper, 1984. Seven stories in an easy-to-read format. Included are stories about sinister men with long teeth, a woman who talks to corpses, and a woman whose head is held on by a green ribbon. Compare the story "In a Dark, Dark Room" to the picture book version, *A Dark, Dark Tale*.

The Scary Book, comp. by Joanna Cole and Stephanie Calmenson. Illustrated by Chris Demarest, Marilyn Hirsh, Arnold Lobel, and Dirk Zimmer. Morrow, 1991. This collection of slightly scary stories, poems, tricks, and jokes includes some excerpts from beginning readers, like *Bony-Legs* and "Strange Bumps" from *Owl at Home*.

The Teeny Tiny Woman, retold by Jane O'Connor. Illustrated by R. W. Alley. Random, 1986. After the woman finds a bone in the graveyard, she is haunted by a mysterious voice. There is a lot of repetition in the book, which helps make it accessible to beginning readers.

The Teeny-Tiny Woman: A Ghost Story, retold and illustrated by Paul

Galdone. Clarion, 1984. This teeny-tiny woman finds a bone and hears a voice that first asks and then demands for the bone to be returned.

Thump, Thump, Thump, written and illustrated by Anne Rockwell. Dutton, 1981. The Thing has lost his hairy toe and the old woman has found it. Now the Thing is looking for his toe.

Wiley and the Hairy Man, adapted from an American folktale and illustrated by Molly Bang. Macmillan, 1976. Wiley and his mother must outwit the Hairy Man three times or he will torment Wiley forever.

About the Author

SCHWARTZ, ALVIN

Fifth Book of Junior Authors and Illustrators, ed. by Sally Holmes Holtze. Wilson, 1983, pp. 276–277.

Something about the Author, ed. by Anne Commire. Gale, 1973, Vol. 4, pp. 183–184; Gale, 1989, Vol. 56, pp. 145–151; ed. by Diane Telgen, Gale, 1993, Vol. 71, p. 171.

About the Illustrator

CHESS, VICTORIA

Illustrators of Children's Books, 1967–1976, Vol. IV, comp. by Lee Kingman, Grace Allen Hogarth, and Harriet Quimby. Horn Book, 1978, pp. 107, 183.

Sixth Book of Junior Authors and Illustrators, ed. by Sally Holmes Holtze. Wilson, 1989, pp. 55–56.

Something about the Author, ed. by Anne Commire. Gale, 1983, Vol. 33, pp. 48–50.

Talking with Artists, comp. and ed. by Pat Cummings. Bradbury, 1992, pp. 10–15.

Scieszka, Jon.   *The True Story of the 3 Little Pigs by A. Wolf*
Illus. by Lane Smith. Viking, 1989 (0-670-82759-2)
Suggested Use Level: Gr. 2–4

Plot Summary

Alexander T. Wolf tells his side of the story of the three pigs. He explains that wolves eat meat, including pork, and his encounters with the three pigs were totally innocent. While making a cake for his granny's birthday, Al runs out of sugar. He goes to his neighbor's straw house to borrow some sugar. At the door, he has a sneezing fit, and the house falls down, killing his neighbor, a pig. Being a wolf, Al has to eat him. The same circumstances occur at the next neighbor's house of sticks. Al asks for the sugar, has a sneezing fit, and blows the house down. Again, the pig inside is killed and Al has to eat him too. At the third neighbor's house, made of bricks, Al's sneezing does not blow the house down. The pig inside makes some rude remarks to him, and Al goes berserk. When the pig police arrive at the third pig's home, Al is out of control. He is arrested, tried, convicted, and sent to prison.

Thematic Material

This folktale takeoff provides an opportunity to reexamine many familiar stories and to discuss point of view.

Book Talk Material and Activities

What really happened to the three little pigs? How does the point of view influence the telling of a story? In this retelling of "The Three Little Pigs," the wolf is the narrator, and the story is changed because of this different point of view. To appreciate the humor of this change, children need to be familiar with the original story. They need to be aware of the recurring elements and conventions of folktales.

After reading many folktales, children are better able to see the humor in variations. In cooperative groups, children could look at other folktales and takeoffs, like *Nanny Goat and the Seven Little Kids* and Tony Ross's *Mrs. Goat and Her Seven Little Kids;* the traditional *Stone Soup* and Tony Ross's version; *The Frog Prince* and Jon Scieszka's *The Frog Prince Continued;* and *The Emperor's New Clothes* and *The Principal's New Clothes.* Jane Yolen's *Sleeping Ugly* is another humorous look at folktale conventions. Jon Scieszka's *The Stinky Cheese Man and Other Fairly Stupid Tales* is a humorous look at several well-known stories.

Audiovisual Adaptation

The True Story of the 3 Pigs by A. Wolf. Viking, cassette/book, 1992.

Related Titles

The Emperor's New Clothes, retold by Anne Rockwell from the nineteenth-century translation by H. W. Dulcken. Illustrated by Anne Rockwell. Cromwell, 1982. Two thieves trick the emperor into buying some clothes that are not really there.

The Frog Prince, adapted from the retelling by the Brothers Grimm and illustrated by Paul Galdone. McGraw-Hill, 1975. After the frog helps her, the king's daughter must be kind to the frog. This version of the story does not end with a kiss!

The Frog Prince Continued, by Jon Scieszka. Illustrated by Steve Johnson. Viking, 1991. This story picks up where *The Frog Prince* ended "happily ever after." The prince is not that happy as a prince. In fact, he misses his life as a frog. He leaves his princess and goes searching for a witch who will cast a spell and change him back into a frog. Familiar folktale witches (from "Sleeping Beauty," "Snow White," "Hansel and Gretel," and "Cinderella") are not very helpful. Children could try writing their own continuations of other folktales.

Mrs. Goat and Her Seven Little Kids, written and illustrated by Tony Ross. Atheneum, 1990. In this retelling of the familiar folktale, six of Big Mother Goat's kids are swallowed by the wolf. The seventh kid hides and tells Mom what happened when she gets home. The Hungry Wolf will be sorry that he bothered her kids.

Nanny Goat and the Seven Little Kids, retold from the Brothers Grimm by Eric A. Kimmel. Illustrated by Janet Stevens. Holiday, 1990. A mother goat warns her kids about the big bad wolf, but he still tricks them into letting him into their house. He eats all the kids and, when Nanny Goat comes home, eats her too. From inside his stomach, Nanny Goat finds a way to outwit the wolf.

The Principal's New Clothes, by Stephanie Calmenson. Illustrated by Denise Brunkus. Scholastic, 1989. Mr. Bundy wears wonderful clothes. At the school where he is the principal, the kids wait to see what he will wear. Two tricksters get Mr. Bundy to buy a suit made with "special cloth." It takes a kindergartner to point out, "The principal's in his underwear!"

Sleeping Ugly, by Jane Yolen. Illustrated by Diane Stanley. Coward, 1981. In most traditional stories, beautiful characters are good and ugly characters are bad. In this one, the beautiful Princess Miserella is a brat and Plain Jane is sweet and lovely. This story pokes fun at some folktale stereotypes.

The Stinky Cheese Man and Other Fairly Stupid Tales, by Jon Scieszka. Illustrated by Lane Smith. Viking, 1992. Fractured fairy tales indeed! Creative book design and illustrations add to the humor and mayhem of these new versions of some familiar tales, including "The Princess and the Bowling Ball" and "Little Red Running Shorts." This book received a Caldecott Honor award in 1993.

Stone Soup, written and illustrated by Tony Ross. Dial, 1987. In Tony Ross's altered version of a familiar folktale, a wolf plans to eat a hen. The hen outwits the wolf by making stone soup, and the wolf ends up too full to eat the hen.

Stone Soup: An Old Tale, retold and illustrated by Marcia Brown. Scribner, 1957. In this traditional retelling of the folktale, three soldiers trick the villagers into sharing their food and making stone soup.

Three Little Pigs and the Big Bad Wolf, written and illustrated by Glen Rounds. Holiday, 1992. Here's another version of the Three Little Pigs story. In this book, the third pig eats the wolf.

About the Author

SCIESZKA, JON

Something about the Author, ed. by Donna Olendorf. Gale, 1992, Vol. 68, pp. 211–212.

About the Illustrator

SMITH, LANE

Talking with Artists, comp. and ed. by Pat Cummings. Bradbury, 1992, pp. 72–77.

Snyder, Dianne. *The Boy of the Three-Year Nap*
Illus. by Allen Say. Houghton, 1988 (0-395-44090-4)
Suggested Use Level: Gr. 2–4

Plot Summary

In Japan, a poor widow lives with her lazy son, Taro. Despite all her efforts, the widow cannot get Taro to do any work. All he wants to do is sleep, earning the nickname The Boy of the Three-Year Nap. As the years pass, the widow despairs that Taro will never accomplish anything, until a rich merchant builds a huge house in their town. Taro, now a young man, is so interested in the splendid home and great wealth that he develops a plan. Disguising himself as the *ujigami,* the god of the town, Taro tricks the merchant into promising to wed his daughter to Taro. Before the wedding, Taro's mother arranges for the merchant to repair the leaks and cracks in her home and to build her many new rooms. She also convinces the merchant to give Taro a job, thus outwitting both the merchant and The Boy of the Three-Year Nap, who will be too busy working to be lazy.

Thematic Material

This story has elements of a traditional folktale, including a lazy main character and a character who succeeds by using trickery.

Book Talk Material and Activities

How many folktales have lazy or foolish main characters? Beginning with Taro in *The Boy of the Three-Year Nap*, children may enjoy hearing book talks of other humorous characters, like the rabbit in *Foolish Rabbit's Big Mistake*, or Big Anthony in *Strega Nona*, or Kojo in *Oh, Kojo! How Could You!* They might think about the *Chicken Little* stories, in which the characters believe that the sky is falling. Or they might mention the man with the sausage on his nose in *The Three Wishes*, or the emperor in *The Emperor's New Clothes*.

As children read many folktales, they develop an awareness of the recurring elements. By focusing a book talk program on some folktales with similar elements that come from different countries, children see that many cultures share a common heritage in their stories. Children begin to look for elements in stories that connect them. Making a list of characters who are tricked or behave foolishly encourages children to read many stories and to look for these humorous characters.

Related Titles

Chicken Little, retold and illustrated by Steven Kellogg. Morrow, 1985. The illustrations show animals wearing clothes and driving an ambulance and a helicopter. In this retelling, Foxy Loxy is tried and sent to prison.

The Emperor's New Clothes, retold by Anne Rockwell from the nineteenth-century translation by H. W. Dulcken. Illustrated by Anne Rockwell. Crowell, 1982. Two thieves trick the emperor into buying some clothes that are not really there.

Foolish Rabbit's Big Mistake, by Rafe Martin. Illustrated by Ed Young. Putnam, 1985. A foolish rabbit hears an apple fall and thinks the earth may be breaking up. Like Chicken Little, he convinces other animals to panic and run away with him. (Condensed in *Primaryplots*, Bowker, 1989, pp. 313–316.)

Oh, Kojo! How Could You! An Ashanti Tale, by Verna Aardema. Illustrated by Marc Brown. Dial, 1984. Kojo causes problems for his mother, Tutuola. He spends her money and does not work. He does not listen to her warnings and is tricked by Ananse. (Condensed in *Primaryplots*, Bowker, 1989, pp. 289–291.)

Rabbit Makes a Monkey out of Lion: A Swahili Tale, retold by Verna Aardema. Illustrated by Jerry Pinkney. Dial, 1989. Two times, Rabbit eats Lion's honey and is not punished. Even Rabbit will not try to trick Lion a third time.

Strega Nona, retold and illustrated by Tomie dePaola. Prentice Hall,

1975. Big Anthony did not listen to Strega Nona's warning, and now the pasta pot will not stop cooking pasta.

The Three Wishes: An Old Story, retold and illustrated by Margot Zemach. Farrar, 1986. If the peasant does not use his third wish wisely, he will have a sausage on his nose forever! For this foolish character, three wishes are not enough.

About the Illustrator

SAY, ALLEN

Sixth Book of Junior Authors and Illustrators, ed. by Sally Holmes Holtze. Wilson, 1989, pp. 266–268.

Something about the Author, ed. by Anne Commire. Gale, 1982. Vol. 28, p. 179; ed. by Donna Olendorf, Gale, 1992, Vol. 69, pp. 181–183.

Young, Ed, translator. *Lon Po Po: A Red-Riding Hood Story from China*

Illus. by the translator. Philomel, 1989 (0-399-21619-7)
Suggested Use Level: Gr. 2–4

Plot Summary

A mother leaves her three daughters at home while she goes to visit their grandmother. The daughters are named Shang, Tao, and Paotze. The mother warns them to be cautious while she is away. A wolf, who has seen the mother leave, comes to the house disguised as the grandmother, Po Po. At first the girls will not let the wolf into the house, but the wolf convinces them he is their grandmother, and they let him in. Once inside, the wolf blows out the candle, so it is too dark for the girls to see they have been fooled. At bedtime, the girls crawl into bed with the wolf/grandmother and begin to be aware of differences. The wolf's foot is bushy, but he says it is hemp for weaving a basket. The wolf's hand has sharp claws, but he says it is an awl for making shoes. Shang, the eldest daughter, lights the light and sees the wolf before he blows it out. She devises a plan and tells her sisters. They tell the wolf about eating the nuts of the gingko tree, which will let you live forever. The wolf allows the girls to climb the tree and then becomes impatient waiting for the nuts. The girls have the wolf climb into a basket and try to pull him into the tree. Three times they pull him up, and three times they drop him. After the third fall, the wolf is dead. The girls climb down and go into the house to bed. When their mother comes home, they tell her of their encounter with the wolf.

Thematic Material

Comparing versions of folktales allows children to apply their knowledge of these familiar stories. *Lon Po Po* could be compared and contrasted with other stories about Little Red Riding Hood. Ed Young received the Caldecott Medal in 1990 for the illustrations in *Lon Po Po.*

Book Talk Material and Activities

When *Lon Po Po* was shown to a group of fourth graders, they were eager to hear it. They had enjoyed some of Ed Young's illustrations for other folktales, including *Foolish Rabbit's Big Mistake* and *Yeh-Shen,* and they were interested in versions of folktales. Because they knew there were often differences in the versions of familiar stories, they decided to talk about their expectations for a Red Riding Hood story. They felt there should be a girl who wore something red on her head. The story should have a wolf and a grandmother. The girl should go to visit her grandmother carrying a basket of treats, and she should be warned about the danger of leaving the path. There should be a trip through a woods, where the girl meets the wolf. In the story there should be a dialogue about big eyes, big ears, and big teeth. The wolf should swallow the grandmother and the girl, but they should be rescued by a woodsman or hunter and live "happily ever after."

After hearing *Lon Po Po,* the students listed some similarities and differences.

Chart 7

Lon Po Po and Other Red Riding Hood Stories	
Same as Expected	*Different from Expected*
There is a wolf and a grandmother. There is a basket. There are questions about the wolf's features. The mother warns them.	The mother leaves and the wolf comes to the house. There are three children. It is the grandmother's birthday—she is not sick. No one is eaten. The girls trick the wolf and he is killed—no woodsman. No one wears red.

The children looked back at the text and illustrations of *Lon Po Po* for additional details. Knowing this book had won the Caldecott Medal, they talked about the images of the wolf that were incorporated into several illustrations. For example, as the mother walks away from the house, she seems to be moving toward a dark hill. Looking carefully, the shape of a wolf's head can be seen, with the three girls and the house sitting on the eye and the mother heading toward the nose. In one of the pictures of the wolf in the basket, the girls appear to be in the eyes of the wolf, and the trunk of the gingko tree seems to be the wolf's snout. These illustrations reminded the ·children of the images of a fish that were in Ed Young's illustrations for *Yeh-Shen*.

After looking at *Lon Po Po*, several children looked at other versions of Red Riding Hood. Others looked for other books illustrated by Ed Young. Reading this book encouraged these children to analyze the story and the illustrations. They used information they knew from other books and applied it to this book. They drew on previous experiences with stories and illustrations to appreciate *Lon Po Po*.

Related Titles

Foolish Rabbit's Big Mistake, by Rafe Martin. Illustrated by Ed Young. Putnam, 1985. A rabbit, dozing under an apple tree, wonders "What if the Earth broke up?" Like Chicken Little, this rabbit gets many animals to join him as he runs away from the noise. Ed Young's illustrations capture the drama of this version of the Henny Penny story. (Condensed in *Primaryplots,* Bowker, 1989, pp. 313–316.)

Little Red Cap, by the Brothers Grimm. Illustrated by Lisbeth Zwerger. Morrow, 1983. Little Red Cap travels to her grandmother's and meets a very personable wolf. He charms her into picking some flowers while he hurries to eat Grandmother. The wolf later swallows Little Red Cap too, but both Grandmother and Little Red Cap are saved by the hunter.

Little Red Riding Hood, adapted from the retelling by the Brothers Grimm and illustrated by Paul Galdone. McGraw-Hill, 1974. Like *Little Red Cap,* this version has a happy ending as both Red Riding Hood and her grandmother are rescued after the wolf has swallowed them.

Little Red Riding Hood, by the Brothers Grimm. Retold and illustrated by Trina Schart Hyman. Holiday, 1983. In this version, the little girl has a name, Elisabeth. The illustrations for this book are filled with details and are framed by borders. This book received a Caldecott Honor award.

Red Riding Hood, retold and illustrated by James Marshall. Dial, 1987.

This is a humorous retelling of the familiar story. Granny says, "You horrid thing," to the wolf, and the wolf says, "I'm so wicked." Details in the illustrations, especially in facial expressions, add to the humor. The hunter cuts open the wolf to release Granny and Red. (Condensed in *Primaryplots*, Bowker, 1989, pp. 310–313.)

Red Riding Hood, retold in verse by Beatrice Schenk de Regniers. Illustrated by Edward Gorey. Atheneum, 1972. The rhyming text and droll illustrations add to the fun of this version. Red Riding Hood and Grandma are both rescued from the wolf's belly.

Yeh-Shen: A Cinderella Story from China, retold by Ai-Ling Louie. Illustrated by Ed Young. Philomel, 1982. The cruelty of Yeh-Shen's stepmother and stepsister is punished by death after Yeh-Shen is chosen to marry the king. This is a good choice to compare with other Cinderella stories.

About the Author and Illustrator

YOUNG, ED

Third Book of Junior Authors, edited by Doris de Montreville and Donna Hill. Wilson, 1972, pp. 309–310.

Illustrators of Children's Books: 1967–1976, Vol. IV, comp. by Lee Kingman, Grace Allen Hogarth, and Harriet Quimby. Horn Book, 1978, pp. 170, 214.

Something about the Author, ed. by Anne Commire. Gale, 1976, Vol. 10, pp. 205–206.

AUTHOR INDEX

Asterisks denote titles that are featured as main entries.

CUMULATIVE AUTHOR INDEX

This index lists all the titles fully discussed in *Primaryplots* (P1) and *Primaryplots 2* (P2).

P1 = Primaryplots; P2 = Primaryplots 2

P1 = Primaryplots; P2 = Primaryplots 2

P1 = Primaryplots; P2 = Primaryplots 2

P1 = Primaryplots; P2 = Primaryplots 2

ILLUSTRATOR INDEX

Asterisks denote titles that are featured as main entries.

CUMULATIVE ILLUSTRATOR INDEX

This index lists all the titles fully discussed in *Primaryplots* (P1) and *Primaryplots 2* (P2).

P1 = Primaryplots; P2 = Primaryplots 2

P1 = Primaryplots; P2 = Primaryplots 2

P1 = Primaryplots; P2 = Primaryplots 2

P1 = Primaryplots; P2 = Primaryplots 2

TITLE INDEX

Asterisks denote titles that are featured as main entries.

CUMULATIVE TITLE INDEX

This index lists all the titles fully discussed in *Primaryplots* (P1) and *Primaryplots 2* (P2).

P1 = Primaryplots; P2 = Primaryplots 2

P1 = Primaryplots; P2 = Primaryplots 2

P1 = Primaryplots; P2 = Primaryplots 2

SUBJECT INDEX

This index includes only the primary titles fully discussed and summarized in *Primary-plots 2*. Additional titles relating to these subjects can be found under the "Related Titles" section that accompanies the discussion of the books listed here. The subject headings refer to the fictional treatment of the subject unless otherwise noted with the label nonfiction.

CUMULATIVE SUBJECT INDEX

This index includes only the primary titles fully discussed and summarized in *Primary-plots* (P1) and *Primaryplots 2* (P2). Additional titles relating to these subjects can be found under the "Related Titles" section that accompanies the discussion of the books listed here. The subject headings refer to the fictional treatment of the subject unless otherwise noted with the label nonfiction.

P1 = Primaryplots; P2 = Primaryplots 2

P1 = Primaryplots; P2 = Primaryplots 2

P1 = Primaryplots; P2 = Primaryplots 2

P1 = Primaryplots; P2 = Primaryplots 2

P1 = Primaryplots; P2 = Primaryplots 2

P1 = Primaryplots; P2 = Primaryplots 2

P1 = Primaryplots; P2 = Primaryplots 2

Ireland
Bunting, Eve. *Clancy's Coat,* P1-205

Japan
Friedman, Ina R. *How My Parents Learned to Eat,* P1-215
Tsutsui, Yoriko. *Anna in Charge,* P2-42
Wisniewski, David. *The Warrior and the Wise Man,* P2-304

Journeys
Baker, Jeannie. *Home in the Sky,* P1-246

King, Martin Luther, Jr.—Nonfiction
Adler, David A. *A Picture Book of Martin Luther King, Jr.,* P2-196

Language Experience
Hoban, Tana. *All about Where,* P2-244

Legends—Native American
Goble, Paul. *Buffalo Woman,* P1-301
Goble, Paul, reteller. *Iktomi and the Boulder: A Plains Indian Story,* P2-314

Letters—Nonfiction
Leedy, Loreen. *Messages in the Mailbox: How to Write a Letter,* P2-121

Libraries
Kimmel, Eric A. *I Took My Frog to the Library,* P2-168

Lindbergh, Charles—Nonfiction
Burleigh, Robert. *Flight: The Journey of Charles Lindbergh,* P2-201

Location
Hoban, Tana. *All about Where,* P2-244

Magic
Johnston, Tony. *The Witch's Hat,* P1-132
Kellogg, Steven, reteller. *Jack and the Beanstalk,* P2-317
McPhail, David. *Pig Pig and the Magic Photo Album,* P1-142
Van Allsburg, Chris. *The Widow's Broom,* P2-218

Wood, Audrey. *Elbert's Bad Word,* P2-86

Math
McMillan, Bruce. *Eating Fractions,* P2-124

Mermaids
San Souci, Robert D. *Sukey and the Mermaid,* P2-292

Meteors—Nonfiction
Branley, Franklyn M. *Shooting Stars,* P2-231

Mexican-American Experience
Mora, Pat. *A Birthday Basket for Tia,* P2-29

Middle Ages—Nonfiction
Aliki. *A Medieval Feast,* P1-157

Milk—Nonfiction
Gibbons, Gail. *The Milk Makers,* P1-89

Monsters
Fisher, Leonard Everett. *Theseus and the Minotaur,* P2-203
Hutchins, Pat. *The Very Worst Monster,* P1-129
Kellogg, Steven, reteller. *Jack and the Beanstalk,* P2-317
Kimmel, Eric. *Hershel and the Hanukkah Goblins,* P2-284
Stevenson, James. *What's Under My Bed?,* P1-152

Moon—Nonfiction
Branley, Franklyn M. *What the Moon Is Like,* P1-203

Moving
Asch, Frank. *Goodbye House,* P1-77
Johnson, Angela. *The Leaving Morning,* P2-71

Museums
Kellogg, Steven. *Prehistoric Pinkerton,* P1-137

P1 = Primaryplots; P2 = Primaryplots 2

P1 = Primaryplots; P2 = Primaryplots 2

P1 = Primaryplots; P2 = Primaryplots 2

P1 = Primaryplots; P2 = Primaryplots 2

P1 = Primaryplots; P2 = Primaryplots 2

P1 = Primaryplots; P2 = Primaryplots 2